Perception, Cognition, and Development: Interactional Analyses

PERCEPTION, COGNITION, AND DEVELOPMENT:
Interactional Analyses

Edited by

Thomas J. Tighe
Dartmouth College

Bryan E. Shepp
Brown University

LEA LAWRENCE ERLBAUM ASSOCIATES, PUBLISHERS
1983 Hillsdale, New Jersey   London

Lawrence Erlbaum Associates, Inc., Publishers
365 Broadway
Hillsdale, New Jersey 07642

Library of Congress Cataloging in Publication Data
Main entry under title:

Perception, cognition, and development.

"Based on a conference held at Dartmouth College's
Minary Conference Center in Holderness, New Hampshire,
June 4–7, 1981''—Pref.
Includes bibliographies and indexes.
Contents: Asymmetric interactions of stimulus
dimensions in perceptual information processing /
Wendell R. Garner—The analyzability of multidimen-
sional objects / Bryan E. Shepp—Holistic and analytic
modes in perceptual and cognitive development /
Deborah G. Kemler—[etc.]
1. Cognition in children—Congresses. 2. Perception
in children—Congresses. I. Tighe, Thomas J.
II. Shepp, Bryan E.
BF723.C5P395 1983   155.4'13   82-24262
ISBN 0-89859-254-2

Printed in the United States of America
10 9 8 7 6 5 4 3 2 1

Contents

For Louise Tighe and June Shepp

Preface

This volume is based on a conference held at Dartmouth College's Minary Conference Center in Holderness, New Hampshire, June 4–7, 1981. The conference brought together a number of investigators whose separate lines of inquiry bear in significant ways on the relationships among perception, cognition, and development. Our purpose was to consider interactions among these basic processes not only as a critical facet of the research programs of the participants but also as a central conceptual problem for current theoretical psychology.

The idea for the conference grew out of discussions between the editors who for a number of years have pursued parallel but independent and theoretically distinct lines of inquiry into the development of children's learning and conceptual behavior. In recent years, it became apparent that our findings, and those of other investigators in the field, were converging in very interesting ways. Specifically, the data pointed to a basic developmental transition from a relatively wholistic mode of perception and/or cognitive processing to a relatively analytic mode. This proposition is consistent with Thomas and Louise Tighe's research relating children's level of perceptual differentiation to performance on discrimination and concept tasks, with the developmental work of both Bryan Shepp and Deborah Kemler on the relation of perceived dimensional structure to attention, classification, and categorization, with David Zeaman and Betty House's analyses of attentional shifts from compounds to components, and with Tracy and Howard Kendler's studies indicating a developmental progression from non-selective, single-stage learning to mediated learning. Common to these research programs are observations suggesting that the stimulus dimensions of discrimination and concept tasks may be treated as integral or compounded features at one level of development but as separate features at another level.

The notion of differential interaction of perceived stimulus dimensions has also become prominent outside of the child discrimination-concept literature. Most notable is the elegant work of Wendell Garner which has delineated the basic architecture, as it were, of dimension integrality-separability and of symmetric/asymmetric dimension interactions. Douglas Medin has recently developed and explored the related concept of correlated stimulus attributes as a fundamental organizing principle of categorization. George Wolford and Carol Fowler have found evidence that wholistic and analytic stimulus processing modes may characterize the poor and good reader, respectively. Norman Anderson's work on "intuitive physics" also emphasizes the role of differential integration of attribute information but, in provocative contrast to the developmental literature noted above, argues that the learning of functional and physical relationships proceeds primarily by synthesis, rather than analysis, of dimensions. Finally, Spiker and Cantor have attempted to link the child discrimination-concept literature to the adult information processing literature, particularly with reference to the onset of dimension-specific hypothesis testing strategies by children.

A specific aim in organizing the conference was to have the foregoing researchers confront one another's methods, data, and formulations with an eye to defining the major points of agreement and disagreement and the critical directions for research. In addition, we believed the empirical and theoretical concerns of these investigators would provide an excellent vehicle for general theoretical analysis of the interface between perception and cognition and the interaction of these processes with development. Toward that end, we sought the contributions of several distinguished investigators, namely, William Estes, Eleanor Gibson, and Herbert Pick, all of whom are broadly knowledgeable in the areas of perception, cognition, and development. These individuals were asked to play the role of critic-discussants in reviewing the contributions of the other participants and in helping to define the broader implications of the conference proceedings.

The content and organization of the text reflect quite directly the content and organization of the conference. Overall, the text provides a multi-perspective analysis of a major frontier area of cognitive-developmental research—the understanding of categorization processes. The participants were selected to bring differing but overlapping perspectives ranging from the relatively perceptual and basic to relatively cognitive and "applied". Thus, the early chapters in the volume stress basic perceptual processes as determinants of classification performance, and with the Kendler and Spiker and Cantor chapters more purely cognitive processes achieve greater prominence. Zeaman and Hanley's chapter presents a transition point, where the concern is with a perceptual-attentional analysis but one that stresses an interaction between biological and experiential contributions to categorization performance. The later papers, by Medin, Anderson, and Wolford and Fowler, extend a stimulus interactional analysis to more complex models or applied domains. The three discussants' papers locate and evaluate essential features of the earlier papers within the context of pertinent traditional and contemporary theoretical efforts. These commentaries provide a perspective on the conference that is at once instructional for the general reader and challenging to the specialist in categorization processes.

In terms of the conference's outcome in relation to the research issue that initially motivated the exchange, the proceedings can be said to have strengthened the hypothesis that differential stimulus interaction may play an important role in developmental differences in discrimination, classification, and related cognitive performances. Or to express the same idea in somewhat more graphic fashion, it might be said that the conference papers collectively suggest that developmental differences in categorization behavior arise in part because children *see similarity differently* than adults do. This idea was explicit or implicit in every paper or participant's work. It is a major presumption in the work of both Shepp and Kemler on how children judge similarity. It is central to Medin's notions that a category is not an attribute but an interaction among attributes and that the nature of the interaction may be different for children as compared to adults. It could well account for the Kendlers' finding of nonselective response in young children but selective response in older children. It clearly is central to the Tighes' theoretical analysis. It provides a basis for an alternative account of the phenomena underlying Zeaman and Hanley's hypothesized redirection of attention from compounds to components, as well as of Anderson's hypothesized developmental change in dimension combination rules. It has implications for more general analyses of cognitive development, as in Shepp's description of the development of conservation in terms of change in perceived stimulus structure, and as in Wolford and Fowler's argument that poor readers do not analyze stimulus features but perceive them in relatively wholistic fashion. It could account, too, for Spiker and Cantor's observation that young children, who display evidence of hypothesis testing ability, are nevertheless likely to exhibit pronounced departures from logical or efficient strategies within simple concept tasks. And of course Garner's work provides a taxonomy of stimulus dimension interaction that can be made to inform many, if not indeed all, of these analyses.

Overall, then, this book highlights key empirical and theoretical advances in cognitive-developmental study of categorization processes and provides a medium for addressing the complex but vital question of the relations among perception, cognition, and development. The thrust of the volume is in the area of basic research and theory rather than toward the practical application of knowledge. However, the perceptual and cognitive processes at issue are so fundamental and pervasive that it is difficult to believe that the papers in this volume will not prove to have significant import for our understanding of perception and cognition in natural life settings. Indeed, the work of Wolford and Fowler, to take one instance, directly attests to the utility of these basic analyses in advancing our understanding of the development of reading skill.

Support for the conference was provided principally by the William T. Grant Foundation. The Foundation not only made an early commitment of funds that enabled planning and organization to proceed with assurance of support, but subsequently, when spiraling costs of air travel strained our resources, augmented the level of its support. We are most grateful for the Foundation's generous assistance. We are also grateful to Larry Erlbaum who provided an advance against royalties that further helped to support the conference. Finally, Lou Tassinary assisted the conference directors throughout the meetings, and quickly, by virtue of his general helpfulness and intellectual contribution, proved an integral and valuable member of the group.

Thomas J. Tighe
Bryan E. Shepp

Perception, Cognition, and Development: Interactional Analyses

1 Asymmetric Interactions of Stimulus Dimensions in Perceptual Information Processing

Wendell R. Garner
Yale University

Introduction

For more than the past decade much of my research has been focused on the nature of the dimensions that generate the stimuli we use in our experiments and, more specifically, on the nature of the interactions between these dimensions. Most of this research (mine as well as that of others) has assumed or experimentally demonstrated an equivalent status of the two or more dimensions used in generating a stimulus; that is to say, any interactions between the stimulus dimensions are assumed or shown to be symmetric. There is an increased interest, however, in those types of stimulus dimensions where the roles of the two or more dimensions are not equivalent, where the interactions between the dimensions are asymmetric. Much of what we know about different types of symmetric dimensional interactions, at least for adults, I have summarized elsewhere (Garner, 1974b, 1976) and I shall refer to this material only when necessary to clarify or to contrast with the idea of asymmetric dimensional interaction. Instead, the purpose of this chapter is to summarize some of what we know about asymmetric dimensional interactions, to clarify some differences between various types of asymmetric interactions, and to suggest other types of asymmetric interaction that may exist.

As in writing any report, I found it necessary to make some delimiting decisions about the topics to be covered. Current information processing research is filled with research on processing levels or stages, and these ideas imply an asymmetry of processing at least and, therefore, potentially an asymmetry of the properties of the stimuli that are processed. So the more general topic of asymmetric information processing, including hierarchical and contingent processing,

1

would encompass most of current human information processing research. I have limited my topic to those types of stimuli that can be defined as generated from dimensions without even being too concerned about distinctions between dimensions and features (Garner, 1978a). Thus I remain interested primarily in the nature of the stimulus properties. This decision, however, requires me to omit material that may at some later time interrelate with the material I shall discuss here. Certainly all the research on hierarchical processing of words and sentences is necessarily omitted, and that is a very large area of research indeed. Another area of research and theorizing that I regret omitting is that concerning asymmetric similarity. To illustrate, Rosch (1975) showed that a nonreference stimulus is judged more similar to a reference stimulus (such as a vertical line or a prototypical color) than the converse, and Tversky (1977) provided a theoretical framework within which such asymmetric similarities might exist, as did Krumhansl (1978). The reason I especially regret omitting this material is that the stimuli used in much of this research are sufficiently simple (i.e., artificial) so that it might be possible to find a connection between asymmetric similarities and some of my ideas.

I shall discuss interactions involving stimulus dimensions. In doing so, I shall consider two major types of interaction: (1) those involving primarily asymmetry of a process without any necessary equivalent asymmetry in the logical structure of the stimuli; and (2) those involving primarily an asymmetry in the logical structure of the stimulus or stimulus set, without any necessary presumption that an experimental outcome will show an equivalent asymmetry. As always with a dichotomization, the flow between the two categories of interaction will be free, because when we are interested in process, we are also interested in the stimulus properties that lead to process differences, and when we are interested in stimulus structure, we are interested in the processing consequences of the differences in structure. Nevertheless, the distinction between asymmetries of process and asymmetries of structure will provide a useful working system. There are many other ways of categorizing the types of issue, and Treisman (1979), in a paper concerned with levels of processing, has made a most useful distinction between sequential and temporal ordering of levels. So there are other distinctions that can usefully be made, and the ones I make here are chosen primarily because they easily fit the types of stimuli and experiments I want to discuss.

ASYMMETRIES OF PROCESS

I shall discuss three types of process asymmetry in which stimulus dimensions are important: selective attention, response interference, and name encoding. Although in each case it is possible to argue that there is a logical stimulus structure that determines the process asymmetry, it seems more likely that the asymmetries are due to processing differences rather than to the logical relations between dimensions.

Selective Attention to Dimensions

When I first began investigations of dimensional interaction with information processing tasks (Garner & Felfoldy, 1970), it seemed necessary to distinguish only between two types of interaction: integral and separable. Integral dimensions were those that showed an increase in speed of processing when the two dimensions were correlated and a failure of selective attention when orthogonal stimulus sets were used with classification required of one dimension as relevant with the other dimension varying irrelevantly. Separable dimensions were those that showed no improvement in processing speed when the dimensions were correlated but did allow selective attention to both dimensions. In all cases examined in that report the results were symmetric in that both of a pair of dimensions showed either the redundancy gain or selective attention. The world then seemed simple and dichotomous with regard to this issue, but it did not remain so very long. By 1974, (Garner, 1974b) it was clear that there were at least some kinds of dimensions for which the information processing results were asymmetrical, and I introduced the idea of asymmetric integrality or separability. By 1976 (Garner, 1976), I had added the idea of asymmetric configural dimensions. In both cases, the critical processing task that led to asymmetry was the selective attention task, with selective attention being possible for one dimension but not the other.

Linguistic Dimensions.   The experiments that first led to the need to consider asymmetry of selective attention were by Day and Wood (1972) and by Wood (1974, 1975), and in both cases the stimuli were auditory, with one dimension involving a linguistic property and the other involving a nonlinguistic property. I shall describe in particular the stimuli and results of Wood (1975). He used four stimuli, as usual in these experiments, which were formed from the orthogonal combinations of a consonant sound and pitch, with the vowel sound being constant. The four stimuli were bae-high pitch, bae-low pitch, gae-high pitch, and gae-low pitch. When discrete reaction times were measured for pairs of stimuli differing on a single dimension, reaction time for discrimination of pitch was 411 msec and that for discrimination of the consonant was 416 msec. Thus these two control measures showed that the two dimensions were equally discriminable, a very important fact to establish in experiments of this kind. When the classification task was used, reaction time for pitch as the relevant dimension with consonant as the irrelevant dimension rose very slightly to 413 msec, not a meaningful increase. When, however, the consonant was the relevant dimension, with pitch now the irrelevant dimension, reaction time rose to 467 msec. In other words, subjects could selectively attend to pitch, ignoring variations in the consonant; but they could not selectively attend to the consonant, ignoring irrelevant variations in pitch.

In a discussion of these and other results, Wood (1974) makes clear that no simple serial or parallel model can explain the totality of his results, especially because in his 1974 experiment a decrease in reaction time was obtained when these two dimensions were used in a correlated fashion. However, as far as the selective attention results are concerned, some form of explanation of the asymmetric results that considers that the linguistic property is processed at a higher level than pitch is not unreasonable. Thus in terms of levels of processing, a property processed at a lower level can be selectively attended from one processed at a higher level, but a property processed at a higher level will be interfered with by one processed at a lower level.

Alternatively, however, there is at least the possibility of an explanation in terms of the logical structure of the stimulus properties (Garner, 1974b, p. 136ff), and that is based on the necessary relations between the two types of dimensions. An auditory stimulus with a consonant and vowel must have a pitch, whereas an auditory stimulus with a pitch need not have a linguistic property. This asymmetry of the required logical relations between the two dimensions may be all that is necessary to explain the asymmetric selective attention. On the other hand, the logical properties of the stimuli may in fact determine processing levels, in which case the two explanations would be quite consistent.

Although it is fairly comfortable to interpret the Wood (1974) experiments as indicating a difference in processing levels, pitch being processed more peripherally, other experimental results with auditory stimuli serve to remind us that answers are not simple or easy. Blechner, Day, and Cutting (1976) found the same asymmetry in selective attention, but with stimulus dimensions that are not easily described as phonetic and nonphonetic. Their stimuli were tones, and their dimensions were intensity of tone and rise time to maximum intensity of the tones. Irrelevant variations in intensity interfered with judgments of rise time, but irrelevant variations in rise time did not interfere with judgments of intensity. No ready explanation of this result in terms of levels of processing is available, although the data do not, of course, in any way vitiate such an explanation.

Another series of experiments (Eimas, Tartter, Miller, & Keuthen, 1978) found asymmetric selective attention with stimuli and dimensions that have no obvious difference in levels of processing. Their stimuli were consonant–vowel syllables, the two dimensions being place of articulation and manner of articulation. As an example, the syllables ba, da, va, and za were used in one experiment. The syllables ba and va are labials, and da and za are alveolar, thus differing in place of articulation. The syllables ba and da have stop consonants, whereas the syllables va and za have fricative consonants, thus differing in manner of articulation. In several experiments these authors found that, although both dimensions prevented selective attention, the amount of interference was much greater when manner varied irrelevantly with judgments of place than the converse. Still further, in one of the very few experiments to manipulate relative discriminability of the dimensions, they found that discriminability differences did not alter the relative interference effects of the two dimensions. As with the Blechner et al. (1976) study, these results do not rule out an interpretation in terms of differences in levels, but the authors chose to interpret their results as indicating the kind of concurrent–contingent processing that Turvey (1973) suggested as an explanation of visual pattern masking. The idea is that processing of both dimensions (or levels) goes on concurrently, at least overlapping in time, but that the processing of one dimension is contingent on processing of the other; such a relationship leads to an asymmetry of selective attention but does not allow perfect selective attention for either dimension. This idea of concurrent–contingent processing is related to the discussion on page 23ff in which I suggest ways of generating stimulus sets that actually require contingent processing for successful performance, in some cases concurrently.

Visual Dimensions. Because of the possibility that the necessary logical relations of dimensional existence could account for the asymmetry of selective attention, I (Garner, 1974b) suggested that possibly color and form would provide the same kind of asymmetry of selective attention, on the grounds that color can exist without a form, but a form must have a color to define its boundaries. Thus irrelevant color variations would be expected to interfere with selective attention to form, but irrelevant form variation would not be expected to prevent selective attention to color. Furthermore, Gottwald and I (Gottwald & Garner, 1972) had done a card-sorting experiment requiring selective attention to form or to color and had found a small difference indicating that selective attention to color might be easier.

Schroeder (1976; data also reported in Posner, 1978, p. 69) carried out an experiment with color and form, using both the classification and discrimination techniques that I have used in such studies and the same–different task made so popular by Posner. With the same–different procedure, evidence for selective attention comes primarily from the results for the *same* response. If a subject is instructed, for example, to say *same* when the two stimuli are the same color, then an actual pair of stimuli requiring the response *same* might be identical in both color and form or might be identical in color but different in form. If it takes longer to respond *same* when the pair of stimuli are different in form than when they are identical in form, then there has been a failure of selective attention, because a difference in form interferes with a judgment about color.

Schroeder's (1976) results showed that it was easier to attend selectively to color than to form, the other being the irrelevant dimension, but the result was stronger with his simultaneous same–different technique than with the classification technique. In this experiment, reaction times were faster when response was to color than when it was to form, with the same–different task (the opposite result occurring with the classification tasks) and this difference, in either direction, is something of a problem. Garner and Felfoldy (1970) had shown for the dimensions of size of circle and angle of a diameter within the circle that if the two dimensions are unequally discriminable, then the more discriminable dimension (i.e., that producing faster reaction time) could produce interference with the less discriminable dimension, even though no such interference was found when the two dimensions were equally discriminable. Thus it is possible to obtain a result showing asymmetric selective attention due solely to differences in discriminability of dimensions, and this fact causes difficulty of interpretation in many experiments. However, because Schroeder obtained the same asymmetry with both tasks, it seems unlikely that the result is an artifact of discriminability differences.

There are many issues unresolved, however. One substantive issue that I thought might influence the integrality or separability of dimensions, even possibly producing asymmetry of selective attention, was the absolute size of the stimuli used. In the Gottwald and Garner (1972) experiment with color and form classification, we had used stimuli of about 3.5° visual angle. Schroeder (1976) had used larger stimuli for the same–different task and smaller ones for the classification task, but within the same general range of sizes. Would smaller visual angles give different results? In an experiment with size and brightness, using card sorting with classification tasks, I (Garner, 1977) varied the size of the stimuli from 1° to 7° visual angle and found absolutely no effect of size within this range. Size and brightness gave the clear result indicating separability (i.e., no redundancy gain but good selective attention), and this result was obtained at all sizes. So there appears to be little reason to expect any clarification of the relation between color and form by systematic variations of size as long as the sizes are foveal or near-foveal.

Other visual dimensions have also recently been shown to produce some asymmetry of selective attention. Redding and Tharp (1981) used the dimensions of right or left location of a line having two different orientations. Although selective attention was not completely possible for either location or orientation, irrelevant location interfered with judgments of orientation more than the converse. Still further, Dick and Hochstein (1981) showed that irrelevant variations in line orientation interfered with judgments of length but not the converse. So the evidence is accumulating that some dimensions have some sort of a priority role with respect to others, thus producing asymmetric selective attention, even when there are no very obvious differences in levels of processing as explanatory constructs.

Methodological Issues.   Although it is not unambiguously clear whether dimensions such as color and form (or any dimensions not having obvious differences in level of processing) produce asymmetric selective attention, some methodological issues are evolving that may require clarification but that may also in their clarification help in our understanding of possible asymmetric relations between dimensions. Many experiments have been done with both the classification technique and with the same–different technique without seeming to suggest that perhaps fundamentally different processes are involved with the two techniques. Recently, however, there has appeared some clear evidence that the two techniques do not necessarily give the same results. Santee and Egeth (1980) investigated selective attention to form with irrelevant variation in size. Two forms were used (circle and square) but three different sizes. With the classification task (both card sorting and discrete reaction time) there was excellent selective attention to form with irrelevant variation in size. With a simultaneous same–different task, however, there was failure of selective attention. Further, with a sequential same–different task, the maximum interference occurred at an interstimulus interval of about 100 msec, but interference was negligible at an interval of about 1000 msec.

The Santee and Egeth (1980) experiment did not investigate the effects of irrelevant variation of form on selective attention to size, so there is no evidence in this experiment of an asymmetric relation between the dimensions. However, given these kinds of time relations with the same–different task, it is possible that the Schroeder (1976) result with respect to color and form would be different with a sequential same–different task rather than the simultaneous same–different task actually used. Such results are, of course, far more than a methodological nuisance; rather, they imply that we need to understand selective attention as a time-determined process, and that fact in turn suggests that there may be asymmetries in relations between dimensions that themselves are time dependent.

The Problem of Unequal Discriminabilities.   Another methodological issue basic to an understanding of the substantive problems themselves concerns the relative discriminabilities of the two or more dimensions about whose interaction we are concerned. As I mentioned, an asymmetry of selective attention can be produced if the two dimensions are very unequal in their discriminabilities: Separable dimensions can be made to be asymmetrical separable, and integral dimensions can be as well, because obviously a dimension that does not perceptually vary at all because the difference in its two levels is too small can hardly interfere with a dimension that has a large perceptual difference.

In the logic of the experiments that I have used, it is clearly necessary to demonstrate with the appropriate control conditions that two dimensions are equally discriminable before any interpretation of an asymmetric result can be made. This seems a simple enough requirement; yet its absence in many experiments makes interpretation very difficult, as we soon shall see. It would be easy to say that there is no justification ever for interpreting an asymmetric result as valid unless controls have shown equal discriminability. But that is too rigid a position to take, because there are experimental situations in which the very difference in reaction times that I am arguing need to be equated are used as evidence of differences in level of processing. To illustrate, the experiment by Garner, Podgorny, and Frasca (1982) described later establishes presumptive differences in levels of processing physical and cognitive dimensions based on differences in reaction times, and to require that each of the three dimensions used in that experiment be equally discriminable is to deny the very phenomenon being investigated. This same issue is true of all the experiments comparing reaction times for physically identical stimuli to those having the same name only (Posner, 1978).

The issue does remain, however, often as an uncomfortable thorn, and the only ultimate solution is to find the kinds of converging operations that Garner, Hake, and Eriksen (1956) argued for some years ago. That is to say, it is unlikely that any arbitrary position on the interpretability of differences in reaction times can be justified, and we shall have to use either more complicated converging operations or very persuasive intuitions.

Asymmetric Response Interference

The basic experimental paradigm that I and others have used in studying dimensional integrality has been the use of single-dimension classifications as control conditions, the use of classification with orthogonal dimensions to determine whether selective attention to dimensions is possible, and the use of correlated dimensions to determine whether there is a gain in processing speed with the redundant information. The logic of this set of experimental operations is that a loss in speed compared to the control conditions can only occur with the selective attention task; interference presumably can occur when there is a dimension varying irrelevantly, thus preventing selective attention to the relevant dimension. The only reasonable expectation when correlated dimensions are used has been that there might be a gain in processing speed but not a loss. However, the kinds of dimensions ordinarily used have been those for which there is no natural relation between either of the dimensions and the nature of the response and, therefore, no natural relation between the dimensions themselves or between their responses. To illustrate, when a card-sorting task is used with the dimensions of color and form, say red or green crossed with square or circle, the correlated dimensions can produce either red square and green circle or, conversely, green square and red circle. Either pair of stimuli provides dimensional correlation, and experimental results have shown no difference between the pairs in terms of redundancy gain or lack of gain. There is, in other words, no meaningful way to specify that one correlation is negative and the other positive.

There are other stimulus sets that are easily thought of as being generated from two dimensions but in which it does seem meaningful to specify one of the correlations as positive and the other as negative. Such stimulus dimensions allow the possibility that interference can occur with correlated dimensions, if the correlation is negative. I have considered such a state of stimuli (Garner, 1976) as involving response interference and thus not really pertinent to an understanding of the kinds of dimensional interaction in which I am primarily interested. However, there are some experiments that have used correlated stimulus dimensions without an explicitly verbal response, the type of response that clearly would lead to response competition with negative correlation. Even though an implicit verbal response can just as easily lead to response interference, some clarification of the nature of interference in such tasks may be helpful, especially insofar as there are asymmetries in the interference.

Verbal Responding.   The classic experiment on response interference is that by Stroop (1935), which has led to so much research that it has practically become its own specialty area in cognitive psychology. The basic stimulus materials are words of color names printed in colors that conflict with the color names. Compared to various types of control (see Dyer, 1973, for a review), it takes longer to name the colors when the words are conflicting or to read the color names when the colors are conflicting. However, there has usually been an asymmetry found in the experiments where the experimental design allowed it to occur, and the asymmetry is that conflicting color words interfere with color naming more than conflicting colors interfere with reading of the color names. The explanation for this asymmetry almost certainly is of the kind suggested by Posner and Snyder (1975), an explanation in terms of differential pathway activations leading to a response. Thus it is not clear that this type of experimental result, pertaining to highly overlearned naming or verbal responses, is valuable in understanding dimensional interaction rather than response interaction.

Further evidence of the primary role of the response in such experiments comes from an experiment by Flowers, Warner, and Polansky (1979), who used a card-sorting procedure with stimulus dimensions of numeric value and numerosity: One, two, or three items appeared on a card, and the items were the digits 1, 2, or 3. Subjects were required to report verbally either the numeric value or the number of items (numerosity). Control conditions established baseline performance against which to compare conditions in which conflicting combinations of numeric value and numerosity occurred, such as 1 1 1 or 2 or 3 3, etc. The results showed that the actual numeric value interfered with reports of numerosity more than the converse, a result quite in line with the asymmetry found in the Stroop test. When, however, the response was to tap manually either the numeric value or numerosity, interference was greatly reduced overall, but even more importantly the asymmetry of interference was reversed: With tapping as the response, conflicting numerosity slowed numeric value responding.

Thus it seems clear that the nature of the response process is critical in Stroop-type experiments, and although there may be dimensional interactions operating in such experimental tasks, the evidence for such interaction is probably overwhelmed by purely response factors.

Nonverbal Responding. Experiments that involve potential response competition need not involve an overt verbal response or even an overt compatible response such as the tapping used by Flowers et al. (1979). The response itself may be neutral with respect to the nature of the stimulus dimensions, and whereas implicit semantic factors may produce any actual interference found, it is possible to carry out the experiment with responses that do not essentially guarantee that response competition is involved. Such experiments may be more pertinent to questions of dimensional interaction.

An excellent experiment of this type, and one that follows exactly the experimental paradigm that has been used in the study of integrality, has been done by Clark and Brownell (1976); I shall report it in some detail because it may involve meaningful dimensional asymmetries, not just asymmetries of response interference. Figure 1.1 illustrates the four stimuli used by these authors. There were the usual four stimuli generated by orthogonal combinations of two dimensions: vertical position and direction of an arrow. The authors used the control tasks of single-dimension discrimination with each dimension; they also used the two selective attention tasks, one for each dimension as relevant; and they used the two tasks involving correlated stimulus dimensions. The two pairs of stimuli involving correlated dimensions have a rather obvious positive and negative correlation, with one diagonal pair of stimuli providing a positive correlation between position and direction of arrow and the other diagonal providing a negative correlation.

These authors required a right or left button press, a direction neither compatible nor incompatible with the up–down properties of the stimuli. Their results are shown in Table 1.1. When direction of the arrow was relevant for response, the positively correlated dimensions produced a substantial facilitation and the

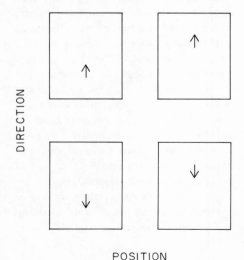

FIG. 1.1.   The kinds of stimuli used by Clark and Brownell (1976).

TABLE 1.1
Reaction Times (msec) for Judgments of Direction and Position of
Stimuli in Fig. 1.1
(After Clark & Brownell, 1976)

	Judgment	
Dimensional Relation	*Direction*	*Position*
Single	462	439
Positive correlation	436	428
Negative correlation	520	454
Orthogonal	511	465

negatively correlated dimensions produced substantial interference. The amount of interference with the two stimuli with negatively correlated dimensions was of the same order of magnitude as the interference produced with the orthogonal stimuli requiring selective attention. When position was relevant for response, exactly the same pattern of results occurred, including the fact that the amount of interference obtained with negatively correlated dimensions was approximately the same as that obtained with orthogonal dimensions.

The point of interest for purposes of this chapter, however, is that the amount of interference (and facilitation as well) was quite different for the two dimensions: Irrelevant or conflicting variations in position interfered far more with judgments of direction than the converse. An interpretation of this asymmetry along the lines of that suggested for the Wood (1974) experiment would be that absolute position is processed at a lower level than direction. Certainly it is true that there is more arbitrariness about the semantic meaning of the direction of an arrow than about position. But it is also true that the arrow does have to have a position, although a position need not have the properties of an arrow or any other semantically interpreted property. Thus an interpretation in terms of either processing levels or logical structure of the stimulus dimensions is possible.

There is, of course, the difficulty that the two control tasks did not show equal discriminability for the two dimensions, and the faster dimension interfered more with the slower dimension than the converse. However, Clark and Brownell (1976) used two different discriminabilities between the two positions (amount of physical difference in location), but this experimental manipulation did not influence reaction times. This lack of effect of discriminability of position suggests that there is a true hierarchical relation between position and direction, with position being a more basic dimension than the more semantically interpreted arrow direction.

A similar set of stimuli was used in an experiment by Logan and Zbrodoff (1979), shown in Fig. 1.2. The response was a key press to the right or left, an arrangement avoiding compatibility issues with stimuli involving up–down relations. The actual stimuli used vertical position of a word above or below a

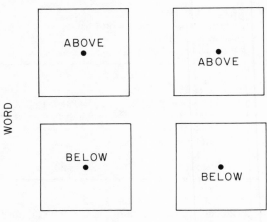

WORD

POSITION

FIG. 1.2.   The kinds of stimuli used by Logan and Zbrodoff (1979).

fixation point as one of the variables, the other variable being the semantically equivalent stimulus words ABOVE and BELOW. These stimulus dimensions could provide both positive and negative dimensional correlations, with congruent or conflicting stimulus values. A stimulus set extending this kind of arrangement even further was used by Logan (1980). In that stimulus set, the stimuli were like those shown in Fig. 1.2, but in addition an asterisk was placed above or below the word, thus introducing relative position as a third variable that could have values congruent or conflicting with values on the other two dimensions.

These two experiments do provide data relevant to the question of dimensional asymmetry. To refer primarily to the Logan and Zbrodoff (1979) experiment, responding was required with either the word or the the position relevant, and trials occurred on which the second dimension had values either congruent or conflicting. The percentage of conflicting trials differed in different blocks of trials. The result of greatest importance here is that position could facilitate or interfere with responses to the word, but the converse effect was very small. That is, judgments of location were relatively unaffected by whether the word was congruent or conflicting or by whether the percentage of conflicting trials was low or high, although judgments of the word were easily influenced by actual position.

Thus absolute position seems to play a more basic or fundamental role than those dimensions whose meaning is derived and arbitrary, such as actual names. The different role of these two dimensions can be understood even further by noting the result of greatest importance to Logan and Zbrodoff (1979) (as well as to Logan, 1980): When blocks of trials involved a higher percentage (e.g., 80%) of conflicting stimuli, then position actually facilitated on conflicting trials and interfered on compatible trials. This result is in contrast to that obtained by Clark and Brownell (1976), who never found that conflicting stimulus dimensions produced facilitation, even though in their tasks the conflicting relation was used on all trials in those blocks involving negative correlations. There are many differences between the experimental procedures and designs of these experiments, including the fact that in the Logan and Zbrodoff experiment there was no true control condition, so the terms facilitation and interference refer only to relative reaction times rather than absolute levels of facilitation and interference. There is nevertheless the suggestion that the stimulus dimensions of Clark and Brownell are more basic, physical, and natural, thus impervious to the kind of reversal of cuing or encoding relations found with stimuli such as actual words.

Discriminability or Levels of Processing?   In the Logan experiments, position was much more discriminable than word or relative position. In the Logan (1980) paper specifically, the appropriate control experiment was run to establish that absolute position was processed faster than word identity, and that word identity in turn was processed faster than relative position, the variable always relevant in that experiment. This result, as also with the Clark and Brownell (1976) experiment, makes interpretation of the experiments difficult, because (despite the fact that an interpretation in terms of levels seems intuitively appealing) much of the evidence for the asymmetric nature of the results could almost certainly be produced with stimulus dimensions that would seem to operate at the same processing level—simply by making the dimensions unequally discriminable.

Different discriminabilities of dimensions can produce asymmetric selective attention to dimensions (i.e., asymmetric interference). Different discriminabilities can also produce asymmetric facilitation, such as that found both by Clark and Brownell (1976) and by Logan and Zbrodoff (1979). Felfoldy and Garner (1971) used dimensions of size of circle and angle of an enclosed diameter, with the angle being much less discriminable (i.e., producing slower reaction times) than size. When the two dimensions were correlated, responses to the slower dimension were facilitated and responses to the faster dimension were not, a result we suggested was due to selective serial processing. Such a result seems so inevitable that the experiment is essentially a demonstration. Yet perhaps such asymmetric facilitation found in these other experiments might also be considered inevitable when the two dimensions are not equally discriminable.

There is no easy resolution to this problem. Just because an equivalent result can be found with other dimensions that are unequally discriminable does not guarantee that the result found with any particular pair of dimensions is due only to the unequal discriminabilities. And it may even be, as Logan (1980) argues, that the differences in reaction times are due to differences in levels of processing. Discriminability or processing levels? The problem seems necessarily to remain with us for some time yet.

Name as a Dimension

In the last section I have been considering experiments in which actual words were treated as though they were stimulus dimensions along with other variables more commonly considered stimulus dimensions, such as color and location. In this section I shall pursue further the question as to whether variables such as names are dimensions in the same sense as the more obviously physical dimensions. This topic is one that could have been considered as one of logical structure of stimulus sets or as a problem of process asymmetry, but because I shall present data dealing with the problem as a process asymmetry, I have chosen to treat the topic within this framework. The basic problem and to a large extent the experimental paradigm stem from the work of Posner (1978) and, more specifically, from Posner and Mitchell (1967).

Name as Hierarchical Structure.   In the original Posner and Mitchell (1967) experiments, pairs of letters in upper and/or lower case were presented in a same–different task. In some conditions, sameness was defined as physical identity: Thus the letter pair AA would be called *same,* but the letter pair Aa would not; nor, of course, would letter pairs such as AB or Ab be called *same.* In other conditions, sameness was defined as same name, so that Aa, for example, would also be called *same.*

What makes this task one of hierarchical structure is simply that when the task instruction is changed from physical identity to name sameness, there is an increase in the number of stimuli that satisfy the definition of same: The class inclusions have become larger. Similarly, when the experiment is extended so that same means all vowels or all consonants, class inclusion has been increased still further. Reaction time, of course, increases with a higher level of class inclusion; therefore the interpretation of the differences in reaction times as differences in processing levels (e.g., see Posner, 1978, p. 32) can as easily be interpreted as due to differences in hierarchical level of the stimulus set. To illustrate the point, if we had a set of random figures with no learned names, and if we increased the number of stimuli that satisfy the definition of same (or increased the number of stimulus items in a class with a classification task), reaction time would increase with this increase in class inclusion, and I would consider such a result to be due simply to properties of the logical structure of stimulus sets.

However, I have pointed out (1980; but also 1974b, p. 137) that experiments can be run in such a way that name is considered a dimension along with letter case, so that the role of the two dimensions and their interactions can be investigated. Nickerson (1972) had even earlier suggested many different ways in which sameness could be specified in same–different tasks involving letters, with both name and case serving as the basis of the definition of sameness. A full use of all the task definitions Nickerson suggested would be an interesting experiment to run, even though the time requirements would be quite substantial. Nevertheless, the point is that name can be considered simply as another stimulus variable, without the problem of a hierarchy in the stimulus set.

Name versus Physical Dimension.   To illustrate the point, I shall use data from an experiment by Garner et al. (1982). Rather than simply treat name and case as two dimensions, we went a step further and introduced three dimensions but with a total set of stimuli of just four items. Our stimuli were 6, 10, VI, X. These stimuli vary in three dimensions: name (6 versus 10), system (Arabic versus Roman), and length (long versus short or one versus two elements). With any two of these dimensions, the stimuli can be arranged into a 2 × 2 matrix such as that in Fig. 1.1, and whichever two dimensions are chosen to define the rows and columns, the third dimension becomes the Latin factor, because these four stimuli based on three dimensions form a Latin square. Each of these dimensions has, of course, equivalent status in terms of a hierarchy of class inclusion, for there are exactly two stimuli within each level of each dimension. Thus any comparisons of speed of processing between these three dimensions do not involve differences in hierarchical level of the stimuli.

Although we used a same–different task, for the moment it is easier to describe the structure of these stimuli in terms of classification schemes. If we choose to consider only two of the dimensions as worthy of mention, but nevertheless use all the three possible 2 by 2 classifications, then two of the classifications are specified by one dimension and would be used to determine whether selective attention is possible. The third classification is the biconditional, which is very difficult, especially with separable dimensions (Garner, 1978b; Gottwald & Garner, 1975). Thus if we consider that length and system are dimensions, then the name classification is the biconditional classification of length and system. On the other hand, should we choose to consider name and length as the dimensions, then system classification is the biconditional classification. Therefore in any classification task or equivalent same–different task, if one of the three dimensions is much more difficult to use than the others, it is not unreasonable to interpret this fact as indicating a primary role of the other two dimensions, with the difficult dimension being interpreted as the biconditional classification of the other two dimensions.

These three dimensions differ in a potentially important way, one that may be useful in understanding the roles of the dimensions and any asymmetries in their interactions. Length is a clearly physical property of the stimuli, one that needs no semantic encoding, even though one might be used. System is a more arbitrarily defined property of the stimuli; yet for these particular stimuli that arbitrary definition can be changed into a reasonably physical one, because the Roman numerals have nothing but straight lines whereas both Arabic numerals have curved lines. Name, however, even though considered as a dimension, cannot be easily translated or encoded into a reasonably physical dimension. The stimuli 10 and X or 6 and VI have little in common other than their names. Thus these stimuli allow us to determine something about the relative utility in processing of clearly defined physical dimensions as contrasted to arbitrarily defined dimensions.

We used a same–different task, and these four stimuli produce 16 pairs to compare in such a task. These pairs of stimuli form four groups with regard to the three dimensions defining the stimuli:

(P) Physically identical: 6 6,   10 10,   VI VI,   X X
(L) Same length, different
    system and name: 6 X,   X 6,   VI 10,   10 VI
(S) Same system, different
    length and name: 6 10,   10 6,   VI X,   X VI
(N) Same name, different
    length and system: 6 VI,   VI 6,   10 X,   X 10

We used four different definitions of same: physical identity, in which only the P stimulus pairs satisfy the definition; same length, in which the P plus the L pairs satisfy the definition; same system, in which the P plus the S pairs satisfy the definition; and same name, in which the P plus the N pairs satisfy the definition. This experimental design provides complete balancing of all three dimensions in the experimental tasks, for not only are the physically identical stimuli used in the definition of same, but all different pairs are defined as same in one of the tasks.

Data for the four groups of stimulus pairs and for the four different task instructions (rules for same), for simultaneous presentation of the stimulus pairs, are shown in Table 1.2. These are a very orderly set of data and allow us to draw some clear conclusions about asymmetric roles of these three stimulus dimen-

TABLE 1.2
Reaction Times (msec) for Same–Different Task, Simultaneous
Presentation, for Four Rules for Same and Four Types
of Stimulus Pairs.
(Data from Garner, Podgorny, & Frasca, 1982)

Stimulus Pairs	Rule for Same			
	Physical	Length	System	Name
Physical identity	400	419	426	449
Same length	441	473	539	620
Same system	450	486	542	599
Same name	419	474	535	597

Note: Numbers in italics are for *same* responses.

sions, if dimensions they psychologically are. First, simply note the diagonal entries that show the reaction times for *same* responses under the four different rules for same. The fastest reaction times, of course, are for the physically identical stimuli, both when physical identity was the rule for same and when any of the other rules was used. But the same-length stimulus pairs show the least increase in reaction time when they are added to the definition of sameness, the same system stimuli show the next largest increase, and the same name stimuli show the largest increase. Stated in terms of asymmetric effects, the stimulus pairs that have the same name but differ in both length and system are the most difficult. Thus these two more physical dimensions interfere with judgments of sameness more than the name dimension interferes with judgments of either same system or same length. In turn, the dimension of length interferes more with judgments of system than the dimension of system interferes with judgments of length. We can thus conclude that there is a difference in processing levels, with the physical dimension of length being the easiest to process and the most effective in interfering with other judgments of sameness, whereas the dimension of name is the most difficult to process and interferes least with judgments of the other dimensions. In fact, judgments of same name are so difficult that one could with comfort interpret these data as indicating that judgments of same name are in reality judgments of nothing more than the biconditional relation between length and system.

What is the role of name in such tasks? The answer lies in Table 1.3, where data are shown for a sequential presentation, with the first stimulus of a pair being displayed for 500 msec before the second stimulus is displayed. All reaction times are lower, probably representing a general readiness factor, but the matter of interest is what happens to the stimulus pairs under each rule for sameness. With length as the rule for sameness, the difference between the physically identical stimuli and those the same in length only is not changed

TABLE 1.3
Reaction Times (msec) for Same–Different Task, Sequential
Presentation, for Four Rules for Same and Four Types
of Stimulus Pairs
(Data from Garner, Podgorny, & Frasca, 1982)

	Rule for Same			
Stimulus Pairs	*Physical*	*Length*	*System*	*Name*
Physical identity	*316*	334	352	355
Same length	364	*381*	433	447
Same system	372	398	*423*	436
Same name	363	394	428	*411*

Note: Numbers in italics are for *same* responses.

compared to the data for simultaneous presentation. With both same system and same name, however, there is a substantial reduction in the times for those stimulus pairs the same in just system or name, and in fact the pairs having the same name are judged as rapidly as those having the same system. Thus it appears that with sufficient time the name serves as a carrier, an encoding device, to recode the stimuli into physical forms that make the judgment of sameness easier. Although I do not want to present all the data in this report, I will simply state that detailed analyses support this conclusion. This conclusion about the role of name encoding is much like what Posner (1978) has suggested for the role of name encoding.

Conclusions

Although most of the experiments discussed in this section were not carried out in the interest of clarifying my present concerns about dimensional asymmetries, there are some reasonably valid conclusions that seem to emerge from this overview:

1. The many different variables that are used as experimental dimensions are not all alike in their effects on information processing, and it is reasonable to consider different dimensions as functioning at different levels in information processing. Thus there are some dimensions that are physical and basic in nature that are processed at a low (peripheral) level, and there are other dimensions that even though physically definable are processed at higher levels. There are at least phonetic and semantic levels at which some dimensions are processed, but there are probably many more meaningful distinctions in level.

2. Asymmetries of both interference and facilitation occur as a result of these differences in levels, and the usual relationship is that the more basic dimensions processed at lower levels facilitate or interfere with dimensions processed at higher levels exclusively or at least more so than the converse.

3. Despite the probable validity of these conclusions, some of the same processing asymmetries that lead to a conclusion of differences in level may be due to differences in discriminability between dimensions processed at the same level. Still further, some of the processing differences may be due to structural asymmetries in the stimulus sets (such as differences in sizes of class inclusion) that can occur with stimuli in reality at a single processing level.

ASYMMETRIES IN STIMULUS STRUCTURE

In this section I shall discuss two major types of structural asymmetry: first, part–whole asymmetry; second, contingent dimensions. In addition, in a third section some aspects of stimulus cuing techniques that relate especially to the use of contingent dimensions will be discussed.

The Part–Whole Asymmetry

Probably the most obvious type of structural asymmetry related to problems of dimensional asymmetry is the part–whole relation. As with the entire topic of processing asymmetries, the topic of parts and wholes in visual perception is a major literature unto itself. However, in keeping with the problems discussed in this chapter I shall be concerned primarily with those experimental tasks in which parts and wholes are used as experimental dimensions.

Part–Whole Asymmetric Integrality.   The earliest research done on the relation between parts and wholes, with a concern for the kinds of dimensional interaction that I have been studying, was carried out by Pomerantz and Sager (1975). They constructed stimulus configurations from elements that were the letters X, Y, O, or V. Although the logic of their stimulus construction was like that shown in Fig. 1.3, their whole configurations were not necessarily letters. In several different experiments, they used the full range of tasks that I have used to establish integrality or separability of the whole configurations and the elements considered as dimensions: the single dimension control conditions, correlated dimensions to determine whether there was a redundancy gain, and orthogonal dimensions to determine whether selective attention was possible for either the part or the whole.

An example of the stimuli used is an X or a + as the whole configuration, composed of either X's or O's as the elements, the visual angle of the large configuration being about 2.5°. There were the usual four possible combinations of the two dimensions. They used a card-sorting task and found that the part or the whole could be used as the basis of sorting equally well, at least in those cases of concern here. It was then found that sorting was faster in the correlated decks, so that there was a redundancy gain, the result that indicates dimensional integrality. There was also interference in the selective attention tasks, but irrelevant variations in the element interfered with judgments of the larger configuration more than the converse. They thus concluded that there was an asymmetric

```
H     H          S S S S S
H     H          S       S
H     H          S       S
H H H H H        S       S
H     H          S       S
H     H          S       S
H     H          S S S S S
```

FIG. 1.3.   The types of stimuli used in studies of part–whole asymmetries. A large letter is constructed from small letters of the same type, and the two letters can be congruent or conflicting.

integrality based on the asymmetric selective attention. They further argued that because both the part and the whole were equally discriminable, the asymmetry was due to an attentional factor, not being an artifactual consequence of a difference in discriminability of the sort I discussed in the previous sections. Thus at least for these types of stimuli and possibly for the particular visual angle used, an asymmetric result was obtained with equal discriminability of the two dimensions, with the part element more capable of interfering with processing of the whole configuration than the converse.

Response Interference.   In the Pomerantz and Sager (1975) experiment, the wholes and the parts were such that the response conflict was not necessarily involved, and their data showed no evidence that response conflict was involved. Navon (1977) used stimuli for which response conflict clearly was a factor. To illustrate with the experiment most like the information processing experiments used in the research I have been reporting, Navon used stimuli like those shown in Fig. 1.3, although his larger letters were formed from 6 × 7 arrays rather than by the 5 × 7 arrays shown in that figure. The vertical visual angle of his stimuli was about 3°. His was an identification task, in which the letters H or S were to be identified; the reaction time with a key response was measured. In some conditions, the larger letter was to be identified, and in others the smaller letter was to be identified. In either case, there were three types of trials: *congruent,* in which both the whole and the part letters were the same; *conflicting,* in which the alternative relevant letter was used (e.g., a large S formed of small H's); and *neutral,* in which the irrelevant component was the letter O, either large or small.

Navon's (1977) results showed that neutral and congruent letters gave about the same reaction times, with responding to either the whole or the part. However, when conflicting stimuli were used, then a conflicting large letter interfered with response to the small letter much more than the converse. From this result Navon concluded that wholes are processed before parts. However, the issue of discriminability is very severe in this experiment, because under the neutral conditions reaction time to the large letters was about 460 msec and that to the small letters was about 570 msec. This difference is so large that any interpretation of asymmetry between parts and wholes is simply not valid.

Other experimenters picked up on this point quickly enough. Martin (1979) used stimuli much like those used by Navon (1977), being only slightly larger (vertical visual angle of about 4°) and being composed of two different element densities. In a dense condition, the whole letters were formed from a 5 × 7 matrix of part elements; in a sparse condition, the large letters were formed from a 3 × 5 matrix of small letters. The same two letters, H and S, were used in an identification task; the same three conditions, congruent, conflicting, and neutral, were used. The response, however, was verbal, with reaction time measured with a voice key. Thus in most important respects the experimental conditions of Navon and Martin were the same. Martin's results showed that with the dense condition Navon's result was obtained, with conflicting whole letters interfering with responses to part letters more than the converse. Interference was, however, found in both directions, and because there was also less difference between whole identification and part identification, there is the strong suggestion of mutual interference when the parts and the wholes are approximately equally discriminable.

The results with the sparse condition were very different: The small letters interfered with identification of the whole letters greatly, whereas the whole letter interfered with identification of the small letter to only a slight extent. Still further, the change from the dense to the sparse condition also greatly changed reaction times in the neutral condition, with reaction times to the part letters being nearly 200 msec faster than to the whole letters. Thus the change from dense to sparse letters changed the direction of interference, but it also changed the relative discriminabilities of the wholes and the parts. It is not clear from these experiments that the structural relation of whole to part has any effect beyond that which would be expected on the basis of discriminability differences.

Another experiment questioning the generality of any result about processing consequences of the relation between parts and wholes was done by Hoffman (1980). He used the same kinds of stimuli shown in Fig. 1.3 and used by Navon (1977) and by Martin (1979) but a larger set of letters: L, T, X, Y, H, N, F, Z. The visual angle of the whole letters was about 2°. He used a memory-search paradigm in which one, two, or four letters were held in memory, and one item was displayed, the subject being required to report whether the displayed item was in the memory set. As in the other experiments, responding was on the basis of either the part or the whole letter. In a first experiment, Hoffman established that, for his particular letters, processing time was equally fast for responding to the whole letter or the part letter, and there was facilitation when the whole and the part letter were congruent compared to the conditions in which they were conflicting. No meaningful neutral condition was used in this experiment. Thus there was no basis on which to state that either wholes or parts have a priority in processing. In a second experiment, however, Hoffman distorted either or both of the large and small letters by moving a single element in the letter. In this experiment the memory set size was always two, and only six different letters were used. With this experimental manipulation, reaction times were changed reflecting the distortion in either the large or small letters: To illustrate, if the small letter was to be reported, distorting it increased its reaction time, but distorting the large letter abolished its ability to produce interference. Because the same result occurred if the large letter was to be reported, it is clear that level of distortion was determining the nature of response interference and not the part–whole relation.

Hoffman's (1980) result makes clear that there are many factors that determine whether a part is processed more rapidly (or with some sort of priority) than a whole, or vice versa. Simple discriminability is one such factor, as I have noted; but so is the quality of the part as contrasted with the quality of the whole. In fact, this result of Hoffman's is reminiscent of a result with a quite different experimental paradigm. Palmer (1977) required subjects to determine whether a part was contained within a whole, using letterlike stimuli but none with obvious names. His experimental variable was the goodness (in the Gestalt sense) of the part, and he found that it is easier to determine that a part is within a whole if the part has a good configuration. So the issue is not just parts versus wholes but quality of parts and quality of wholes.

A last experiment to be reported (last because it seems to summarize the nature of the part–whole issue as far as speed of processing is concerned) is one by Kinchla and Wolfe (1979). They too were concerned about the generality of Navon's (1977) conclusion that wholes are processed before parts. They used the same kinds of stimuli as those shown in Fig. 1.3, using the letters E, H, S generated from a 6×7 matrix. On each trial the subject was instructed to respond positively for one of the three letters, negatively otherwise, using key press as response, with a positive response being required if either the large or the small letter satisfied the requirement. The point of importance is that they used five different visual angles, ranging from just under 5° to slightly over 22° for the larger letter. At the different visual angles, the proportionate sizes of the large and small letters were the same (i.e., the *relative* physical properties of the wholes and parts were not changed, just the overall size). Their results showed that at the smaller visual angles positive responses were faster to the whole letters than to the part letters but that at the larger visual angles the reverse was true. A crossover of the two functions suggests that parts and wholes were equally fast at about 8° of visual angle. To quote Kinchla and Wolfe (1979), "Even though both the large and the small letters were always perfectly perceptible, the large letters were processed more slowly when they were too large, and the small letters more slowly when they were too small [p. 228]."

This result clearly shows that there is no single principle about wholes being processed before parts or parts being processed before wholes. Rather, there is some optimum size (visual angle) of an entity, and processing is faster at that optimum size, whether what is being processed is, in a structural sense, a part or a whole. This issue and this conclusion is similar to a remark I made about configural and letter processing of words (Garner, 1981). In studying whether the greater configural differentiation available with words made of lowercase letters compared to the same words made of uppercase letters would improve discriminability and identification, I had stated that it was self-evident that with very large words only letters could be processed, whereas with very small words only the whole configuration could be processed. Therefore, there was a legitimate experimental question only at intermediate sizes, sizes at which it was at least possible that either individual letters or word configurations could serve as the primary basis of identification. This conclusion does not leave us with a clear sense of how to understand the part–whole problem. The structural relation exists and is very meaningful; but understanding the role of the structural relation in information processing is made difficult by such sensory and perceptual factors as discriminability of parts and wholes, their absolute sizes, and the perceptual quality of parts and wholes. Thus the type of stimulus structure with the clearest logical asymmetry does not provide an equally clear answer about the processing consequences of this structural asymmetry.

Contingent Dimensions

An asymmetric structural relation between parts and wholes can be specified for a single stimulus, although the experiments discussed used both parts and wholes as dimensions, thus making our concern be with sets of stimuli and not just single stimuli. There is another type of stimulus set that involves a logical structural asymmetry. I shall use the term *contingent dimensions* as a general descriptive term, but these include what might more easily be described as sets of stimuli with nested dimensions. There has not been a lot of research done on information processing of such stimulus sets, so much of what I shall be saying is concerned with an understanding of the logical relations between dimensions in such sets rather than with clear experimental results. The common factor in these stimulus sets and their associated tasks is a logically asymmetric relation between dimensions or their functions.

Contingent S–R Mapping. The first experiment I shall describe was by Shaffer (1965), and although it does not strictly conform to the asymmetry requirements I specified, it provides a very good introduction to the topic. Shaffer used a discrete reaction task to two lights placed to the left or right of center, with right and left key presses as responses. These were considered to be the primary signals. Between the two lights was another stimulus that could be either a vertical or a horizontal line. These stimuli specified whether a subject was to use a homolateral or a contralateral mapping of responses to the two light stimuli: Thus the middle line specified the S–R mapping between the lights and the response, and the S–R mapping was contingent on the value of the middle stimulus.

Although this task can indeed be interpreted as a contingent information processing task, Biederman (1972) pointed out that in terms of the logical structure the two stimulus dimensions (light location and line orientation) had equivalent status, and the task when both dimensions were used was simply that of a biconditional classification. The logical nature of this task can be seen in Table 1.4, where color and form are the two stimulus dimensions. The biconditional classification task requires that a single response be given to the stimulus pairs on the diagonals. Yet it is also true that the biconditional classification specifies a contingency, because, for example, when form is square, then an S–R mapping

TABLE 1.4
Schema of a Simple Biconditional Classification Task Showing that
Either Dimension May Be Considered Primary with the Other
Dimension Contingent, Indicating Response Assignment

		Color	
		Red	Green
	Square	1	2
Form			
	Triangle	2	1

Note: The number in the table indicates the response assignment.

is specified in which red is assigned the response 1 and green is assigned the response 2; although when form is triangle, the reverse S–R mapping is required. The mapping between the response and color is indeed contingent on the level of the form dimension. However, it is equally true that the mapping between the response and form is contingent on the level of the color dimension.

The biconditional classification does involve contingency, but the relation is symmetric unless the task is constructed so that one of the dimensions plays the rule-giving role and the other plays the contingent role. Alternatively, subjects in our information processing tasks may choose to treat one of the dimensions as rule giving and the other as contingent, even if the task set by the experimenter does not require it. So although there is no logical necessity for the biconditional classification task to be structurally asymmetric, the biconditional task can be useful in determining whether there are processing asymmetries.

In Shaffer's (1965) actual experiment, the results indicated that there was little difference in the role of the two stimulus dimensions. Reaction times to the light positions used alone were 387 and 441 msec, respectively, for homolateral and contralateral S–R mappings (equivalent controls for line orientation were not used). When the mapping changed on a trial-by-trial basis, reaction time increased to about 700 msec, and that is exactly the result that should occur with a biconditional classification. In other conditions the line preceded the light by ⅓ sec, and these temporal relations produced a structural asymmetry between the dimensions. The results were that reaction time was 497 msec for homolateral and 542 msec for contralateral mapping. Thus moving the line orientation dimension forward in time, providing it with an asymmetric rule-giving status, resulted in lower reaction times. However, when the light location preceded the line orientation, reaction time to line orientation was 580 msec. This result clarifies that either dimension in this biconditional task could serve as the rule-giving dimension if it preceded the other dimension in time. So there is no clear result showing one dimension to be prior in an information sense; and either could play the rule-giving role if advanced in time. Thus the structural asymmetry of the temporal relations is important in information processing, but there is no clear evidence about any other asymmetry for these two dimensions.

Even though these results do not clarify much about any contingent relations between this pair of dimensions, I have gone into this much detail because the biconditional classification task does provide the opportunity of investigating asymmetric processing of dimensions. The biconditional task is truly one involving contingent relations, but the contingencies may be in either direction. Yet this very fact makes the task useful for investigations of processing asymmetries because the asymmetries are not fully constrained by the logical structure of the stimulus dimensions and the tasks.

Contingent Identification.   Biederman (1972) used a procedure for providing contingent dimensions somewhat different from that requiring biconditional classification. Hodge (1959) had earlier used a general technique in which levels on some dimensions to be processed also specified which other dimensions were relevant. Biederman, in a much more elaborate experiment, used a set of stimuli like those diagrammed in Fig. 1.4. Each of three dimensions had two levels, and

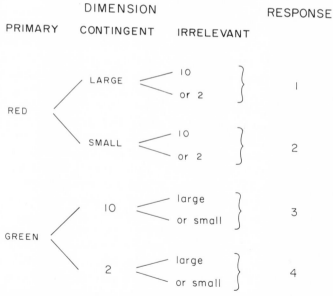

FIG. 1.4.   A diagram of the kind of contingent identification task used by Biederman (1972). Color is the primary dimension, and either size or tilt (indicated by number) is the contingent dimension. The contingent dimension was used as a varying irrelevant dimension when not used as the contingent dimension in the Biederman experiment, but it can also be held constant in a simple identification task.

a primary dimension (in this example, color) then specified which of the two other dimensions (size of a circle or tilt of a line within the circle) was contingently relevant for determining the correct response. In the case illustrated, if the primary dimension was red, then size had to be processed; if it was green, then the tilt of the line was to be processed. Note that this system requires four different responses. The dimension not needing to be processed can, logically, be held constant at one of its levels, in which case there are only four different stimuli, one for each response; and in this case the term *contingent identification* is clearly appropriate. Biederman actually allowed the unprocessed dimension to vary irrelevantly, so that all eight possible stimuli were used, assigned two each to the four responses, so that the task was more properly speaking one of classification. But because the contingent dimensions in combination with the primary dimensions require separate responses, I have called these tasks *contingent identification*. Biederman used the classification *schema* so that he could compare results with two other types of classification, one a condensation task similar in nature to the biconditional task in Table 1.4 but with three dimensions used, and one a filtering task in which the orthogonal combinations of a pair of dimensions was sufficient to specify which of the four responses was required, the third dimension varying irrelevantly. In the actual experiments all three pairs of dimensions were used as relevant in the filtering task, and all three dimensions were used as the primary dimension in the contingent task.

Reaction time was the main measure of performance, and although I cannot describe all the results of this quite complicated and sophisticated experiment, I shall describe those results most pertinent to questions of asymmetry. Of first importance is simply the evidence that subjects can handle this type of contingent identification. Performance on the contingent task was considerably faster than on the condensation task, a result indicating that the contingent use of two dimensions is more efficient than the use of all three. Although on the average the speed of identification in the filtering task was faster than in the contingent task, the differences were not great; it is not unreasonable to interpret the data as suggesting that with some dimensions at least such contingent processing is as fast as filtering. Furthermore, examination of the error data confirmed that the contingent relations were in fact being used. Thus the experiment provides clear evidence that the asymmetric logical structure of this type of contingent task can provide equivalent asymmetric processing of dimensions.

A second major issue, however, concerns the role of specific dimensions. Are some dimensions more effective as primary dimensions or more easily processed as contingent dimensions? A simple overall summary of the data would suggest that color is the best primary dimension, a conclusion not unlike that from the Schroeder (1976) result. Fortunately, however, Biederman (1972) introduced two levels of discriminability for the dimensions of color and tilt of line, and these changes in discriminability produced the kinds of changes in performance that make it difficult to isolate the effect of a dimension per se from the effect of discriminability: When discriminability of a dimension was increased, it lowered reaction time, especially when the more discriminable dimension was used as the primary dimension.

The fact that the effect of changes in discriminability affected reaction time most when the pertinent dimension was primary could suggest that the primary dimension is therefore more important in the sense that it has to be processed first because the relevant contingent dimension cannot be known until the primary dimension is classified. Once again, however, caution about such a processing interpretation must be expressed because the primary dimension also gives the maximum amount of response information: The two levels on the primary dimension give one bit of response information, narrowing the response choices from four to two. Although each of the contingent dimensions provides a conditional one bit of response information, the additional response information for the second bit is shared between the two contingent dimensions.

Thus it seems safe to conclude that ordered processing of stimulus dimensions does occur when there is a structural property of the stimulus set that requires a contingent sequence. But there are problems of interpretation concerning the relative importance of primary and contingent dimensions due to the nature of the response assignments in such tasks.

Contingent Classification.   Although several themes have run through this discussion, one theme of considerable importance to me has been the question concerning whether some stimulus dimensions have an inherent processing advantage such that they are processed first, serve best as a primary dimension, indicate a level of processing, etc. The contingent identification task used by Biederman (1972) seems to me to have a lot of unused potential as a paradigm for information processing studies, but its main disadvantage for the question about particular dimensions is the fact that the primary dimension necessarily gives more direct response information than do the contingent dimensions.

There is another experimental paradigm that can be used to investigate this question, however, although it has been rarely used, and to my knowledge not at all used for this question. It is what I shall call *contingent classification.* The basic paradigm is diagrammed in Fig. 1.5. The properties of this paradigm are that it is a classification task in which two stimuli are assigned to each of two responses. The important feature of this task is that the primary dimension gives no response information directly; it simply provides a stimulus contingency that changes the task from a 4 to 2 classification to a 2 to 2 classification.

It is possible to consider the question asked from such an experimental paradigm in at least two meaningful ways. First, note that the contingent dimension (form in the illustration) can be used without the primary dimension, and a straightforward 4 to 2 classification task is required. The contingent dimension may have nominal levels, or it may have ordered levels, even metrically different levels, and in any case a classification task is feasible. Looked at this way, the

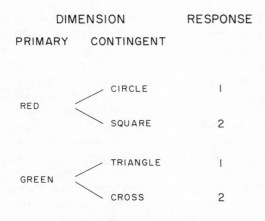

DIMENSION   RESPONSE

PRIMARY   CONTINGENT

RED
  — CIRCLE   1
  — SQUARE   2

GREEN
  — TRIANGLE   1
  — CROSS   2

FIG. 1.5. A diagram of a contingent classification task in which four levels of a contingent dimension are classifiable into two groups of two but in which the primary dimension specifies that two levels must be identified. Note that the primary dimension provides no direct response information. The contingent dimension need not be the same for each level of the primary dimension (e.g., green stimuli could vary in size rather than form).

question then becomes whether the addition of the primary dimension provides an improvement in speed of classification, even though it provides no response information in and of itself.

Second, and not entirely separate from the first question, do some dimensions provide contingent stimulus information more effectively than others? For the case illustrated in Fig. 1.5, we could try spatial location instead of color as the primary dimension; or we could try size, or brightness, etc. Alternatively, we can simply reverse the role of the dimensions of color and form and have two levels of form serve as the primary dimension, with four different colors as the contingent dimension. If we had run control classifications with the sets of colors and forms alone, we could determine whether there is some kind of a processing priority for either form or color, by adding each dimension as a primary dimension to the other.

For the particular set of stimuli diagrammed in Fig. 1.5, the language of nested variables would be as appropriate as the language of contingencies I have been using. I have used the terms *primary* and *contingent dimensions* because, at least for the moment, it seems to allow greater generality, but neither language is entirely appropriate for every case we can think of. What does run through all of these stimulus sets and experimental paradigms, however, is the very general concept of contingency. Consider another stimulus set (more properly, subset) in Fig. 1.6: There are two dimensions (color and form, our old standbys), but each of them serves both as primary and contingent dimension. One level on each specifies that two other levels on the other dimension must be processed to determine which of the two responses should be used. Even though this set is diagrammed as having primary and contingent dimensions, it is possible to consider it as one to be classified into two groups without differentiating between primary and contingent dimensions.

Table 1.5 diagrams this same task in tabular form, where possibly the relation between the two dimensions can be seen more readily. It is very much like the

DIMENSION   RESPONSE

PRIMARY   CONTINGENT

FIG. 1.6. A diagram of a contingent classification task in which each dimension serves to state a contingency for the other dimension. The color red or the form triangle give no direct response information but indicate that two nonprimary levels of the other dimension are to be identified.

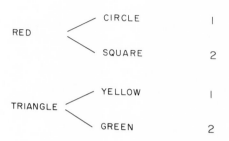

biconditional task in that both dimensions must be processed in order to determine the correct response, but it is a somewhat more complicated biconditional task than that usually formed from a 2 × 2 dimensional set of stimuli. Nevertheless, just as the biconditional task can be used to determine whether there is a natural order or hierarchy of processing of dimensions, so can the contingent classification task diagrammed in Table 1.5, because reaction times to individual stimuli would clearly establish the order of processing of the pair of dimensions.

The paradigm of a contingent classification requires only two defining properties: It must be a classification task in which two or more stimuli are assigned a single response; and the primary dimension that specifies the contingent relations must itself give no direct response information. There are many ways of generating stimulus sets that satisfy these two requirements in addition to the kinds of illustrations used here. For example, the contingent levels need not be on a single dimension; they may be features instead of dimensions (Garner, 1978a); they may be neither dimensions nor features, simply being categorizable objects; and various types of dimensional or feature crossing can be used to generate the sets.

TABLE 1.5
Schema of the Contingent Classification Task Diagrammed in Fig. 1.6,
in Which the Level of One Dimension Indicates the Response
Assignment for Two Levels of the Other Dimension

		Color		
		Red	Yellow	Green
	Circle	1	—	—
Form	Square	2	—	—
	Triangle	—	1	2

Note: The number in the table indicates the response assignment.

However, the examples I have used are sufficient to show the basic possibilities of the use of contingent classification to investigate the processing effects of different dimensions.

Because letters of the alphabet are so frequently used as stimulus materials, it is of some interest to see how easy it is to use subsets of letters that can be described as having primary and contingent dimensions and that could be used in contingent classifications. Consider the letters C, O, I, L. These can be described in contingent form, with curved–straight as a primary dimension whose level specifies processing on two other dimensions. If a classification task is used such that, for example, C and I are classed together with O and L also classed together, then the primary dimension gives no response information but does specify the dimension to be processed further, that is, open or closed for the C and O and one or two lines for the I and L. In like manner the letters X, K, I, T can be considered to have a primary dimension of existence of diagonal lines, with each level of the primary dimension (or feature) specifying the contingent dimension to be processed. The examples are too numerous to continue.

Dimensions as Channels.   In an earlier report (Garner, 1974a), I had distinguished various attentional constructs and had defined a channel as "any property of a stimulus that makes information available but is not itself part of the information aspect of the stimulus [p. 26]." Thus a modality is ordinarily a channel, because it is the means by which information becomes available but is usually not considered as a level on a dimension to which differential response is required. I had noted at that time that color and location seemed able to operate as visual information channels, thus specifying a class of information but not providing information about the appropriate response. That role of channel, of course, is exactly what is required of the primary dimensions in Fig. 1.5 and 1.6, those tasks that I have called *contingent classification*. Thus in Fig. 1.5 the color red provides a channel within which discrimination between circle and square must be made, whereas the color green provides another channel within which another discrimination must be made.

Is there any evidence that color and location really are especially suited to act as information channels? Not only have the several experiments reported here suggested such a special role, but experiments from another realm of research have as well. That evidence comes from experiments using the partial report procedure in studies of the size of the sensory register, or iconic store, such as those of Sperling (1960) and Averbach and Coriell (1961). The point of interest here is that when an array of alphanumeric symbols is displayed but the experimental subject is then concurrently with the display told that some smaller set of all items is to be reported, those items must be designated by some physical property. In the two original experiments, that property was spatial location, the subjects being required to report a row or a column of stimuli. Von Wright (1968) later did a systematic investigation of several stimulus properties that could be used to designate the subset of items: location, color, brightness, size, and orientation. Color and location were roughly equally effective in specifying the subset and were clearly superior to any of the other dimensions. Conceivably, only these dimensions can be made very highly discriminable, in which case the Von Wright result could be an artifact. But the persistence of these two dimensions as special cannot be lightly dismissed.

Dimensional Cuing

The last topic I shall discuss is that of dimensional cuing. This type of experimental paradigm does not involve a strict structural asymmetry of stimulus dimensions such as that provided by the part–whole problem or stimulus sets with contingent dimensions; yet its form is such that it is very similar to the use of contingent dimensions. Furthermore, the technique can be used in conjunction with contingent classification tasks to investigate problems of dimensional asymmetry.

The Cuing Paradigm.   Although the cuing paradigm has become widely used in recent years (see especially Posner, 1978, for a variety of problems), for present purposes I shall describe two experiments in which the stimulus sets involve contingent classification, because these experiments most easily lend themselves to a discussion of dimensional cuing. LaBerge, Van Gelder, and Yellott (1970) first used the cuing technique, in the following way: They used four stimuli with two responses, thus having a basic classification task. The stimuli were a high tone or a low tone, and a red square or green square. The high tone and the red square were assigned to one response, and the low tone and green square were assigned to the other response (key presses). This experimental task can be seen as exactly the equivalent of the contingent classification task diagrammed in Fig. 1.5, with modality as the primary dimension and color or pitch as the contingent dimensions.

The cuing technique involved presenting one of the four stimuli in advance of the actual stimulus presentation. On 73% of the trials, the cued stimulus actually occurred, and on those trials the cue was *valid;* on the other 27% of the trials, one of the other three stimuli occurred with equal probability, and on those trials the cue was *invalid.* It is necessary in such an experiment to use a cue that is not always valid, because if it is always valid, it simply becomes the stimulus proper and the task becomes meaningless. The pertinent results are that cuing the stimulus produced a much faster reaction time for the stimulus cued when valid. When the cue was not valid, however, it could be valid for cuing the correct response but the wrong modality, the correct modality but the wrong response, or both the wrong modality and the wrong response. In trials of the latter type, with both modality and response invalidly cued, reaction time was very slow. But when the cue gave either correct response information or correct modality information, the response was faster than when the cue was invalid in both respsects. It does not seem surprising that response cuing gives some facilitation, but the fact that cuing of the modality (i.e., the primary dimension in a contingent classification task) also facilitates is perhaps more surprising; at least it is of considerable interest in the present context. LaBerge (1973) reported another experiment with the same basic technique and once again demonstrated that cuing of the modality was effective, even though no response information was given by the cue.

The second experiment pertinent to contingent classification was by Ruth (1976; also described in Garner, 1980). Her stimuli were four patterns of dots, two of good configuration and two of poor. One good pattern and one poor pattern were assigned to each of two responses (key presses again). Thus the basic task was one of contingent classification like that diagrammed in Fig. 1.5, with configural goodness being the primary dimension and there being nominally different forms within each goodness level as the contingent dimension. In her experiment she used an advance cue, which at times was like one of the stimuli but at other times was neutral in character, and the nature of the cue made no difference. But instead of cuing one stimulus, she cued either the response or the stimulus goodness, with the cue being valid on 75% of the trials. Her results showed that cuing either the response or the goodness level had equal facilitative effects on reaction time. Once again such effective cuing of the response is not at all surprising; the point of special interest is that the primary dimension could be cued effectively, even when no response information was given by the cue.

The fact that the primary dimension in a contingent classification task can be cued makes clear that the primary dimension in these tasks is performing some useful function and is not simply an unnecessarily redundant stimulus property. There are two ways in which this conclusion can be useful in understanding and using the cuing technique with contingent classification. One way is to consider the primary dimension as a cue; the other is to advance the cue (or the primary dimension) to determine which stimulus dimensions are useful as primary dimensions.

Contingent Classification as Cuing.   The first point of interest is that the contingent classification task can itself be seen as a cuing task, one in which the primary dimension serves as the cue that reduces the set of stimulus alternatives without at the same time providing response information. Consider once again the contingent classification task diagrammed in Fig. 1.5. There are four different forms assigned to two responses. Such a classification task (which Gottwald & Garner, 1972, called *grouping*) is easily carried out without the existence of the primary dimension that provides the contingency at all. If, as mentioned earlier, the addition of the primary dimension lowers reaction time in the classification task over that obtained with grouping of just the four forms, then we have evidence that the primary dimension is providing useful stimulus information without response information.

Considering the primary dimension as a cue requires accepting two differences from the usual cuing experiment: First, the cue is presented simultaneously with the other stimulus properties (i.e., the primary and contingent dimensions are presented simultaneously). But simultaneous presentation does not change the logical function of the primary dimension, and in many cuing experiments in which the time course of the cuing information is desired, simultaneous presentation of the cue does occur as a limit, or control, condition.

Second, the cue is valid on all trials, whereas in the usual cuing experiment it is valid on just some of the trials. There are two reasons why the cue is probabilistically valid in the usual cuing experiment: One reason, as I pointed out previously, is that if response information is given by the cue, it simply becomes the stimulus instead of the intended stimulus. For example, when Ruth (1976) used response cuing, if the cue had been valid on every trial, the subject would have known the correct response before the stimulus was actually presented. Another reason for using probabilistically valid cues is that there is some real experimental interest in the difference in reaction time to expected and unexpected stimuli (or responses). In such a case, of course, probabilistic cuing must be used so that there can be unexpected stimuli.

Neither of these reasons is pertinent to understanding the role of stimulus dimensions in contingent classification. Although it is experimentally quite feasible to use probabilistic primary dimensions, it would usually be unnecessary in studies concerned with dimensional roles. Rather, the kind of investigation that would be of interest is the determination of which stimulus dimensions serve a useful role as the primary dimension in a contingent classification task or as the cue in a simultaneous cuing task. Thus the specific nature of the primary and contingent dimensions are of interest rather than their probabilistic relations.

Advance Cuing.   Ordinarily when the cuing technique is used, the cue is presented in advance of the stimulus proper. The use of advance cuing can be helpful in studies of dimensional asymmetry with at least two possible experimental paradigms. The first of these is simply to advance the primary dimension itself, using it as the cue. Consider once more the contingent classification task diagrammed in Fig. 1.5. Suppose we use color as the primary dimension with form as the contingent dimension and then reverse the roles of color and form, making form the primary dimension. If color has an advantage in serving as the primary dimension (because, e.g., it is processed at a lower level or can serve as a channel), then the use of color as the primary dimension should provide faster classification than the use of form as the primary dimension. Suppose further, however, that there is no difference in classification time with these two dimensions. One possible reason might be that both are so effective (or ineffective) that our experimental manipulation cannot differentiate between them. In that case we might choose to advance the primary dimension, so that the color of a display occurs before its form, or vice versa. It is quite conceivable that with the primary dimension presented as an advance cue there would be a difference in the effectiveness of the two dimensions that does not show up with simultaneous presentation.

The second experimental paradigm that might be useful in differentiating dimensional roles is to separate the function of the dimension in its role as primary dimension in contingent classification from the cuing role. In advance cuing, the cue need not be the same as any single stimulus or even be a level on one of the dimensions that define the stimuli. The question that is being addressed with this procedure is whether the dimension that the experimenter defines as primary is serving an effective role, for if the dimension cannot be cued, we cannot conclude that it is useful in defining the stimulus set.

Note that this role was played in both the LaBerge et al. (1970) experiment and in the Ruth (1976) experiment: The fact that in each experiment cuing for a stimulus property without providing response information (as in Ruth) was effective means that there was a cuable property of the stimulus set. In the LaBerge et al. experiment, the cuable property was modality, and as I indicated earlier, modality is an information channel, the sort of stimulus property that ought to have a special role, such as color and spatial location might also play. Thus the fact that it was cuable is not too surprising. In the Ruth experiment, the cuable property was pattern goodness, and the fact that such a property was cuable is not at all obvious. I would suspect, however, that differences in cuability between these two primary dimensions (in a contingent classification task) might show up with short advance times in cuing.

Advance cuing can also be used to determine whether there is a cuable property in a set of stimuli at all. Consider the set of uppercase letters I mentioned earlier: C, O, I, L. There are three possible ways of providing a 2 by 2 classification and in each case responses can be assigned so that cuing of the stimulus class can be done without cuing the response. If the classification is C I/ O L, one response for each pair separated by the slash, then cuing can be done for the C and O as contrasted to the I and L, without response cuing. If curvature really is serving as a primary dimension in the contingent classification task, then there should be an improvement in classification speed. As an alternative, we could use the classification C O/I L; in this case the response is correlated with curvature and would probably be faster than with the C I/O L task, without cue in both cases. However, a cue could be used to specify, in the second task, C and I as contrasted with O and L. Possibly cuing would be effective, but I would doubt it. The point is, however, that by carrying out a variety of classification tasks, with and without advanced cuing, it should be possible to learn which kinds of stimulus dimensions or other properties are being used in the information processing tasks.

As a last brief comment about the use of contingent classification and cuing as experimental techniques to determine relative roles of different kinds of stimulus dimension, it should be possible to combine the structural properties of the contingent classification task with those of the part–whole structure, along with the use of cuing to differentiate further the structural roles of parts and wholes. Just as one example, four stimuli could be generated from a constant whole but with different parts, so that the four different parts would correspond to the contingent dimension in Fig. 1.5. Then two different wholes could be added as a primary dimension to see if there is any improvement in classification. Or the reverse could be done as easily, starting with four wholes that are different and then adding a differentiating part as a primary stimulus. An asymmetric outcome of such an experiment would help clarify the part–whole problem.

CONCLUSION

Are there any conclusions to this discursive review of problems of asymmetric dimensional interactions in perceptual information processing? The primary purpose of this report has been to provide the review itself but also to try to draw both substantive and methodological conclusions insofar as possible.

A primary conclusion has to be that problems of substance and problems of method are interrelated. As I indicate on page 18, there are almost certainly asymmetries of dimensional interaction that reflect differences in levels of processing, and yet firm conclusions are difficult to draw because of the many methodological problems involved. When turning to the topic of asymmetries in stimulus structure, we might have hoped that the firmer foundation that knowledge of a stimulus structure can give us would also lead to firmer conclusions about processing asymmetries that are associated with the structural asymmetries. But no strong conclusions emerge. In the part–whole issue, there appears to be no single answer to the question of the priority of wholes over parts, or vice versa; rather, there seems to be some intermediate level of size that is optimal. And there has been too little use of the various contingent information processing techniques to provide a clear picture about dimensional asymmetries, again without some possible artifacts especially associated with the problem of dimensional discriminability.

As my later sections attempt to show, however, there may be some very useful applications of some of the structurally different types of stimulus sets, such as those used in contingency tasks or in stimulus cuing tasks. In other words, we may not have fully used the experimental paradigms available to us in studying these problems. Certainly the evidence of special roles of those dimensions that can act like information channels, such as modality, visual location, or even color, is sufficiently strong that the topic of dimensional asymmetries is worth pursuing.

ACKNOWLEDGMENTS

This research was supported by Grant MH 14229 from the National Institute of Mental Health to Yale University. Many of the ideas expressed here were improved by discussions with Daniel Algom, Paula Durlach, and Daniel Kaye.

REFERENCES

Averbach, E., & Coriell, A. S. Short-term memory in vision. *Bell System Technical Journal*, 1961, *40*, 309–328.

Biederman, I. Human performance in contingent information-processing tasks. *Journal of Experimental Psychology*, 1972, *93*, 219–238.

Blechner, M. J., Day, R. S., & Cutting, J. E. Processing two dimensions of nonspeech stimuli: The auditory–phonetic distinction reconsidered. *Journal of Experimental Psychology: Human Perception and Performance*, 1976, *2*, 257–266.

Clark, H. H., & Brownell, H. H. Position, direction, and their perceptual integrality. *Perception & Psychophysics*, 1976, *19*, 328–334.

Day, R. S., & Wood, C. C. Interactions between linguistic and nonlinguistic processing. *Journal of the Acoustical Society of America*, 1972, *51*, 79.

Dick, M., & Hochstein, S. *Interactions in the discrimination and absolute judgment of orientation and length*. Unpublished manuscript, 1981.

Dyer, F. N. The Stroop phenomenon and its use in the study of perceptual, cognitive, and response processes. *Memory & Cognition*, 1973, *1*, 106–120.

Eimas, P. D., Tartter, V. C., Miller, J. L., & Keuthen, N. J. Asymmetric dependencies in processing phonetic features. *Perception & Psychophysics*, 1978, *23*, 12–20.

Felfoldy, G. L., & Garner, W. R. The effects on speeded classification of implicit and explicit instructions regarding redundant dimensions. *Perception & Psychophysics*, 1971, *9*, 289–292.

Flowers, J. H., Warner, J. L., & Polansky, M. L. Response and encoding factors in "ignoring" irrelevant information. *Memory & Cognition*, 1979, *7*, 86–94.

Garner, W. R. Attention: The processing of multiple sources of information. In E. C. Carterette & M. P. Friedman (Eds.), *Handbook of perception* (Vol. 2). New York: Academic Press, 1974. (a)

Garner, W. R. *The processing of information and structure*. Potomac, Md.: Lawrence Erlbaum Associates, 1974. (b)

Garner, W. R. Interaction of stimulus dimensions in concept and choice processes. *Cognitive Psychology*, 1976, *8*, 98–123.

Garner, W. R. The effect of absolute size on the separability of the dimensions of size and brightness. *Bulletin of the Psychonomic Society*, 1977, *9*, 380–382.

Garner, W. R. Aspects of a stimulus: Features, dimensions, and configurations. In E. Rosch & B. B. Lloyd (Eds.), *Cognition and categorization*. Hillsdale, N.J.: Lawrence Erlbaum Associates, 1978. (a)

Garner, W. R. Selective attention to attributes and to stimuli. *Journal of Experimental Psychology: General*, 1978, *107*, 287–308. (b)

Garner, W. R. Functional aspects of information processing. In R. S. Nickerson (Ed.), *Attention and Performance VIII*. Hillsdale, N.J.: Lawrence Erlbaum Associates, 1980.

Garner, W. R. The analysis of unanalyzed perceptions. In M. Kubovy & J. Pomerantz (Eds.), *Perceptual organization*. Hillsdale, N.J.: Lawrence Erlbaum Associates, 1981.

Garner, W. R., & Felfoldy, G. L. Integrality of stimulus dimensions in various types of information processing. *Cognitive Psychology*, 1970, *1*, 225–241.

Garner, W. R., Hake, H. W., & Eriksen, C. W. Operationism and the concept of perception. *Psychological Review*, 1956, *63*, 149–159.

Garner, W. R., Podgorny, P., & Frasca, E. M. Physical and cognitive dimensions in stimulus comparison. *Perception & Psychophysics*, 1982, *31*, 507–522.

Gottwald, R. L., & Garner, W. R. Effects of focusing strategy on speeded classification with grouping, filtering, and condensation tasks. *Perception & Psychophysics*, 1972, *11*, 179–182.

Gottwald, R. L., & Garner, W. R. Filtering and condensation tasks with integral and separable dimensions. *Perception & Psychophysics*, 1975, *18*, 26–28.

Hodge, M. H. The influence of irrelevant information upon complex visual discrimination. *Journal of Experimental Psychology*, 1959, *57*, 1–5.

Hoffman, J. E. Interaction between global and local levels of a form. *Journal of Experimental Psychology: Human Perception and Performance*, 1980, *6*, 222–234.

Kinchla, R. A., & Wolfe, J. M. The order of visual processing: "Top–down," "bottom–up," or "middle–out." *Perception & Psychophysics*, 1979, *25*, 225–231.

Krumhansl, C. L. Concerning the applicability of geometric models to similarity data: The interrelationship between similarity and spatial density. *Psychological Review*, 1978, *85*, 445–463.

LaBerge, D. Identification of two components of the time to switch attention: A test of a serial and a parallel model of attention. In S. Kornblum (Ed.), *Attention and performance IV*. New York: Academic Press, 1973.

LaBerge, D., Van Gelder, P., & Yellott, J. A cueing technique in choice reaction time. *Perception & Psychophysics*, 1970, *7*, 57–62.

Logan, G. D. Attention and automaticity in Stroop and priming tasks: Theory and data. *Cognitive Psychology*, 1980, *12*, 523–553.

Logan, G. D., & Zbrodoff, N. J. When it helps to be misled: Facilitative effects of increasing the frequency of conflicting stimuli in a Stroop-like task. *Memory & Cognition*, 1979, *7*, 166–174.

Martin, M. Local and global processing: The role of sparsity. *Memory & Cognition*, 1979, *7*, 476–484.

Navon, D. Forest before trees: The precedence of global features in visual perception. *Cognitive Psychology*, 1977, *9*, 353–383.

Nickerson, R. S. Binary-classification reaction time: A review of some studies of human information-processing capabilities. *Psychonomic Monograph Supplements*, 1972, *4*, No. 17(Whole No. 65).

Palmer, S. E. Hierarchical structure in perceptual representation. *Cognitive Psychology*, 1977, *9*, 441–474.

Pomerantz, J. R., & Sager, L. C. Asymmetric integrality with dimensions of visual pattern. *Perception & Psychophysics*, 1975, *18*, 460–466.

Posner, M. I. *Chronometric explorations of mind*. Hillsdale, N.J.: Lawrence Ealbaum Associates, 1978.

Posner, M. I., & Mitchell, R. F. Chronometric analysis of classification. *Psychological Review*, 1967, *74*, 392–409.

Posner, M. I., & Snyder, C. R. R. Attention and cognitive control. In R. L Solso (Ed.), *Information processing and cognition: The Loyola symposium*. Hillsdale, N.J.: Lawrence Erlbaum Associates, 1975.

Redding, G. M., & Tharp, D. A. Processing line location and orientation. *Journal of Experimental Psychology: Human Perception and Performance*, 1981, *7*, 115–129.

Rosch, E. Cognitive reference points. *Cognitive Psychology*, 1975, *7*, 532–547.

Ruth, D. S. *The effects of pattern goodness on automatic and strategy-dependent processes*. Unpublished doctoral dissertation, Yale University, 1976.

Santee, J. L., & Egeth, H. E. Selective attention in the speeded classification and comparison of multidimensional stimuli. *Perception & Psychophysics*, 1980, *28*, 191–204.

Schroeder, R. *Information processing of color and form*. Unpublished honors thesis, University of Oregon, 1976.

Shaffer, L. H. Choice reaction time with variable S–R mapping. *Journal of Experimental Psychology*, 1965, *70*, 284–288.

Sperling, G. The information available in brief visual presentations. *Psychological Monographs*, 1960, *74*, 11(Whole No. 498).

Stroop, J. R. Studies of interference in serial verbal reactions. *Journal of Experimental Psychology*, 1935, *18*, 643–662.

Treisman, A. The psychological reality of levels of processing. In L. S. Cermak & F. I. M. Craik (Eds.), *Levels of processing in human memory*. Hillsdale, N.J.: Lawrence Erlbaum Associates, 1979.

Turvey, M. T. On peripheral and central processes in vision: Inferences from an information-processing analysis of masking with patterned stimuli. *Psychological Review*, 1973, *80*, 1–52.

Tversky, A. Features of similarity. *Psychological Review*, 1977, *84*, 327–352.

Von Wright, J. M. Selection in visual immediate memory. *Quarterly Journal of Experimental Psychology*, 1968, *20*, 62–68.

Wood, C. C. Parallel processing of auditory and phonetic information in speech discrimination. *Perception & Psychophysics*, 1974, *15*, 501–508.

Wood, C. C. Auditory and phonetic levels of processing in speech perception: Neurophysiological and information-processing analyses. *Journal of Experimental Psychology: Human Perception and Performance*, 1975, *1*, 3–20.

2

The Analyzability of Multidimensional Objects: Some Constraints on Perceived Structure, the Development of Perceived Structure, and Attention

Bryan E. Shepp
Brown University

Introduction

The nature of the psychological stimulus and the relation between different psychological stimuli are fundamental to theories of perception and cognition. Despite the periodic recognition of these problems (Boring, 1933; Gibson, 1960), systematic investigation of the psychological stimulus has been relatively neglected. Typically, the experimenter has adopted some description of the physical stimulus and has assumed that this description adequately characterizes the stimulus relations that are perceived by the observer. As Gibson (1966) and Garner (1974b) have so cogently argued, however, physical descriptions of the stimulus may not correspond to a subject's perceptions. Indeed, it can be shown that a specific object is perceived in one instance as wholistic but in another by its particular attributes.

Such considerations have led several investigators to begin to speak to questions regarding the internal representation or perceived structure of stimulus objects and to describe the forms of organization that may characterize different perceived structures (Garner, 1974b; Krantz & Tversky, 1975; Monahan & Lockhead, 1977; Palmer, 1978; Rosch, 1973; Shepard, 1974; Tversky, 1977). Still others have begun to discuss the relation between different representations and the attentional options of the subject (Garner, 1974a, 1976; Kahneman, 1973; Lockhead, 1972).

Questions of perceived structure have also been raised as central in perceptual and cognitive development (Gibson, 1969), and a number of recent investigations have provided a specific characterization of developmental trends in object perception and the relation of such trends to the development of attention (Shepp,

1977, 1978; Shepp, Burns, & McDonough, 1980; Shepp & Swartz, 1976; Smith & Kemler, 1977, 1978).

Taken together, the adult and developmental work provide dramatic evidence that an understanding of the nature of objects or multidimensional stimuli is indeed fundamental to issues of perceptual organization and attention and once again underscores the importance of a developmental approach in the theoretical analysis of perceptual and cognitive phenomena.

The purpose of this chapter is to review some of the developmental work on perceived structure, to provide a progress report of more recent efforts (Shepp, 1977, 1978), and to summarize recent findings that bear on some of the unresolved issues.

THE DEVELOPMENT OF PERCEIVED DIMENSIONAL RELATIONS

There is general agreement that the developmental changes in the representation of real-world objects proceed in a direction from the perceptual or concrete to increasingly abstract, semantic, or logical representations (Bruner, Olver, Greenfield, 1966; Clark, 1973; Gibson 1969; Inhelder & Piaget, 1964; Kendler & Kendler, 1962; Nelson, 1974). There is, of course, considerable disagreement concerning how the specific trends in representations are to be characterized and the nature of the processes that contribute to the progression. A focal point for some of this disagreement arises in the characterization of object perception by the young child. Some theorists hold that the young child initially perceives multidimensional objects as unitary or undifferentiated wholes and that the attributes of objects (e.g., color, shape, size) become differentiated only during the course of development (Bruner et al., 1966; Gibson, 1969; Nelson, 1974; Werner, 1948). For these theorists, age-related performance differences are related, in part, to developmental differences in object perception. Other theorists, however, have assumed, either tacitly or explicitly, that the attributes of objects are perceived by children of different ages as levels or values of independent dimensions (Clark, 1973; Hagen & Hale, 1973; Inhelder & Piaget, 1964; Kendler & Kendler, 1962, 1970; Zeaman & House, 1963). For the latter theorists, age-related performance differences are due to some aspect of cognitive development other than differences in object perception.

Despite the clear conceptual differences between these alternative views of perceptual organization in the young child, there has been little evidence to support either view directly. Typically, the performances of younger children are compared with those of older children and adults in tasks with experimenter-defined dimensionally organized stimuli. The performances of the young child may be less good or different from those of the older subjects. Such differences may be indicative of developmental differences in perceptual organization (Gibson, 1969), but such evidence may also be interpreted as reflecting differences in processes such as logical operations or attention.

Recently, Tighe and his associates (Tighe, Glick, & Cole, 1971; Tighe, 1973; Tighe & Tighe, 1972, 1978) have provided rather convincing evidence of developmental differences in perceptual organization. Their task is a standard discrimination task in which, say, two arrays, red square versus green circle and red circle versus green square, are presented. By one description of the stimuli, color is the relevant dimension and form and position are irrelevant. One mode of solution is consistent with this description: Subjects learn that color is relevant and consistently choose red. In this case, the different arrays are treated as instances of the same problem, and the solution is governed by some form of dimensional learning.

Tighe et al. (1971) have pointed out that there is another equally plausible description of the stimulus arrays that would lead to an alternative type of solution. There are two stimuli, red square and red circle, that lead to a correct response. These stimuli (as well as the ones that lead to incorrect responses) could be treated as unitary objects, in which case each array of the task constitutes an independent subproblem, and the solution is based upon the choice of specific objects (see Table 2.1).

The type of solution adopted by the subjects can be revealed by an examination of performances on reversal and nonreversal shift tasks. If subjects have learned the initial task on the basis of object–reward relations, both subproblems must be relearned in the reversal shift, and the errors committed on each subproblem should be equivalent. In the nonreversal shift, however, the object–reward relations remain unchanged in one subproblem (Array 1) and are reversed in the second (Array 2). Only the reversed subproblem must be relearned, and the errors committed on the reversed subproblem should exceed those committed on the unchanged subproblem, which ideally would be zero. "Dimension–reward" learning (Tighe & Tighe, 1972) would, however, lead to a very different outcome in the shift tasks. Because each array is perceived as an

TABLE 2.1
Reversal–Nonreversal Shift Paradigm

Array	Original	Learning*
1	Red + Square	Green − Circle
2	Red + Circle	Green − Square

Array	Reversal Shift		Array	Nonreversal Shift	
1	Red − Square	Green + Circle	1	Red + Square	Green − Circle
2	Red − Circle	Green + Square	2	Red − Circle	Green + Square

*Note: Only two of the possible four arrays are shown. In practice two additional arrays, in which the positions of the stimuli are interchanged, would also be presented. The symbols + and − indicate that a choice of a particular stimulus is rewarded or nonrewarded, respectively.

instance of the same problem in both types of shift task, error rates should be equivalent for the arrays within each shift task. In particular, the changed and unchanged subproblems of the nonreversal shift should be learned at the same rate.

Tighe (1973) and Tighe and Tighe (1972, 1978) have summarized consider- able evidence to the effect that the mode of solution adopted by infrahuman animals and young children differs from that of older children. Infrahuman animals and young children show a marked asymmetry in errors that are commit- ted on the two types of subproblems of the nonreversal shift; often such subjects commit no errors on the unchanged subproblem in solving the nonreversal task. In contrast, the error rates of older children on the two subproblems are more nearly symmetrical. Such results have led the Tighes to develop a view, derived from perceptual learning theory (Gibson, 1969), that assumes that children per- ceive both objects and dimensions but that younger children are more likely to learn object–reward relations than dimension–reward relations, whereas the re- verse is assumed for older children.

The evidence provided by the Tighes and their colleagues establishes rather convincingly an object to dimensional trend in perceptual development, and it poses a serious challenge for theories that do not address these alternative modes of perception. The evidence does not speak, however, to some other fundamental issues of perceptual development.

The first concerns the nature of object and dimensional perception. At one level the characterization of objects and dimensions is fairly straightforward. Objects can be considered as aggregations of features or values on dimensions. Thus, objects are wholistic, whereas features or values are components or parts. Such a characterization is too simplistic, of course, and several theoretical analy- ses of the object-feature problem have suggested three basic object–feature rela- tions. First, objects may be simple wholes, meaning that specific features are independent and are processed in parallel (Garner, 1978a). Second, the specific values may fuse and yield a unique compound (Zeaman & House, 1974). Final- ly, specific features may be initially stuck together as a whole but subsequently analyzable into specific components (Lockhead, 1972). Any of these types of objects could, in principle, anchor a trend in perceptual development, and each would have different implications for the development of perceived dimensional relations.

A second issue concerns the relation between alternative stimulus structures and attention. Tighe and Tighe (1978) have argued that the phenomenon of object–reward learning is not consistent with attentional interpretations of dis- criminative learning and concept identification (Sutherland & Mackintosh, 1971; Trabasso & Bower, 1968; Zeaman & House, 1963). These theories have com- monly assumed that subjects learn only about the subset of cues to which atten- tion has been directed, and most of these views have made the simplifying assumption that the units of the stimulus that control attention are stimulus dimensions. Thus, the criticism that perceptual units other than the stimulus dimension have been omitted is correct. The theories do not provide for attention to different perceptual units. The problem can, however, be relatively easily finessed. Zeaman and House (1974) have assumed that compounds (i.e., objects) are dimensions just like other dimensions and follow, therefore, the same attentional rules.

The role of attention in learning has, of course, been debated extensively. The major developmental issues have centered on the importance of attention in contributing to age-related performance differences in discriminative transfer (Shepp & Turrisi, 1966; Wolff, 1967) and selective learning (Hagan & Hale, 1973; Shepp & Adams, 1973). Although attention theories (Sutherland & Mackintosh, 1971; Trabasso & Bower, 1968; Zeaman & House, 1963) have been highly successful in predicting the details of learning and transfer, there are several nonattentional views of learning that account equally well for many of the observed phenomena (Kendler & Kendler, 1962, 1970, 1975; see also Kendler's chapter in this volume; Spiker, 1971; Spiker & Cantor, 1973). Thus, although the learning task yields evidence of a developmental trend in perception, it has been less good in revealing developmental differences in attention.

If, on the other hand, developmental differences in performance in other types of tasks are considered as well, age-related differences in attention become obvious. Indeed, one of the most consistent trends in the developmental literature is the finding that younger children have more difficulty in ignoring irrelevant sources of information than do older children. This finding occurs not only in learning tasks (Hagen & Hale, 1973; Kemler, Shepp, & Foote, 1976; Wohlwill, 1962) but also in tasks such as selective listening (Doyle, 1973; Maccoby, 1969) and speeded classification (Pick & Frankel, 1973; Smith, Kemler, & Aronfreed, 1976; Strutt, Anderson, & Well, 1975). Interestingly, however, this class of experiments provides no direct evidence for developmental differences in perceived structure. To summarize, then, we would argue that there are trends in both perceptual and attentional development but that the evidence does not reveal a systematic relation between alternative modes of perception and attention nor does it indicate how such relations might change in the course of development. Fortunately, some clarification of these issues is suggested by some recent work on the nature of dimensional interactions.

Garner (1970, 1974b, 1976) and Lockhead (1966, 1972), following earlier work of Attneave (1950), Shepard (1964), and Torgerson (1958), have shown that different combinations of physical dimensions produce different forms of perceptual interactions for the observer. In some instances, stimuli when combined yield fused wholes for the perceiver. In other instances, the combination of multidimensional stimuli yields a dimensional organization; dimensional relations may be symmetric or asymmetric. Finally, stimuli may combine in such a way that emergent relations among the stimuli dominate the perception of the observer (Garner, 1974b, 1976, 1978a).

For the present discussion, the distinction between dimensional combinations that are integral and those that are separable is the most relevant. According to Garner (1970), two dimensions are integral if the realization of a level on one dimension requires the specification of a level on the second. Two dimensions are separable, on the other hand, if a level on one can be specified without regard to the other. Stimuli that are generated by combining levels of integral dimensions (e.g., hue and brightness) are perceived as unitary wholes, whereas stimuli that are generated by separable dimensions (e.g., size of circle and angle of a radial line) are perceived as conjunctions of perceptually distinctive components.

Operationally, according to Garner and Felfoldy (1970), integral dimensions are "those which lead to a Euclidean metric in direct distance scaling, produce a redundancy gain when the dimensions are correlated and some measure of speed or accuracy is used, and produce interference in speed of classification when selective attention is required with orthogonal stimulus dimensions [p. 238]." By contrast, separable dimensions produce a city-block metric in direct-distance scaling, yield no redundancy gain with correlated values in speeded sorting, and allow selective attention to one dimension in a speeded-sorting task despite orthogonal variation of a second dimension (Garner, 1976).

THE SEPARABILITY HYPOTHESIS

Shepp and Swartz (1976) and Shepp (1978) have observed some interesting parallels between properties of integral and separable dimensions in adult perception and the developmental trends in object perception and attention. Taking the two developmental trends together, younger children have been described as perceiving objects as unitary wholes and as failing to attend selectively. This characterization is strikingly similar to the perception and attention of an adult when performing with integral dimensions. In contrast, older children are characterized as perceiving objects according to values on specific dimensions and as succeeding in selective attention. Such a description accurately describes an adult's perception and attention when confronted with separable dimensions. On the basis of these parallels, we have suggested the hypothesis that dimensional combinations that are perceived as separable by the older child and adult are perceived as integral by the young child.

The meaning and implications of this hypothesis can be clarified by a further consideration of integral and separable dimensions. When dimensions are integral, the perception of a specific value or feature on one dimension depends on the specific feature of a second dimension that appears concurrently. Reference axes for these kinds of dimensional combinations are arbitrary (Shepard, 1964), and the similarity between objects generated by integral dimensions depends on the direct distance between them (Garner, 1974b). In a similar vein, Lockhead (1972) has suggested that objects generated by integral dimensions are first perceived as locations in an *n*-dimensional space or as "blobs." As a consequence, selective attention to the features or values of an integral stimulus is not possible.

Alternatively, when dimensions are separable, the perception of a specific feature on one dimension is independent of any feature on a second that is presented concurrently. Thus, the similarity between objects that are generated by separable dimensions is taken to be some combination of the similarity of specific features to other features on their respective dimensions. Moreover, selective attention to a feature of an object generated by separable dimensions is a logical possibility.

These differences in perceived structure and attention can be illustrated by considering the speeded-sorting task of Garner and Felfoldy (1970). In this task, subjects are instructed to sort a deck of cards into two piles as quickly as possible. On each card one value on each of two dimensions is displayed, and the subject is instructed to sort on the basis of one of the dimensions. During the course of this experiment, subjects sort decks composed of different subsets of stimuli. To illustrate the composition of the different decks, consider the four stimuli shown in Fig. 2.1. In a one-dimension task the deck includes stimuli that only vary on one dimension. A one-dimension task for dimension X includes A and D (or B and C). In a correlated-dimensions task, the values of the dimensions are redundant; the deck includes A and C (or B and D). In the orthogonal-dimensions task, all four stimuli are included in a deck (e.g., A, B versus C, D).

Differences in the perceived structure of integral and separable dimensions are shown by comparing performances on the one-dimension and correlated-dimensions tasks. Because the similarity between stimuli generated by integral dimensions is determined by the direct distance between the stimuli, the stimuli A versus C are more dissimilar to each other than are A versus D. As a consequence the correlated-dimensions task should be performed more quickly than the one-dimension task. In contrast, the differences between stimuli generated by separable dimensions are perceived according to the levels on specific subjective di-

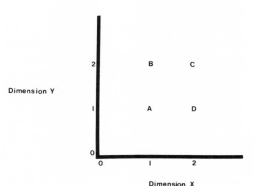

FIG. 2.1. An illustration of four stimuli for speeded classification.

mensions. If the subject is instructed to sort on dimension X, for example, the classification in both the one-dimension and the correlated-dimensions task is based upon the specific values on that dimension. Consequently, the two tasks should be performed at the same speed. The expected results have been observed for both integral and separable dimensions (Garner & Felfoldy, 1970; see also Garner, 1974b).

That object structures affect the attentional options of the subject are shown by performances on the orthogonal-dimensions task relative to the one-dimension task. Because the objects generated by integral dimensions are unitary, selective attention to specific features is not possible, and the orthogonal-dimensions task should be performed more slowly than the one-dimension task. The features of separable dimensions, however, are seen as perceptually distinct components and do allow selective attention. Thus, the time to sort with orthogonal-dimensions should be no longer than the time to sort with the variation on a single dimension. As predicted, there is substantial interference on an orthogonal dimensions task with integral dimensions but none with separable dimensions (Garner & Felfoldy, 1970).

The first direct test of the separability hypothesis was made by Shepp and Swartz (1976) using the speeded-sorting task. First- and fourth-grade children were asked to perform the speeded-sorting task with either hue versus brightness or color versus form as dimensions. Because hue and brightness are integral for the adult, no qualitative difference in sorting times would be expected across different ages. Compared with the one-dimension task, there should be a redundancy gain with correlated dimensions and interference with orthogonal dimensions. As expected, there were absolute differences in sorting speeds, but both first- and fourth-graders showed the expected effects.

According to the separability hypothesis, there should be an age by task interaction for subjects who sorted with color and form. If younger children perceive the stimuli generated by combinations of color and form as integral, a redundancy gain should occur with correlated dimensions and interference should occur with orthogonal dimensions. If, on the other hand, fourth-graders perceive these same stimuli according to features on specific dimensions and are capable of attending selectively, the sorting times for the three tasks should not differ. This pattern of results was obtained, and similar results with different stimuli have been reported by Smith and Kemler (1978).

The differences in perceived structure between integral and separable stimuli are also shown clearly by the results of restricted classification (Garner, 1974b). In this task, subjects are instructed to partition subsets of stimuli according to which ones go together best. Subjects readily oblige by grouping together stimuli that are most similar. Consider the triad of stimuli shown in Fig. 2.2. Stimuli A and B share a value on dimension X but differ considerably on dimension Y. Stimulus C shares no value with either A or B but differs slightly from B on both dimensions. If these stimuli are generated by integral dimensions, then the sim-

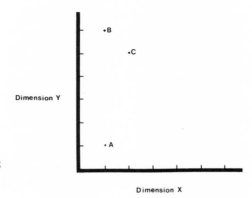

FIG. 2.2. A hypothetical triad depicting dimensional and overall similarity relations.

ilarity between the stimuli would depend on the distance or overall similarity structure. Accordingly, *B* and *C* would be perceived as more similar to each other than either *A* to *B* or *A* to *C*. If the stimuli are generated by separable dimensions, however, the stimuli would be perceived as features or values on specific dimensions. Thus, stimuli *A* and *B* would be seen as more similar because they share an identical value on dimension *X*. When adult subjects are presented with such subsets of stimuli and are instructed to make the best classification, they will group *B* and *C* together if the stimuli are generated by integral dimensions (e.g., hue versus chroma) but will group *A* and *B* together if the stimuli are generated by separable dimensions (e.g., size of circle versus angle of a radial line) (Burns, Shepp, & McDonough, Ehrlich, 1978).

Smith and Kemler (1977) ran groups of kindergarten, second-grade, and fourth-grade children on the restricted classification task with subsets of stimuli generated by combinations of size and brightness, and they report results that provide strong evidence for the separability hypothesis. Kindergarten children classified both triads and tetrads according to distance or overall similarity relations, but with increasing age there was a reliable trend in the direction of increasing dimensional classifications. A similar pattern of results was observed by Shepp et al. (1980) with different dimensional combinations.

Some Implications of the Separability Hypothesis

The results of these recent experiments with speeded and restricted classification provide strong support for the separability hypothesis. These results are also consistent in some respects with earlier views of perceptual development (Gibson, 1969; Tighe, & Tighe 1978). We would argue, however, that the separability hypothesis and the related views of colleagues (Kemler, this volume) provides the framework for a more rigorous formulation of issues that pertain to both perceived structure and the relation of perceived structure and attention than do alternative views. Moreover, taken in conjunction with other evidence, we believe that this formulation can suggest some new ways of looking at issues of cognitive development.

Consider the development of perceived structure. We have claimed that the young child's perception is biased in the direction of direct distance or overall similarity relations among objects and that with increasing age perception shifts to dimensionally organized relations among objects for at least some dimensional combinations. There is strong evidence demonstrating this trend and a simple interpretation is tempting. There is other evidence, however, that suggests the operation of several complicating perceptual mechanisms and cognitive processes. It is to some of these issues to which we now turn.

The young child's bias toward overall similarity relations among objects can be attributed to several perceptual factors. Garner (1974b) has argued that objects have both overall similarity relations and dimensionally similar relations. It is also clear that these types of relations may be attributed to both the properties of objects and sets of objects. Dimensions may combine in such a way that features either fuse or strongly interact. In such cases, it may be either very difficult or require considerable effort to recover and identify the specific dimensional features that compose an object. As a result, overall similarity relations will dominate the perception of sets of such objects. These properties are assumed to characterize integral stimuli for at least the first stages of perceptual analysis (Garner, 1974b; Lockhead, 1972) and may also characterize the young child's perception of some stimuli that may later become separable.

It is also possible that the features that compose an object are readily identified in some contexts and not in others. In other words, similarity relations may vary in salience. To illustrate, consider a study by Shepp et al. (1980). They presented triads of two-dimensional stimuli in a version of the restricted classification task. Shepp et al. showed that the types of classifications made depended on the psychophysical differences between the objects. Shepp et al. used triads with similarity relations like those portrayed by the Type I and III triads shown in Fig. 2.5. Adults and older children (7 years) classified Type I triads by overall similarity relations under some conditions but typically classified Type III triads by dimensional relations. Four-year-olds, on the other hand, classified both types of triads by overall similarity relations. This pattern of results supports the argument that the salience of similarity relations can be varied and interact with variables such as age, dimensional preference, and analyzability of the stimulus set (Shepp et al., 1980).

A similar type of effect has been reported by Smith (1981). She presented subsets of stimuli in a restricted classification task; the stimuli varied on either two or four dimensions. The two-dimensional stimuli produced the usual developmental trend. Kindergarten children classified by overall similarity relations, but with increasing age there were increasingly more dimensional classifications.

With four-dimensional stimuli, however, children of all ages classified objects according to overall similarity relations.

It is important to note that Smith's stimuli contained some spatially separate features, such that subjects could easily identify features in different objects. Like real-world objects, however, the properties did not provide a basis for classification by defining feature but rather were readily grouped overall by similarity or family resemblances (Rosch & Mervis, 1975).

In many respects, then, the bias toward specific types of similarity relations depends on the manner in which the features that compose an object are "glued together," the composition of the stimulus set, and how readily the subject of a particular developmental level can pull them apart. The gluing together of features and other elements of the stimulus can be considered a problem of unit formation or perceptual grouping (Kahneman, 1973; Kahneman & Henik, 1977; Pomerantz, 1981) and must be adequately addressed in any view of perceptual development. There is reasonably good evidence that perceptual units are formed automatically at an early stage of processing and preserved for subsequent cognitive operations. It seems probable that these early processes do not differ developmentally and that the principles of object formation are invariant with age. By this assumption the primary mode of perceptual organization is overall similarity; dimensional similarity is derived. Observed performance differences across age are due to the development and acquisition of cognitive operations such as perceptual learning and attention. Until the young child is able to perform such operations, perception and performance are organized by overall similarity relations; with increasing maturity and experience the child becomes proficient in using other similarity relations and in exercising some choice of alternative similarity relations.

Given that features are combined automatically to produce objects, it is important to establish the conditions that promote both feature recognition and the use of features in the performance of particular tasks. We have previously suggested (Shepp, 1978) the importance of the child's learning to analyze multidimensional stimuli and believe that subjective analysis is basic to other operations that may affect the nature of perceived similarity relations. The operations or processes that have been traditionally concerned with the interface between perception and performance include perceptual learning, problem solving, and attention.

Gibson (1969) has stressed the importance of perceptual learning in the differentiation of features and higher-order perceptual invariants. For her, such processes as abstraction and selective filtering are critical. In many respects Gibson's theory is consistent with and, indeed, anticipates some aspects of the present hypothesis. We would argue that in analyzing the stimulus the child discovers that the relations of values along one dimension remain perceptually invariant despite variations along one or more other dimensions. This type of analysis, as Gibson has shown, would lead to improved discriminations between features and, ultimately, to what one could call feature invariance. It also seems reasonable that perceptual learning also teaches the subject something about the dimensional nature of features. There is certainly evidence from dimensional shift studies (Wolff, 1967) that subjects who learn to analyze the features of a dimension in one situation will continue to analyze the features of that same dimension in another situation.

Although Gibson (1969) makes a clear case for the role of perceptual learning in the differentiation of objects into dimensional features, it is important to note that there are properties of dimensions other than features. Some of these properties may be, in principle, more complex than others; some may follow others in the course of development; and some may become apparent only when required by a particular task. Many of our current results show only that children tend, with increasing age, to detect dimensional features and that these features organize performance (Shepp & Swartz, 1976; Smith & Kemler, 1977). The results also imply that differentiation takes time. As features become detectable, cue discriminability more dramatically affects performance and subjects are more strongly influenced by dimensional perferences (Shepp et al., 1980). The child may be asked to organize stimuli by dimensional relations but may require some prodding to do so (Smith & Kemler, 1977). The properties of the stimulus required for these tasks, or for dimensional learning, can be considered as relatively fundamental perceptual relations. But the knowledge of these relations does not imply the knowledge of relations that are necessary for transitive inference, conservation of quantity, and, more generally, the concept of a dimension. To assume that a child who shows responses based upon the recognition of simple features will show other properties of dimensions may be misleading and may oversimplify the processes that contribute to the discovery of these other properties.

Even though perceptual learning seems crucial in the discovery of stimulus properties, the tradition does not speak explicitly to learning that results from feedback or learning about task demands. Consider a class of objects such as shoes. Shoes are highly similar but not identical in a number of respects; they also share some common properties (e.g., heels). During the course of learning about shoes in different contexts, the child may learn that aspects of objects that are useful in one context are not so useful in another. In absolute identification, for example, overall similarity relations are important. Such relations can improve the speed and accuracy of identification (Lockhead, 1972; Monahan & Lockhead, 1977). In analytical tasks, on the other hand, a common feature, heels, may provide the most effective relation. These kinds of interactions can be considered as problem solving, which involves both an appreciation of task demands as well as feedback for specific responses.

A view that incorporates such assumptions is due to Klahr and Wallace (1976). They assume that every object can be perceived either as a whole or according to specific features. The type of perceived structure that is prominent in a particular task is determined by the representation on which attention is focused. This "attentional grain" is affected by feedback. According to their view the subject strives to be an efficient problem solver and in so doing attends to wholes or features of dimensions depending on which structure is consistent with effective feedback. They report evidence that is consistent with their model and we believe that their argument for a dual representation of objects is plausible for many, if not all, multidimensional objects. Moreover, they must surely be correct in asserting the importance of feedback in what we would consider to be analysis of the stimulus if reinforcers are taken to be a form of "cue" rather than "glue." In addition to feedback, however, we would argue that the nature of the task is a factor in the choice of perceived structure, and it seems likely that the child's appreciation of task demands would improve with age. As we have noted, Lockhead (1972) has stressed the importance of task demand in using particular types of perceived structures to improve task performances.

Klahr and Wallace (1976) have reported some evidence to support their model, and there is, of course, additional evidence that some objects may be perceived as wholes or features (Lockhead, 1972). But it is not clear that all objects enjoy dual representation nor that subjects (even adult subjects) can so flexibly adjust attentional grain. Importantly, however, Klahr and Wallace have specified some relations between efficient problem solving and feedback that may be central to perceptual and conceptual development.

Finally, we would argue that the development of attention also plays a key role in the perception of similarity relations. Moreover, as we have previously indicated (Shepp, 1977; 1978), the separability hypothesis proposes specific relations between perceived structure and attention. The first important relation between structure and attention is seen in the wholistic perception of the young child. If younger children perceive objects as integral stimuli and do not perceive specific features, it is erroneous to conclude that these children cannot focus or divide attention to features. It is appropriate, however, to ask questions about focused or divided attention to objects and, in this context, whether there are developmental differences in attention. Unfortunately, most developmental studies have investigated attention to features rather than objects (Shepp et al., 1980).

To illustrate, consider two experiments reported by Shepp (1977). Kindergarten, second-, and fifth-grade children were asked to perform a speeded-sorting task. Each subject performed in each of three conditions: control, correlated, and orthogonal. In one experiment the stimulus dimensions were spatially separated; in the second they were not. The stimuli were three concentric circles. The outer two circles formed a ring and a number of parallel lines were placed around the ring. The number of lines was one dimension. The inner circle was colored, and different colors served as the second dimension. The third dimension was an arrow that was attached to the circle and displayed in the same color.

The arrow varied in angle of inclination. The spatially separated dimensions were number of lines versus color. The spatially contiguous dimensions were color versus angle. Separate groups of subjects were presented with each dimensional set. Other procedure details followed those of Shepp and Swartz (1976).

The spatial separation of integral dimensions is one condition that makes the dimensions psychologically independent (Garner & Felfoldy, 1970) and allows the subject to focus on one source of information in a task that requires selective attention. Thus, even for the young child, who normally perceives objects as integral stimuli, spatial separation of the dimensions should provide separate sources of information and allow the investigation of developmental trends in the subject's control of attention. In contrast, the usual developmental trend in performance would be expected for the spatially contiguous dimensions.

The results show clearly that the observed interference in tasks with orthogonal dimensions can be due either to the perception of stimuli as integral or to the failure to control attention. The subjects who performed with spatially contiguous dimensions show the developmental trend reported previously. Kindergarten children showed a redundancy gain with correlated values and interference with orthogonal values. With increasing age both of these effects were eliminated. Performances with spatially separated dimensions showed a different pattern. First, there was no redundancy gain that could be attributed to integral dimensions at any development level. Thus, the dimensions can be considered as independent sources of information. Second, there was interference with orthogonal dimensions, but the amount of interference declined with age. Kindergarten children showed interference; fifth-graders did not. These results with spatially separated dimensions indicate that the sources of information are perceived as separable and that with increasing age the child gains command of attention resources.

The results of Shepp (1977) show that attention improves with increasing age and that developmental changes in attention can be assessed provided that the sources of information are perceptually independent. What such results do not show are the specific ways in which attention might improve with age. First, attentional control can improve. The young child's performance deficits can be due to some difficulty in focusing attention on a relevant target or in maintaining attention in the presence of irrelevant stimuli. The difficulty either in focusing attention or in switching attention could disrupt performance in a variety of tasks. The improved performance that is observed with increasing age could be the result of either or both sources of better attentional control.

The time course of attention could also shorten with age. Younger children may have satisfactory control over attentional resources, but the time required to direct attention may be longer than that for older children. Similarly, younger children may be able to maintain attention for a shorter interval than older children. This possibility suggests that attention deficits may be less pronounced between ages when accuracy measures rather than times measures of attention are used. Some evidence for this view has recently been presented by Day (1980).

A second important relation between perceived structure and attention is that attention may affect the similarity relations that are dominant in perception. Stimuli that are first perceived as integral by children are often subsequently organized by dimensional features. Such objects may be perceived either as integral wholes or as features. In the young child the wholistic structure is primary; later, the features become salient. Each structure could exist at a different level or stage, and attention directed to a particular level would prime a specific structure. Whether attention becomes highly flexible (Klahr & Wallace, 1976) or goes from whole to part (Lockhead, 1972) remains to be seen. In any event we take the evidence for this type of relation to be sufficiently strong as to be a viable source of developmental performance differences.

In the preceding sections of this chapter, we have summarized the Separability Hypothesis, presented experimental tests of the hypothesis, and discussed some implications of the hypothesis for perception and cognition. It is possible, of course, to show relevance of the hypothesis to virtually any problem where perception or analysis begins with the concept of stimulus dimensions. We have not as yet developed, however, a more general model of perception that would speak to properties other than stimulus dimensions and would show how the perception of such properties changes with age as well as the general principles relating these properties to attention. Until such a general model is developed, it is pointless to try to exhaust the possible implications. Our current strategy has been to pose questions of general or developmental theoretical interest and to use the data base that such questions generate to build gradually such a model. In the remainder of this chapter, we consider two sets of experiments that address two basic questions. The first is whether all dimensions are analyzable into subjectively independent values. The second examines the relation between the perceptual structure of complex stimuli (rectangles) and conservation of quantity.

ANALYZABLE AND NONANALYZABLE STIMULI

As we mentioned earlier, there are several performance criteria that converge on the concept of integral dimensions. Some dimensional combinations such as hue and chroma of a single Munsell chip meet these criteria extremely well. Other dimensional combinations, however, are more problematic. Size and brightness, for example, produce a redundancy gain with correlated values (Biederman & Checkosky, 1970) and show interference with orthogonal values (Garner, 1977). But these effects are often small and sometimes do not obtain (Smith & Kemler, 1978). Moreover, in tasks with no speed demands such as dissimilarity judgment and restricted classification, such dimensions show the result that is typical of separable dimensions rather than integral ones (Burns, Shepp, & McDonnough, Ehrlich, 1978). These kinds of results have led Garner (1974b) to argue that there is a continuum of stimulus integrality rather than a simple dichotomy.

Burns et al. (1978) take a similar point of view in suggesting that stimulus dimensions may vary in the degree to which they may be analyzed by the subject. It is commonly believed, of course, that at some level of perceptual or cognitive analysis the features or values that compose a multidimensional stimulus can be analyzed and identified. Indeed, many of the converging operations that contrast integral and separable dimensions implicitly or explicitly assume dimensional analyzability. Consider, for example, the city-block and Euclidean metrics. Each metric is a combination rule for predicting the distance between objects that vary on two dimensions. The distance between the objects, d_{xy}, that vary on dimension X and Y is $d_x + d_y$ for the city-block metric and $(d_x^2 + d_y^2)^{1/2}$ for the Euclidean metric. In either case the stimuli must be analyzed to give values of d_x and d_y.

The argument that all dimensional combinations can be analyzed identifies a fundamental property of stimulus dimensions, namely that they must be subjectively independent. A specific value or feature of a dimension must retain its perceptual integrity or identifiability regardless of the value on another dimension with which it is paired. Despite the fundamental nature of the property of subjective independence of dimensions, it has seldom been tested and only recently have some formal criteria for subjective independence been provided.

Beals, Krantz, and Tversky (1968) and Tversky and Krantz (1970) have developed an additive difference model that specifies formal axioms for subjectively independent dimensions. To illustrate, consider interdimensional additivity, which requires two types of relations to hold in dissimilarity judgments. The first is the equality prediction that is illustrated most clearly by reference to Fig. 2.3. Suppose the subject is asked to rate stimuli that differ on levels 1 and 2 on dimension y. Four pairs of stimuli, 1 versus 5, 2 versus 6, 3 versus 7, and 4 versus 8, are compared. In each pair the value of dimension x is held constant. If dimension x and y are independent, then each stimulus pair is judged according to the difference between levels 1 and 2 on dimension y; the constant value of x should not contribute to the judgment of any pair. Thus, the ratings of the four pairs should be equal. In a similar fashion, the remaining one-step, two-step, and three-step unidimensional intervals as well as the corresponding diagonals would be compared. If all equivalent intervals on both dimensions x and y are judged as equal, the equality prediction would be satisfied.

The second prediction of interdimensional additivity is ordering. If each of two dimensions contribute independently to the judgments of dissimilarity, the ordering of dissimilarity ratings for pairs of stimuli differing on one dimension should not change if a level on the second dimension is changed by a constant interval. If, for example, the stimulus pair, 1 versus 13, is judged as more dissimilar than the pair 1 versus 5, then ordering is preserved if 2 versus 13 is

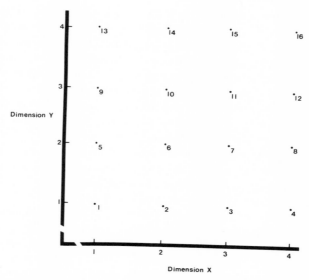

FIG. 2.3.   A 4 × 4 matrix of stimuli used in dissimilarity judgments.

judged as more dissimilar than 2 versus 5, 3 versus 13 is judged as more dissimilar than 3 versus 5, and so on.

The confirmation of the equality and ordering predictions indicates that dimensions are subjectively independent, and some dimensions such as the features of schematic faces satisfy these predictions (Tversky & Krantz, 1969). In contrast, the dimensions of rectangles (height, width, area, and shape) violate the equality and ordering predictions (Krantz & Tversky, 1975; Wender, 1971). The latter finding is especially interesting because there is other evidence that the attributes of rectangles are integral (Felfoldy, 1974; Shepp et al., 1980).

In a recent series of experiments Burns, et al. (1978) have assessed the subjective independence of three sets of multidimensional combinations: hue versus chroma of a single Munsell chip, size versus brightness of square, and size of circle versus angle of a radial line. In the first set of experiments the dissimilarity judgments of adults were evaluated for interdimensional additivity. The data for hue and chroma showed strong violations of interdimensional additivity, but the data for the remaining two-dimensional sets met the requirements of equality and ordering.

An attempt to converge on the property of subjective independence was made in a second set of experiments using the same stimuli in a restricted classification task. Subjects were presented with triads of stimuli and were instructed to "classify together the stimuli that go best together." Consider the triad shown in Fig. 2.1. Stimuli *A* and *B* share a value on dimension *X* but differ considerably on *Y*.

Stimulus C shares no value with either A or B but is only slightly different from B on both dimensions. For dimensional combinations that are separable, the grouping of A and B together provides the best classification; for integral dimensions, however, the grouping of B and C together is best (Garner, 1974b). The results obtained by Burns et al. (1978) were very clear. When subjects were presented with triads of stimuli generated by combinations of hue and chroma, stimuli B and C were classified together. In contrast, when presented with triads generated by combinations of either size versus brightness or size of circle versus angle of a radial line, subjects chose to group A and B together.

Taken together, the results of these two sets of experiments identify an important relation between perceptual independence and perceptual similarity. When stimuli violate the criteria of perceptual independence, they are classified by overall similarity relations. When, on the other hand, stimuli fulfill the criteria for subjective independence, they are classified according to dimensional similarity. The conclusions to be reached from these results are clear. Dimensional combinations such as size of circle versus angle of a radial line are readily analyzed according to their dimensional features or levels, and the subjects perform both dissimilarity judgments and classifications according to dimensional similarity relations. The results also suggest that dimensional combinations such as hue and chroma are not analyzed by features and, as a result, subjects perform both tasks on the basis of perceived overall similarity relations. Unfortunately, it is not clear whether the latter results are due to the nature of the perceived stimulus or to the demands of the task. It would clearly help to have additional evidence that would speak to this question of stimulus analyzability.

One very convincing source of evidence comes from a study by Smith and Kemler (1978). As part of an elegant series of experiments, they had adult subjects perform on two different-speeded classification tasks that are illustrated in Fig. 2.4. The broken line in each panel shows the basis for the classification. Thus, stimuli A, B, C, and D are classified together and the stimuli on the other side of the broken line are classified together. In the dimensional task the stimuli are so arranged that classification by values of a dimension is possible. Clearly, if subjects analyze the stimuli that are presented in these alternative fashions, the dimensional classification task should be easier than the 45° rotational task. In the dimensional task the subject is required only to identify a value on the target dimension (e.g., X_1 and X_2), but in the rotational task the subject must identify a value on each dimension in order to perform the task successfully. If, on the other hand, the subject does not or cannot analyze the stimuli, the dimensional task and the rotational task should yield equivalent performances.

Smith and Kemler (1978) report data on these tasks for two-dimensional combinations: value versus chroma and size versus value. With value and chroma as stimuli the two tasks were performed equally well. In contrast, the dimensional task with size versus value was easier than either task with value versus

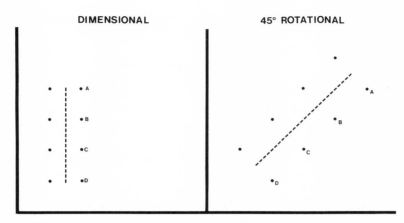

FIG. 2.4.   An illustration of stimuli used to illustrate a dimensional and a 45°
rotational task.

chroma, but the rotational task with size versus value was harder than either task
with value versus chroma.

These results by Smith and Kemler (1978) suggest that there is little option for
the subject in performing with these dimensional combinations. Apparently, size
and value must be analyzed according to dimensional value even when an alternative perceptual mode would benefit performance such as in the rotational task.
On the other hand, the subject is apparently unable to analyze stimuli composed
of levels of value and chroma even when performance would be improved by
such analysis as in the case of the dimensional task. It is possible, of course, that
the pressures of a speeded task or multiple stimuli make analysis very difficult,
especially if an alternative and more dominant mode of perceptual representation
is available. Nevertheless, the results suggest that analysis of value and chroma
is most difficult.

In a recent series of experiments, Burns and Shepp (1982) have further attempted to evaluate the analyzability of multidimensional stimuli. In this series
of experiments we have assessed analyzability of all three combinations of dimensions of the Munsell system: hue, chroma, and value. These stimulus sets
have been examined in the context of dissimilarity judgment, restricted classification, and instructed restricted classification.

Before considering the results of these studies, consider first some of the
general procedures that were employed. The stimulus sets were constructed
using Munsell glossy chips that varied in hue, value, and chroma. Set 1 (hue
versus chroma) was composed of 36 chips of a constant value (6) that varied in 6
equal steps of hue from 10RP to 2.5YR and 6 equal steps of chroma that varied
from 2 to 12. Set 2 (hue versus value) had a constant level of chroma (12) and 36

stimuli were generated from 6 levels of hue that varied from 10RP to 2.5YR and 6 levels of value that varied from 3 to 8. Set 3 (value versus chroma) had a constant value of hue (7.5R). All possible combinations of 6 levels of brightness that varied from 3 to 8 and 6 levels of chroma that varied from 2 to 12 were used. The chips were judged against an intermediate gray background (value = 5) under a tungsten artificial daylight lamp with a blue filter approximating illuminant C. Separate groups of subjects, Brown undergraduates, were used in different experiments. Specific procedures, unless otherwise noted, followed those of Burns et al. (1978).

The results of our experiments using dissimilarity judgments and restricted classification agreed closely with those of Burns et al. In the case of all three stimulus sets there were substantial violations of interdimensional additivity and these violations appeared consistently in the data of individual subjects. In the restricted classification task, subjects classified stimuli according to overall similarity relations. Thus, both sets of results are consistent with the conclusion that the features on these dimensions are not analyzed and are not therefore subjectively independent.

In order to provide a more rigorous test of dimensional analyzability and the subject's capacity to analyze these sets of stimuli according to specific features we devised an instructed restricted classification task. In this task our subjects were shown a triad of three stimuli and were told that two of the stimuli in the triad shared an identical value on one dimension. They were told that they were to choose the two stimuli that shared the identical value. Prior to the administration of this task all subjects were given the following types of pretraining: (1) The concept of a dimension was explained in the context of the present experiment, and a description of identical features or values was given. (2) The subjects were shown a series of Munsell chips from a different location in the Munsell series and dimensional variations were illustrated using the particular stimulus set (e.g., hue versus chroma) that a particular subject would later be required to classify. (3) Each subject was given a series of trials with rectangles that varied in height and width. The subject was instructed to classify the stimuli of each triad according to whether the stimuli had identical heights or identical widths. Following this series of trials each subject then preformed the instructed classification task with one of the Munsell sets. Otherwise the procedures followed those of Burns et al. (1978).

The results for the classifications made by subjects instructed on the restricted classification task are shown in Table 2.3 and for comparison purposes the classifications made by subjects on the standard classification task (without instruction) are shown in Table 2.2. The triads used in these experiments are illustrated in Fig. 2.5. The triads used with the standard classification task were I, III, and V, whereas the triads used in the instructed classification task were II, IV, and V. As shown in Table 2.2 the results are quite straightforward. In both Type I and Type III triads, subjects consistently classified by overall similarity

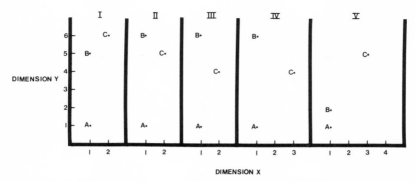

FIG. 2.5.   An illustration of triads that vary the salience of dimensional of overall similarity relations.

relations regardless of which dimension displayed a common feature and this trend is apparent across all three sets of dimensions. By hypothesis, Type III triads were designed to induce a higher proportion of dimensional responses, but with these stimulus sets there were no substantial differences between the proportions of dimensional classification across the two types of triads.

Consider now the results with instructed classification. First, it is important to note that some integral stimuli were readily analyzable. Recall that as part of pretraining subjects were first given rectangles arranged in Type I triads and were required to classify according to shared values of height or width. The proportion of dimensional classifications made by all subjects averaged across all conditions was 0.99. As shown in Table 2.3, however, the subjects did not fare quite so well with the attributes of color. The first major point of interest is that subjects

TABLE 2.2

Proportions of Dimensional, Haphazard, and Similarity Responses, in the Standard Classification Task, for Each Dimension, Composing the Hue–Croma, Hue–Value, and Value–Croma Stimulus Set

	Hue–Chroma						Hue–Value						Value–Chroma					
	Shared Hue			Shared Chroma			Shared Hue			Shared Value			Shared Value			Shared Chroma		
	D	H	S	D	H	S	D	H	S	D	H	S	D	H	S	D	H	S
Type I	.06	.03	.91	.04	.02	.94	.14	.08	.78	.04	.06	.90	.09	.08	.83	.10	.17	.73
Type III	.08	.06	.86	.07	.09	.84	.24	.13	.63	.14	.05	.81	.10	.10	.80	.23	.15	.62
Type V	.95	.02	.03	.92	.04	.04	.88	.09	.03	.92	.05	.03	.96	.00	.04	.93	.04	.03

D = dimensional classification (A and B)

H = haphazard classification (A and C).

S = overall similarity classification (B and C).

TABLE 2.3

Proportion of Dimensional, Haphazard, and Similarity Responses in the Restricted Classification Task—Instructed Condition—for Each Dimension, Composing the Hue–Chroma, Hue–Value, and Value–Chroma Stimulus Set

	Hue–Chroma						Hue–Value						Value–Chroma					
	Shared Hue			Shared Chroma			Shared Hue			Shared Value			Shared Value			Shared Chroma		
	D	H	S	D	H	S	D	H	S	D	H	S	D	H	S	D	H	S
Type II	.01	.35	.64	.30	.23	.47	.07	.22	.71	.33	.14	.53	.31	.27	.42	.16	.28	.56
Type IV	.10	.42	.48	.59	.15	.26	.30	.21	.48	.63	.09	.28	.40	.25	.35	.36	.28	.36
Type V	.63	.06	.31	.74	.05	.21	.81	.06	.13	.71	.02	.27	.59	.17	.34	.66	.15	.23

D = dimensional classification (A and B).
H = haphazard classification (A and C).
S = overall similarity classification (B and C).

in the instructed classification task made fewer overall similarity responses than did subjects in the standard version of this task. Thus, the effect of instructing the subjects to classify by dimension at least had the effect of reducing overall similarity responses. We interpret this reduction to mean that the subjects were at least trying to perform the task as instructed. Their accuracy in so doing is another matter. Consider the classifications made to Type II triads. Although there were some variations from set to set, subjects nevertheless continued to classify the stimuli by overall similarity relations even though they had been instructed to classify by dimension. Classification of Type IV triads showed selective improvement. Although subjects could not identify identical levels of hue, they could reliably identify levels of value and chroma when each was paired with hue. When value and chroma were combined, the subject could not classify by dimension.

The classifications of Type V triads are of special interest. These triads were introduced to determine if the subject had adopted the strategy of putting together the most different stimuli as the ones that shared a common dimensional feature. Notice that in triad Types I–IV the stimuli that were most dissimilar on both dimensions were also the stimuli that shared a feature. During the course of pretraining, subjects could have noted this characteristic of these triads; during the course of instructed classification, they could have applied this rule to their classifications even though specific dimensional identities could not be detected. In Type V triads stimuli A and B share a value on a dimension and they are also most similar overall. Stimulus C shares no value with either A or B and is very dissimilar to both. A comparison of the proportions of dimensional classifications in Type V triads confirms that such a strategy was indeed being employed. Notice that the number of "dimensional" classifications in these Type V triads was substantially less for the instructed task than for the uninstructed task. Even so, it seems reasonable to conclude that subjects were able to detect common levels of chroma and value when these dimensions were paired with hue.

The results of our experiment with instructed classification show that the typical college sophomore cannot analyze the attributes of color very effectively. This is perhaps not surprising because the kind of task that we are asking our subjects to do was one where they had had very little experience. Certainly it is true that we can tell colors apart at least across broad categories (e.g., red versus blue) and that even within a category we have names that describe different color experiences (e.g., light blue versus blue) (Bornstein, Kessen, & Weiskopf, 1976). We believe, however, that there may be some specialized populations whose experience and/or special talent for color might give us a different answer to the analyzability of color attributes than did our college freshmen. Thus, we enlisted the cooperation of a class of students in painting at the Rhode Island School of Design. These students had all just completed a course in color theory that had gone over extensively the attributes of the Munsell system. These students were also considered to be advanced students in painting.

Our painters were asked to perform the same experiment as our freshmen who performed the instructed classification task. Only one of the sets was used, namely hue and chroma. The only other deviation in procedure from our previous experiment was the use of size and brightness as the classification stimuli during pretraining. Thus, before classifying hue and chroma these subjects classified size and brightness.

The results of this experiment are very clear. First, as expected, these students were able to classify triads of size and brightness very effectively. The proportion of dimensional classifications exceeded 0.99. In classifying triads composed of variations in hue and chroma our painters did not do much better than our college students. They showed no evidence of being able to classify by dimension on triads that shared a common hue for either Type II or Type IV triads. For saturation, on the other hand, there was evidence for analysis by dimension. Type II did not show substantial proportions of dimensional classifications, but on Type IV triads the painters classified by dimension on 75% of the trials. This performance is slightly superior to the college student. The classifications made by our painters on Type V triads closely approximates the performances of our college students on these same triads.

Across several types of experimental situations we can reach the conclusion that the attributes of color are not readily analyzable. There is no evidence in these experiments that subjects can discover stimuli that contain identical hues. In some contexts subjects can identify stimuli that contain identical levels of value or chroma, but they are not very good at such identification. Even with extensive experience or talent, performance does not improve much. On balance, then, it is reasonable to conclude that some integral stimuli are highly analyzable, but others are either not analyzed or analyzed with only moderate accuracy.

As we suggested earlier in this chapter, many integral dimensions such as size and brightness are perceived as features on dimensions in tasks such as dissimilarity judgment and restricted classification, but in speeded tasks such dimensions sometimes act as integral wholes. Thus, it appears that the wholistic properties of analyzable dimensions must be detected by measures of attention. Several investigators (Kahneman & Henik, 1977) have shown that attention is distributed equally among all members of a perceptual group or unit, but it has also been shown that the distribution of attention may change if the features are either spatially separated (Pomerantz, 1981) or made more dissimilar (Garner, 1978b). A similar argument can be applied to dimensional features that combine to produce objects. Some features (e.g., hue and value) produce what seem to be very robust objects. Conjunctions of features should be easy to identify, but a specific feature in a selective attention task should be difficult to identify. Other features (e.g., size of circle versus angle of a radial line), however, are seen as separate objects; it should be difficult to divide attention to conjunctions of such features but very easy to attend to them selectively.

Recently, Shepp, Kolbet, and Fink (1982) employed a version of a discrete trial priming task to study the relation between stimulus analyzability and attention. This task, illustrated in Table 2.4, presented a stimulus, the prime, centered in the upper half of the visual field for 500 msec. Immediately following the prime, two stimuli were presented in the lower half of the visual field, equidistant from the center. The subject's task was to identify the aspect of one of the stimuli that corresponded to the cued aspect of the prime and to press the button located below that stimulus as quickly as possible without making errors. The

TABLE 2.4
Selective and Divided Attention Paradigms[a]

Type of Irrelevant Stimulus	Selective Attention Task Prime $S_1 V_1$		
	Orthogonal	Control-Size	Control-Value
Same (SI)	$S_1 V_1 \, S_2 V_2$	$S_1 V_1 \, S_2 V_1$	$S_1 V_1 \, S_1 V_2$
Different (DI)	$S_1 V_2 \, S_2 V_1$	$S_1 V_2 \, S_2 V_2$	$S_2 V_1 \, S_2 V_2$

Divided Attention Task Prime $S_1 V_1$ Condition		
Conjunction	Control-Size	Control-Value
$S_1 V_1 \, S_2 V_1$ $S_1 V_1 \, S_1 V_2$	$S_1 V_1 \, S_2 V_1$	$S_1 V_1 \, S_1 V_2$

*The tasks are illustrated for two levels of size (S_1 and S_2) and two levels of value (V_1 and V_2). Note that only half of the lateral arrangements are presented.

subject's response turned off the display. After a short but variable interval, the next trial was begun. Conditions were run in blocks of 80 trials (plus practice trials).

In the selective attention task the subject was instructed to attend to one of two dimensions. Thus, if the subject were instructed to attend to size, the prime, S_1V_1, would cue the subject to look for S_1 in the test pair. In the selective attention condition, the irrelevant cues, V_1 and V_2, were orthogonal to S_1 (or S_2) in the test pairs. In the control condition the irrelevant stimuli were held constant. Corresponding conditions were run for value. In the divided attention task, the subject was instructed to look for the specific conjunction of features (S_1V_1) in the test pair or to look for a specific feature S_1 or V_1 in the control conditions.

Six separate experiments were run with Brown students. Each of three dimensional sets was run on selective and divided attention with different groups of subjects in each experiment. All stimuli were photographed against a dark gray background and the slides were shown by a projection T-scope. One dimensional set consisted of rectangles (each rectangle subtended a visual angle of 5.4° × 3.4°) that varied hue (2.5P versus 10R) and value (4 versus 7). A second set consisted of squares that varied value (4 versus 7) with a constant 10R/8 hue/chroma and size (large versus small). The visual angles of the squares were 5.4° and 3.7°. The third set of stimuli was size of circle and angle of a radial line. The circles were white discs that subtended a visual angle of 3.4° and 3.7°. The radial line (0.07° wide) was black and extended from the center of the circle by a constant distance (1.1°).

Consider first the selective attention experiments. If the subject can attend selectively to a specific feature, the reaction times to the two types of test pairs should be equivalent. If the prime is S_1V_1 and the subject is attending to size, S_1, it should not matter whether the irrelevant stimulus is V_1 (SI) or V_2 (DI). This would be the expected result for separable stimuli.

If the subject cannot attend selectively to a feature, the reaction time to SI should be faster than DI. The interference observed with DI test pairs, however, would result from different factors in different sets. With difficult-to-analyze dimensions such as value and chroma, the basis for interference is perceptual. The correct stimulus in the SI test pair is identical to the prime, but the correct stimulus in the DI pair is a completely different object. For hue versus value, a stimulus–response mapping problem, two stimuli on one response, must be solved. The source of interference for easy-to-analyze dimensions such as size and value is attentional. The prime, S_1V_1, is analyzed and the features are extracted in parallel. In the SI test pair S_1 and V_1 are preserved in the same stimulus, and the subject responds quickly. But in the DI test pair the features of the prime are presented in different stimuli. Since we assume that subjects mandatorily attend to the features of analyzable dimensions, attention will be directed to the irrelevant stimulus on some proportion of trials. This misdirected attention will interfere with performance.

The differences between integral dimensions that are easily analyzed and those that are not easily analyzed can be detected by comparing reaction times to the *SI* and *DI* test pairs in the control condition. For hue and value, subjects are faced with the same difficulty as in the orthogonal condition. There are still two distinctive stimuli to map onto one response; the *DI* test pairs should be more difficult than the *SI* pairs. For size and value, however, the source of interference has been removed. The *DI* trials present a different but constant irrelevant feature. Because this feature was not present in the prime, it does not compete for attention and no disruption in performance should occur.

The results of the selective attention experiments are shown in Table 2.5. For hue and value the results are consistent with the argument that the features of these dimensions are difficult to identify. The reaction times to the *DI* test pairs are slower than *SI* test pairs for both dimensions in both the orthogonal and control conditions. Such results are consistent with the stimulus–response mapping hypothesis.

The results for size and value suggest that the dimensions are asymmetric. Size is more difficult than value, but more importantly irrelevant variation in value interferes with attention to size but the reverse is not true. Thus, the reaction time to *DI* is slower than *SI* only in the orthogonal condition for size. Surprisingly, there is also an asymmetric relation with size and angle. Irrelevant variations in size interfere with attention to angle. Although the effect is small (18 msec), *DI* is reliably slower than *SI* when angle is the target and size is orthogonal. Note that interference occurs even though size is the more difficult dimension.

The asymmetric relation between dimensional combinations that are readily analyzed suggests that some features contribute more to object composition than

TABLE 2.5
Mean Reaction Time (msec) in Selective Attention Task for Three
Dimensional Sets

Stimulus Set	Type of Irrelevant Stimulus	Condition			
		Orthogonal		Control	Control
		Hue	Value	Hue	Value
Hue vs. value	Same (*SI*)	358	356	350	342
	Different (*DI*)	431	401	389	379
		Size	Value	Size	Value
Size vs. value	Same (*SI*)	343	313	336	305
	Different (*DI*)	389	309	340	306
		Size	Angle	Size	Angle
Size vs. angle	Same (*SI*)	409	372	418	373
	Different (*DI*)	407	391	408	376

do others. Some features such as color and spatial location seem to provide more "glue." Similarities of color and/or location appear to integrate or even create other aspects of the stimulus in generating objects while dissimilarities segregate clusters of features into different objects (Garner, 1974a; Kahneman & Henik, 1977). This suggests a levels of processing approach where integrating features such as color or location can be extracted independently of the process of object formation. Thus, subjects can selectively attend to value (or other attributes of color) but cannot attend selectively to shape or size because these are features of objects that result in part from the integration of information by color and spatial location. Similarly, variations in size are correlated with variations in other aspects of the object (e.g., brightness) that would facilitate selection of size but could interfere with selection of angle.

Consider now performance on the divided attention task. As shown in Table 2.6, the reaction time to the conjunction is not different from the slower control for either the hue versus value set or the size versus value set. This type of finding can, of course, be predicted by certain parallel processing models (Egeth, 1966; Taylor, 1976; Townsend, 1971). However, in order to do so, extreme assumptions need to be met. For example, the reaction time distributions for the control conditions cannot overlap. If there is overlap in the distributions, the parallel model predicts that the reaction time to the conjunction will be slower than the slower control. The parallel model does better with size versus angle, where the conjunction is slower than either control, than it does with hue versus value or size versus value. With the latter sets the mean reaction times of the distributions were within one standard deviation of each other. Thus, it appears that the objects generated by hue and value or size and value were first perceived as integral wholes or "blobs" (Lockhead, 1972) and that the divided attention task was performed using this form of perceived structure.

On balance, the results from the experiments on selective and divided attention are consistent with our hypotheses that objects vary in analyzability and that with some objects subjects are able to make use of perceptual properties that are particularly suited to the task. Size versus value yielded performances like those of hue versus value in divided attention, suggesting attention to wholistic proper-

TABLE 2.6
Mean Reaction Times (msec) in Divided Attention Task for Three
Dimensional Sets

Stimulus Set	Conjunction	Condition	
		Control	Control
Hue (H) vs. value (V)	331	335 (H)	337 (V)
Size (S) vs. value (V)	374	378 (S)	342 (V)
Size (S) vs. angle (A)	521	490 (S)	413 (A)

ties. Selective attention to a dimension was partially successful when called for. There was, however, less option for the subject than we had supposed. Asymmetric interference in the case of both size versus value and size versus angle indicate principles of object formation that deny attentive options. Under what conditions these options could be improved remains to be determined.

PERCEIVED DIMENSIONAL STRUCTURE AND LOGICAL OPERATIONS

A persisting and difficult issue for theories of cognitive development is the relative contribution of perceptual and conceptual operations to a variety of performances. Consider a typical conservation task. The child is shown two identical glasses with equivalent amounts of liquid. After the child has agreed that the glasses contain the same amounts, the contents of one of the glasses is poured into a glass of a different shape (e.g., one that is taller and narrower). The child is then tested for conservation.

According to Piaget (1967; 1968) the preoperational child will say that the taller glass has more liquid because the child centrates or focuses attention on but a single aspect of the stimulus. The somewhat older child decenters or attends to several variations of the stimulus simultaneously, a skill that is important in the development of operations such as compensation that, in turn, lead to conservation. For Piaget, then, perception contributes to the performance of the preoperational child, but it is logical operations that result in the successful conservation by the concrete operational child.

Many investigators (Anderson & Cuneo, 1978; Gelman, 1969; Wohlwill, 1962) have argued that perception is fundamental to all behavior and that relations between perception and conceptual operations persist throughout development. We agree with this general viewpoint but would contend that a successful approach to the problem must ultimately address the development of perceived structure and the kinds of operations that would be permitted by both perceived structure and the developmental level of the perceiver who performs the task.

To illustrate, consider a set of rectangles that has the attributes that characterize objects used in the conservation of quantity. Each rectangle has height (H) and width (W), and these dimensions combine to yield area ($H \times W$) and shape (H/W). It is typically assumed that perception of these dimensions does not vary with the age of the child but that developmental differences in attention, judgment, and logical operations are critical in the conservation of quantity. There are two reservations about this approach. The first is that there may well be developmental differences in perceived structure. If so, such differences must be identified in order to determine constraints on other processes. The second is that these types of stimuli do not readily allow the processes in adult perception that are assumed to be critical in the management of such stimuli by children. Generally, for example, these dimensions are integral and do not allow selective attention (Felfoldy, 1974). Moreover, these attributes are perceived according to overall similarity relations (Monahan & Lockhead, 1977), and violate the criteria of subjective independence (Krantz and Tversky, 1975; Wender, 1971).

In a recent series of experiments, Shepp and Burns (1982) have attempted to reconcile some of these issues. They point out that although these stimuli are generally integral, some aspects of the stimuli are at least analyzable even though dimensional relations may vary in salience in some sets of stimuli. Moreover, they argue that previous work with the adult may be misleading because the aspects of shape have been oversimplified.

Consider the rectangles illustrated in Fig. 2.6. The stimuli that fall along the primary diagonal are squares, whereas the remaining stimuli in the matrix are either tall or wide rectangles. Stimuli falling along the secondary diagonal or arrays parallel to it share equal areas.

The aspects of shape that a subject may perceive in a set of rectangles include (1) simple shape relations, (2) prototypic relations, and (3) configural relations. Simple shape refers to stimuli on arrays that lay parallel to the primary diagonal; stimuli having the same shape may be either tall or wide. For example, the

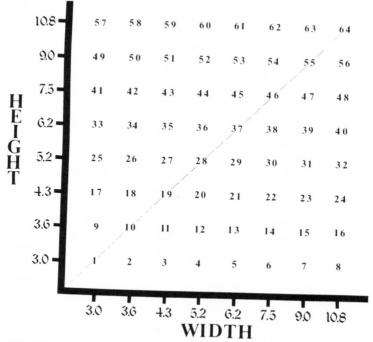

FIG. 2.6. An 8 × 8 matrix depicting the attributes of rectangles for restricted classification.

stimuli 33, 42, 51, and 60 are tall rectangles that have the same shape (height/ width). Prototypic properties refer to perceptually good stimuli, ones that are most representative of objects of a particular category and most unlike objects that belong to other categories (Rosch, 1973, 1975). Squares are most representative of four-sided figures and least representative of other categories of form. Along the same lines, Garner (1974b) has defined pattern goodness in terms of the number of patterns that can be generated by rotating or reflecting the stimulus in 90° steps about any of the four axes, horizontal, vertical, left diagonal, and right diagonal. Because squares show maximal redundancy and symmetry, rotation and reflection about the principal axes yield just one unique stimulus. Finally, there are configural properties of stimuli that are also related to the concept of subset and are produced by a 90° rotation. For example, stimuli 9 and 2 are configural stimuli. The stimuli are identical except for a 90° rotation.

Shepp and Burns (1982) report two experiments that support this characterization of rectangles. The first was a scaling study of a subset (4 × 4) shown in Fig. 2.6. The scaling solution yielded two dimensions. One scaled factor correlated +.96 with area, whereas the other correlated +.97 with absolute distance of a particular array of shapes from the prototype (square). From the latter factor, the dimensions of shape are readily derived.

An attempt to converge on these stimulus properties was made by asking subjects to classify triads of rectangles in a restricted classification task. The results from this experiment are shown in the last column of Table 2.7. The classifications of aspects of shape show a reliable organization by dimensional value, whereas the triads that present shared values of height, width, or area were classified by overall similarity. These results suggest a complicated perceptual organization of the stimuli by the adult; some aspects of the stimuli are perceived by dimensional relations but some are perceived by overall similarity.

The results of experiments with adults are relatively clear and are useful in formulating developmental hypotheses. Two questions are important. First, are there trends in perceptual development? Second, is there any relation between developmental changes in perceived structure and the occurrence of conservation?

In considering the development of perceived structure for these stimuli, two kinds of trends seem plausible. For some aspects of the stimulus, such as height, width, and area, we would expect consistent overall similarity relations regardless of age. We would expect, however, some developmental differences in perceived structure in the classification of shape. Considering some of the evidence reviewed by Gibson (1969) on perception of symmetry, it is reasonable to suppose that prototypes will anchor the child's perception relatively early and that configural relations will also be obvious. Simple shape, however, can be considered a more complex relation and thus require more analysis or more perceptual learning in order for dimensionally perceived relations to become more salient than overall similarity relations.

TABLE 2.7
Proportion of Dimensional Classifications of Rectangles at Different
Developmental Levels

| Triad Type | Nursery School | Developmental Levels | | Adults |
| | | Third-Graders | | |
		Nonconservers	Conservers	
Height	.15	.03	.09	.22
(57, 63', 53')				
Width	.13	.05	.15	.28
(57, 9', 26')				
Area	.14	.20	.22	.11
(16, 44', 38')				
Shape				
(1) Simple				
(35, 62', 56')	.16	.18	.83	.85
(2) Prototype				
SST	.60	.79	.78	.94
(46, 19', 26')				
TTS	.56	.60	.75	.68
(49, 35', 28')				
WWS	.35	.20	.30	.70
(7, 21', 28')				
(3) Configural				
CCS (N)	.22	.65	.80	.94
(35, 28, 21)				
CCS (F)	.78	.85	1.00	.97
(58, 37, 16)				
CCS	.80	.97	.97	1.00
(59, 24', 39')				

S = square; T = tall; W = wide; C = configuration
Numbers in parentheses refer to stimuli that compose example triads (see Fig. 2.6).
The grouping of *italicized* stimuli is a dimensional classification. The grouping of stimuli with superscripts is an overall similarity classification.

Given that the hypothesized development of perceived dimensional relations occurs, there remains the question concerning the relation between the development of perceived dimensional relations and conservation. Because several aspects of the stimuli are integral for the young child a change in one aspect of the stimulus will change the perceived overall similarity relations. Such a change might mislead the judgment by a young child. It is quite another matter, however, to believe that the appearance of perceived dimensional relations contributes directly to conservation. It is reasonable, of course, to argue that the older child who perceives dimensional relations will perceive perceptual invariants that the younger child does not perceive, and it is also possible that the older child has acquired skill at perceptual analysis. Thus, the concurrent appearance of particular perceived dimensional relations and successful conservation may reflect the knowledge and analysis that contribute to each performance.

To investigate these possible relations, we presented a restricted classification task to nursery school children and third-graders. Following the classification task these subjects participated in a conservation task. Before describing the results, consider a few matters of procedure. The stimuli were rectangles that were constructed from black, opaque, plexiglass, ¼ in. thick. The stimuli varied in width and height from 3 to 10.8 cm as shown in Fig. 2.6. Examples of the triads that were used are shown in Table 2.6. The classification task presented 72 trials.

Plexiglass "cookie cutters" were constructed for use in the conservation task. Play dough was used to fashion cookies with the cookie cutters and this provided a context for the standard conservation task. Following the task, questions were asked of the subjects to justify their conclusions regarding conservation.

The results of classification are shown in Table 2.7. The third-grade group is divided to show classifications for those children who conserve and gave correct justifications and those children who did not do so. As expected, the classifications of triads with shared values of height, width, or area are consistently based upon overall similarity relations for all ages. The picture with shape is somewhat more complicated. Consider first, classifications in which prototypic relations were involved. Three such relations were used and are illustrated in Table 2.7. In the first of these triads, two squares and a tall rectangle were presented. Clearly, there is developmental difference in classification, but it is not a very interesting difference. Nursery school children do tend to classify the two squares together but they do not do so consistently. With increasing age the tendency to classify the two squares together improves. The next prototypic triad presents two tall rectangles and a square. Our subjects tend to get better in classifying the two tall rectangles together with increasing age but the effect is quite small. In the remaining prototypic triad the subject is presented with two wide rectangles and a square. In these triads there is a strong developmental difference. Both nursery school and third-grade children tend to classify by overall similarity whereas adults classify by dimensional relations.

There were three triads that portrayed configural relations. Two of these triads presented two configural stimuli with a square whereas the third presented the two configural stimuli with a nonsquare. The one substantial developmental difference in perceived relations occurred in the triad where the two configural stimuli were close to the square. For these triads the youngest children tended to group the square with one of the configural stimuli rather than grouping the configural stimuli together. With increasing age there was, of course, a strong tendency to group the configural stimuli together. Developmental differences in the remaining two configural triads are quite small. All groups showed a reliable tendency to classify on the basis of the configural dimension.

The classifications of simple shape triads show clear developmental differences that discriminate between conservers and nonconservers. Nursery school children and nonconserving third-graders classify these triads reliably by overall similarity relations. In contrast, conserving third-graders and adults classify reliably by dimension.

The results of this experiment have identified several interesting trends in perceptual development and have clarified somewhat the relation between perception and tasks that involve judgment of quantity. The classifications of triads with shared values of height, width, or area yielded the expected results. Subjects of all ages do not ordinarily perceive these aspects according to dimensionally organized relations but rather in terms of overall similarity relations. As we observed earlier in this chapter, adult subjects can classify accurately by either height or width dimensional values when instructed to do so, and there is no reason to believe that children could not also be trained to do so. We have also observed (Shepp & Burns, 1982) that adults cannot accurately classify triads that share a value of area even when they are instructed to do so.

In contrast there was a marked change in the development of shape perception. Even the young child perceived some prototypic relations. Still there is improvement in classifying by prototype with increasing age for tall and square stimuli. The marked delay in classifying wide rectangles together suggests an asymmetry in the perception of wide and tall that deserves additional investigation. Finally, there was a marked developmental trend in the direction of increasing dimensional perception of shape with age, a finding that provides new support for the Separability Hypothesis.

The results also agree with our earlier comments about the possible relation between perceived dimensional structure and conservation. The child who classifies by dimension exhibits a specific type of knowledge and analytical skill but there is no compelling reason to believe that the appearance of perceived dimensional relations contributes directly to conservation. Indeed, there are instances (e.g., wide, wide, square triads) where the conserving third-grader is perceiving overall similarity relations when the adult is perceiving dimensional relations. Yet, both conserve. Moreover, Gelman (1969), after training with very specific dimensions, observed very general transfer effects to other types of conservation tasks.

SUMMARY

The present chapter has described the Separability Hypothesis and has attempted to characterize some of its implications. We have attempted to show that the features of some objects are analyzed more effectively than are others, and the consequences of this differential analyzability have been illustrated in several tasks. We have also argued that with increasing age, subjects become more effective in analyzing stimuli. This improving analytical skill may contribute to both the detection of dimensional relations and the knowledge of invariant quantity. We also found evidence that perceived structure constrained the subjects' processing options more than anticipated, but the conditions that might improve these options are not sufficiently clear.

ACKNOWLEDGMENTS

This research and preparation of this paper was supported by research grant HD 13406 from the National Institute of Child Health and Human Development. I am grateful to Karen Harris for her assistance in the general administration of the experiments, analysis of the data, and preparation of the graphs. Special thanks are due Sue Fink for her invaluable comments on an earlier draft of the manuscript.

REFERENCES

Anderson, N. H., & Cuneo, D. O. The height + width rule in children's judgements of quantity. *Journal of Experimental Psychology*, 1978, *107*, 335–378.

Attneave, F. Dimensions of similarity. *American Journal of Psychology*, 1950, *63*, 516–556.

Beals, R., Krantz, D. H., & Tversky, A. Foundations of multidimensional scaling. *Psychological Review*, 1968, *75*, 127–142.

Biederman, I., & Checkosky, S. F. Processing redundant information. *Journal of Experimental Psychology*, 1970, *83*, 486–490.

Boring, E. G. *Physical dimensions of consciousness.* New York: Century, 1933.

Bornstein, M. H., Kessen, W., & Weiskoph, S. The categories of hue in infancy. *Science*, 1976, *191*, 201–202.

Bruner, J. S., Olver, R. R., & Greenfield, P. M. *Studies in cognitive growth.* New York: Wiley, 1966.

Burns, B., & Shepp, B. E. *The analyzability of multidimensional stimuli: Some constraints on the perception of color.* Unpublished manuscript, 1982.

Burns, B. B., Shepp, B. E., McDonough, D., & Ehrlich, W. The relation between stimulus analyzability and perceived dimensional structure. In G. H. Bower (Ed.), *The psychology of learning and motivation: Advances in research and theory*, Vol. 12. New York: Academic Press, 1978.

Clark, E. V. Whats in a word? On the child's acquisition of semantics in his first language. In T. E. Moore (Ed.), *Cognitive development and acquisition of language.* New York: Academic Press, 1973.

Day, M. C. Selective attention by children and adults to pictures specified by color. *Journal of Experimental Child Psychology*, 1980, *30*, 277–289.

Doyle, A. Listening to distraction: A developmental study of selection attention. *Journal of Experimental Child Psychology*, 1973, *15*, 100–115.

Egeth, H. E. Parallel versus serial processes in multidimensional stimulus discrimination. *Perception & Psychophysics*, 1966, 1, 245–248.

Felfoldy, G. L. Repetition effects in choice reaction time to multidimensional stimuli. *Perception & Psychophysics*, 1974, *15*, 453–459.

Fisher, M. A., & Zeaman, D. An attention–retention theory of retardate discrimination learning. In

N. R. Ellis (Ed.), *International review of research in mental retardation*, Vol. 6. New York: Academic Press, 1973.

Garner, W. R. The stimulus in information processing. *American Psychologist*, 1970, *25*, 350–358.

Garner, W. R. Attention: The processing of multiple sources of information. In E. C. Carterette & M. P. Friedman (Eds.), *Handbook of perception*, Vol. 2. New York: Academic Press, 1974. (a)

Garner, W. R. *The processing of information and structure*. Hillsdale, N.J.: Lawrence Erlbaum Associates, 1974. (b)

Garner, W. R. Interaction of stimulus dimensions in concept and choice processes. *Cognitive Psychology*, 1976, *8*, 98–123.

Garner, W. R. The effect of absolute size on the separability of the dimensions of size and brightness. *Bulletin of the Psychonomic Society*, 1977, *9*, 380–382.

Garner, W. R. Aspects of a stimulus: Features, dimensions, and configurations. In E. Rosch & B. B. Lloyd (Eds.), *Cognition and categorization*. Hillsdale, N.J.: Lawrence Erlbaum Associates, 1978. (a)

Garner, W. R. Selective attention to attributes and to stimuli. *Journal of Experimental Psychology: General*, 1978, *3*, 287–308. (b)

Garner, W. R., & Felfoldy, G. L. Integrality of stimulus dimensions in various types of information processing. *Cognitive Psychology*, 1970, 1, 225–241.

Gelman, R. Conservative acquisition: A problem of learning to attend to relevant attributes. *Journal of Experimental Child Psychology*, 1969, *7*, 167–186.

Gibson, E. J. *Principles of perceptual learning and development*. New York: Appleton-Century-Crofts, 1969.

Gibson, J. J. The concept of the stimulus in psychology. *American Psychologist*, 1960, *15*, 694–703.

Gibson, J. J. *The senses considered as perceptual systems*. Boston: Houghton Mifflin, 1966.

Hagan, J. W., & Hale, G. H. The development of attention in children. In A. Pick (Ed.), *Minnesota symposia on child psychology*, Vol. 7. Minneapolis, Minn.: University of Minnesota Press, 1973.

Inhelder, P., & Piaget, J. *The early growth of logic in the child*. New York: Norton, 1964.

Kahneman, D. *Attention and effort*. Englewood Cliffs, N.J.: Prentice-Hall, 1973.

Kahneman, D., & Henik, A. Effect of visual grouping on immediate recall and selective attention. In S. Dornic (Ed.), *Attention and performance, VI*. Hillsdale, N.J.: Lawrence Erlbaum Associates, 1977.

Kemler, D. G., Shepp, B. E., & Foote, K. E. The sources of developmental differences in children's incidental processing during discrimination trials. *Journal of Experimental Child Psychology*, 1976, *21*, 226–240.

Kendler, H. H., & Kendler, T. S. Vertical and horizontal processes in problem solving. *Psychological Review*, 1962, *69*, 1–16.

Kendler, H. H., & Kendler, T. S. From discrimination learning to cognitive development: A neobehavioristic odyssey. In W. K. Estes (Ed.), *Handbook of learning & cognitive processes*, Vol. 1. Hillsdale, N.J.: Lawrence Erlbaum Associates, 1975.

Kendler, T. S., & Kendler, H. H. An ontogeny of optional shift behavior. *Child Development*, 1970, *41*, 1027.

Klahr, D., & Wallace, J. G. *Cognitive development: An information-processing view*. Hillsdale, N.J.: Lawrence Erlbaum Associates, 1976.

Krantz, D. H., & Tversky, A. Similarity of rectangles: An analysis of subjective dimensions. *Journal of Mathematical Psychology*, 1975, *12*, 4–34.

Lockhead, G. R. Effects of dimensional redundancy on visual discrimination. *Journal of Experimental Psychology*, 1966, *72*, 95–104.

Lockhead, G. R. Processing dimensional stimuli: A note. *Psychological Review*, 1972, *79*, 410–419.

Maccoby, E. E. The development of stimulus selection. In J. P. Hill (Ed.), *Minnesota symposia on child psychology*, Vol. 3. Minneapolis, Minn.: University of Minnesota Press, 1969.

Monahan, J. S., & Lockhead, G. R. Identification of integral stimuli. *Journal of Experimental Psychology: General*, 1977, *106*, 94–110.

Nelson, K. Concept, word, and sentence: Interrelations in acquisition and development. *Psychological Review*, 1974, *81*, 267–285.

Palmer, S. E. Fundamental aspects of cognitive representation. In E. Rosch & B. Lloyd (Eds.), *Cognition and categorization*. Hillsdale, N.J.: Lawrence Erlbaum Associates, 1978.

Piaget, J. Cognitions and conservation: Two views. *Contemporary Psychology*, 1967, *12*, 530–533.

Piaget, J. Quantification, conservation, and nativism. *Science*, 1968, *162*, 976–979.

Pick, A. D., & Frankel, G. W. A study of strategies of visual attention in children. *Developmental Psychology*, 1973, *9*, 348–358.

Pomerantz, J. Perceptual organization in information processing. In M. Kubovy & J. R. Pomerantz (Eds.), *Perceptual organization*. Hillsdale, N.J.: Lawrence Erlbaum Associates, 1981.

Rosch, E. On the internal structure of perceptual and semantic categories. In T. E. Moore (Ed.), *Cognitive development and the acquisition of language*. New York: Academic Press, 1973.

Rosch, E. Cognitive reference points. *Cognitive Psychology*, 1975, *7*, 532–547.

Rosch, E., & Mervis, C. B. Family resemblances: Studies in the internal structure of categories. *Cognitive Psychology*, 1975, *7*, 573–605.

Shepard, R. N. Attention and the metric structure of the stimulus space. *Journal of Mathematical Psychology*, 1964, *1*, 54–87.

Shepard, R. N. Representation of structure in similarity data: Problems and prospects. *Psychometrika*, 1974, *39*, 373–421.

Shepp, B. E. *The relation between stimulus structure and the development of voluntary selective attention*. Paper presented at a conference on dimensions judgments by children, Kassel, Germany, June 1977.

Shepp, B. E. From perceived similarity to dimensional structure: A new hypothesis about perceptual development. In E. Rosch & B. B. Lloyd (Eds.), *Cognition and categorization*. Hillsdale, N.J.: Lawrence Erlbaum Associates, 1978.

Shepp, B. E., & Adams, M. J. Effects of amount of training on type of solution and breadth of learning in optional shifts. *Journal of Experimental Psychology*, 1973, *101*, 63–69.

Shepp, B. E., & Burns, B. *The perception of geometric forms: Prototypes, configurations, and dimensions*. Unpublished manuscript, 1982.

Shepp, B. E., Burns, B. B., & McDonough, D. The relation of stimulus structure to perceptual and cognitive development: Further tests of a separability hypothesis. In F. Wilkening & J. Becker (Eds.), *The integration of information by children*. Hillsdale, N.J.: Lawrence Erlbaum Associates, 1980.

Shepp, B. E., Kolbet, L., & Fink, S. *Some relations between dimensional analyzability and performance in selective and divided attention tasks*. Unpublished manuscript, 1982.

Shepp, B. E., & Swartz, K. B. Selective attention and the processing of integral and non-integral dimensions: A developmental study. *Journal of Experimental Child Psychology*, 1976, *22*, 73–85.

Shepp, B. E., & Turrisi, F. D. Learning and transfer of mediating responses in discriminative learning. In N. R. Ellis (Ed.), *International review of research in mental retardation*, Vol. 2. New York: Academic Press, 1966.

Smith, L. B. Importance of the overall similarity of objects for adults' and children's classifications. *Journal of Experimental Psychology: Human Perception and Performance*, 1981, *7*, 811–824.

Smith, L. B., & Kemler, D. G. Developmental trends in free classification: Evidence for a new conceptualization of perceptual development. *Journal of Experimental Child Psychology*, 1977, *24*, 279–298.

Smith, L. B., & Kemler, D. G. Levels of experienced dimensionality in children and adults. *Cognitive Psychology*, 1978, *10*, 502–532.

Smith, L. B., Kemler, D. G., & Aronfreed, J. Developmental trends in voluntary selective attention: Differential effects of source distinctness. *Journal of Experimental Psychology*, 1976, *20*, 352–362.

Spiker, C. C. Application of Hull–Spence theory to the discrimination learning of children. In H. W. Reese (Ed.), *Advances in child development and behavior*, Vol. 6. New York: Academic Press, 1971.

Spiker, C. C., & Cantor, J. H. Applications of Hull–Spence theory to the transfer of discrimination learning in children. In H. W. Reese (Ed.), *Advances in child development and behavior*, Vol. 8. New York: Academic Press, 1973.

Strutt, G. F., Anderson, D. R., & Well, A. D. A developmental study of the effects of irrelevant information on speeded classification. *Journal of Experimental Child Psychology*, 1975, *20*, 127–135.

Sutherland, N. S., & Mackintosh, N. J. *Mechanisms of animal discrimination learning*. New York: Academic Press, 1971.

Taylor, D. A. Stage analysis of reaction time. *Psychological Bulletin*, 1976, *83*, 161–191.

Tighe, T. Subproblem analysis of discrimination learning. In G. H. Bower (Ed.), *The psychology of learning and motivation*, Vol. 7. New York: Academic Press, 1973.

Tighe, T. J., Glick, J., & Cole, M. Subproblem analysis of discrimination-shift learning. *Psychonomic Science*, 1971, *24*, 159–160.

Tighe, T. J., & Tighe, L. S. Stimulus control in children's learning. In A. Pick (Ed.), *Minnesota symposia on child psychology*, Vol. 6. Minneapolis, Minn.: University of Minnesota Press, 1972.

Tighe, T. J., & Tighe, L. S. A perceptual view of conceptual development. In R. D. Walk & H. L. Pick (Eds.), *Perception and Experience*. Plenum, 1978.

Torgerson, W. S. *Theory and methods of scaling*. New York: Wiley, 1958.

Townsend, J. T. A note on the identifiability of parallel and serial processes. *Perception & Psychophysics*, 1971, *10*, 161–163.

Trabasso, T., & Bower, C. G. *Attention and learning: Theory and research*. New York: Wiley, 1968.

Tversky, A. Features of similarity. *Psychological Review*, 1977, *84*, 327–352.

Tversky, A., & Krantz, D. H. Similarity of schematic faces: A test of interdimensional additivity. *Perception & Psychophysics*, 1969, *5*, 124–128.

Tversky, A., & Krantz, D. H. The dimensional representation and the metric structure of similarity data. *Journal of Mathematical Psychology*, 1970, *7*, 572–596.

Wender, K. A test of independence of dimensions in multidimensional scaling. *Perception & Psychophysics*, 1971, *10*(1), 30–32.

Werner, H. Comparative psychology of mental development (Rev. Ed.). Chicago: Follett, 1948.

Wohwill, J. From perception to inference: A dimension of cognitive development. *Monographs of the Society for Research in Child Development*, 1962, *72*, 87–107.

Wolff, J. L. Concept-shift and discrimination-reversal learning in humans. *Psychological Bulletin*, 1967, *68*, 369–408.

Zeaman, D., & House, B. J. The role of attention in retardate discimination learning. In N. R. Ellis, (Ed.), *Handbook of mental defiency*. New York: McGraw-Hill, 1963.

Zeaman, D., & House, B. J. Interpretation of developmental trends in discriminative transfer effects. In A. Pick (Ed.), *Minnesota symposia on child psychology* (Vol. 8). Minneapolis, Minn.: University of Minnesota Press, 1974.

3 Holistic and Analytic Modes in Perceptual and Cognitive Development

Deborah G. Kemler
Swarthmore College

Introduction

Perhaps more than any single theme, the description of psychological growth as a tendency toward differentiation has been a unifying principle between accounts of perceptual and cognitive development. The principle has been invoked to describe development at almost all levels of cognitive functioning. Thus, Gibson (1969) makes differentiation the cornerstone of her influential theory of perceptual development, and the principle has been invoked also to describe trends in the development of conceptual knowledge, classification, problem solving, and personality (Werner, 1948, 1957). Flavell (1977) identifies differentiation as a principle operative "in many or all cases where cognitive growth occurs [p. 240]." Werner (1957) suggests that it is a defining property of all natural developmental processes.

This chapter is in the tradition of past efforts to describe perceptual and cognitive development in terms of differentiation. Like Werner (1957), in particular, the overriding claim will be that development proceeds from a relatively undifferentiated state in which information is processed in a global holistic mode to a differentiated state in which information is processed analytically. Perhaps most distinctive about the current treatment is that undifferentiated–holistic and differentiated–analytic are given far more precise definitions than they have had in the past. The consequences, I hope to show, are the possibilities of rendering the differentiation hypothesis more convincingly testable as a description of developmental phenomena and, in addition, allowing for the proposition of more specific questions concerning the nature and source of developmental sequences.

In attempting to elucidate the terms of the differentiation hypothesis, we have received a considerable impetus from individuals working entirely outside the concerns of developmental psychology, investigators of human adult perception. They have distinguished between two different kinds of stimuli, which Garner (1974) has called "integral" and "separable," Lockhead (1966) has called "integral" and "nonintegral," and Shepard (1964) has called "nonanalyzable" and "analyzable." The distinction is between stimuli that are apprehended by adults primarily as global, unitary wholes (i.e., holistically) and those that are apprehended primarily as articulated sets of properties or dimensions (i.e., analytically). This distinction sufficiently resonates with Werner's (1957) contrast between differentiated and undifferentiated perception that it warrants the attention of developmental psychology. Such attention is rewarded by a set of converging operations that distinguish between separable and integral stimuli (Garner, 1974). These operations are ready-made tools to test the viability of the integral–separable distinction as a means for clarifying the undifferentiated–differentiated distinction in development. More specifically, the same operations that define "integral stimuli" for adults might be the operations required to provide a positive specification of the undifferentiated–holistic mode, presumably characteristic of the young child, and those operations that define "separable stimuli" for adults might provide the specification for the differentiated–analytic mode (Shepp, 1978, this volume; Shepp & Swartz, 1976; Smith & Kemler, 1977).

THE REVISED DIFFERENTIATION HYPOTHESIS

Of the several operations proposed by Garner (1974), one is of special interest because it suggests a specific and clarifying formulation for how undifferentiated perception differs from differentiated perception: Undifferentiated wholes (integral stimuli) are most naturally related to one another on the basis of *overall similarity* relationships whereas differentiated wholes (separable stimuli) are most naturally related by the *possession of a common property* or dimensional value. The operation that supports this derivation most directly is based on the types of partitions that subjects produce in a classification task, when told to "put together the items that belong together." Critical partitions occur in the context of stimulus sets in which putting together stimuli that share overall or global resemblances leads to a different partition than does putting together items that have a selected property in common. Two such sets are schematized in Fig. 3.1, where, in both cases, the stimuli A and C constitute the most similar pair within the set, but the stimuli A and B are the only pair to have a dimensional value in common.

In a classification task, adults sort color chips differing in saturation and brightness into groupings dictated by overall similarity relationships (i.e., A and C together) rather than groupings determined by possession of a common value on either dimension. For these integral stimuli, the dimensions of the stimuli are

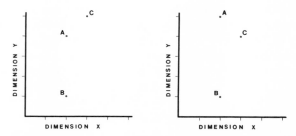

FIG. 3.1.   The structures of two stimulus sets that pit dimensional relations against overall similarity relations (Kemler, 1982).

not of immediate psychological significance to the perceiver; global relations of similarity are. By contrast, adults sort items differing in size and brightness by relating items that match on a particular dimension (i.e., *A* and *B* together), regardless of their overall similarity relations. Dimensions are psychologically primary for these separable stimuli; overall similarity relations are not.

Now it is well known that there is a developmental progression toward increased use of dimensions for the purpose of constructing classes. This finding has been highlighted by, among others, Piaget (Inhelder & Piaget, 1964), Vygotsky (1962), and Bruner (Bruner, Olver, & Greenfield, 1966). The consensus is that the finding reveals a trend in conceptual development toward "logical" or "true" concepts, by which they mean concepts defined by a critical feature (or features). Thus when a child forms groups based on common colors (all the red ones together; all the green objects together, regardless of size or form), that child is forming classes that have a "logical" structure. Prerequisite for the classification is extracting one property from the object wholes and singling it out as the basis for forming groups. Thus, such classifications appear to presume a differentiated–analytic perception of the object: The properties of the object take precedence over the whole.

The hypothesis that undifferentiated perception is characteristic of young children predicts correctly that preschool children are much less likely to form classes based on the dimensional structure of the set of objects. That hypothesis is considerably enriched by the specific assumption that "undifferentiated" implies sensitivity to the similarity structure of the stimulus set, as suggested by the proposed link to Garner's (1974) description of integral stimuli. Is this enriched hypothesis consistent with the evidence? Developmentally prior to "true" conceptual groupings are classifications described as "complexive" (Vygotsky, 1962). For example, the child groups with a red square both a red triangle and an orange square. There are two alternative ways to describe such groups. One can assert that the dimensional criteria used by the child are unstable: In joining the red triangle to the red square, the child attends to color; in joining the orange square to the red square, the child attends to form. An equally accurate description of the group is that it is united by its similarity structure. In forming the group the child is guided by the overall similarity relations—global resemblances—of the objects rather than by component dimensional relations: Both the red triangle and the orange square are similar overall to the red square. The latter interpretation is exactly what the revised differentiation hypothesis recommends. Thus, the evidence is consistent with it. Moreover, the very fact that younger children, once they do use the dimensional structure consistently, lack the flexibility to switch between dimensional criteria in successive classifications (Bruner et al., 1966) seems inconsistent, at least at a first pass, with the alternative interpretation of complexes as determined by shifting dimensional criteria.

The recommended interpretation of young children's classifications as based on overall similarity gains support from recent studies specifically designed to test the revised hypothesis. The methodology is exactly the classification operation singled out by Garner (1974) to distinguish integral and separable stimuli. The set of stimuli to be classified is selected so that the dimensional structure dictates one classification and the similarity structure dictates another, as given in the examples in Fig. 3.1. Each contains two stimuli (A and B) that share an identical value on one dimension but differ substantially on the other. Putting A and B together constitutes a dimensional classification. The sets also contain two stimuli (A and C) that are not identical on either dimension but constitute the most similar pair in the set. Putting A and C together constitutes a similarity classification. Importantly, a third type of classification is potentially available for each set, a classification in which B and C are put together. This classification (hereafter called *anomalous*) obeys neither the similarity structure nor the dimensional structure. Thus, if young children are simply *not* using the dimensional structure, if they are not positively inclined toward the similarity structure, anomalous classifications should be as frequent as similarity classifications for the set. In fact, Inhelder and Piaget (1964) and Vygotsky (1962) describe the earliest classifications of children as being "chaotic" and "idiosyncratic" (the complexive stage constituting an advance over this first stage), which translates into a prediction of frequent anomalous classifications in young children.

Thus, it is of considerable interest to know that no group of children tested on the triads of Fig. 3.1 has produced a high proportion of anomalous classifications. This statement applies not only to a group of 6-year-old kindergartners (Smith & Kemler, 1977) but also to 3- to 5-year-old preschoolers (Kemler, 1982a; Shepp, Burns, & McDonough, 1980) and a group of mildly retarded preadolescents—mean MA being in the same range as the kindergartners (Kemler, 1982a). It also has some generality over stimulus sets: It applies whether or not the stimuli are constructed by varying size and brightness (of achromatic colors), by varying chromatic color and form, or by varying size of a circle and orientation of a radial line. Significantly, in all these cases, the preferred classification is exactly the one dictated by the similarity structure. In fact, the consistency with which younger children produce similarity-based classifications is no less than the consistency with which 10- and 11-year-olds produce dimensionally based classifications (Smith & Kemler, 1977). Thus, these studies reveal a true and convincing qualitative difference between age groups in classification. Younger children are no less systematic (or correct because the instruction was "put together the ones that go together") than older children, but they are certainly different from them. A description of that difference is captured precisely by the revised differentiation hypothesis: Younger children treat stimuli as undifferentiated wholes and thus relate them by overall similarity; older children treat stimuli as analyzed sets of dimensional components and thus relate them by shared dimensional values.

Classification and Conceptual Structure

This new way of describing the nature of developmental differences in classification also suggests a different perspective on the relationship between classification and conceptual structure than the one favored in the past. Vygotsky (1962) offers a clear statement of the traditional view: Young children who do not classify in the same way as adults are incapable of entertaining the same concepts as adults, for the adults' concepts are uniformly structured by the extraction of consistent criterial properties, which young children cannot or at least do not spontaneously do. Fodor (1972), however, challenges this extrapolation from Vygotsky's classification data, partially on the grounds of its implausibility. He argues that communication between children and adults would be impossible if Vygotsky were correct and, therefore, dismisses classification behavior as a valid index of conceptual structure.

However, some recent analyses of conceptual structure by Rosch and Mervis (Mervis & Rosch, 1981; Rosch, 1977) suggest that Vygotsky may not have been wrong about the connection between classification behavior and the structure of concepts underlying natural language but may have erred instead in presuming that all adult concepts have a structure determined by criterial properties. With a considerable empirical base, Rosch and Mervis (1975) have shown that the extensions of many natural language categories for concrete objects are structured by overall similarity or "family resemblances" rather than by possession of a few criterial properties. Moreover, they have argued that there is one natural or basic level for such concepts, a level that maximizes overall similarity relationships. At the basic level of categorization, members of the same category have strong relations of mutual resemblance to one another and weak relations of resemblance to members of neighboring categories (Rosch, Mervis, Gray, Johnson, & Boyes-Braem, 1976). Examples of basic-level categories are chair, table, car, and truck. These contrast with superordinate-level concepts like furniture and vehicle, which lack strong internal similarity, and with subordinate-level concepts like dump truck and moving van, which have strong similarities across categories.

There is strong evidence that the basic-level categories are just the ones that children first name when they are learning language (Anglin, 1977; Rosch et al., 1976). In addition, basic categories provide an advantage for young children in conceptual classification. Rosch et al. (1976) replicated the traditional finding that 3- to 4-year-olds often do not use taxonomic class membership as a basis for classifying real-world items. Thus, given the set containing dog, horse, and tree, they often fail to group together a dog and a horse even though they are both animals. However, Rosch et al. found this "deficit" to be specific to categorizations at the superordinate level where family resemblance relations are weak. When grouping can be accomplished at the basic level (sorting two different dogs together), 3- and 4-year-olds produce such taxonomic classifications. These results converge in an elegant way with the studies on perceptual classification discussed earlier. Young children are attuned to overall similarity relations. When the set to be classified possesses a compelling similarity structure, then young children consistently use it as a systematic way to partition the set.

It is clear that Rosch's analysis of the structure of natural language concepts is not unlimited in its applicability, for surely there are many human concepts that are better described in terms of criterial properties than in terms of family resemblances, as Rosch herself was quite aware. Many of these concepts apply to abstract elements, like the concept of odd number, but some, like island,[1] apply to concrete objects as well. Vygotsky (1962) distinguishes between "everyday concepts" and "technical concepts," a distinction that might be helpful here. Everyday concepts are learned from their examplars, in a bottom-up fashion in the course of everyday social (particularly linguistic) contact between the child learner and adults. Technical concepts, Vygotsky thought, are often taught in school and taught specifically in a top-down fashion from their definitions. Thus a child is instructed in a geography lesson that an island is a mass of land surrounded on all sides by water. Definitions single out criterial properties. Accepting Rosch's (1977) analysis for everyday concepts and importing something like Vygotsky's distinction between everyday and technical concepts lead to the speculation that preschool children, with their bias toward overall similarity relations, are well-prepared to learn everyday concepts (Medin, this volume) but less prepared to learn technical concepts. Such speculation is at least consistent with common observations of what natural language concepts young children command first.

A Closer Examination of the Hypothesis

If the revised differentiation hypothesis has sufficient plausibility to be taken seriously, as I believe it does, then its implications merit closer examination. In

---

[1]The example is due to Frank Keil.

particular need of clarification is what is entailed by the claim that the undifferentiated state, characteristic of young children, is one where similarity relations—rather than component properties—take precedence. Does this imply that there is no sensitivity to dimensions in young children? Even that simple question turns out to be quite ambiguous. If what is at stake is whether young children are sensitive to the differences between objects that vary unidimensionally, the answer, of course, is that they are. A red square and a yellow square, differing only in color, or a red square and a red triangle, differing only in form, are easily discriminated in the undifferentiated state: Simply they are discriminable wholes.

Distinct from the issue of discrimination is the issue of whether the child appreciates the nature of the differences he or she perceives. In particular, the question is whether the child distinguishes the kinds of differences that are detectable. Without differentiation in this sense, two stimuli varying only in color may be seen as different and equally dissimilar to one another as are two stimuli varying only in form *without any appreciation that the two relations represent dissimilarities of quite a different kind*. The revised differentiation hypothesis raises such a possibility. As such, it focuses on a level of functioning one cognitive level above the major phenomena addressed by Gibson's (1969) differentiation theory. The two views are complementary: When differentiation is complete in Gibson's sense, such that discrimination occurs, it may still be incomplete in the current sense that analysis does not occur and objects are only related by the similarity of wholes.

If the holistic, undifferentiated state is difficult to contemplate in the abstract, an appeal to intuitions might be helpful. There are cases in which adults experience such an undifferentiated state. One relatively widespread phenomenal example is the encounter of a familiar person whose appearance has been slightly changed. Often the first impression is that the person looks somehow different without the knowledge—at least accessible knowledge—of what the nature of the difference is. Did he change his hair? Cut it? Part it on a different side? Did he shave off his mustache? Trim his beard? Get a tan? The difference is clear; its nature is not.

This example is sufficiently revealing that I shall pursue it with a few additional comments. Often after puzzling over the source of the perception of difference (and we adults *do* puzzle over it; the undifferentiated state is an uncomfortable one for us), we are able to access the relevant knowledge. Aha, our friend is no longer wearing his glasses! Thus, at least in adults, the undifferentiated state may give way to differentiated knowledge after some effort. One possible account is that accessing the new information depends on contacting an entirely different mental representation of the individual's former appearance—one that was differentiated into properties, in contrast to the first one that was not. Another possibility is that the mental representation contacted in the first undifferentiated act of recognition and in the second differentiated comparison is the very same one but that different processes operated on the representation during the two acts of comparison. By this account, information about the specific property of the mental representation that did not match the current percept was available but not accessible in the undifferentiated state.

Extrapolations from this example to developmental concerns are of three kinds. First, as the last possibility makes clear, the claims that there is a developmental trend toward differentiation and that there is a qualitative distinction between lack of differentiation and its presence does not entail that the very nature of mental representation itself undergoes qualitative change in development. The processes that operate on the mental representations may be the sole components that change qualitatively. Second, the example suggests that even when the undifferentiated mode takes precedence, cognitive effort may be sufficient to enlist successfully the differentiated mode. Thus the bias of young children toward the undifferentiated mode does not necessarily preclude the *ability* to employ the differentiated mode. In this sense, developmental differences might be quantitative, even though the difference between differentiated and undifferentiated modes is qualitative. Development may consist in an ever greater likelihood that the differentiated mode is deployed in a wider and wider range of situations. Third, the undifferentiated mode is not exclusive to children. Of course, this is quite clear in Garner's (1974) discussion of stimuli like color chips that are integral for adults, but the facial recognition example has the particular advantage of reinforcing this point with a case familiar to everyone.

Properties and Transformations

An entailment of the revised differentiation hypothesis, in contrast to its ancestors, is that younger children may perceive differences without being knowledgeable about the nature of these differences. Such a claim generates some particularly interesting and somewhat startling predictions concerning the kinds of mundane knowledge that young children might be lacking. What children may fail to know is that certain real-world transformations on objects leave some of the properties of the objects intact while modifying others. If this last statement resonates with Piaget's discussion of conservation concepts in the child, the connection is not unintentional. Piaget was specifically concerned with knowledge of quantitative concepts: number, length, mass, weight, and volume. The concern here is far more general, and so is the prediction. Young children, despite their rather extensive experience with activities like cutting, coloring, and painting (a rather complete summary of the preschool curriculum) may not be aware that cutting selectively changes size (and usually form) and that coloring or painting selectively changes color.

One way to test this is to arrange an analog of the standard Piagetian conservation task. Imagine this scenario. An adult faces a child across a table. The adult puts down two identical squares of gray paper, one in front of the child and one in front of herself. She asks the child whether her paper and the child's paper are just the same size. When the child agrees that they are, she says, "Now watch what I'm going to do," as she picks up one of the papers and colors it uniformly with a black marking pen in full view of the child. She then replaces the paper to its original position, asking: "Now are our papers still the same size or are they not the same size? Are these still the same size or show me the one that is bigger?"

Tasks of this kind were administered to preschoolers and to mentally retarded preadolescents (Kemler, 1982b). The example given might be called a conservation-of-size task. We also arranged a conservation-of-color task in which the irrelevant transformation involved cutting with scissors so as to produce a smaller square than the original. Pilot work revealed an extremely high frequency (almost 100%) of nonconservation responses in both groups. The children said that cutting changed color and coloring changed size.

The results were so dramatic that we were inclined to treat them cautiously. Might we be picking up a general tendency of the child to believe (or say) that any action on an object changed the object rather than a more specific tendency to misinterpret the nature of a change that actually occurred? The question is best clarified by an example: Suppose we perform an action that transforms *no* properties of the object (e.g., changing its spatial location or tapping on it). Will the children still say that color or size has been changed? If so, our previous results with irrelevant transformations may be due to a general response bias rather than a specific inability to interpret the nature of difference.

Accordingly, a procedure was designed in which each child was queried about nontransformations as well as irrelevant transformations and relevant transformations (Kemler, 1982b). The revised differentiation hypothesis predicts more errors on irrelevant transformations (coloring changes size; cutting changes color) than on nontransformations (tapping changes size; moving changes color). Moreover, in a pretraining period, we established a bias toward a conservation response by giving the child practice with nontransformations, different from the ones used in the test phase, along with feedback that no change in the queried dimension had occurred. Unless the child consistently produced the conservation response in pretraining, he or she was not given the test trials. Sometimes pretraining took several trials, and sometimes it failed entirely.

Table 3.1 shows there was a differential error rate[2] for the three kinds of transformations in the test phase, both for 3-year-old normal children (mean age: 3 yr, 9 mon; range: 3 yr, 4 mon to 4 yr) and for the group of mildly retarded preadolescents (mean CA: 11 yr, 8 mon; range: 9 yr, 3 mon to 14 yr, 7 mon; mean MA: 6 yr, 4 mon; range: 4 yr, 1 mon to 8 yr, 7 mon). Note that an error on a relevant transformation involves saying that the transformed dimension has *not* changed, whereas an error on either an irrelevant transformation or nontransformation involves saying that an untransformed property *has* changed. In general,

---

[2]A subject was scored as making an error on a trial if either of the two forms of the question asked after the transformation was answered incorrectly.

TABLE 3.1
Percentage Errors in Conservation Task
(Adapted from Kemler, 1982b)

	Type of Transformation		
	Relevant	*Irrelevant*	*Nontransformation*
Color Question			
Normal 3-year-olds (n = 9)	11.1	22.2	5.6
Retarded children (n = 16)	18.2	54.6	13.7
Size Question			
Normal 3-year-olds (n = 8)	25.0	37.5	12.5
Retarded children (n = 14)	21.4	50.0	17.9

the highest error rate occurs in the irrelevant category, just as the revised differentiation hypothesis predicts. These children have a tendency to interpret any difference as evidence of the type of difference that is queried. By comparison, performance of a group of seven 4-year-olds (mean age: 4 yr, 5 mon; range: 4 yr to 4 yr, 10 mon), administered exactly the same procedures, was flawless on all types of transformations. Apparently, conservation of color and size improves markedly even within the preschool years of the normal child.

There is one way that the conservation task may overestimate mundane knowledge of property-specific transformations and another in which it may underestimate it. Overestimation may occur because a correct response need not result from any *general* (Piaget would say "logical") knowledge of the effects of cutting and coloring, as long as the child is capable of making property-specific judgments on the spot. A strategy open to the child is simply to compare the colors or the sizes of the papers after the transformation, regardless of the transformation, and to respond according to whether the colors or sizes are the same or different at that point. Thus, a child might look to see that this particular act of cutting did not change color without knowing the general rule that cutting always leaves color intact. Of course, the ability of children to do even this comparison on the spot requires use of the differentiated–analytic mode, but such use is specifically elicited by the question rather than being a spontaneous tendency derived from everyday activity that is simply tapped by the question.

The conservation task may underestimate children's mundane knowledge of property-specific transformations because it requires an understanding of the terms *color* and *size, bigger* and *blacker*. Of course an inability to comprehend these terms may itself be a derivative of the inability to grasp the concepts, but conceptual knowledge is not itself sufficient to guarantee the linguistic knowledge. So we cannot be sure that the errors are conceptually based rather than linguistically based.

To deal simultaneously with both reservations, a different task was devised (Kemler, 1982b). In the prediction task, the child was asked to make judgments outside a linguistic context and without the potential aid of a direct comparison. As in the conservation task, the experimenter began with two identical pieces of medium gray paper, one for the child and one for herself. The child was told that the two were "just the same" (i.e., in all ways; no dimension was mentioned). Then, the adult dramatically picked up a tool (scissors or black marking pen) while telling the child to "watch what I'm going to do." (In a preliminary phase, the child had been allowed to play with both tools.) She then proceeded to color or to cut (never both) her piece of paper, but in such a way that the child could see the action without seeing the effects of the action. The crucial test required the child to select from two alternative papers, offered by the adult, "What does my piece of paper look like now?" When the action was coloring, the correct alternative was a darker piece of paper of the same size and shape as the original; when the action was cutting, the correct alternative was a smaller piece of paper, of the same color and shape as the original. The incorrect alternatives on different trials were: (1) an untransformed item; (2) an item transformed only in the relevant way but in the wrong direction (e.g., a larger piece when the action was cutting); (3) an item transformed only in the irrelevant way (e.g., a darker piece of the same size and shape when the action was cutting); (4) an item transformed along both dimensions with the relevant transformation in the correct direction (e.g., a smaller, darker item when the action was cutting), or (5) a doubly transformed item with the relevant transformation in the incorrect direction (e.g., a larger, darker item when the action was cutting). Recall that a choice was made always with a replica of the original state in the child's view.

The derivation from the revised differentiation hypothesis is that young or retarded children will have difficulty with the prediction task despite the fact that no knowledge of the dimensional vocabulary is required. Confirmation is found in the results that are displayed in Table 3.2, separately for trials on which the operation was coloring and cutting. Overall the error rates of young preschoolers (mean age: 3 yr, 11 mon; range: 3 yr, 8 mon to 4 yr, 2 mon) and mildly retarded preadolescents were quite high, averaging 38% and 35%, respectively. On cutting trials, neither group performed reliably above chance. On coloring trials, errors were still considerable.[3] Even an older group of preschoolers (mean age: 5 yr, 0 mon; range: 4 yr, 10 mon to 5 yr, 4 mon) committed some prediction errors, and these errors were highly concentrated on trials that involved an incorrect alternative that had been transformed in an irrelevant way (Types 3, 4, and 5). These are exactly the trial types on which lack of differentiation should be most severely debilitating.

Together the results from conservation and prediction tasks suggest that at least one consequence of undifferentiated cognition is that the child is deficient in

---

[3]For all groups, performance on cutting trials is reliably worse than on coloring trials, a result that probably derives from stimulus preferences for larger and darker items. See Kemler, 1982b, for more details.

TABLE 3.2
Percentage Errors in Prediction Task
(Adapted from Kemler, 1982b)

	Type of Operation	
	Coloring	Cutting
Younger preschoolers	20	56
Older preschoolers	4	10
Retarded children	26	44

being able to distinguish kinds of differences that he or she can detect. This consequence is a unique prediction of the revised differentiation hypothesis that links undifferentiated perception to holistic perception with psychologically primary relations based on overall similarity rather than component property relations. It is perhaps particularly remarkable that the predicted deficits occurred in the context of familiar activities and materials, conditions that should optimize performance.

INCIPIENT KNOWLEDGE OF DIMENSIONS

If young children only perceive objects as wholes, if they are only sensitive to similarity relations among them, how does differentiation occur? How do normal children eventually come to know about the properties of objects—become able to use them to formulate technical concepts and to make sense of the regularities of their environment—if at an earlier point in development those properties have no psychological reality at all? The question is sufficiently challenging that it prompts a reconsideration of the premise. Is it the case that young children (or retarded children) are totally insensitive to the dimensional structure of the objects they perceive and discriminate? Evidence that they are not, that dimensions have some psychological reality for them, simplifies the problem of explaining cognitive growth at least by identifying an incipient capacity on which development builds.

In fact, there is a fair amount of converging evidence that the dimensions of color and size do have some psychological reality for preschoolers and retarded children. Looked at from this perspective, even the conservation and prediction data suggest this. Four-year-old preschoolers and retarded preadolescents are sufficiently accurate on the coloring trials of the prediction task to achieve above-chance levels of performance, and even the group of 3½-year-olds are performing above chance on the conservation task (Kemler, 1982b). Thus familiar activities of cutting and coloring are probabilistically, if largely insecurely, related to dimensions of the objects.

Preschoolers and, to a lesser extent, retarded youngsters, also reveal dimensional knowledge when they are asked to make same–different judgments concerning static pairs of stimulus objects (Kemler, 1982b). The question was phrased: "Are these two things the same color (size) or not the same color (size)? Are these two things the same color (size) or is one of them blacker (bigger)?" Different dimensions were probed in different sessions in order to eliminate any difficulty the child might have switching back and forth between dimensions.

To assess dimensional knowledge, the most critical type of trial is one in which the correct response is "same" because the items are identical on the relevant dimension, but the items differ on the irrelevant dimension (so overall the two wholes are not the same). A control trial is one in which the items are identical on all dimensions and thus overall the same. The difference between error rates on these two types of trials is as good a measure of dimensional knowledge as this task allows. The 4½-year-olds are near perfect on both kinds of trials; 3½-year-olds almost double their error rate from 9.5% at baseline to 17% for the critical trials. Retarded children produce as many as 42% errors on the critical trials as compared to 9.5% on the control trials. Nevertheless, each one of the separate groups reponds above chance on the critical trials. Once again, the double message comes through: Young preschoolers and retarded children have difficulty analyzing wholes into properties, but analytic ability is not entirely lacking (Kemler, 1982b).

A stronger test of whether the dimensional structure has psychological reality is to seek evidence of its influence in an optional context like classification. Here, the instruction does not explicitly point the child to the properties of the objects. If the child undertakes an analysis into properties, it must be a self-initiated activity. Is there any evidence, then, that dimensions do play a psychological role in young children's classification? What would the nature of such evidence be? It would have to show that the similarity structure of the stimuli is not sufficient to account for all the systematic classifications young children produce. Such evidence is more difficult to come by than first appearances suggest. For example, suppose a child classifies into one group a red rectangle and a red square and classifies into another group a green rectangle and a green square. Although such a classification *could* be based on the dimensional components of the stimuli—specifically, the systematic use of the color dimension for grouping—the classification is no less consistent with the similarity structure of the stimuli because the child may consider the red rectangle and red square to be more similar to one another than the red rectangle is to the green rectangle. In fact, if the classifier is using the similarity structure, the most likely classifications that he or she will produce for this set of four objects are just the ones that *appear* to be generated by the dimensional structure.

In order to provide unambiguous evidence of the psychological reality of dimensions in a task, one must show that there are differences in performance on two stimulus sets that are equivalent in similarity structure[4] but different in dimensional structure. Another way of stating this operational principle is that dimensions have psychological reality for a particular group of subjects in a particular task if performance is different for stimulus sets that are organized around the axes defining the dimensions of the stimulus space than it is for stimulus sets organized in an equivalent manner around arbitrary axes of the space. This is the privileged-axis criterion for the psychology reality of dimensions (Smith & Kemler, 1978). It is an entirely general criterion, applicable in principle to any dimensions in any task, administered to any group of subjects.

Now an apparently tricky requirement of this operation is the necessity of establishing the equivalence of the comparison sets on overall similarity. In fact, this requirement may be bypassed by including two different stimulus sets that conform to the dimensional axes and that in their similarity relations straddle a single nondimensional stimulus set (that conforms to arbitrary axes). Demonstrating that performance in the nondimensional condition differs in the same way from performance in the two dimensional conditions is entirely satisfactory for concluding that the dimensions play a role in determining performance—that the dimensions have psychological reality for the subject in the task.

This type of design was employed to test for the psychological reality of size and color in classification by preschoolers and retarded children (Kemler, 1982a). The sets to be classified always contained four items. Three different types of tetrads were used, as shown in Fig. 3.2. The first two, which are labeled REDUNDANT, have correlated similarity and dimensional structures for purposes of classification. They differ from one another only by the degree of interstimulus similarity within the tetrad. The NONREDUNDANT set consists of the 45° rotation of a set intermediate in interstimulus similarity between the two REDUNDANT sets. Importantly, the effect of the rotation is to eliminate the redundancy of dimensional and similarity structures.

It is easy to predict what should happen in classification if dimensions have no psychological reality. The predictions are generated by imagining that the X and Y axes in the figure are totally arbitrary (that they are not privileged axes) and thus the rotation that produces the NONREDUNDANT tetrad makes no psychological difference at all (i.e., there are 45° rotated axes, relative to which the NONREDUNDANT set is equivalent in configuration to the two REDUNDANT sets). Accordingly, the expectation, most simply, is that the *distributions of classifications should be absolutely equivalent across the three types of tetrads* (because all within-tetrad similarity relations are identical) or else that the pattern of classification for the NONREDUNDANT set should be intermediate between

---

[4]When stimulus similarity relationships are computed according to a Euclidean metric (see Garner, 1974).

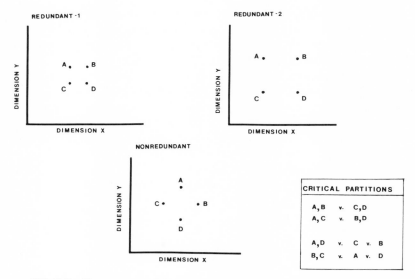

FIG. 3.2.   The structures of three types of stimulus sets. The one-step and two-step redundant sets differ only in degree of interstimulus similarity. The nonredundant set differs from the other two by having a more complex description in dimensional terms. For explanation of the ''critical partitions'' that potentially distinguish redundant sets from nonredundant sets, see the text (Kemler, 1982a).

the two REDUNDANT sets (because its absolute similarity relations are intermediate between them).

If, on the other hand, dimensions do have psychological reality in classification, then the *distributions of classifications for the two REDUNDANT sets should be more similar to one another than either is to the NONREDUNDANT set.* Relative to the X and Y axes defined by the dimensions, the NONREDUNDANT set is distinctly different from the REDUNDANT sets. More specific predictions require consulting Fig. 3.2 in detail. Any tendency to be influenced by the dimensional structure should produce partitions that obey the dimensional axes: (1) sorts into two groups of (A and B) versus (C and D) or (A and C) versus (B and D) for the REDUNDANT sets but not the NONREDUNDANT set; (2) sorts into three groups of (A and D) versus (C) versus (B) or (B and C) versus (A) versus (D) for the NONREDUNDANT set but not the REDUNDANT sets. All of these sorts are called *critical* sorts because they are differentially expected for REDUNDANT and NONREDUNDANT sets under the assumption of dimensional reality. The appended designations, 2 and 3, distinguish these sorts according to the number of stimulus groups that are produced. So, if dimensions have some psychological reality in classification, critical-2 sorts should be less frequent and critical-3 sorts should be more frequent for the NONREDUNDANT set than for either of the REDUNDANT sets.

Actual tetrads were constructed by varying size of a square and its shade of gray, dimensions that had been used in the original studies of classification by these subjects. Each child sorted eight unique tetrads, two REDUNDANT-1, two REDUNDANT-2, and four NONREDUNDANT sets.

Figure 3.3 displays the relative frequencies of the different patterns of classifications for each of the types of tetrads. The top half of the figure shows the data of the preschoolers (mean age:4 yr, 6 mon) and the bottom half the data of the retarded children (mean age: 11 yr, 4 mon; mean MA: 6 yr, 3 mon). The patterns for the two groups are quite comparable. They both indicate that the dimensional structure *does* play some role in classification.

The designations of the kinds of classifications counted in Fig. 3.3 are best understood by referring to Fig. 3.2. For each type of tetrad, what is shown are

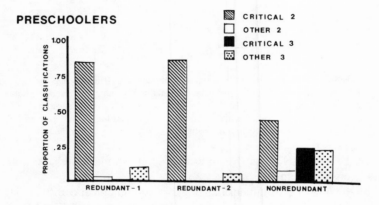

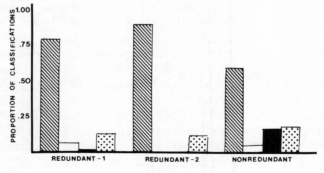

FIG. 3.3. Sorting patterns for the stimulus sets separately for preschoolers and retarded children according to type of stimulus set. For explanation of the categories of sorting patterns, see Fig. 3.2 and the text (Kemler, 1982a).

the proportions of the classifications that fell into each of four categories: critical-2, all other classifications into two groups each of two items [e.g., (A and D) versus (B and C) in Fig. 3.2], critical-3, and all other classifications into three groups [e.g., (A and B) versus (C) versus (D) in Fig. 3.2].

It is immediately apparent that the most frequent kind of classification, regardless of tetrad type, was the critical-2. However, although the critical-2 pattern is almost the exclusive pattern for the REDUNDANT tetrads, other patterns—notably the critical-3—also appear for the NONREDUNDANT tetrad. More specifically, critical-2 sorts are relatively more frequent and critical-3 sorts relatively less frequent for the REDUNDANT sets, exactly what is expected if the children are influenced by dimensional structure in their classifications.

Apparently, then, the tendency of these children to attend to properties of objects is not restricted to situations in which such analysis is requested or required by external sources. Differentiation of the stimulus is in part under spontaneous self-control. It may not be frequent, as the original classification studies with triads establish and the new data reinforce: Truly "dimensional" classifications of the NONREDUNDANT tetrad occurred under 35% of the time for the preschoolers and under 25% of the time for the retarded children. Nevertheless, property-based classification does occur sufficiently often to meet the statistical criterion for dimensional reality in both groups.

In summary, neither the ability to analyze into dimensions nor the tendency to use that ability in the service of classification is entirely absent early in the development of intelligence or in the special cases where intelligence is subnormal. This suggests that the account of development in this domain be told in quantitative rather than in qualitative terms. Although the distinction between analytic and holistic modes itself is qualitative, both modes exist as early possibilities and it is the balance between them that changes in development. Such a conclusion is entirely congruent with that reached by Zeaman and House (1974) in a review of developmental trends in discrimination learning. As they pointed out, there is considerable evidence that young children are typically less likely to learn about component dimensions than are older children and are more likely to learn about stimulus wholes. Nevertheless, a highly sensitive test for dimensional learning—the comparison of intradimensional and extradimensional shifts— reveals some dimensional learning in both preschoolers and retarded children.

THE ANALYTIC ATTITUDE

What prompts the changing balance from holistic to analytic modes of processing in the course of normal development in childhood? One factor that cannot be ruled out is that analysis into properties simply becomes easier and easier for the child and that alone shifts the balance between the alternatives. Certainly it is possible to interpret much of the data as being consistent with that idea. The findings from conservation tasks, prediction tasks, and same-different judgment tasks consistently show the older preschoolers analyzing more or more successfully than the younger preschoolers when such analysis is specifically required. Quite likely the ability to analyze is itself improving. However, given the pitfalls of inferring underlying ability from specific task performances, such an interpretation can be only tentative.

There is reason to speculate that the relative ease of analyzing is not the sole determinant of developmental trends but that at least part of the explanation of developmental trends is to be found at the level of higher-order control processes. This speculation is an extrapolation from findings that at a given developmental level, the nature of the task can have a powerful effect on whether the individual utilizes the holistic or the analytic mode. In particular, both children and adults are more likely to be analytic—to analyze wholes into properties and relate them by shared components—when the task calls for deliberate problem-solving activities than when it does not.

The first evidence for a powerful context effect emerged serendipitously in a series of studies designed to investigate the use of analytic and holistic modes in a complex concept-learning task. The task is a concept-learning problem in which solution depends on learning a rule that applies to the *relation* between pairs of stimulus items. Actually, it was arranged that two different relational rules applied equally well to the pairs used during training. One rule was based on dimensional relations; for example, a pair of items might be the same in color (one category) or different in color (the other category). The other rule was based on overall similarity relations; for example, a pair of items might be identical overall (one category) or different overall (the other category). These two rules describe equally well the following assignments of pairs to two categories, designated here as categories *A* and *B*: red square and red square (*A*), green triangle and green triangle (*A*), yellow circle and yellow circle (*A*), red square and yellow square (*B*), red circle and green circle (*B*), green triangle and yellow triangle (*B*). However, the two rules dictate different assignments for a test pair such as red square and red circle. According to the dimensional rule, the assignment for the test pair is (*A*) because the items are identical in color; according to the similarity rule, the assignment is (*B*) because the items are different overall. Thus, by inserting such test pairs after the subject has learned the correct assignments of the original pairs, one can assess which rule the subject has actually used to solve the problem.

Knowing that kindergarten children prefer to classify spontaneously by similarity over dimensional relations (Smith & Kemler, 1977), we predicted that they would more likely learn the similarity rule in the concept-learning task. Analogously, based on fifth-graders' preference for dimensional relations over similarity relations in classification, we predicted that they would tend to learn the dimensional rule. We were only half right. In fact, both age groups showed an overwhelming preference for the dimensional rule and there was no evidence at all of differences between the age groups (Kemler & Smith, 1979, Experiment IV).

Kindergarten children, then, show a preference for similarity relations in classification and a preference for dimensional relations in a complex rule-learning task. This contrast was refined and replicated by Smith (1979) who investigated classification behavior under two conditions. In both, the child was presented initially with six items, partitioned into two categories, and then was asked to judge which of a set of test items belonged in either category (or did not belong at all). The child's extensions of the categories were examined for their conformity to the similarity structure or the dimensional structure of the original groups. In one condition, the original items were present while the child made judgments about which of the test items "went with" the preformed categories of items that "go together." In a second condition, the child *learned* first to sort the original items into the preformed categories, which were said to conform to a "rule." Only after rule learning had occurred were the children asked to extend the categories using the test items. Both kindergartners and second-graders were more likely to use a dimensional organization and less likely to use a similarity-based organization for extension in the "rule-learning" condition than in the spontaneous classification condition. Once again, a rule-learning context appears to produce a shift to a preference for dimensional structure in young elementary school children. Thus, the major conclusion on which the studies converge is that an intentional rule-learning condition encourages the use of dimensional organization even in 6-year-olds.

These results from kindergartners suggest that the nature of the task can have a powerful effect on whether or not individuals spontaneously employ the analytic mode. Specifically, they prompt the hypothesis that differentiation is particularly characteristic of the self-conscious, reflective modes of processing elicited by a rule-learning situation. This hypothesis obtains further support from studies of concept learning in college students. Parallel with the kindergarten findings, Kemler and Smith (1979) showed that when adults learn a relational rule concerning pairs of *integral* stimuli (stimuli that adults consistently classify by similarity, just as kindergartners classify separable stimuli by similarity), the adults also manifest a surprising tendency to seek a dimensional rule. This tendency is clearly far less dramatic for integral than for separable stimuli in adults—so there is convergence between classification and concept learning—but the likelihood of spontaneously analyzing integral stimuli into properties is higher in the rule-learning setting than in any other relevant task we know (Smith & Kemler, 1978).

Recently, we arranged a direct comparison between concept learning under intentional and incidental conditions[5] (Kemler, in preparation). An intentional condition is one in which the subject knows that there is a categorization to be

---

[5]Two different studies, using different cover tasks for the incidental conditions, were conducted. Both led to the same conclusions, and only the second of the two is reported here. In the first, the incidental task was a continuous yes/no recognition–memory test for the cartoon figures, which were presented one at a time as a face paired with a uniform.

learned. An incidental condition is one in which the subject is exposed to the category information but is unaware that the information is being acquired, which is possible by attuning the subject to a different task. Thus, whatever is learned about the categories is learned without intention. Only the first condition should elicit deliberate problem-solving activities, directed toward learning the structure of the category distinction. The comparison between what is learned about the categories under the two conditions should shed light on the hypothesis that the differentiated analytic mode is the more exclusive province of intentional information processing.

In order to provide a fair test of the hypothesis with adult subjects, the stimuli were cartoon faces, selected mostly on intuitive grounds to be the kinds of stimuli that adults can process either analytically or holistically. The faces differed along four attributes, hair (curly–straight), mustache (handlebar–clipped), ears (large–small) and nose (aquiline–pudgy). There were three ordered values for each attribute. Some exemplary faces are shown in Fig. 3.4. The categories were realized as a distinction between "doctors" and "policemen."

During the acquisition phase, subjects, regardless of condition, were shown six different exemplars, three from each category. The exemplars were selected in such a way that the categories could be distinguished both on the basis of a

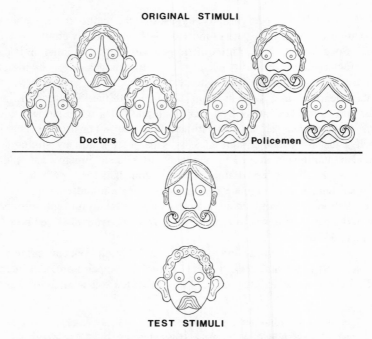

FIG. 3.4.   Examples of stimuli used in the concept-learning study.

single criterial attribute (e.g., all the policemen have a broad, pudgy nose; all the doctors have an aquiline nose) and also on the basis of overall similarity structure (i.e., overlapping sets of properties producing family resemblance relationships among the members of the same category and distinguishing them from members of the other category). Such a set of exemplars is shown in Fig. 3.4. Also shown in that figure are two critical test instances, exemplars that were withheld until a test phase designed to discover the basis for learning the original categories. Notice that if the subject extracted the single criterial attribute, then the top test stimulus is classified as a doctor (because it has an aquiline nose) and the bottom one is classified as a policeman (because it has a pudgy nose). However, if the subject learned on the basis of overall similarity [e.g., constructed prototypes for the two categories, or learned exemplars and classified by similarity to them (Medin, this volume], then the top test instance is classified as a policeman and the bottom one as a doctor.

The intentional condition for acquisition was the standard variety for concept-identification experiments. Subjects were told that they would see cartoon faces, one at a time, and that some of them were doctors' faces and some were policemen's faces. They were to learn the correct assignments over the course of the series. On each trial, the subject made a tentative categorization and received feedback.

The incidental condition was arranged by informing subjects that we were interested in their stereotypes of how doctors and policemen look. On each trial, subjects were shown two stimuli successively, either two doctors or two police-men, *always atop the appropriate uniform,* and asked to judge which of the two faces best represented their stereotype of the particular category. Incidental sub-jects received no encouragement to ascertain which faces went with which cate-gory; in fact, they were not informed that the same face would occur in only one category.[6]

After subjects saw 32 stimuli (either 5 or 6 of each of the six exemplars), they were put into a test phase, identical for both conditions. The subjects from the intentional condition were simply told to continue their classifications, now without feedback. The subjects from the incidental condition did the same thing after first being apprised of the new requirement to draw on whatever informa-tion they might have acquired incidentally about the category assignments.

The major results of this study concern the type of concept learned by subjects in the two conditions as ascertained from their classifications of the critical test instances. Of course, the data come from only those subjects who did learn—determined by accurate classification of the original exemplars in the test phase. Table 3.3 shows the breakdown of the individual learners in each condition by

---

[6]In addition to the incidental–intentional variable, the study also included variation in instruc-tions to process the stimuli either analytically or holistically. Because analyses showed no effects of this secondary variable, it is omitted from the current report (but see Kemler, in preparation).

type of concept acquired. On the basis of 20 decisions that each subject made about the critical test instances, a learner was classified as acquiring a similarity-based or critical-attribute-based concept if the subject responded consistently on 16 or more of the trials. Otherwise, the learner was categorized as "unclassifiable." Inspection of Table 3.3 reveals a dramatic difference in the predicted direction: far more concepts based on the single criterial attribute in the intentional, as compared to the incidental, condition. As expected, instructions that elicit deliberate hypothesis testing lead to an increase in the use of the analytic mode.

The verbalizations of subjects concerning what they had learned also support this conclusion. In an interview following the test phase, subjects were asked to make a forced choice as to which description best captured what they knew about the categories:

1. I have a general impression of what a doctor or a policeman looks like, but it does not apply to individual features.
2. I have a general impression of what a doctor or policemen looks like, which involves certain key features.
3. I have more than one feature that I can use to tell doctors and policemen apart.
4. I identify policemen and doctors by one particular facial feature and the other features are irrelevant.

Of the incidental learners, 50% selected description 1 or 2, both of which mention a general impression; 10% selected alternative 4, which implies a single criterial feature. By contrast, 28% of the intentional learners selected 1 or 2, the more holistic descriptions, and 47% selected alternative 4. Interestingly, some of the incidental learners mentioned that they had started out only with general impressions at the beginning of the test phase but that, in making the test responses, they had been prompted to analyze those impressions.

The conclusion to which all these findings point is that the tendency to analyze or not is partially under the control of the task. The requirement to discover a rule (or even the implicit requirement to apply a rule) prods individuals to be analytic. Acts of deliberate discovery and analytic processes go hand in hand. Perhaps this is because the mental tools of discovery, hypothesis

TABLE 3.3
Frequency of Types of Concepts Acquired

	Criterial Attribute	Family Resemblance	Unclassifiable
Intentional condition	22	22	4
Incidental condition	7	29	12

formulation and hypothesis testing, are far more easily fashioned in analytic than in holistic terms.

If analyzing is partially under voluntary control, and if, more particularly, it is the hallmark of a reflective, goal-directed attitude, then one plausible explanation of developmental trends toward analytic processing is that the older child is more likely to adopt such an attitude spontaneously—even when an explicit rule-learning requirement is not attached. This speculation is consistent with current formulations of the nature of development in other domains, such as memory (Brown & DeLoache, 1978), where a tendency toward self-reflectiveness and self-control provides at least as convincing an account of the nature of development as do changes in the basic cognitive processes themselves. My guess is that the account most successfully applies to developmental trends toward analytic processing within the elementary school years and that some basic change in the ability to analyze accounts for development in the preschool years.

The findings from the incidental–intentional comparison are enlightening in a further respect. As Medin points out in this volume, strategic hypothesis-testing—a win–stay, lose–shift procedure applied to attributes—is well-suited to the acquisition of categories based on criterial properties. It is poorly suited to the acquisition of ill-defined categories where no attribute is necessary and no logical combination of attributes is sufficient for determining categorization. The type of learning exhibited by the incidental (presumably, nonstrategic) subjects in our experiment is far better geared toward discovering ill-defined categories, like the basic-level categories identified by Rosch et al. (1976). There is a happy convergence, worth entertaining, then. Young children are naturally nonstrategic concept learners; they have a general bias toward overall-similarity relations; many of the natural categories that they do (must) acquire are structured by strong family resemblance relations, potentially based on overall similarity. Medin (this volume) provides some further interesting discussion.

CONCLUDING COMMENTS

This chapter began with a specific formulation of the principle of differentiation, from holistic to analytic, based on the distinction between integral and separable stimulus structures. The account particularly clarifies the nature of perception when differentiation is lacking: The stimulus is apprehended as a whole without the internal structure of properties or dimensions. As a result, the primary relation available between undifferentiated stimuli is overall similarity.

The revised principle of differentiation served as a guide for examining developmental differences, for making comparisons between normal and retarded children, and for investigating the effects of task variables. In general, the holistic mode was found to be characteristic of the young child, the retarded child, and the unintentional learner—although neither preschooler, retarded youngster, nor incidental learner is entirely restricted to it. The normal development of intelligence reflects a shifting toward the more frequent use of the analytic mode, associated with differentiation.

The current formulation that associates differentiation with stimulus analysis and lack of differentiation with the apprehension of stimulus wholes is consistent with previous uses of the principle in its implication that differentiation produces a more powerful system. Still, quite important for our view of development is the clarity with which the current view also imputes some psychological power to the individual even when differentiation is lacking. For one, apprehension of stimulus wholes does not mitigate against discrimination (except perhaps when resources are limited). Two different unanalyzed wholes are perfectly discriminable as global units. Thus, in the present sense of differentiation, the detection of differences between unique stimuli and the recognition of unique stimuli are both possible without differentiation. Second, the apprehension of stimuli as wholes does not mitigate against the formation of equivalence classes. Overall resemblances between wholes provide a coherent and systematic basis for relating discriminable wholes and, thus, the formation of classes of stimuli. Concept formation and transfer of learning *are* possibilities when differentiation is absent. Therefore, even if the young child were totally restricted to processing wholes, that child would not be psychologically helpless.

The power, however, that comes with differentiation (i.e., stimulus analysis) is most profound for the formation of equivalence classes. Holistic perception limits both the kinds of stimuli that can be considered equivalent and the flexibility of equivalence operations. On both counts, the holistic mode is less enabling than the analytic mode. Given analysis into properties, two stimuli that are very different from one another can be considered fundamentally the same for some purpose. They can be considered equivalent because they share a particular common attribute. The analytic mode uniquely allows the detection of equivalence among diverse items, an affordance that would seem to be especially valuable for intelligent functioning. Relations based on overall similarity are, by definition, limited or diffuse in scope.

The flexibility afforded by analysis into properties is that classes can be differently constituted for different purposes. Two stimuli can be considered simultaneously the same according to one criterion and different according to another. Differentiation provides the flexibility to entertain different patterns of equivalence for the very same set of stimuli by focusing on different properties. In contrast, the overall similarity structure that governs relations when differentiation is lacking is entirely fixed, given the same stimulus set. So, the flexibility of intelligent functioning is also the unique affordance of the analytic mode. Both in the scope of equivalence classes it enables and in the flexibility of equivalence operations it allows, the analytic mode is more abstract than the holistic mode. At the least it seems appropriate to state that in the course of normal perceptual and cognitive development the balance shifts from holistic to analytic.

ACKNOWLEDGMENTS

Preparation of this chapter and much of the research reported in it were supported by a grant from NSF, BNS 79-24035, and from NICHHD, PO1 HD 10965-4. Jeanette Brack helped considerably with editorial comments.

REFERENCES

Anglin, J. M. *Word, object, and conceptual development.* New York: Norton, 1977.

Brown, A. L., & DeLoache, J. S. Skills, plans and self-regulation. In R. S. Siegler (Ed.), *Children's thinking: What develops?* Hillsdale, N.J.: Lawrence Erlbaum Associates, 1978.

Bruner, J. S., Olver, R. R., & Greenfield, P. M. *Studies in cognitive growth.* New York: Wiley, 1966.

Flavell, J. H. *Cognitive development.* Englewood Cliffs, N.J.: Prentice-Hall, 1977.

Fodor, J. A. Some reflections on L. S. Vygotsky's *Thought and Language. Cognition,* 1972, *1,* 83–95.

Garner, W. R. *The processing of information and structure.* Potomac, Md.: Lawrence Erlbaum Associates, 1974.

Gibson, E. J. *Principles of perceptual learning and perceptual development.* New York: Appleton-Century-Crofts, 1969.

Inhelder, B., & Piaget, J. *The early growth of logic in the child.* New York: Norton, 1964.

Kemler, D. G. Classification in young and retarded children: The primacy of overall similarity relations. *Child Development,* 1982, *53,* 768–799. (a)

Kemler, D. G. The ability for dimensional analysis in preschool and retarded children: Evidence from comparison, conservation and prediction tasks. *Journal of Experimental Child Psychology,* 1982, *30.* (b).

Kemler, D. G. The effect of intention on how concepts are acquired. In preparation.

Kemler, D. G., & Smith, L. B. Accessing similarity and dimensional relations: The effects of integrality and separability on the discovery of complex concepts. *Journal of Experimental Psychology: General,* 1979, *108,* 133–150.

Lockhead, G. R. Effects of dimensional redundancy on visual discrimination. *Journal of Experimental Psychology,* 1966, *72,* 95–104.

Mervis, C. B., & Rosch, E. Categorization of natural objects. In M. R. Rosenzweig & L. W. Porter (Eds.), *Annual review of psychology,* 1981, *32,* 89–115.

Rosch, E. Human categorization. In N. R. Warren (Ed.), *Studies in cross-cultural psychology,* Vol. 1. New York: Academic Press, 1977.

Rosch, E., & Mervis, C. B. Family resemblances: Studies in the internal structure of categories. *Cognitive Psychology,* 1975, *7,* 573–605.

Rosch, E., Mervis, C. B., Gray, W. D., Johnson, D. M., & Boyes-Braem, P. Basic objects in natural categories. *Cognitive Psychology,* 1976, *8,* 382–439.

Shepard, R. N. Attention and the metric structure of the stimulus space. *Journal of Mathematical Psychology,* 1964, *1,* 54–87.

Shepp, B. E. From perceived similarity to dimensional structure: A new hypothesis about perceptual development. In E. Rosch & B. B. Lloyd (Eds.) *Cognition and categorization*. Hillsdale, N.J.: Lawrence Erlbaum Associates, 1978.

Shepp, B., Burns, B., & McDonough, D. The relation of stimulus structure to perceptual and cognitive development: Further tests of a separability hypothesis. In J. Becker & F. Wilkening (Eds.), *The integration of information by children*. Hillsdale, N.J.: Lawrence Erlbaum Associates, 1980.

Shepp, B. E., & Swartz, K. B. Selective attention and the processing of integral and nonintegral dimensions: A developmental study. *Journal of Experimental Child Psychology*, 1976, *22*, 73–85.

Smith, L. B. Perceptual development and category generalization. *Child Development*, 1979, *50*, 705–715.

Smith, L. B., & Kemler, D. G. Developmental trends in free classification: Evidence for a new conceptualization of perceptual development. *Journal of Experimental Child Psychology*, 1977, *24*, 279–298.

Smith, L. B., & Kemler, D. G. Levels of experienced dimensionality in children and adults. *Cognitive Psychology*, 1978, *10*, 502–532.

Vygotsky, L. S. *Thought and language*. Cambridge, Mass: MIT Press, 1962.

Werner, H. *Comparative psychology of mental development* (Rev. ed.). New York: International Universities Press, 1948.

Werner, H. The conception of development from a comparative and organismic point of view. In D. Harris (Ed.), *The concept of development*. Minneapolis: University of Minnesota Press, 1957.

Zeaman, D., & House, B. J. Interpretation of developmental trends in discriminative transfer. In A. D. Pick (Ed.), *Minnesota symposia on child psychology* (Vol. 8). Minneapolis: University of Minnesota Press, 1974.

4 Stimulus Preferences As Structural Features

David Zeaman and Patricia Hanley
University of Connecticut

OVERVIEW

Although stimulus preferences are usually regarded as *control processes* in being (to a strong degree) determined by experiential factors such as learning and habituation, there may be some unlearned determinants, or *structural feature* aspects, of stimulus preferences even in the human. The varying saliencies of auditory and visual stimuli quite likely have some native species-specific basis in subhuman animals, for example, in the identification of secondary sex characteristics or recognition of calls by birds of like kinds. Ethologists provide us with many such examples. Whether humans have, to any extent, unlearned stimulus preferences or innate saliency hierarchies is a more controversial question as shown: (1) by the fact that theories of discriminative learning are wildly variable in the provisions made for the possibility of any hard-wiring of preferences for cues or stimulus dimensions; (2) by an appreciable body of experimental data that suggest that observed age changes in stimulus preferences may be accounted for solely by maturation. We review some of the kinds of evidence that have been adduced for unlearned stimulus preferences and look for theoretical homes for such phenomena.

METHODOLOGY OF STRUCTURAL FEATURE HUNTING

Some Indirect Inferences

A 25-year program of research on discrimination learning in the House–Zeaman laboratory led to the conclusion that initial preferences for attention to various dimensions such as color and form and position were related to intelligence

(Zeaman & House, 1979). More specifically, both MA and IQ were repeatedly found to be related to the starting probabilities of attending to the various dimensions of stimuli before training had begun. Color and form component preferences were positively related to intelligence, whereas position was inversely related to intelligence. Such findings caused considerable cognitive dissonance in the House–Zeaman camp, because in their attention theory stimulus preference, or dimensional saliency was a control process (in the Atkinson & Shiffrin, 1969, sense, i.e., a variable easily changed by training). The lifetime constancy of individual differences in intelligence in our population of retarded persons (Fisher & Zeaman, 1973) had predisposed us to regard intelligence as a structural feature. That individual differences in a soft-wired structural feature should relate to such a presumably hard-wired structural feature trait as intelligence was a dissonant idea. The resolution of this conflict led us to posit that stimulus preferences were also in part hard-wired. If this were the only logic leading to the inference of stimulus preferences as structural features, the picture would hardly be convincing. But other arguments and data bear on the issue, and these will be considered.

More Direct Methods

The general strategies of nature–nurture parsing in the field of individual differences vary in their directness. The most direct evidence for structural feature status would be a demonstration that a trait could be bred. Kinship studies of stimulus preferences, with reasonable controls for environmental determinants, are not to our knowledge available but are in principle possible. Thomas Bouchard's Minnesota Study of Twins Reared Apart has not yet been published, but advance press releases contain descriptions of highly similar form and color preferences in monozygotic strangers.

Another methodological tack can be taken. If learned and unlearned are exhaustive classifications, the demonstration that a stimulus preference is unlearned can proceed by showing that learning has been controlled or ruled out as a likely cause of observed preferences. Because the opportunities for learning are so ubiquitous, this strategy is by no means easy. It might seem, for example, a safe assumption that a behavior occurring at birth must be unlearned, because the opportunity for learning is so slight, but recent research has shown that birds learn something about the parents' call prior to hatching—while they are still inside the egg. Presence at birth is in this instance a fallible indicator of stimulus hard-wiring.

Other criteria for unlearned status include demonstrations such as universality across individuals and environmental contexts, uniform developmental progressions, and appearance of a behavior despite contrary training. All of these may be fallible indices of unlearned status. For example, a preference for form over color may be observed in a situation where color has received more training. This could indicate that a native form preference is overcoming the recent training or that there is regression to the transferred effects of a greater amount of prior form training. It is not easy to rule out the possibility of hidden transfer, but circumstances make such transfer unlikely. Despite the weakness of strong controls, nature–nurture parsing is done in the current state of the art by weighing the possibly fallible evidence and coming to tentative, best-estimate conclusions. It would be pleasant to have theories waiting that can accommodate any outcome of the nature–nurture issues in stimulus preferences. The adequacy of some current theories in this respect will be examined in what follows, together with a scanning of the evidence in four areas of stimulus preference: color–form, position, novelty, and compound–component.

COLOR–FORM PREFERENCES

Over the last half century there have appeared with sporadic frequency experimental reports of a developmental progression in the relative saliencies of color and form. Younger or less developed subjects prefer to attend to color; older or smarter subjects focus more on the dimension of form. The idea appears to have originated with Descoudres (1914). Although the subsequent findings are far from univocal, this is the modal pattern of results among American, French, and German children as reported in about a dozen studies. Most of the studies have made use of some variant of a forced matching task in which, for example, a sample stimulus of a particular color and form is shown (say, a red square), and subjects are then asked to choose as a match with the sample one of two test stimuli each sharing just one property of the sample. The test stimuli might be a red triangle (choice of which would indicate a color preference), and a blue square (a choice here would be classified as a form preference).

A summary of the results of a number of studies using matching techniques with normal children is shown in Fig. 4.1. To make all data roughly comparable we took whatever measure of form preference that was reported and expressed this as a percentage of the sum of both color and form measures. Functions A and B were from a study by Brian and Goodenough (1929) with function A representing the use of two-dimensional stimuli and B representing three-dimensional stimuli. It was unfortunate that the latter function was not carried out beyond the age of 5 years. Functions C and D are from Suchman and Trabasso (1966) using two methods of computing a central tendency (C is based on grouped data; D is based on individual preferences). Functions E and F are from a study by Lee (1965) with E representing boys and F, girls. Functions G and H are also for boys and girls, respectively, reported in a study by Corah (1964). Functions I and J are again for girls (I) and boys (J) as reported by Kagan and Lemkin (1961). These studies used a variety of color–form stimuli and different performance indices.

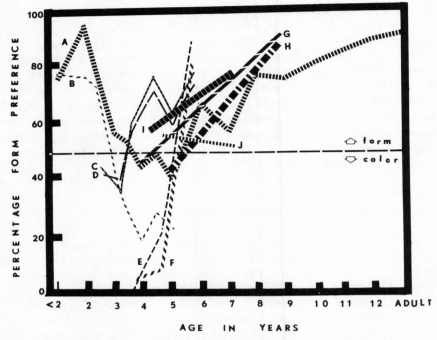

FIG. 4.1.   The relation of age to color–form preferences as reported in a variety of studies identified in the text.

To eliminate a lot of the unsystematic variability of the data of Fig. 4.1, we next took medians of all functions at 6-month intervals to yield the data of Fig. 4.2. Between the ages of 4 years and 12 years (and higher) there appears a continuous growth in form preference in comparison to color preference. The monotonic trend is broken by the data below 4 years that are from a single study by Brian and Goodenough (1929). These may not be replicable, although curvilinear maturational trends are hardly unknown. Spears (1964, 1966) tested visual preferences for color and form stimuli in 4-month-old infants using visual fixation times and found color dominant over form, as would be expected if the color–form progression were monotonic.

Plotted in Fig. 4.2 are also some data points derived from a different experimental paradigm, a conflict of cues design in a discriminative learning study (House & Zeaman, 1963). Table 4.1 outlines the method. On the first trial of a two-trial problem, the color–form stimulus C_1F_1 is designated the positive stimulus in a two-choice discriminative problem, and C_2F_2 is the negative or non-rewarded stimulus (the subscripts denote different colors and forms). On the second trial, a choice is given in which the redundant color and form cues of the training trial are put into conflict to reveal which dimension has acquired the

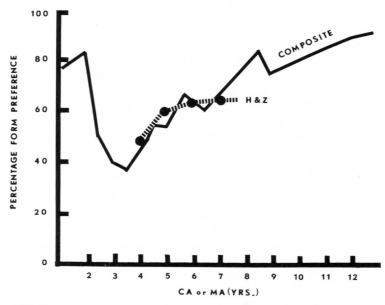

FIG. 4.2.   The relation of age to color–form preferences. A composite of the data of Fig. 4.1 together with additional data from House and Zeaman (1963).

greater approach–avoidance strengths on the single training trial. This in turn is assumed to be a function of the relative saliency of color and form. Different colors and forms were used on a long series of trial pairs of this type with retarded subjects varying in mental age. The relative preference of form over color increased with mental age as shown in the dotted function of Fig. 4.2. The dominance of color over form in the concept learning of preschool children has also been reported by Suchman and Trabasso (1966).

Although the color–form progression shown in Fig. 4.2 has appreciable generality in methods, stimuli, and subjects, there exists at least one negative finding reported by Suchman (1966) who found among West African children no devel-

TABLE 4.1
Conflict of Cues Design in the House and
Zeaman Study (1963)

	Positive Stimulus	Negative Stimulus
Training Trial	C_1F_1	C_2F_2
Test Trial	C_1F_2	C_2F_1
	Color Choice	Form Choice

opmental trends in color–form preferences between the ages of 3 years and 16 years. Nigerian children at all these ages preferred color almost exclusively in color–form preference tests of several types. Suchman interprets these findings to mean that color–form progressions in Euro-American children must have been learned (i.e., were control processes) because they were not observed in Nigeria. Another possible interpretation is that color–form progressions are maturationally determined in many national groups but not those having strong native color preferences. A resolution of this structural-feature versus control-process interpretation of color–form preferences does not emerge forcibly from the array of evidence available. A simple box-score methodology is suggestive of a maturational unfolding even if the finding is not universal. We suspect that color-to-form sequences will continue to be reported in a broader variety of settings, stimuli, and subjects where there are no obvious training factors that account for them. The absence of strong controls for environmental determinants should not mean that color–form progressions are automatically interpreted as control processes. The control-process interpretation is just as lacking in controls for genetic or maturational (structural feature) interpretations. These could be provided by the demonstration that training effects were independent of age. Neither interpretation is more parsimonious, neither incapable of disproof with better data. One of our main points is that our theories ought to have provisions for any outcome of this issue.

POSITION

Any one who has tried to teach a two-choice visual discrimination to rats or monkeys knows well how pesky their error tendencies can be of responding to the left–right positions of stimuli rather than the color and form attributes that are generally made relevant. These take the form of responding persistently to one side or alternating sides or responding to the side last rewarded. Rats, for example, will not uncommonly run off 100–200 consecutive responses to one side of a T-maze (or jumping stand or discrimination box) before learning a black–white discrimination (Lovejoy, 1968). Regression to position responding in nonhuman subjects is also extremely common when learned discriminative performances are disturbed by retention intervals, stimulus changes, or other extraneous factors.

With human subjects, age changes in position responding are commonly reported. These take the form of positional error tendencies in the discriminative learning of nonpositional cues of color and form. Such errors decrease with age. It may be a surprise that the speed of learning a position discrimination *decreases* with age (because older usually means smarter), but such findings should not be a surprise if positional stimuli are natively more salient for the young, and other dimensions such as color and form show maturational increases in salience.

One of the earlier studies to show clearly the greater tendencies of younger children to attend to positional cues was that of Weir (1964). He used a three-choice position discrimination with probabilistic schedules of reinforcement to study age changes in problem-solving strategies. His two youngest age groups (3-year-olds and 5-year-olds) learned to solve these simple positional problems faster than older groups up to 18 years of age. Older subjects developed more complicated (error) strategies of response sequencing that interfered initially with the learning of a simple positional response and depressed the earlier portions of their learning curves.

House and Zeaman (1963) used Levine's Strategy Indices to assess the strengths of position hypotheses in retarded children of varying mental ages. Figure 4.3 depicts the course of change with mental age of three position hypotheses. Two of these, left-or-right-position preference and win–stay, lose–shift with respect to position show reliable decreases with mental age. It should be emphasized that these are error tendencies being measured here because the correct hypothesis was win–stay, lose–shift with respect to stimuli in a two-choice, visual discrimination learning task.

In a number of other studies, position alternation strategies have shown decreasing frequencies as developmental levels increase. Studies by Gholson, Levine, and Phillips (1972); Gerjuoy and Winters (1967); and Ress and Levine (1966) taken together lead to the inference of a negative age trend in positional responding. More recently, in a kind of tour de force, Spitz, Carroll, and Johnson (1975) designed a learning study in which retarded subjects were predicted to outperform college students because of their presumably greater tendency to attend to positional cues. The task was a two-choice visual discrimination with a pair of Japanese symbols as stimuli arranged in left–right order. The correct

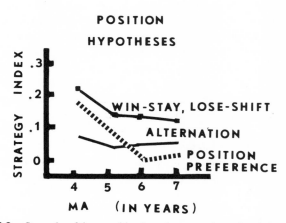

FIG. 4.3.   Strengths of three position hypotheses are shown in relation to mental age. Data are from House and Zeaman (1963).

strategy was maliciously chosen as a position alternation rather than a win–stay, lose–shift with respect to the Japanese symbol that the college students expected it to be (as inferred from error analyses). The results were as expected, the smarter subjects did significantly poorer because of their initially lower tendencies to attend to position as a relevant dimension.

Position strategies are not only more likely to occur in less developed subjects at the outset of training, but when nonpositional discriminations are made difficult, retarded subjects will regress to positional strategies after having been trained to adopt nonpositional strategies (House & Zeaman, 1963).

The possibility that preferences for the position dimension have an unlearned basis appears reasonable given that subjects will regress to position responding despite the reinforcement histories running quite counter to such responding. In the House–Zeaman laboratory we have observed retarded subjects regressing to position errors who in some instances have had over 10 years of successful discriminative learning experience in which position has never been a relevant dimension.

The relative imperviousness of position responding to training histories (in rats) led Lovejoy (1968) to construct a theory that posited some nonadjustable or "native" component of attention, a matter to be discussed later.

NOVELTY

The stimulus preferences for color–form and for position were both *dimensional* preferences. Developmental changes have also been reported for *cue preferences* within the dimension of novelty–familiarity. Younger children prefer to approach novel cues more than older children, who have a greater preference for familiar stimuli. And, because MA and CA are such close correlates, during childhood, smarter subjects tend to have less novelty preferences than not-so-smart subjects. The evidence for these developmental effects has been reviewed in detail by Zeaman (1976), so only a sketch will suffice here.

The major experimental vehicle for demonstrating developmental changes in novelty–familiarity preference has been the Moss–Harlow effect. In the Moss-Harlow (1947) paradigm a single stimulus is presented on Trial 1 and rewarded. On Trial 2 the old positive and a new negative stimulus are presented for choice. Figure 4.4 provides an illustration at top left. Subjects at age 2 or mental age 2 are so attracted to novelty that they prefer the new negative stimulus despite having been rewarded on the positive stimulus on the prior trial. This is shown as a below-chance point on the positive function at age 2 in Fig. 4.4.

Under the negative condition of the Moss–Harlow paradigm a nonreinforced negative stimulus is presented on Trial 1 and followed by a choice of a new positive and the old negative on Trial 2. Note that the Trial 2 stimuli are identical for both positive and negative conditions and that the information given on Trial

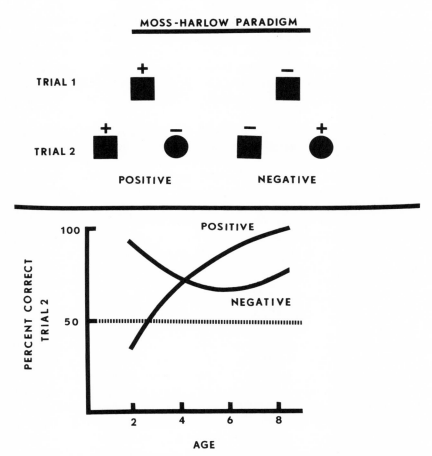

FIG. 4.4. Illustrated at top are the kinds of stimuli used in a Moss–Harlow paradigm. Two conditions are distinguished: A positive and a negative subcondition in which the only simulus presented on Trial 1 is reinforced or nonreinforced, respectively. Performances on Trial 2 under each condition for subjects of varying age (or mental age) are shown in the graph.

1 is in principal sufficient for problem solution. In fact quite different performances are observed under the two conditions at different ages (or mental ages). The functions shown in Fig. 4.4 are summary approximations of those reported by a number of investigators including House and Zeaman (1958), Cross and Vaughter (1966), Grabbe and Campione (1969), and Fisher, Sperber, and Zeaman (1973).

The vertical distance between the positive and negative functions provides an index of the relative preference for novel and familiar stimuli. Between the ages of 4 and 5 years a change in preference from novelty to familiarity takes place. How should these findings be interpreted? Are these changing preferences to be viewed as maturational changes in structural features? It has been shown by Greenfield (1976) that novelty–familiarity preferences are reversible at any age by training on many problems in which the novel (or familiar) stimulus is correct. This means only that a control-process interpretation is viable, not strongly confirmed.

Zeaman (1976) argues for a structural-feature interpretation of novelty preferences in the young and less well-developed subjects because almost all the appetitive training that occurs in everyday environments predisposes toward a familiarity preference. Well-adapted organisms must approach or maximize previously rewarded stimulus situations. Previously rewarded means familiar. The law of effect thus dictates a familiarity preference, and the developmental progression from novelty to familiarity preferences may likely reflect a learning function. But we apparently start life not neutrally but with a bias toward novelty preferences. Such a bias may reflect a native tendency because it runs counter to training.

COMPOUND–COMPONENT

Dozens of papers have been written about the presumably maturational determinants of preferences for compound and component aspects of stimuli. A progression has been postulated in which developmentally young subjects prefer to attend to compound, thinglike, or holistic aspects of stimulation, whereas older and smarter subjects prefer to attend to component (or abstract and conceptual) dimensions of the surround. Writers such as Werner, Spence, Bitterman, Gibson, the Tighes, the Kendlers, Cole, House, and Zeaman have provided both theory and data in this area that today is still as controversial as it was in the 1930s when Spence argued that component dimensions were primary, in contrast to Werner who believed that compounds had developmental primacy. The data domains providing empirical support for the inference of developmental changes in compound and component preference have been largely those of discriminative learning, especially dimensional shift effects and subproblem analyses. Much of this literature was reviewed by Zeaman and House (1974) so only representative highlights will be sketched that are relevant to the structural-feature issue of stimulus preferences.

A more recent literature has developed on a related issue, the development of competing modes of perception termed *integral* and *separable* by writers such as Garner, Lockhead, Shepp, Kemler, and Burns. Development appears to proceed from integral to separable. The data domains from which these conceptualizations emerge are usually variants of speeded sorting tasks and classification problems.

There is a rough correspondence between attentional preferences for compound dimensions and the integral mode of perception and between component preferences and separable modes of perception. These correspondences will be discussed.

The heart of the compound–component controversy can be seen clearly in the context of a simple two-choice, simultaneous discrimination. Two settings of the stimuli in such a problem are shown in Table 4.2. If the two trial settings depicted are alternated irregularly with left–right positions of the stimuli randomized, there are at least two solutions of this problem. One is a component solution: Triangle is correct. The other is a compound solution: The black triangle is correct *and* the white triangle is correct. Similar solutions could be expressed in terms of the negative stimulus but the compound–component distinction would be the same. The compound solution appears to the adult eye cumbersome and unnecessarily complex in treating the two trial settings as different problems, but this in fact is the way younger children (and some other species) solve such problems. Zeaman and House (1974) summarize the many different kinds of experimental evidence converging on this conclusion but the most convincing evidence comes from an ingenious invention of Tighe, Glick, and Cole (1971) and Tighe (1973) called *subproblem analysis*.

The paradigm demonstrating subproblem analysis is shown in Table 4.3. In an original learning condition (a two-choice color discrimination is illustrated in Table 4.3 with a two-valued irrelevant form dimension), two stimulus settings as shown are irregularly alternated with left–right positions of stimulus pairs randomized. Following achievement of a criterion of learning, the experimental conditions are changed to either a reversal shift as shown at the bottom left of Table 4.3 or an extradimensional shift as shown at the bottom right of Table 4.3. In the reversal shift condition, the reward values of both settings are reversed. In the extradimensional shift condition, just one setting is reversed in reward value (designated the "changed" setting in the table), whereas the other remains "unchanged." With these reward values the problem is changed from a color discrimination (blue is correct) to a form discrimination (circle is correct).

The extreme forms of two outcomes on the shift problems are shown in Fig. 4.5. The function labeled *C* designates the gradual improvement observed on the "changed" setting of the EDS condition (and both settings of the reversal shift).

TABLE 4.2
Stimulus Settings Illustrating A Simple
Two-Choice Form Discrimination

Trial	Positive Stimulus	Negative Stimulus
N	Black triangle	White circle
N + 1	White triangle	Black circle

TABLE 4.3
Paradigms for Subproblem Analysis

Original Learning

Setting	Positive Stimulus	Negative Stimulus
1	Blue circle	Red square
2	Blue square	Red circle

Reversal Shift

Setting	Positive Stimulus	Negative Stimulus
1	Red square	Blue circle
2	Red circle	Blue square

Extradimensional Shift

Setting	Positive Stimulus	Negative Stimulus
1 (UNCH.)	Blue circle	Red square
2 (CHNG.)	Red circle	Blue square

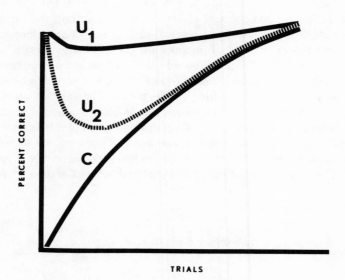

FIG. 4.5. Some results of a subproblem analysis. Two contrasting types of response, U_1 and U_2, on the unchanged trial settings of an extradimensional shift are shown in relation to performance on trials with changed trial settings, C.

The function labeled U_1 represents the performance on the "unchanged" setting of the EDS condition of subjects showing subproblem independence. The function labeled U_2 represents the performance on the unchanged setting of subjects who show subproblem dependence. It is inferred that the subjects who show the U_1 outcome have solved the original learning problem as two independent subproblems (i.e., on a compound basis). The U_2 outcome denotes solution of the original problem on a dimensional basis. The negative transfer from the changed setting to the unchanged is attributable to the extinction of a dimensional mediating response such as attention.

The U_1 function is approximated by preschool children, rats, and turtles (Tighe, 1973), whereas the U_2 function is characteristic of older children and adults. The ontogenetic (and phylogenetic) difference has been demonstrated a number of times by the Tighes and their associates (Cole, 1973; Tighe, 1973; Tighe et al., 1971; Tighe & Tighe, 1978). The experimental literature has been reviewed by Zeaman and House (1974) and updated by Tighe and Tighe (1978) so it will not be documented here. Suffice it to say that the developmental trend from compound to component solutions of discriminative problems has been experimentally well established not only by the data of subproblem analyses but by a variety of other convergent operations within the domain of discriminative learning. It is about as well confirmed an effect as we find in developmental psychology.

The degree of empirical confirmation is not, however, matched by agreement among theorists in interpretation of the data. The Tighes and their associates identify subproblem independence in the developmentally young as the result of holistic *object* perception in contrast to the component *dimension* perception inferred from subproblem dependence in older subjects. Zeaman and House (1963, 1974, 1979) take a somewhat different view, not with respect to the dimensional response of the older subjects but with respect to the presumably dimensionless, global, thinglike, object perception of the younger children and lower animals. These subjects are, according to House and Zeaman, responding to a dimension, a compound dimension of color and form in the problems shown in Table 4.3. A compound is defined as a joint aspect of a stimulus that is independent of its components. A red square, for example, if responded to as a color–form compound, will show no generalization to red or to square presented separately as components. The concept is perhaps a subtle one but central to attention theory. The independence of compounds from their component elements is easily seen in the instance of written words. The components of words are letters, but we respond to words as compounds of letters that are to a strong extent independent of the component letters. The words *post* and *pots* are very different words despite the fact that all the component letters are the same with a single inversion of letter ordering.

Compound perception is, in our view, not global or holistic or undifferentiated or thinglike. A joint property of two or more dimensions does not mean a combination of all dimensions. An adequate specification of compound perception must say which dimensions are presumed to define the compound. For example, a color-form compound must be distinguished from a position-texture compound or a size–brightness compound. In almost all the studies in the discriminative learning literature in which the developmental progression from compound to component is shown, there are just two or three dimensions varied experimentally to yield the compounds that presume to control the perception of the younger subjects. A specification in terms of the joint properties of two dimensions is hardly holistic. "Object" perception is an equally poor characterization. Objects have an indefinite number of component dimensions (including relations with the context) that can compound to allow objects to be identified. To say that a stimulus array is perceived as an object does not tell us much because it is certain that something less than all the component and compound aspects of an object are being used by the perceiver in object identification. An experimental analysis is required to find out how many or how complex are the stimulus compounds used in a particular situation. Tighe (1973) has indicated how the techniques of subproblem analysis can be used for this purpose. What is termed *object perception* in the experimental analyses reported in the literature of this field often turns out to be responses based on simple color–form compounds.

The complexity of compounds is not the only issue on which theorists differ. Whether compounds are dimensional in nature is also controversial. In the one camp are writers such as the Tighes, Shepp, Cole, and Linda Smith who regard component perception as dimensional in nature but regard compound or object perception as dimensionless. In contrast to this view is the position of House and Zeaman and their associates for whom compounds are dimensional in exactly the same sense that components are inferred to be. The major experimental operation used to infer dimensional perception is the differential transfer observed in intradimensional and extradimensional shifts. In an intradimensional shift the same dimension is made relevant on two consecutive discriminative problems with entirely different cues. For example, a red–green discrimination might be followed by a yellow–blue problem for an intradimensional color sequence. An extradimensional shift might be illustrated by a color-to-form sequence of problems (e.g., a purple–orange discrimination followed by one requiring the learning of a square–triangle discrimination). A large experimental literature has established that intradimensional shifts are associated with positive transfer and extradimensional shifts tend to occasion negative transfer (Wolff, 1967). In a novel extension, these operations can be employed to show positive transfer between two different compound problems or two different component problems (intradimensional shifts) and negative transfer between a sequence of compound-to-component problems or component-to-compound problems (extradimensional shifts). The empirical demonstration of these effects requires a class of problems likely solved on a compound basis and another class soluble on a component basis. Table 4.4 illustrates the two classes of problems. The compound problem

TABLE 4.4
Sample Trial Settings for Compound and Component Problems

	Compound Problem		Component Problem	
Setting	Positive Stimulus	Negative Stimulus	Positive Stimulus	Negative Stimulus
1	Red circle	Red square	Red circle	Red square
2	Blue square	Blue circle	Blue circle	Blue square
3	Blue square	Blue circle	Green circle	Green square
.	.	.	.	.
.	.	.	.	.
.	.	.	.	.
n	Red circle	Red square	Yellow circle	Yellow square

is sometimes called a conditional problem. The two settings are randomly alternated as are the left–right positions. Note that responses to all the component cues (red, blue, circle, and square) are equally rewarded, making a component solution impossible. A compound solution is "Choose the red circle" (with setting 1) and "Choose the blue square" (with setting 2). Note that if there is any generalization from either of these compound solutions to the constituent components, errors will ensue.

The component problem illustrated in Table 4.4 is most likely solved on a component basis, "Circle is correct," because only one component (form) remains constant over trials in association with reward. No compound solution of color–form is possible because stimulus colors change on every trial.

The question of interest on the dimensionality issue is this: What are the transfer relations of these two types of problems? Zeaman and House (1974) presented preliminary data on this problem showing the expected positive transfer associated with intradimensional shifts of two successive compound or component problems (using different cues, of course, on each problem) and the negative transfer of a compound-to-component or component-to-compound sequence. This finding was well established in subsequent studies using the same paradigm with college students (Barnes, Cassidy, Ninfa, Yago, & Barnes, 1978) and with retarded subjects (Barnes, 1978). House (1979) also demonstrated the dimensional nature of compound solutions by combining the operations shown in Tables 4.3 and 4.4. She trained separate groups of retarded subjects on either a compound problem or a component problem as illustrated in Table 4.4. With attention thus presumably fixed on either the compound or component dimension, the differentially pretrained groups were given training on a new problem solvable on either a compound or a component basis. The problem sequence shown in Table 4.3 was then instituted to show, through subproblem analysis, whether the pretrained attention to compound or component dimensions had transferred to the new problem. The results were as expected from the House–Zeaman views on compounding. The subjects given the component pretraining showed subproblem dependence (function U_2 in Fig. 4.5). Those given compound pretraining showed subproblem independence (function U_1 in Fig. 4.5).

Compound and component solutions are not different modes of perception. They are simply different directions of attention that can be readily altered by a little training. Without the special training, however, it appears that subjects at the lower developmental and phylogenetic levels have some preference for directing their attention to compound aspects of stimuli.

Evidence for fixed stimulus preferences has not been restricted to the experimental literature of discriminative learning. Such preferences have also been inferred from results in a parallel literature on tasks requiring subjects to sort or classify multidimensional stimuli. Adults and older children asked to sort multidimensional stimuli will typically use just one of the dimensions to form their categories or classes of similar objects. Younger children (under 8 years) tend to classify the same stimuli not on the basis of a single dimension but on the basis of similarities on more than one (usually two) dimension. The differences can be seen graphically in Fig. 4.6.

The stimulus A (with coordinates 1, 1) is judged by young children to be more similar to stimulus C (coordinates 2, 3) than to stimulus B (coordinates 1, 4) although C is different from A in *both* dimensions and B is different in only *one*. The measure of dissimilarity for younger children is the Euclidean distance from A to C ($\sqrt{d_1^2 + d_1^2} = \sqrt{1^2 + 2^2} = 2.24$ units), which is less than that between A and B (3 units). When this Euclidean metric provides an accurate measure of

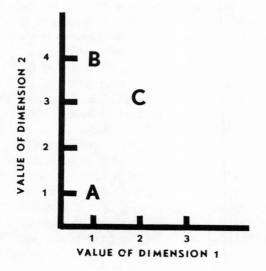

FIG. 4.6.   Three two-dimensional stimuli, A, B, and C, have coordinates (1, 1), (1, 4), and (2, 3), respectively, on the two dimensions.

similarity, judgments are said to be classified on the basis of *overall* similarity because both dimensions jointly determine the index. Pairs of dimensions that give rise to judgments based on *overall* similarity are termed *integral*. Pairs of dimensions that give rise to judgments based on primarily one or the other are classified as *separable*. The distinction between integral and separable dimensions was emphasized by Garner and Felfoldy (1970) and Lockhead (1972) among others, and the analogy between integral–separable and compound–component has been pointed out by Shepp and his associates (Shepp, Burns, & McDonough, 1978). Dimensions perceived integrally are responded to as unanalyzed compounds; separable dimensions are analyzed into separate components and response may be to either. If this analogy holds, then the compound–component hypothesis of Zeaman and House (1974) becomes the separability hypothesis of Shepp (1978), which assumes that dimensional combinations perceived as integral by younger children are perceived as separable by older subjects. A number of confirming instances of the integral–separable progression with development have been reported. Color and form, which are separable for adults (Garner, 1974), are found to be integral for young children and separable for older children (Shepp & Swartz, 1976). Smith and Kemler (1977) showed that size and brightness shifted from integral to separable status as children grew older. This result was replicated by Shepp et al. (1978). Size and brightness are separable for adults (Handel & Imai, 1972). Some other dimensional pairs showing the integral–separable shift with age are size of circle and angle of radius (Shepp et al., 1978) and length and density (Ward, 1980). These developmental differences have an obvious stimulus parameter because there are dimensional pairs such as hue and saturation that are integral for adults. As would be expected, these dimensions are integral for children as well (Burns, Shepp, McDonough, & Weiner-Ehrlich, 1978). Height and width of rectangles act in the same way (Shepp et al., 1978).

The developmental trends observed are impressive, but we lodge a complaint about their characterization as a shift from global, holistic perception to component dimensional perception. The term *overall similarity* is accurate as a description of integral relations provided that we have a counting system that goes "one, two, everything." By *overall* is really meant *overboth* because integrality is typically defined as a property of dimensional pairs. When multidimensional stimuli vary on more than two dimensions, the developmental progression disappears (Smith, 1981). When someone does an experiment showing that exposure to a series of problems in which the separable mode of perception is likely will predispose subjects toward separability on a subsequent problem (ID shift) and away from integrality (ED shift), then our analogy with the compound–component literature will be virtually complete.

Whether integral and separable are synonymous with compound and component, respectively, may be argued independently of the control-process versus structural-feature question. Some dimensional pairs such as hue and saturation do not appear to be perceived as anything but integral (hence a likely structural feature), but for other pairs such as color and form the integral versus separable modes appear to have both control-process and structural-feature determinants in that instructions or training can change the mode (defining a control process); yet there are strong age changes (suggesting structural features). Writers such as Shepp, Burns, Kemler, and Smith theorize that children start life predisposed to see stimulus dimensions integrally or holistically (a better word would be "bothistically" given the typical data of this field); then, with an increase in age and with perceptual learning, a shift to the separable mode occurs. The kind of perceptual learning appealed to here is that described by Gibson (1969) featuring the processes of abstraction and selective filtering. The picture emerges of a native perceptual preference overcome by a trained perceptual preference.

We believe that no great violence is done to the theory and data related to the separability hypothesis if an identity is proposed: The preference for separable modes of perception is identical to probabilities of attention to component dimensions; and the preference for integral modes of perception is identical to probabilities of attention to compound dimensions. In this domain as in all the others we have discussed, there is a modest amount of evidence that these perceptual preferences or attentional probabilities have both a fixed and an adjustable component. We look now to some possible theoretical homes for these ideas.

THEORY

Restrictions

Our search for theoretical homes for fixed and adjustable stimulus preferences is restricted to theories of discriminative learning because, whatever one's views on the likelihood of fixed preferences, everyone is agreed some preferences are adjustable by learning. We consider only theories having sufficient degrees of formal explication and quantification to allow the identification of specific parameters representing stimulus preferences regardless of their fixed or adjustable status. Given that the data we have adduced deals with preferences at the level of both cues and dimensions, we restrict our pool of theories to those that can accommodate both types of preference. The final constraint was a recency bias. We looked at theories of fairly recent vintage (less than 20 years old).

Within these constraints, we found eight theories or models, but no strong claim to exhaustive scholarship is made. These eight fell into three broad classes:nurture theories, nature theories, and nature–nurture theories, by which is meant, respectively, those with only learned or adjustable stimulus preferences, those with only fixed stimulus preferences, and those with both fixed and adjustable preferences.

Theories with Adjustable Stimulus Preferences Only

The Attention Models of Zeaman and House.   The one-look and multiple-look attention models of Zeaman and House (1963) have a theoretical variable representing dimensional preferences, $Po_{(i,T)}$, the probability of attending to the ith dimension on trial T, and another variable representing cue preferences, $Pr_{(i,j,T)}$, the probability of approaching cue j of dimension i on trial T. A subject may enter an experiment with starting values of these variables that have some unlearned origins but both preferences are in theory completely adjustable by reward contingencies. The theoretical preferences have no fixed components that could deliver deductively the dimensional dominance, regression, or developmental effects that give rise to the inference of fixed components. In short, these are nurture models.

Attention–Retention Theory of Fisher and Zeaman.   The multiple-look model of Fisher and Zeaman (1973) has a feedback mechanism that allows cue properties to affect dimensional saliencies. If, for instance, a subject had a strong native preference for some cue on a dimension, this preference would theoretically make the salience of the carrier dimension $[EPo_{(i,T)}]$ quite high at the outset of discriminative learning. However, once the cue preference is changed by reinforcement contingencies, the initial innate determinant is theoretically lost. So it can be concluded for this model that the nature and nurture determinants are not conceptually distinct for either dimension or cue preferences.

The Kendler, Basden, and Bruckner (1970) Dimensional Dominance Model.   This model modifies Spence's early discriminative learning theory to provide an account of dimensional dominance effects without invoking any selective attention mechanism. Stimulus preferences are represented by excitatory and inhibitory tendencies associated with cues. These are gradually changed by reinforcement schedules, according to the authors. No theoretical distinction is drawn between the nature and nurture sources of initial cue preferences and once these are changed by experience, they are not in principle recoverable.

Dimensional dominance is built into this model by assuming that generalization among cues within a dimension is greater than generalization among cues between dimensions. Differential dominance is delivered by postulating different generalization parameters associated with the various dimensions of stimulation. These generalization parameters are fixed psychological features but they do not correspond to the notion of dimensional preferences in any obvious way. If the data reviewed in this chapter implicate any fixed stimulus preferences, such effects would fall outside the deductive range of this model.

Medin's (1972) Context Theory.   In this ingenious model the assumption is made that attention influences generalization. For attended dimensions, the positive and negative cues are perceived as more distinctive (i.e., show less generalization) than the same cues on an unattended dimension. The model receives its name from the fact that generalization is presumed to operate among the cues of all dimensions both relevant and irrelevant—the latter being a synonym for *context*. The rate of mastery of a discriminative problem is determined by two sets of theoretical parameters, learning-rate constants and parameters controlling the degree of generalization among cues of each dimension.

This model has dimensional salience or attention value as a variable completely adjustable by reward schedules. Natively determined starting levels, or base levels, to which regression occurs are not part of this model.

The generalization parameters control the distinctiveness of cues. These do not change with experience, but they do vary with particular cues selected by the experimenter. The generalization parameters represent the psychophysical differences among cues. Although it is not explicit, it may be assumed that these constants would be fixed by nature rather than by nurture.

In summary, for this model dimensional salience is completely learned, cue distinctiveness is completely unlearned. Cue distinctiveness is not, however, a cue preference, hence the conclusion that Medin's is not a nature–nurture model of stimulus preference for either cues or dimensions. It would require modification to handle phenomena of fixed stimulus preferences.

Theories with Fixed Stimulus Preferences Only

The Attention Theory of Trabasso and Bower.   Trabasso and Bower (1968) have an attentional model of discriminative learning in which the saliencies of dimensions are represented as probabilities of attending to various dimensions. Oddly enough, these probabilities are completely nonadjustable. Each subject is postulated to have a fixed vector of preferences for dimensions competing for attention. Although the matter is not discussed by the theorists, the nonadjustable nature of attentional probabilities may lead the reader to infer that the dimensional preferences are inborn. Cue preferences in this model are, in contrast, completely adjustable by schedules of reinforcement with no fixed components even hinted at. No one, to our knowledge, has tried to relate the Trabasso and Bower model to the data reviewed in this chapter. In principle it should do better than the pure nurture theories listed here.

The House and Zeaman (1963) Multiple-Look Model.   In this multiple-look submodel of attention theory, the subject is posited as having *fixed* probabilities f, c, and k of attending to at least the dimensions of color, form, and kompound. Cue preferences are completely adjustable (in just one trial) with no fixed components. In these respects it bears a strong resemblance, and anticipates, the Trabasso and Bower (1968) model, although the models are otherwise quite different. This model was rationalized within the context of a specific experimental context (Estes' Miniature Experiment Designs), so much of the data we have cited on dimensional and cue preferences would not be appropriately related to this particular model. However, if someone wished to construct a new model including components of fixed dimensional preferences, they might find the Markovian machinery of this model appealing.

Theories with Both Fixed and Adjustable Stimulus Preferences

Lovejoy's (1968) Attention Model.   In this model, the attention value or control strength, C, of a stimulus dimension is a joint function of both a learned and an unlearned component. The learned or adjustable component, which Lovejoy calls "directable distinctiveness," is symbolized as Δ. The unlearned component, D, is called nondirectable distinctiveness. The relation between these variables is given by the equation

$$C = \frac{D + \Delta}{v(1 - v)}$$

where v and $(1 - v)$ are the strengths of an approach response to the positive and negative cues, respectively, on the dimension considered.

The value of the nature–nurture constants D and Δ are such that D is usually small compared to the maximal value of Δ, which increases during discriminative learning. At the outset of learning, therefore, dimensional preference would be largely controlled by D because Δ is zero, whereas at asymptotic levels of Δ growth the unlearned distinctiveness component is overridden by the learned component. These theoretical properties are just the ones needed to account for the commonly observed starting preferences for color–form, position, novelty, and compound–component that we have speculated may be native (but that are overridden by training).

The value of the learned component Δ can be changed not only by learning but also reduced by extinction [or by forgetting if we wished to expand Lovejoy's (1968) model]. This means that the fixed component, D, can control attention at other times than merely the outset of training. Figure 4.7 shows the values of D and Δ and the sum of the two as they may typically be during acquisition and extinction of a discrimination. The weak native stimulus preference, D, remains constant throughout. The theoretical sum $(D + \Delta)$, which determines behavior, is equal to D at the outset of training but is almost the same as Δ, the trained component, at the end of acquisition. Note that at the end of extinction the theoretical state of affairs is the same as at the outset of training; control returns to the native component, D. This property would be useful in handling the regression and dimensional dominance effects reported in the literature we have cited (especially in the ID–ED shift domain).

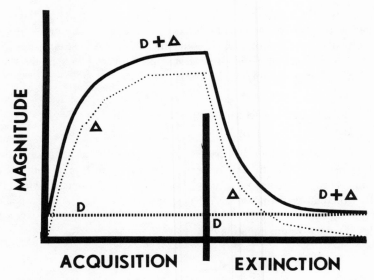

FIG. 4.7.   The magnitudes of Lovejoy's (1968) theoretical variables D and Δ (and their sum) as these are likely to be during acquisition and extinction. Discriminative performance is related to the $D + \Delta$ function, which is controlled by D, the fixed stimulus preference, at the beginning of acquisition and end of extinction.

For the rat, the value of D is relatively high for dimensions such as position and much lower for dimensions such as color and form. A theory of this form has been found useful in accounting for the pervasiveness of position responding despite contrary reinforcement schedules. It can obviously provide a post hoc theoretical home for any finding of native components of direction of attention.

The Attention Theory of Sutherland and Mackintosh (1971).   This theory resembles Lovejoy's (1968) in being an attentional model of discriminative learning with both fixed and adjustable components of attention. Attention to a particular dimension, i, is termed the switching in of analyzer i. The strength of an analyzer, A_i, is incremented and decremented by the usual linear operators on reward and nonreward trials during which some analyzers are making strong predictions about the locus of reward. If no analyzer makes a strong correct prediction, then all analyzers change in the direction of their base values, B_i. The base values of analyzer strengths are the fixed, presumably native saliences for dimensions. These operate theoretically only when the learned components of attention are ineffective in predicting the cues that hide reward. Regression to position habits in difficult nonposition discriminations would be predicted by assigning position a relatively high B_i value.

These theoretical interactions of fixed and adjustable components of attention differ considerably from those of Lovejoy (1965), but the model of Sutherland

and Mackintosh (1971) could just as easily provide a deductive home for fixed stimulus preferences in humans. Both models were constructed for animal data but there is no reason that their theoretical mechanisms for fixed preferences could not be borrowed and incorporated in theories of human discriminative learning.

Need for New Theory

It is odd that Lovejoy (1968) made provision for a fixed component of dimensional salience but did not make one for native cue preferences. It is well known that rats (Lovejoy's subjects) have a strong native preference for approaching black rather than white cues. For original learning, Lovejoy's model could handle native cue preferences by assigning a relatively large value for $v_{i,1}$, the response strength of approach to the positive cue of the ith dimension on the first trial, but under the model once this value of v is changed by learning, the initial value is theoretically gone.

What is needed is a model that treats dimensional and cue preferences in a parallel fashion relating both preferences to fixed and adjustable components. For example, in Lovejoy's model the preference for cue 1 (v_1) could be related to an adjustable component, A_1, and a fixed component, F_1, by the equation

$$v_1 = \frac{A_1 + F_1}{1 + F_1 + F_2}$$

where F_2 is the fixed preference for cue 2. The corresponding value for cue 2 would be $(1 - A_1 + F_2)/(1 + F_1 + F_2)$.

A composite model of this kind might likely be better able to handle the array of data we have presented because in the section on novelty–familiarity the preference exhibited was for a cue (novelty) at least in part.

SUMMARY

Evidence has been presented with human subjects for some dimensional and cue preferences that may have some fixed properties. The structural feature status of these preferences is inferred from: (1) their common occurrence prior to training; (2) their occasional appearance despite countertraining; (3) regression to these preferences when opposed training is weakened by extinction, forgetting, or generalization decrement; and (4) developmental progressions not readily accounted for by training.

Preferences for four types of stimuli are reviewed: color–form, novelty–familiarity, position, and compound–components. The empirical grounds offered, although appreciable, are not so strong as to be considered uncontroversial, a conclusion reflected in the widely different positions adopted by theories of discriminative learning on the issue of fixed versus learnable stimulus preferences. Some suggestions were made for the construction of new theory including provision for both fixed and adjustable preferences at the level of both dimensions and cues.

REFERENCES

Atkinson, R. C., & Shiffrin, R. M. Human memory: A proposed system and its control processes. In K. W. Spence & J. T. Spence (Eds.), *The psychology of learning and motivation: Advances in research and theory* (Vol. 2). New York: Academic Press, 1969.

Barnes, T. R. Transfer of compounds and components in the discriminative learning of retardates. *Journal of Experimental Child Psychology*, 1978, *25*, 71–79.

Barnes, T. R., Cassidy, E. M., Ninfa, J. M., Yago, M. M., & Barnes, M. J. Transfer of compound and component solution modes. *Memory & Cognition*, 1978, *6*, 607–611.

Brian, C. R., & Goodenough, F. L. The relative potency of color and form perception at various ages. *Journal of Experimental Psychology*, 1929, *12*, 197–213.

Burns, B., Shepp, B. E., McDonough, D., & Wiener-Ehrlich, W. K. The relation between stimulus analyzability and perceived dimensional structure. In G. H. Bower (Ed.), *The psychology of learning and motivation* (Vol. 12). New York: Academic Press, 1978.

Cole, M. A developmental study of factors influencing discrimination transfer. *Journal of Experimental Child Psychology*, 1973, *16*, 126–147.

Corah, N. L. Color and form in children's perceptual behavior. *Perceptual and Motor Skills*, 1964, *18*, 313–316.

Cross, H. A., & Vaughter, R. M. The Moss–Harlow effect in preschool children as a function of age. *Journal of Experimental Child Psychology*, 1966, *4*, 280–284.

Descoudres, A. Couleur, forme, ou nombre? *Archives de Psychologie*, 1914, *14*, 305–341.

Fisher, M. A., Sperber, R., & Zeaman, D. Theory and data on developmental changes in novelty preference. *Journal of Experimental Child Psychology*, 1973, *15*, 509–520.

Fisher, M. A., & Zeaman, D. An attention–retention theory of retardate discrimination learning. In N. R. Ellis (Ed.), *International review of research in mental retardation* (Vol. 6). New York: Academic Press, 1973.

Garner, W. R. *The processing of information and structure.* Hillsdale, N.J.: Lawrence Erlbaum Associates, 1974.

Garner, W. R., & Felfoldy, G. L. Integrality of stimulus dimensions in various types of information processing. *Cognitive Psychology*, 1970, *1*, 225–241.

Gerjuoy, J. R., & Winters, J. J., Jr. Binary-choice responses of retardates, normal children, and college students to similar and dissimilar stimuli. *American Journal of Mental Deficiency*, 1965, *20*, 474–477.

Gerjuoy, J. R., & Winters, J. J., Jr. Response preference and choice-sequence preferences: Regression to alternation. *Psychonomic Science*, 1967, *7*, 413–414.

Gholson, B., Levine, M., & Phillips, S. Hypotheses, strategies, and stereotypes in discrimination learning. *Journal of Experimental Child Psychology*, 1972, *13*, 423–446.

Gibson, E. J. *Principles of perceptual learning and development.* New York: Appleton-Century-Crofts, 1969.

Grabbe, W., & Campione, J. C. A novelty interpretation of the Moss–Harlow effect in preschool children. *Child Development*, 1969, *40*, 1077–1084.

Greenfield, D. B. Novelty and familiarity as redundant cues in retardate discrimination learning. *Journal of Experimental Child Psychology*, 1976, *21*, 289–302.

Handel, S., & Imai, S. The free classification of analyzable and unanalyzable stimuli. *Perception & Psychophysics*, 1972, *12*, 108–116.

House, B. J. Attention to components or compounds as a factor in discrimination transfer performance. *Journal of Experimental Child Psychology*, 1979, *27*, 321–331.

House, B. J., & Zeaman, D. Miniature experiments in the discrimination learning of retardates. In L. P. Lipsitt & C. C. Spiker (Eds.), *Advances in child development and behavior* (Vol. 1). New York: Academic Press, 1963.

House, B. J., & Zeaman, D. Reward and nonreward in the discrimination learning of imbeciles. *Journal of Comparative and Physiological Psychology*, 1958, *51*, 614–618.

Kagan, J., & Lemkin, J. Form, color, and size in children's conceptual behavior. *Child Development*, 1961, *32*, 25–28.

Kendler, T. S., Basden, B. J., & Bruckner, J. B. Dimensional dominance and continuity theory. *Journal of Experimental Psychology*, 1970, *83*, 309–318.

Klahr, D., & Wallace, J. G. *Cognitive development: An information-processing view*. Hillsdale, N.J.: Lawrence Erlbaum Associates, 1976.

Lee, L. C. Concept utilization in preschool children. *Child Development*, 1965, *36*, 221–227.

Lockhead, G. R. Processing dimensional stimuli: A note. *Psychological Review*, 1972, 79, 410–419.

Lovejoy, E. *Attention in discrimination learning*. San Francisco: Holden-Day, 1968.

Medin, D. L. A theory of context in discrimination learning. In G. H. Bower (Ed.), *The psychology of learning and motivation* (Vol. 9). New York: Academic Press, 1972.

Moss, E., & Harlow, H. The role of reward in the discrimination learning of monkeys. *Journal of Comparative and Physiological Psychology*, 1947, *40*, 333–342.

Ress, F. C., & Levine, M. Einstellung during simple discrimination learning. *Psychonomic Science*, 1966, *4*, 77–78.

Shepp, B. E. From perceived similarity to dimensional structure: A new hypothesis about perceptual development. In E. Rosch & B. Lloyd (Eds.), *Cognition and categorization*. Hillsdale, N.J.: Lawrence Erlbaum Associates, 1978.

Shepp, B. E., Burns, B., & McDonough, D. The relation of stimulus structure for perceptual and cognitive development: Further tests of a separability hypothesis. In F. Wilkening & J. Becker (Eds.), *The integration of information by children*. Hillsdale, N.J.: Lawrence Erlbaum Associates, 1978.

Shepp, B. E., & Swartz, K. B. Selective attention and the processing of integral and nonintegral dimensions: A developmental study. *Journal of Experimental Child Psychology*, 1976, *22*, 73–85.

Smith, L. B. Importance of overall similarity of objects for adults' and children's classification. *Journal of Experimental Psychology: Human Perception and Performance*, 1981, *7*, 811–824.

Smith, L. B., & Kemler, D. G. Developmental trends in free classification: Evidence for a new conceptualization of perceptual development. *Journal of Experimental Child Psychology*, 1977, *24*, 279–298.

Spears, W. C. Assessment of visual preference and discrimination in the four month old infant. *Journal of Comparative and Physiological Psychology*, 1964, *57*, 381–386.

Spears, W. C. Visual preference in the four month old infant. *Psychonomic Science*, 1966, *4*, 237–238.

Spitz, H. H., Carroll, J. G., & Johnson, S. J. Hypothesis-testing from a limited set: An example of mentally retarded subjects outperforming college students. *American Journal of Mental Deficiency*, 1975, *79*, 736–741.

Suchman, R. G. Color–form preference, discriminative accuracy, and learning of deaf and hearing children. *Child Development*, 1966, *37*, 439–451.

Suchman, R. G., & Trabasso, T. Color and form preference in young children. *Journal of Experimental Child Psychology,* 1966, *3,* 177–187.

Sutherland, N. S., & Mackintosh, N. J. *Mechanisms of animal discrimination learning.* New York: Academic Press, 1971.

Tighe, T. J. Subproblem analysis of discrimination learning. In G. H. Bower (Ed.), *Psychology of learning and motivation* (Vol. 7). New York: Academic Press, 1973.

Tighe, T. J., Glick, J., & Cole, M. Subproblem analysis of discrimination shift learning. *Psychonomic Science,* 1971, *24,* 159–160.

Tighe, T. J., & Tighe, L. S. A perceptual view of conceptual development. In R. D. Walk & H. L. Pick (Eds.), *Perception and experience.* New York: Plenum Press, 1978.

Trabasso, T. R., & Bower, G. H. *Attention in learning: Theory and research.* New York: Wiley, 1968.

Ward, T. B. Separable and integral responding by adults and children to the dimensions of length and density. *Child Development,* 1980, *51,* 676–684.

Weir, M. W. Developmental changes in problem-solving strategies. *Psychological Review,* 1964, *71,* 473–490.

Wolff, J. L. Concept-shift and discrimination reversal learning in humans. *Psychological Bulletin,* 1967, *68,* 369–408.

Zeaman, D. The ubiquity of novelty–familiarity (habituation?) effects. In T. J. Tighe & R. N. Leaton (Eds.), *Habituation: Perspectives from child development, animal behavior, neurophysiology.* Hillsdale, N.J.: Lawrence Erlbaum Associates, 1976.

Zeaman, D., & House, B. J. The role of attention in retardate discrimination learning. In N. R. Ellis (Ed.), *Handbook of mental deficiency.* New York: McGraw-Hill, 1963.

Zeaman, D., & House, B. J. Interpretations of developmental trends in discriminative transfer effects. In A. D. Pick (Ed.), *Minnesota symposium on child psychology* (Vol. 8). Minneapolis, Minn: University of Minnesota Press, 1974.

Zeaman, D., & House, B. J. A review of attention theory. In N. R. Ellis (Ed.), *Handbook of mental deficiency, psychological theory and research* (2nd ed.). Hillsdale, N.J.: Lawrence Erlbaum Associates, 1979.

5 Labeling, Overtraining, and Levels of Function

Tracy S. Kendler
University of California, Santa Barbara

FOUR TIME SCALES

In an essay on "Time and Biology," J. B. S. Haldane wrote that every biological event can be considered against four different time scales; this observation also applies to psychological events. Most behavioral changes studied by experimental psychologists take place on a time scale that can be counted in minutes or hours. Eliciting these changes are the immediate neurological events that occur in milliseconds. The same psychological event may also be construed in terms of the life history of some organism, measured in months or years. Finally the same behavioral event can be described in terms of societal, or biological, evolutionary changes occurring over centuries or millenia. Thus the single behavioral event can be conceived as a psychological, neurological, developmental, or evolutionary phenomenon. By abstracting variables whose significant change takes place over the appropriate time scale and either ignoring or holding all the rest constant, we can treat an event on only one time plane. By implication the fullest description would, however, obtain from a theory that provides for the intersection of these time scales thereby allowing us to understand how the phenomenon evolved, how it develops ontogenetically, how it is affected by contextual variables, and what are the underlying neurological or physiological processes. There is no way to foresee whether one should wait until each level of analysis has made substantial progress before attempting such integration or whether there is a heuristic value in beginning to think in such terms at an earlier point. But there is some pressure to attempt such integration if one uses a programmatic, comparative–developmental–experimental approach, as I have, in the study of cognitive development. The products of this program are: (1)

129

some significant phylogenetic continuities and discontinuities; (2) some quantifiable human developmental changes, stable enough to be referred to as laws; (3) some experimentally produced changes; and (4) an evolving theoretical framework designed to systematize these and other pertinent phenomena. This evolving theory currently incorporates the different time scales in the following way. First the theory refers to the immediate events that occur between the reception of information and the behavioral output. These events are modeled after neurological processes in the central nervous system. "To be modeled after" means here that the CNS provides a way of representing these hypothetical, unobservable, mediating events and also some conceptions of how these events might be related. It is not, strictly speaking, a neurological theory, although an attempt has been made to theorize in ways that are compatible with what little is known about how the brain mediates cognition. Second, to account for phylogenetic differences, the theory assumes that different levels of function have evolved during the course of phylogenesis that result in qualitative behavioral differences. Third, to account for human ontogenetic change, the hypothetical functional levels are assumed to mature at different rates, roughly paralleling the order of phylogenetic development. Finally, to account for the relatively short-term laboratory-produced effects on behavior, the activity in these hypothetical levels of function is assumed to be responsive to extrinsic, contextual effects.

A LEVELS-OF-FUNCTION THEORY

This theory is a skeletal account of the development of some hypothetical processes that mediate between the input of the information and the output of the response under a particular set of experimental situations. In an earlier formulation (Kendler & Kendler, 1962) this development was described as a transition from single link (S–R) to mediated (S–r–s–R) behavior. In single-link behavior, the response was considered to be under the relatively direct control of the stimulus, whereas in mediated behavior the locus of control moved to a covert, symbolic representation of the stimulus produced by the individual. In the levels-of-function theory, the term *mediation* is used in a different sense, namely to refer to all the internal events that intervene between the input of the information and the output of the response. This mediating system is analyzed into two major components based, in part, on Luria's (1973) analysis of the principal functional units of the brain. There is the affective or encoding component that functions to obtain, process, and store information, and the behavioral regulation component that functions to generate and control behavior. These components, which are modeled after the sensory and motor components of the nervous system, are assumed to be organized into levels of function. As initially proposed by Hughlings Jackson (Lassek, 1970), these levels emerged gradually during the evolution of homo sapiens and follow at least a grossly similar course during the development of the individual human. In line with the general principles laid down by Jackson, the lower level is the simplest, most automatic, and fixed; the higher level is more complex, voluntary, and plastic.

These notions of components and levels were used to formulate a theory of the processes underlying certain developmental changes in discriminative learning and transfer (Kendler, 1979a) that will be elaborated here. This very general formulation, as illustrated in Fig. 5.1, represents a hypothetical, central processing system that mediates between the reception of the stimulus input and the ensuing behavioral output. The encoding component processes the information and the behavioral regulation component monitors the motoric output. The structures underlying the two component processes are organized into levels that mature at different rates. As in the central nervous system, the higher levels mature at a slower rate than the lower levels and, to some extent, refine and duplicate their functions. Although most theories of CNS functioning propose three levels of functioning only the two highest levels are represented in this scheme because it is limited to constructs that are coordinated with the experimental operations to be detailed presently. None of these measure the simple reflexive behavior usually associated with the lowest level; therefore it is excluded from present consideration.

Each level is construed to operate in a different mode. The lower level of the encoding component operates in a nonselective mode that processes all the registered stimulus information, whereas the higher level acts in a selective mode that abstracts only the relevant information for further processing. In the behavioral regulation component the lower level operates in an incremental learning mode that regulates the gradual increase and decrease in the tendency of the respective encoded outputs to evoke approach or avoidance responses as a function of the reinforcement contingencies. The higher level operates in a rational,

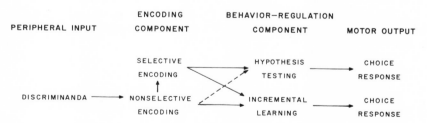

FIG. 5.1.   A schematic diagram of the hypothetical central processing systems that mediate discrimination learning and transfer behavior. There are two major components, encoding and behavior–regulation; each component is differentiated into two levels that operate in different modes. Each module is capable of both receiving and generating signals, but this capability depends in part on the developmental status of the organism. The arrows trace the paths this activation may take in the fully mature human (Kendler, T. S., 1979a.)

problem-solving mode that successively tests for the response, rule, or strategy that yields a correct solution. Each mode constitutes a process that can be activated by an input signal and is itself capable of generating an output signal. The potential paths taken by the signals in the mature human adult are illustrated in Fig. 5.1. The system may be activated by an input that originates in the peripheral reception of the discriminanda that goes first to the lower level of the central-encoding component, where all the imput is processed. The output may take two paths, to the selective-encoding mode or to the incremental-learning mode or to both. The output from the selective-encoding module may also take two paths, to the hypothesis-testing module or to the incremental-learning module or to both. Each of the behavior-regulation modules, if activated, generates a signal that may eventuate in an overt response.

As in the central nervous system, all levels can function in parallel providing that their effects are compatible. If the effect, say on behavioral outcome, is incompatible, then the stronger signal will prevail. The strength of the signal generated by any of these processes is assumed to depend on the ontogenetic and phylogenetic status of the organism as well as on the eliciting conditions. All the underlying systems are assumed to develop gradually within the individual organism, but in the modal environment the structures that underlie the nonselective-encoding and the incremental-learning modules are assumed to begin and culminate their development earlier than those subserving the selective-encoding and the hypothesis-testing modules. The developmental status of these structures is presumably jointly determined by genetic preprograming and relatively long-term environmental conditions.

The theory was primarily designed to deal with the time frames that encompass ontogenetic and evolutionary changes. This chapter discusses its usefulness for dealing with experimentally manipulated changes in discrimative learning and transfer that take place in the much shorter time contexts wherein experimental manipulations are feasible. At the same time the information engendered by some previously unpublished results is used to flesh out the skeletal framework. Before the research is presented, the relationship of the theory to other conceptions of discrimination learning is described.

LEVELS OF ENCODING AND THE
CONTINUITY–NONCONTINUITY CONTROVERSY

Discriminative learning was first used by Lashley (1929) to measure the sensory discriminative capacity of animals. This research often dealt with the visual modality and usually consisted of arranging the stimuli to be discriminated side by side, for easy comparison. If one wanted, for instance, to test a rat's capacity to discriminate form, the animal could be shown, say, a circle and a triangle. One of the forms (e.g., the circle) would be baited with hidden food and the animal would be required to learn to choose the baited circle in preference to the unbaited triangle. Each choice constituted a trial; these trials were repeated as often as required to find out whether the animal could learn to choose the baited stimulus consistently. If the proper controls are used, such learning is evidence of the capacity to discriminate between those stimuli. An almost incidental finding of this line of research was that, although rats could make certain visual discriminations, they often required many trials before they learned to choose the correct stimulus consistently. Because this phenomenon had obvious implications for learned adaptations in the natural environment, an interest in the learning process, per se, began to occupy central stage.

One of the early, confirmed observations Lashley (1929) made about the discriminative learning behavior of rats is that they usually begin with a position bias. At the outset of learning, they are likely to respond consistently to the right, consistently to the left, or to alternate positions regardless of where the correct visual discriminandum is placed. To control for the possibility that the animals would learn to respond to position, which is relatively easy for them, rather than to the visual properties of the discriminanda, it is standard procedure to vary the position of the discriminanda randomly from trial to trial in all visual discriminative-learning research. Nevertheless, early position bias is typical. (Incidentally, position bias is also typical of young children.)

On the basis of these observations, Lashley made some conjectures about the nature of discriminative learning in rats that were to have a telling impact. He suggested, for one thing, that such learning consists of a series of attempted solutions (1929).

> responses to position, to alternation, or to cues from the experimenter's movements usually precede the reaction to (the correct cue) and represent attempted solutions that are within the rat's customary range of activity . . . such behavior . . . suggests that the actual association is formed very quickly and that both the practice preceding and the errors following are irrelevant to the actual formation of the association [p. 135].

Lashley (1938) also proposed that the rat attends selectively to one stimulus at a time.

> A definite attribute of the stimulus is "abstracted" and forms the basis of the reaction; other attributes are either not sensed at all or are disregarded. So long as the effective attribute is present, the reaction is elicited as an all-or-none function of the attributes. Other characteristics may be radically changed without affecting the reaction [p. 81].

Spurred by Lashley's conception, Krechevsky (1932) performed a series of visual discriminative learning experiments with the white rat that confirmed the tendency for the animals' presolution behavior to be systematic rather than random. Krechevsky dubbed these systematic responses as "hypotheses" and, following Lashley, inferred that the rat learns by attempting various solutions and giving them up when they don't work until he finally hits upon the correct one. Such evidence was important at the time because it was taken as invalidating the so-called "trial-and-error" theories of learning. The Lashley–Krechevsky conceptions became known as the noncontinuity theory.

In 1936 Spence came to the rescue of trial-and-error learning theory by first pointing out that the appellation was, itself, misleading. These theories would be better described as incremental, associative, learning theories in that they supposed that associations were gradually strengthened as a function of practice. Systematic presolution behaviors are entirely consistent with such theories because they would expect animals to perform systematically in accordance with either innate predispositions or previous learning. More important, Spence proceeded to demonstrate precisely how an incremental theory that assumed neither the capacity to abstract nor the ability to test successive hypotheses could nevertheless account for the systematic presolution and postsolution behavior characteristic of discriminative learning in the rat. The essential notions in this seminal theory begin with observing that in a discriminative-learning problem the subject is presented discriminanda composed of both relevant and irrelevant cues. In the example we have been using, form (circle versus triangle) is relevant, and position (left versus right) is irrelevant. For the relevant cues, response to one cue (e.g., circle) is always rewarded whereas response to the other relevant cue (e.g., triangle) is never rewarded. Relevance is thus defined with respect to the reinforcement contingencies. Spence's theory assumed that on every rewarded trial the tendency to respond to each of the cues that compose the correct discriminandum is increased in some measure. On every nonrewarded trial these tendencies are decreased. The implication is that every training trial increases the differential tendency to choose the correct cue, because it either increases the approach tendency to the correct cue or decreases the approach tendency to the incorrect cue. For this reason Spence's theory was referred to as the continuity theory of discriminative learning. Because continuity theory did *not* assume that the rat attended selectively, the tendencies to respond to the irrelevant cues also increase whenever they are compounded with the correct cue and decrease whenever they are compounded with the incorrect cue.

A second basic assumption is that the strength of the tendency for a given discriminandum to evoke the choice response will be a function of the sum of the approach tendencies of its component cues. The third assumption is that the animal will choose the discriminandum that evokes the greatest approach tendency. A detailed review of this theory and its predictive capacity is beyond our present scope, but a sense of how it would work can be gleaned by applying it to our example.

Suppose we imagine a highly simplified situation wherein a hypothetical rat begins learning with a strong left-going tendency, a weaker right-going tendency, and very weak tendencies to approach either circles or triangles. Early in training this animal would be expected to continue for a number of trials to choose the discriminandum on the left, be it a circle or a triangle. How long this behavior would persist should depend on how strong the initial left-going tendency is. Gradually this tendency to go left would, however, be weakened because it would decrease more on nonrewarded trials than it would gain on rewarded trials, until it would equal in magnitude the right-going tendency. Meanwhile every trial should either increase the tendency to choose *circles* or decrease the tendency to choose *triangles* depending on which one was on the left, until ultimately the correct cue, *circle,* gains ascendancy. When this occurs, the aggregate tendencies for the discriminanda that contain the circle, be it on the left or right, would be the strongest and the animal would therefore show a systematic tendency to make the correct response.

Spence was well aware that a complete account of animal discrimination learning would require a much more complex theory, but he did succeed in demonstrating that it was not at all necessary to ascribe to the animal the intellectual powers attributed to it by noncontinuity theory. In so doing he produced a nonselective, incremental learning theory that not only supplied mechanisms that accounted for the behavior of the rat but also generated testable predictions, several of which were tested and confirmed. The most pertinent of these predictions for us was that, if the reinforcement contingencies of the cue stimuli are reversed before the animal is responding to the correct stimulus more often than chance, a greater number of trials will be required to learn the reversed problem than would have been necessary for the original problem. This prediction, translated in terms of our example, would be that if one reversed the reward contingencies so that the triangle became the correct cue while the animal was still going to the left consistently, it would require more trials to reach criterion than an animal that was maintained on the same reward pattern. This prediction effectively differentiated between continuity and noncontinuity theory, because a theory that assumes the animal is selectively attending to one cue or hypothesis at a time should predict that it is not learning anything about the other cues in the stimulus complex. This prediction was tested with rats in a number of studies and learning was, for the most part, found to be slower among the reversed than among nonreversed animals (Deese & Hulse, 1967; Riley, 1968). The rationale and the experimental procedure used in the present research is derived from this background.

While noncontinuity theory was an anthropomorphic conception intended to apply across species and ages, continuity theory had a more comparative–developmental perspective in that it was limited to what Spence referred to as "nonarticulate organisms," which included infrahuman animals and preverbal humans. He reasoned that in the case of a verbal organism, behavior in discriminative situations becomes cued to some extent to words that refer to the abstracted features of the discriminanda. Because, in the case of the human adult, verbal processes presumably dominate behavior, selective encoding should occur. This hypothesis was tested and confirmed by Spence's student, Kuenne (1946), in a transposition experiment.

In the 1950s, Kendler and Kendler began a series of investigations, using a reversal-shift paradigm to test this hypothesis further and to implement the rather vague conceptions about the differences between "verbal" and "preverbal" organisms. Before describing this research a quick comment on the current status of the theoretical controversy is in order. The original "strong" form of noncontinuity theory held that rats, and presumably organisms in general, attend selectively to one cue at a time and that learning consists of testing a succession of hypotheses about which cue is associated with reward until the correct one is reached. Such a theory has been shown convincingly to apply to adult humans in discrimination or concept-learning experiments (Kendler, 1979a; Levine, 1966; Trabasso & Bower, 1968). With regard to animals and young children the issue is still moot (Riley & Leith, 1976) but, although there are influential advocates of this theory on the current scene, it is fair to say that the strong version has been replaced with weaker ones. For one thing, the selective-attention and hypothesis-testing notions have been segregated so that some current theorists, although maintaining the need for a selective-attention mechanism agree that, for infrahuman organisms (Sutherland & Mackintosh, 1971) and for human retardates (Fisher & Zeaman, 1973), discriminative learning is incremental. For another, these selective-attention theorists now agree that the notion that animals attend to only one dimension at a time is not consistent with the evidence. For instance, without abandoning the notion of selective attention, Zeaman and House replaced their original "single-look" (1963) model that assumed attention to one dimension at a time with a "multiple-look" model that assumed the organism can attend to several dimensions simultaneously (Fisher & Zeaman, 1973). In fact, Tighe, Glick, and Cole (1971); Tighe and Tighe (1972); and Medin (1973) have demonstrated that the assumption that some infrahuman organisms attend selectively according to either single-look or multiple-look versions of selective-attention theory, is inconsistent with evidence. Therefore Zeaman and House (1974) further diluted the conception of selective attention by assuming that subjects can selectively attend to the compound, per se, as well as to the dimensions and that the tendency to respond to compounds is stronger than the tendency to attend to dimensions in infrahuman animals and young children.

The levels theory takes a further step toward resolving the continuity–noncontinuity controversy by proposing that the lower level operates in accordance with noncontinuity principles and the higher level in accordance with continuity principles. The research to be described was intended on the one hand to provide new tests of the validity of this proposition and on the other to provide additional data to fill in more details of the theory. Behavior in a discriminative-learning problem that employs a variant of the reversal–nonreversal shift procedure is used to determine which level of functioning is controlling the subject's choice behavior. The assumption underlying this procedure is that the two levels can lead to incompatible behavioral outcomes and when this happens, the mode that generates the strongest signal will prevail. The degree to which one or the other prevails provides a measure of the relative strength of the signal it produces.

The experimental procedure consists of presenting the individual with a discriminative problem that can be solved at either level. After solution is attained, a transfer test is presented that pits the two levels against each other, followed by a test series that indicates which level prevailed. The particular variant of this procedure used in the present research is illustrated in Fig. 5.2. It consists of three phases: the initial discrimination, the shift discrimination, and the test series. In each phase the discriminanda differ simultaneously on two visual dimensions, size and form. For a given subject, one of these dimensions is made relevant and the other irrelevant to the reinforcement contingencies. In the illustrative example, regardless of which pair is presented or which position the discriminanda occupy, *big* is correct and *small* is incorrect; therefore size is relevant and form irrelevant. When the individual has made 10 successive correct choices on the initial discrimination, the shift discrimination is initiated without any ostensible break in the procedure. During this phase only one pair of discriminanda are presented and the reinforcement contingencies are reversed. As a

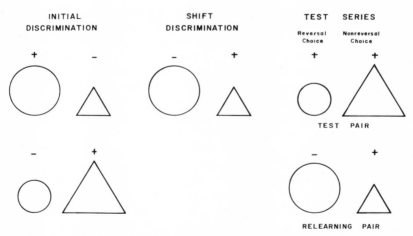

FIG. 5.2.   An illustration of the three phases of the optional shift task. In the initial discrimination each pair of stimulus compounds is presented one at a time in a prearranged alternating sequence. In the shift discrimination only one pair of stimulus compounds is presented and the reinforcement is reversed. In the test series both pairs of stimulus compounds are presented, one at a time, in the same sequence as the original discrimination, but any choice on the test pair is reinforced. Throughout the task the position of the stimulus compounds, left or right, is randomly alternated (Kendler, T. S., 1979a.)

result, both dimensions become relevant and redundant and to reach criterion in this phase the subject must make a shift. In our example, *small triangle* becomes correct and *large circle* becomes incorrect.

When the subject makes 10 successive correct choices on the shift discrimination, the test series is initiated also with no ostensible break. This series differs from the shift discrimination only in that a series of 10 opposed-cues test trials are randomly inserted between an approximately equal number of retraining trials. The purpose of the test trials is to determine which encoding mode prevailed. If the subject chooses the small circle eight or more times, the selective mode is implicated because the subject has made a reversal shift within the relevant dimension. Such a subject, in effect, goes through the entire test series choosing *small* regardless of whether it is compounded with circle or triangle. We infer from this pattern of behavior that the subject learned the initial discrimination by selectively encoding the relevant dimension and that he or she, furthermore, maintained this selective control during the shift discrimination and test series even though it required shifting his or her overt choices. Reversal shifting is typical of human adults (Buss, 1956; Kendler, 1979a; Kendler & D'Amato, 1955).

On the other hand, if the subject responds to the test trials either by choosing the *large triangle* consistently (eight or more times) or by responding inconsistently, sometimes choosing the *large triangle* and other times the *small circle,* while continuing to respond correctly to the relearning pair, we may infer that the behavior is controlled by the nonselective mode. A subject who is controlled by this mode should reach criterion on the initial discrimination when the tendency to choose *large* is strong relative to the tendency to choose *small* because the former has been reinforced consistently and the latter has never been reinforced. The tendency to choose *circle* and *triangle* should be of middling and approximately equal strength because they were each reinforced on half of the trials. During the shift discrimination, when the reinforcement contingencies are reversed, the necessary differential tendency in favor of *triangle* over *circle* should be reached more rapidly than the differential in favor of *small* over *large* because the latter is the opposite of what was learned in the initial discrimination. When the relevant and irrelevant cues are pitted against each other in the test series, either the initially irrelevant cue, *triangle,* should prevail or both sets of cues should share control. In the former instance the subject should choose *triangle* consistently regardless of whether it is compounded with *large* or with *small.* This pattern of behavior is referred to as an extradimensional shift. In the latter instance where both *small* and *triangle* are equally effective, the subject should respond inconsistently to the test pair, sometimes choosing the *small* circle and sometimes the large *triangle.* As shown in more explicit detail elsewhere (Kendler, 1971), either an extradimensional or an inconsistent shift is in keeping with nonselective encoding. For that reason these two patterns of behavior are combined into one category that will hereafter be referred to as nonreversal shifts. If the experiment is properly controlled, nonreversal shifts are characteristic of rats regardless of whether they are overtrained (Sutherland & Mackintosh, 1966; Tighe & Tighe, 1966). One necessary control is that the two dimensions be of approximately equal salience (Kendler, 1971). The present research uses the particular constellation of stimuli illustrated in Fig. 5.2 because they are as close as we have come to equal salience for human subjects.

Thus we may infer from whether the subject makes a reversal or nonreversal shift which mode prevails at the time of testing, allowing, of course, for some margin of error. When humans between 3 years of age and young adulthood are presented with this task, in a cross-sectional design, the proportion of subjects who make reversal shifts increases as a logarithmic function of age. There is a considerable array of evidence to support the hypothesis that this developmental function represents a gradual, longitudinal increase in the mean probability of making a reversal shift (Kendler, 1979b). This longitudinal increase is, in turn, interpreted as reflecting a gradual developmental increase in the relative strength of the signal generated by the selective-encoding module.

LEVELS OF BEHAVIORAL REGULATION AND THE CONTINUITY–NONCONTINUITY CONTROVERSY

Although it was not originally designed to do so, the optional shift also allows us to determine whether learning occurs in an incremental or hypothesis-testing mode. To put this measure into perspective we need once again to delve briefly into a little history. Although Spence and his collaborators won the first round in the continuity–noncontinuity controversy, it was by no means the end of the match. By the 1950s, interest in human behavior had revived, experimental tasks became more complex, explanations became more rigorous and mathematical, and the way was paved for a new spate of more sophisticated hypothesis-testing theories. One of these theories (Levine, 1959) was designed to account for infrahuman primate discriminative learning-set. Discriminative learning-set is a phenomenon discovered by Harlow (1949) who found that if monkeys are presented with a long series of 6 or 12 trial-discriminative problems over a period of months, each problem consisting of different discriminants, the result is a gradual increase in the probability that they will solve the problem by the second trial. A similar phenomenon has been demonstrated in children (Eimas, 1969; Gholson, Levine, & Philipps, 1972). Levine proposed to explain learning-set by assuming that these subjects formed hypotheses (*H*'s), defined as a sequence of responses, which may, like other responses, be differentially reinforced. He listed nine possible *H*'s that were pertinent to discrimination-learning problems and devised a method for determining which *H* was controlling choice behavior. The following four *H*'s will serve to illustrate the theory: (1) a position preference H defined as a sequence of responses to one side; (2) a stimulus preference H defined as a sequence of responses to one of the stimuli; (3) a win–stay lose–shift H with respect to position defined as a sequence of responses to the position rewarded on the previous trial; and (4) a win–stay lose–shift H with respect to the stimulus defined as a sequence of responses to the stimulus that was correct on the preceding trial. The last H described would lead to problem solution in the typical discriminative learning-set task and therefore the H that is acquired in the course of a learning-set experiment.

In this way Levine succeeded in making learning-set amenable to conventional incremental learning theory, but what was learned could more properly be considered to be a guiding strategy or rule than a specific choice response. It is therefore appropriate that shortly after Levine (1963) reformulated his theory in a way that has particular bearing on the mediational development formulation. He shifted the focus of his research to human adults and changed his conception of H's from directly observable response patterns to mediating processes of which these patterns are a manifestation.

At the same time Levine differentiated two distinctly different H's, response-set H's and prediction H's. Response-set H's, exemplified by a set to repeatedly choose the same stimulus or position, were conceived to be automatic response tendencies that are insensitive to feedback. Prediction H's, exemplified by the prediction that one of the stimuli is correct and will repeat, was conceived of as a problem-solving process that attempts to predict events and produces behavioral patterns in conformity with the prediction. The latter Hs were assumed to be highly sensitive to feedback. Levine noted that response-sets are widespread among rats (Krechevsky, 1932), monkeys (Harlow, 1950; Levine, 1959), and chimpanzees (Schusterman, 1961). Later research, using the blank trial procedure that Levine developed for identifying H's, showed that response-sets were also prevalent in young children (Gholson et al., 1972). On the other hand, as Levine showed, adult humans, specifically college students, showed only prediction H's, a finding that has since been widely replicated.

These two kinds of H's, with a slight modification, could be the ideological forerunner of the two levels of behavioral regulation in the levels theory. The prediction H's are analogous to the higher-level, hypothesis-testing mode. If the response-set H's could be regarded as habit tendencies rather than as hypotheses and if they could be regarded as only relatively insensitive to feedback in the sense that it may take many trials for the reinforcement effects to be gradually manifested, they could be analogous to the lower-level, incremental mode. The phylogenetic and ontogenetic differences with respect to these two behaviors would be consonant with the hypothesis that the higher-level function develops more slowly than the lower level.

The more directly relevant support, however, entailed the recent use of the optional shift procedure to infer which mode, incremental or hypothesis testing, controls choice behavior. It would be well to remind the reader that in the optional shift procedure the test phase is preceded by the initial discrmination that must be learned to criterion. There is no simple way to infer how the initial discrimination was learned but if, on the shift discrimination a subject's first correct choice is also the first trial of his or her criterion run, then we may infer that he or she is using a win–stay strategy and, therefore, behaving in conformity with *H* theory (Kendler, 1979a). On the other hand when a subject continues to make wrong choices after the first correct choice he or she is behaving in conformity with incremental theory because the shift from the initially correct choice (e.g., *large*) to the newly correct choice (e.g., *small circle*) should in principle be achieved gradually rather than abruptly.

The need to differentiate between the encoding and the behavioral regulation modes arose from the incidental discovery of a highly replicable and systematic ontogenetic increase in the efficiency with which both the original and shift discriminations were learned. A similar ontogenetic change in monkeys has been reported by Harlow (1971), with prior experience controlled. To explain this increase, Kendler (1979a) hypothesized that it was due to an increasing tendency over age for problem solution to be controlled by the *H* mode. The following series of results were presented in support of this hypothesis: (1) The pattern of errors produced by the adults was consistent with *H* theory. (2) The learning curves of young children and slow learners showed a gradual decrease in errors prior to the last error that is inconsistent with *H* theory and consistent with incremental-learning theory. (3) The proportion of subjects who manifested a win–stay *H* with respect to the stimulus increased monotonically over age. (4) The population could be empirically dichotomized into two groups, *H* testers who learned relatively rapidly and incremental learners who learned relatively slowly.

Because the optional shift task provided separate measures for each of the encoding and behavioral regulation components, it was possible to determine whether they are separable by determining whether subjects who encoded selectively (made reversal shifts) invariably hypothesis-tested (win–stayed) and conversely whether subjects who encoded nonselectively (made nonreversal shifts) invariably learned incrementally (did not win–stay), allowing of course for some margin of error. When the data were reanalyzed from this point of view, it was found that the appropriate interpretation depended on including the entire age scale. For if we looked only at the lowest and highest ends, it would appear that these components were functionally inseparable because the great majority of the 3- to 4-year-olds encoded nonselectively and learned incrementally, whereas almost all the adults encoded selectively and *H*-tested. However, among the children between the two ends of the tested age scale, there was a substantial proportion who encoded selectively but learned incrementally, large and reliable enough to establish that we are dealing with separable modules.

EXTRINSIC EFFECTS

Competence–Performance Distinction

The competence–performance distinction derives from the supposition that behavior is a joint function of the pertinent, impinging, extrinsic circumstances and the germane, enduring, intrinsic characteristics of the organism. Although extrinsic and intrinsic factors are difficult to define, typical instances are easily identified. Thus, for discriminative learning and transfer, the number of training trials, the salience of the relevant dimension, and the instruction to label the cues constitute relatively changeable, pertinent, extrinsic conditions, whereas species membership, age, and individual differences are relatively stable, germane, intrinsic characteristics. Intrinsic characteristics may be directly observable, like species membership, or they may take the form of indirectly defined theoretical constructs, like competence, which is of central concern in the analysis of cognitive development. Because competence is a theoretical construct that is inferred from behavior, it necessarily requires some extrinsic context. Because context also affects behavior, a competence–performance distinction is implied that parallels the learning–performance and phenotype–genotype distinctions.

Competence is a theoretical construct whose properties are defined in terms of a nomological network and whose connections to behavior are as indirect as the level of abstraction it occupies in this network. In the levels theory, competence refers to a characteristic degree of activity in a given module under some stipulated set of conditions. One may speak therefore of competence with respect to nonselective encoding or to selective encoding. Likewise one may speak of competence at incremental learning or at hypothesis testing. Whether a given module is activated, and in what degree, is assumed to be a joint function of intrinsic competence and extrinsic context.

The present research investigated how two extrinsic variables, labeling and overtraining, interact with each other and with an intrinsic variable, age, to determine the degree of activity in the selective encoding module, as measured by the probability of reversing in the test phase of the optional shift procedure. Overtraining and labeling were selected for investigation because they have each been critical for a different conception of the processes underlying selective encoding and for how these processes change developmentally. The strategy was to use the experimental results to clarify the issues that distinguish these two conceptions.

Method

Design.   There were four independent experimental groups, each composed of five age levels between 4 and approximately 18 years of age. One group served as a standard and was, therefore, neither overtrained nor required to use verbal labels. The training of each of the other groups differed from the standard group's only on the initial discrimination and in only the following ways: On the initial discrimination the overtrained group was given 30 overtraining trials, the label group was required to label the relevant cue before each choice, and the overtrained–label group was given 30 overtraining trials and required to label the relevant cue. The dependent variables were the proportion of subjects at the various age levels who made a reversal shift and who win-stayed in the shift discrimination.

Subjects.   The 768 subjects, drawn from nursery and elementary schools in Goleta, California, and from the University, are described in Table 5.1. The subjects within an age level were randomly assigned to the counterbalanced conditions and to the control, overtraining, and label conditions but not to the overtrained label conditons because it was not introduced until after some of the subjects in the other condition were run. In order to test for the effects of sampling, 128 children in the kindergarten level were randomly assigned to each of the four conditions.

Apparatus.   The discriminanda, projected onto a pair of display panels by preprogramed electronic readouts, consisted of a pair of geometric amber figures on a black background that, as illustrated in Fig. 5.1, always differed in size and form. The diameter of the small and large circles were 3.02 and 4.78 cm. The bases of the small and large triangles were 3.33 and 5.78 cm; their altitudes were 2.86 and 5.08 cm. A trial was initiated with the projection of the stimuli when the subject touched a start panel located between and below the two windows. The trial was terminated when the subject pressed one of the display panels thereby activating a microswitch that shut off the readouts. If the subject pressed the panel on which the correct discriminandum was displayed, a marble was automatically released into a trough and placed in a marble board by the subject. The sequencing was arranged so that the correct discriminandum appeared equally often in each panel. A modified correction procedure was used in which the sequence advanced only after a correct response. The apparatus and procedure are described in greater detail in Kendler and Kendler, 1970.

Procedure.   The three phases of the procedure are illustrated in Fig. 5.2. In the initial discrimination the two pairs of stimuli were presented, one pair at a time, in a preprogrammed alternating sequence. For a given subject, one value on one of the dimensions was correct. If, as in our example, *large* was correct, the subject was rewarded with a marble only when he chose the larger of the two discriminanda regardless of whether it was a circle or a triangle. In this example, size is the relevant dimension. The four possible values assigned as correct were counterbalanced. Training was continued until the criterion of 10 successive correct trials was attained, after which the shift discrimination began with no

TABLE 5.1
Distribution of Subjects

	Standard Group				Label Group			
	No.	CA		PPVT IQ		No.	CA		PPVT IQ	

Educational Level	No.	M	Range	M	S.D.	No.	M	Range	M	S.D.
Nursery School	32	4.0	3.3–4.9	107.4	.99	32	4.1	3.1–4.9	109.3	1.21
Kindergarten	64	5.7	5.3–6.3	106.9	.78	48	5.6	5.0–6.3	105.8	1.20
Second Grade	32	7.9	7.1–8.6	108.7	1.37	32	7.8	7.3–8.6	102.5	1.08
Sixth Grade	32	11.8	11.0–13.7	111.9	1.34	32	11.7	11–12.3	112.8	1.00
College[a]	32	18	—	—	—	32	18	—	—	—

	Overtrained Group				Overtrained–Label Group			

Educational Level	No.	M	Range	M	S.D.	No.	M	Range	M	S.D.
Nursery School	32	4.0	3.1–4.9	111.6	1.01	32	4.0	2.9–4.9	105.2	1.50
Kindergarten	48	5.7	5.0–6.6	108.4	.88	48	5.6	4.9–6.5	—	—
Second Grade	32	7.8	7.2–8.6	110.5	1.21	48	7.9	7.2–8.9	—	—
Sixth Grade	32	11.6	10.3–12.3	119.4	1.34	48	11.9	11.3–13.3		
College	32	18	—	—	—	48	18	—	—	—

[a]The college students were arbitrarily assigned a mean CA of 18 years as representative of the upper limit of development.

ostensible break in the procedure. Only one pair of stimuli was presented in this phase, rendering both dimensions relevant and redundant, but the reinforcement was reversed so that in our example *small triangle* was now correct. Attainment of criterion on the shift discrimination was followed by the test series that consisted essentially of a continuation of the shift discrimination but with 10 opposed-cues test trials interspersed. On the test trials either choice was rewarded but the subject was obliged to choose between the previously incorrect cue on the relevant dimension (e.g., *small*), which was classified as a reversal choice, and the previously irrelevant cue (e.g., triangle), which was an extra-dimensional choice. If a subject made 8 or more reversal choices on the 10 test trials, he was considered to have made a reversal shift within the relevant dimension.

The standard group was presented with the basic procedure described here. Each of the other experimental groups varied only in the following ways: (1) The label group was instructed on the second trial of the initial discrimination to tell the experimenter, prior to each choice, which he or she thought would make the marble drop, the _____ or the _____ one, the labels referring to the relevant cues such as "big" or "small." (2) The overtrained group was given 30 over-training trials on the initial discrimination. (3) The overtrained label group was given the same instructions as the label group and the same overtraining as the overtrained group.

RESULTS AND DISCUSSION: ENCODING MODULE

To simplify the presentation, the results are divided into two sections: encoding and problem solving. Whenever feasible the relationship between age and behavior—the developmental function—is described mathematically in order to increase precision, render the results easier to grasp at a glance, and permit comparisons that would otherwise be clumsy or impossible.

The dependent variable in this section is the proportion of subjects who reversed, which is interpreted as reflecting the consistency or probability that the selective level of encoding prevailed. Figure 5.3 presents the proportion of

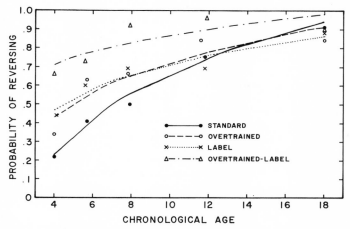

FIG. 5.3. The fitted logarithmic functions and the obtained proportions of subjects who made reversal shifts in each experimental condition.

reversers at each age level under each experimental condition. To arrive at this figure the results of each experimental group were fitted to a simple logarithmic function of the form $y = a + b \ln x$ where y is the proportion of subjects who made reversal shifts, $\ln x$ is the natural logarithm of age, a is the fitted intercept parameter, and b is the fitted slope parameter. In line with the theoretical formulation proposed at the outset, y is conceived to estimate the mean *probability* that a subject selected at random from a given age level will reverse.

Table 5.2 presents the fitted parameters of each function along with its statistical evaluation. For these evaluations the mean ages were converted to logs thereby transforming the log functions into linear functions. This transformation permitted the use of a chi-square (χ^2) test that partitions the total variance within each condition into a linear component (χ^2_{lin}) and a remainder component (χ^2_{rem}) due to departure from linearity (Maxwell, 1961). A significant linear component indicates a reliable age trend; a nonsignificant remainder indicates that the logarithmic form of the function is a tenable hypothesis. Thus from the first column of chi-squares and their corresponding p's, we may infer that under every condition there is a highly reliable, monotonic, developmental trend. From the last column of chi-squares and their corresponding p's, we may infer that all functions produced acceptable fits.

Standard Condition

Because subjects in this condition were trained to criterion with no instructions to label, their behavior provided a standard against which to evaluate the effects of the extrinsic variables. From the first row of Table 5.2 we glean that in this condition there is a highly reliable monotonic, developmental trend to which the log function provides an excellent fit, accounting for 99% of the variance.

Apparently at all ages tested both the selective and nonselective encoding modules are functional in some degree but there is a quantitative increase over age in the probability that the selective mode will prevail due, presumably, to the

TABLE 5.2
Fitted Parameters for Each Experimental Condition and the Related
Statistical Evaluations

Experimental Condition	Parameters		Chi-Square				
	Slope	Intercept	$\chi^2_{(1\ \text{in})}$ $(1\ df)$	p	$\chi^2_{(\text{rem})}$ $(3\ df)$	p	r^2
Standard	0.46	−0.42	40.53	<.001	0.38	>.90	.99
Overtrained	0.32	−0.01	20.18	<.001	3.94	>.25	.84
Label	0.26	+0.11	12.86	<.001	1.51	>.50	.91
Overtrained–Label	0.18	+0.45	13.42	<.001	7.60	>.05	.69
Marginal	0.31	+0.03	76.98	<.001	3.29	>.25	.96

slower rate at which the higher level of functioning matures. If so, the time span covered by this ontogeny is surprisingly long, beginning as it does in early childhood and continuing until adulthood. Changes in consistency of higher-level control is only one of the possible behavioral measures of this ontogenetic change, but in the standard condition it is apparently a sensitive measure capable of reflecting small ontogenetic differences that might otherwise be obscured.

Label Condition

Purpose.   Assigning a special role to linguistic labels in the learning process can be traced back to Pavlov who regarded words as abstractions of reality and the means of generalizing that led to a new principle of conditioning, a principle applicable only to language users. Spence (1937) also proposed that, with the advent of verbal processes, the simple mechanisms of discrimination learning could be transcended. Although the original S–r–s–R version of developmental mediation proposed by Kendler and Kendler (1962) conceived of the mediating *r* as a hypothetical response that was *not* necessarily coordinated to language or any other specifiable response, there appeared to be good reason to predict that labels that referred to the abstracted relevant cues (e.g., ''large'' and ''small'' or ''circle'' and ''triangle'') could either serve as the mediating response or could activate it. Therefore instructions to label the cues were expected to potentiate the tendency to reverse among young children and, given that the tendency to ''mediate'' spontaneously increased with age, the potentiation was expected to decrease with age. This expectation was confirmed (Kendler, 1964; Kendler & Kendler, 1961; Silverman, 1966), and the result was considered as supporting the S–r–s–R conception of mediational development.

The present purpose for manipulating the label variable was to determine more precisely how labeling interacts with age by determining how it affects the developmental trend both for its own sake and for the sake of comparison with the effect of overtraining. This comparison was expected to show whether labeling and overtraining had qualitatively similar or different effects on the developmental trend. The second purpose was to provide a baseline for the third experimental manipulation, which was the experimental combination of overtraining and labeling.

Results.   As seen in Fig. 5.3, instructions to label the relevant cues neither eliminated nor changed the logarithmic character of the developmental trend. Labeling did, as expected, flatten the slope by potentiating the probability of reversing at the lower end of the age scale relative to the standard condition. [The difference between the two slopes is statistically significant; C.R. $= 2.07, p$ (one tail) $= .02.$]

There was another interesting finding about the labeling behavior itself. All the children, even the 3-year-olds, used the labels appropriately. Before they chose, they said ''big'' or ''little,'' ''circle'' or ''triangle,'' or their equivalents, as instructed and they chose accordingly. To recall the procedure, subjects were told at the outset of the initial discrimination to use these labels before each choice. During the course of the experiment we observed that adults and older children, without any further instructions, continued to speak the labels aloud throughout all three phases of the experimental task. The younger children, however, tended to behave differently. After the instructions they would label for a few trials and then omit the labels, although they went on "playing the game." When reminded of the instructions, they would resume labeling for a while but they needed continual reminders if the labeling was to be sustained. By design, these reminders occurred only during the initial discrimination; when the reminders ceased, the tendency to label on the part of the younger children declined. These incidental observations led us to tabulate the proportion of labeled trials in each phase of the task for both the label and overtrained-label conditions (Fig. 5.4). The latter condition was included to show that the general trends are replicable. Apparently there is an age-related tendency to stop labeling in every phase of the task that becomes more manifest when children are left to their own devices. To see whether or how this developmental trend is related to the reversal trend, a simple log function was fitted to the mean proportion of labeled trials in the test series for the label and overtrained-label conditions combined. The a and b parameters of this function were, respectively, .29 and .46 ($r^2 = .86$). It is interesting that the slope parameter, .46, is the same as the slope parameter of the developmental trend for reversing in the standard condition.

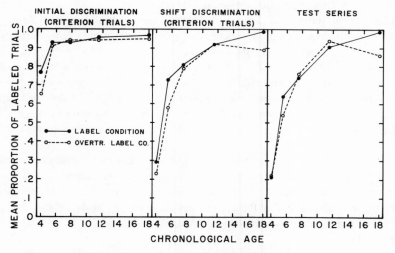

FIG. 5.4.   Mean proportion of labeled trials on the 10 criterion trials on the initial and shift discriminations and on the entire test series in the label and overtrained–label conditions.

Discussion.   Interpreting these results in terms of levels theory one would say that appropriate labeling is a form of categorization that depends on the selective encoding of the relevant cues. That children can label appropriately when so instructed indicates that activity in the selective encoding module can be increased by appropriate instructions. The systematic age-related tendency to stop labeling suggests that to do so produces some cognitive strain in immature systems that is relieved by returning to a more comfortable level of activation.

Overtrained Condition

Purpose.   There is prior research showing that overtraining on the initial discrimination potentiates the probability of reversing among children (Eimas, 1969; Shepp & Adams, 1973; Tighe & Tighe, 1966). In the past this finding has been construed as supportive of selective-attention theories that, like the 1963 Zeaman and House version, according to Eimas (1969): "assumed (the process) to be independent of developmental status but strongly under the control of stimulus and training factors [p. 169]." However, as shown with reference to labeling, developmental and extrinsic effects are not mutually exclusive. One purpose of the overtrained condition was to extend this analysis to the effects of training.

Results.   The effect of 30 overtraining trials, as shown in Fig. 5.3, is highly comparable to the effect of labeling, qualitatively and quantitatively. They are qualitatively comparable in that neither condition eliminates the developmental trend nor changes its logarithmic character, but they each flatten the slope relative to the standard in the same manner. That they are quantitatively similar may be coincidental because there is no obvious reason for the arbitrarily selected 30 overtraining trials to produce the same magnitude of potentiation unless, perhaps, both extrinsic effects are asymptotic.

Discussion.   Recently selective attention theorists have acknowledged the validity of developmental differences in discriminative learning and transfer. One hypothesis they have offered in explanation is that there are maturationally determined changes in learning rates (Campione, 1970; Dickerson, Novik, & Gould, 1972; Zeaman & House, 1974). According to any mediational theory, predictions about shift behavior must take into account both the positive transfer of the mediating response to the initially relevant dimension and the negative transfer of the reversed choice response. A reversal shift will occur when the former is greater than the latter. According to the Fisher and Zeaman (1973) version of the selective-attention theory, the strength of the mediating attentional response to a dimension is increased at a given rate, θ_{oa}, if the trial outcome confirms the subject's expectancies about the reward values of the cues on that dimension and decreases at a given rate, θ_{oe}, if these expectancies are violated. When predictions are required of the theory, the usual procedure is to simulate the effects, given a certain set of parameters. In the standard set used for most simulations the attentional acquisition parameter, θ_{oa}, is .5 and the attentional extinction parameter, θ_{oe}, is .1. The assumption, given these parameters, is that the attentional response is acquired much more rapidly than it is extinguished. The mediating attentional response is the first stage in the mediating process; it chooses the dimension to notice. In the second stage the cues on the attended dimension are associated with the different reward outcomes. A rewarded trial increases the tendency for a cue on the attended dimension to elicit the instrumental choice response at a given rate, θ_{ra}, and a nonrewarded trial extinguishes it at a given rate, θ_{re}. In the standard set of simulation parameters, the two instrumental response parameters, θ_{ra} and θ_{re}, are both assumed to equal .5.

Given this set of four parameters, the simulated "stat child" would be likely to make an optional shift because the attentional response extinguishes much more slowly than the instrumental response. If, however, the parameters were changed so that the extinction rate of the selective attention response is more rapid than that of the instrumental response, the stat child would be more likely to make a nonreversal shift. Accordingly, the developmental increase in reversing could be accounted for either by a developmental decrease in the extinction rate of the attentional response or a developmental increase in the rate of instrumental extinction and learning.

In the course of proposing this learning rate hypothesis, Zeaman and House (1974) criticized the earlier version of our developmental mediation theory on the grounds that it had uncertain developmental significance. This criticism, they argued, does not apply to their learning rate hypothesis because the revised version of selective-attention theory adheres to the distinction between control processes and structural features where control processes refer to parameters that change with factors such as experience, training, or instructions whereas structural features refer to relatively unchangeable parameters that are characteristic of the organism. Developmental laws should be concerned with structural features and a learning rate parameter is a structural feature. Zeaman and House proposed the learning rate hypothesis primarily to show that, by manipulating parameters, their theory could account for the developmental differences in reversing. However, no firm proposal was made about which possible parametric change, or changes, would best account for the developmental trend.

Because one purpose of the revised developmental mediation theory was to introduce an explicit maturational component, there is no current disagreement in that quarter. For instance, the distinction between control processes and structural features is akin to the distinction between what we referred to earlier as extrinsic and intrinsic factors. Moreover the notion that learning rates change developmentally is quite compatible with a levels-of-function formulation. The levels formulation would, however, place some constraints on how these rates should change. Specifically, the assumption that the lower levels begin and end their maturational cycles before the higher levels and that the tendency to encode selectively is controlled by the higher level would imply that in the age range we are studying the locus of developmental change should be mostly in the selective encoding module.

A working hypothesis consistent with these assumptions that would account for the present results is as follows: (1) The tendency to encode the cues selectively on a given dimension increases in some measure on each trial in which this response predicts the outcome and decreases on each trial when it does not. (2) The rate of change is a function of the developmental status of the selective encoding module. (3) The stronger the relevant selective encoding tendency becomes, the more resistant it will be to extinction. (4) At its maximum the selective encoding tendency is stronger than the nonselective encoding tendency. Because the probability of reversing is a function of the difference between the selective and nonselective encoding tendencies, it follows that, if other things are equal, the probability of reversing should increase, and the potentiating effect of overtraining should decrease, developmentally. The probability of reversing should increase developmentally because the older children get, the more rapidly the relevant selective encoding tendency should increase during the initial discrimination. Therefore the greater should be the discrepancy between the selective and nonselective encoding tendencies. The potentiating effect of overtraining should decrease developmentally because the more the selective encoding rate is increased, the less overtraining should be needed to attain comparable differences.

It should be briefly noted that an alternative hypothesis was proposed by Zeaman and House (1974). This hypothesis, mentioned earlier as rather like the one proposed by Tighe and Tighe (1978), states that children respond to compounds as well as dimensions and that the former is stronger in young children than the latter. Although Zeaman and House treat the learning-rate and compound–component hypotheses as alternatives, I am proposing that they are complementary.

Overtrained-Label Condition

Purpose. This condition was included to determine whether, or to what extent, the potentiating effects produced by overtraining and labeling are interchangeable. One could, for instance, conceive of a verbal mediation hypothesis that would explain the potentiation due to overtraining by hypothesizing that children have a relatively weak tendency to label the cues covertly. This tendency is strengthened as the training proceeds, but young children require more training for the covert response to become strong enough to control choice behavior. If this hypothesis were valid, one should predict that combining overtraining with overt labeling should not produce much more potentiation than labeling taken alone.

In a similar vein, a selective-attention theory that conceives of attention as perceptual could explain the potentiation in the label condition by assuming that the effect of labeling is to increase attention to the relevant dimension. Most selective-attention theorists assume that the increase per trial is some constant proportion of the amount of possible increase. If labeling increases the tendency to attend selectively to the relevant dimension at criterion, the amount of possible increase produced by overtraining should be proportionately reduced. Therefore, the combined effect of overtraining and labeling should be less potentiating than the sum of the potentiation under each condition taken alone. Combining the two conditions experimentally and comparing the combination with each condition separately should determine how valid these hypotheses are.

Results. First, with regard to the developmental trend, as seen in Fig. 5.3 and Table 5.2, although the age differences are sharply attenuated and the fit of the function is much poorer than in the other conditions, there is a significant developmental trend and it takes a logarithmic form.

To compare the potentiation derived from combining overtraining and labeling with each variable taken by itself, one needs only to glance at Fig. 5.3 to see that the combination produced a much greater effect than either variable taken by itself at every age level except the eldest, where there is little room for increase. In fact the combined effect is not only cumulative but comes close to being literally additive, as shown in Table 5.3. If we let O, L, and OL serve as subscripts for the overtrained, label, and overtrained-label conditions, respectively, and let ΔRS represent the potentiation relative to the standard condition, additivity would be expressed as $\Delta RS_{OL} = \Delta RS_O + \Delta RS_L$. In testing for additivity the expected value (column 3) was compared with the obtained value (column 4) by converting these proportions to their corresponding frequencies and applying a chi-square goodness-of-fit test. The test showed the additivity

TABLE 5.3
Comparing the Increase in the Proportion of Reversers Attributable
to Overtraining and Labeling Taken Separately and Combined

Age Level	Empirical Values			
	$\Delta RS_O{}^a$	$\Delta RS_L{}^a$	$\Delta RS_O{}^a + \Delta RS_L$	$\Delta RS_{OL}{}^a$
4.0	.12	.22	.34	.44
5.6	.22	.19	.41	.32
7.9	.16	.19	.35	.42
11.9	.09	−.06	.03	.21
18.0	−.07	−.03	−.10	−.01
Mean	.10	.10	.21	.28

$^a\Delta RS$ = proportion of reversers in the given experimental group subtracted from the corresponding proportion in the standard group and the subscripts O, L, and OL refer to the overtrained, label, and overtrained-label group, respectively.

hypothesis to be tenable ($\chi^2 = 2.5537$, $df = 4$, $.50 < p > .25$). Because most subjects in the overtrained-label condition were run at a later date than the other subjects, they were not all strictly randomized; therefore these differences might be attributable to sample differences. However when the results of the 128 kindergarten children who were randomly assigned to the four experimental conditions were analyzed separately, the proportion of reversers in the standard, overtrained, label, and overtrained-label conditions were .41, .56, .59, and .75, respectively. Thus for these children $\Delta RS_{OL} = .34$ and $\Delta RS_O + \Delta RS_L = .33$, lending support to the representativeness of the finding for the results obtained with the sample taken as a whole.

Discussion.   The additivity of the potentiation attributable to overtraining and labeling is inconsistent with either hypothesis just mentioned. A more fitting alternative hypothesis is that the selective encoding module, like the higher centers of the cortex, is supramodal and may receive input from either the visual (perceptual) modality or the acoustic (linguistic) modality or both. According to this hypothesis overtraining potentiates reversing via the visual modality, labeling potentiates reversing by way of the acoustic modality and the input from the two channels is additive.

Levels of Behavioral Regulation

Although overtraining and labeling were selected for study because of how they affected the encoding process, the procedure provided data that made it possible to test the generality of previous findings that: (1) the probability of hypothesis testing increases monotonically over age; and (2) the encoding and behavioral regulation components are separable but related. Opportunity was also taken to explore briefly how these variables affect the level of function in the behavioral regulation component. In these analyses if a subject's first *correct* choice on the shift discrimination was also the beginning of his criterion run, he was classified as win–staying. Win–staying was taken as indicative that problem solution was controlled by the cognitive, hypothesis-testing module.

Developmental Trend

Previous research, in which subjects were neither overtrained nor required to label but which varied the dimensions that composed the stimulus compounds, showed that in each stimulus condition the probability of win–staying was a monotonic function of age (Kendler, 1979b). The present results, summarized in Table 5.4, show that the same monotonicity applies in the present training conditions ($L = 218$, $p < .001$). Although the trends for each condition taken separately were too irregular to describe mathematically, the marginals revealed a smooth developmental progression that, like the probability of reversing, fitted particularly well ($r^2 = .99$) to a log function [$y = -.59 + .50 \ln x$ ($\chi^2_{1in} =$

TABLE 5.4
Proportion of Subjects Who Win–Stayed in the Shift Discrimination

| | Experimental Conditions | | | | |
Mean Age	Standard	Label	Overtrained	Overtrained–Label	Marginal
4.1	.09	.22	.03	.19	.13
5.6	.19	.33	.17	.44	.28
7.8	.16	.41	.22	.75	.38
11.7	.47	.34	.81	.88	.62
18	.84	.81	.91	.96	.88
Marginal	.35	.42	.43	.64	—

176.5272, $p < .001$, $\chi^2_{rem} = 2.4223$, $p > .50$)]. Apparently the tendency to hypothesis test, like the tendency to encode selectively, increases gradually over a long time period between early childhood and young adulthood. There is some suggestion that this developmental trend may, like the reversal trend, be described as logarithmic, but the present indication is that for this form to become clearly manifest requires very large samples.

Relations Between Selective Encoding and Hypothesis Testing

The simplest and most direct way to show how win–staying and reversing are related are presented in Fig. 5.5 and Table 5.5. Figure 5.5 shows that these two behaviors are separable because, at each age level below adulthood, a substantial proportion of the subjects who reverse do not win–stay. These results, which replicate the earlier findings, indicate that selective encoding is not a sufficient condition for hypothesis testing.

Table 5.5 presents the probability of win–staying for each level, flanked on the right by the conditional probability of win–staying, given that the subject reverses, and on the left by the conditional probability of win–staying given that he did not reverse. It can be seen that at every age level except the eldest, the probability that a reverser will win–stay is greater than the corresponding probability for a nonreverser, for the eldest age level the relationship may have been attenuated by ceiling effects. This result suggests either that the hypothesis-testing module is more receptive to the output of the selective than the nonselective-encoding module or that the individual differences in the reactivity of these two modules are correlated. The present data do not enable us to decide which explanation is more plausible.

Extrinsic Effects on Hypothesis Testing

Because the trends for each separate condition are so irregular, they do not lend themselves to curve fitting; consequently the interaction of extrinsic effects

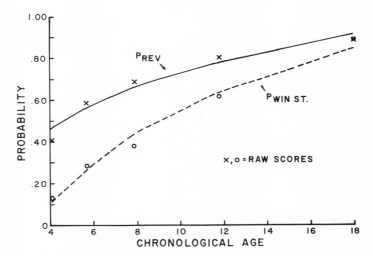

FIG. 5.5.   The fitted logarithmic functions and the obtained proportions, of all subjects combined, who reversed and who win–stayed in the shift discrimination, respectively. To obtain these values each experimental condition was weighted equally.

with age becomes very complex to evaluate statistically. To economize on space the analysis of extrinsic effect will be restricted to the main effects for all ages combined. As to these main effects, one should expect that an extrinsic variable that potentiates selective encoding should also potentiate hypothesis testing because selective codes, in this situation, produce the most efficient hypotheses. The lower marginals in Table 5.4 show that each experimental group had` a

TABLE 5.5
Relations Between Win–Staying (Hypothesis Testing) and Reversing
(Selective Encoding) for All Conditions Combined

Age Level	$P_{W/R}$*	P_W**	$P_{W/\bar{R}}$***
4.1	.17	.13	.11
5.6	.33	.28	.21
7.8	.46	.38	.20
11.7	.68	.62	.38
18	.88	.88	.87
Marginal	.56	.46	.24

*$P_{W/R}$ refers to the conditional probability of win–staying given that the subject made a reversal shift.

**P_W refers to the unconditional probability of win–staying.

***$P_{W/\bar{R}}$ refers to the conditional probability of win–staying given that the subject made a nonreversal shift.

higher mean probability of win–staying than the standard group. Although these results are in the expected direction, only the large difference in favor of the overtrained-label group was statistically significant ($\chi^2 = 26.4541$, $df = 1$, $p < .001$).

One other outcome worthy of mention is that although the overtrained group had more hypothesis testers than the standard group, it, nevertheless, made reliably more mean perseverative errors (2.57 versus 1.88) to the initially correct stimulus display ($F = 6.2531$, $\frac{1}{310}$, $p < .01$). These outcomes are not incompatible because a subject is classified as a hypothesis tester if he or she made no errors beyond the last perseverative error. It seems that although overtraining reliably increases the tendency to persevere on the previously correct response, it may also increase the tendency to hypothesis test once the now incorrect response is abandoned. This finding is consistent with the levels theory if one makes the common assumptions that: (1) the hypothesis-testing module is activated when there is no adaptive, automatic, well-learned response available; and (2) the activity in this module subsides as the adaptive, incrementally learned association gains strength.

CONCLUSIONS

Basic Issues

Developmental Functions

In this chapter there has been a great deal of emphasis on developmental trends, because of the belief that developmental change is the subject matter of the developmentalist rather than behavior at any given developmental status. Age was used to measure developmental status because, at least for the present, it is the most reliable and practical index. The developmental trends were fitted to mathematical functions wherever feasible because they brought order to the data and allowed for comparisons and statistical evaluations that would otherwise be clumsy, insensitive, or impossible. By such quantification we have shown that there is a common form to the development of selective encoding and perhaps to hypothesis testing that can be replicated with different subject samples and applies over a range of conditions.

Given that there have been serious questions about the validity of developmental differences in selective encoding and hypothesis testing in some quarters, one might ask why we obtain such consistent developmental trends. To answer this question, we would point out first that the behavior being measured is not stable; the trends apply to the probability that these behaviors will occur and therefore are inherently variable. Moreover, the trends that emerged from the research only become manifest when measured over a wide age range with sizable samples at each age level. Furthermore, although it is common practice to do so, for this purpose it is important to neither eliminate children for failure to learn nor to use special techniques to induce criterion among the slower learners. Our conclusion, then, is that the reason there are such replicable behavioral trends is because they reflect a lawful developmental change and they would generally be more manifest if they were measured in similar ways.

In this and other research we have consistently found that the simple log function provides the closest fit. Why it should be a log function, per se, is not obvious, so leaning on the side of caution, we regard it as a first approximation that is particularly useful because it is so mathematically tractable. Probably the important property that will hold up is the negative acceleration, which is shared by growth functions in general.

Finally we might ask, why does this change continue for so many years? It was the initially unexpected length of time spanned by these developmental trends that led to the hypothesis that they reflected a long-term maturational change, probably in the central nervous system, a notion that is consistent with the little we know about maturation in the cerebral cortex. Myelination is one of the primary measures of neural maturation and the last centers to myelinate in the cortex, or anywhere else in the central nervous system are the intramodal or supramodal association areas (Flechsig, 1901). These areas continue to myelinate but at a negatively accelerated rate well into and possibly beyond the second decade of life (Yakovlev & Lecours, 1967). Axonal myelination is positively related to impulse conduction velocity, to the amplitude of the action potential, to membrane excitability, and sometimes to the maximal frequency of impulses. The amplitude of the action potential determines the amount of transmitter secreted at the nerve endings. The thickness of the myelin sheath at the first Ranvier node determines how many excitatory postsynaptic potentials are needed to generate a certain number of action potentials (Schulte, 1969). It is therefore plausible that these centers become functional at an early age but become more efficient and responsive with increasing maturity and this increase takes place gradually over a long time period. It is, in the same vein, plausible that behavioral developmental trends bear some relationship to such increasing neural efficiency.

Ontogenetic Change

As discussed earlier, there is evidence that the reversal-shift trends refer to longitudinal changes in individual probability of reversing. We have not yet accumulated the same evidence with regard to hypothesis testing, but it seems likely that the same would apply. To explain why the behavior is probabilistic we would suggest that when faced with a situation that allows for solution at either the lower or higher level of function, one or the other will prevail. The evidence indicates that in children both levels are to some degree functional in early childhood. If we make the simplifying assumption that the lower level is at or near asymptote by about 4 years of age, the developmental trends would reflect the degree to which the discriminative learning task activates the higher functional level. On any given occasion which level will prevail is assumed to depend on their ratio of activity and this ratio depends on: (1) the relatively stable developmental status of the competing modules; (2) the temporary contextual factors operative at the time of measurement; and (3) momentary random internal and external factors that can affect the ratio of activation, probably more by affecting the higher than the lower-level activity.

Extrinsic Effects

Another advantage of fitting functions to developmental trends is that they provide a handy vehicle for assessing how developmental and extrinsic variables are related. In this research we found that labeling and overtraining on the initial discrimination flattened the slope parameter of the developmental function, which was interpreted to mean that they potentiate higher-level functioning and the effect of that potentiation is inversely related to developmental status.

Perhaps the most troublesome question raised by these results is why the higher functional levels should be so responsive to extrinsic effects. Let it be noted that sensitivity to extrinsic effects is not limited to these measures but is rather characteristic of responses to a wide variety of tasks used to measure problem solving, particularly in young children (Gelman, 1978). A speculative but interesting explanation for this sensitivity consists in applying Gottlieb's thesis about the relationship between experience, which he defines as activation, and maturation. This thesis is described succinctly as follows by Gottlieb (1976).

> Function, whether spontaneous or evoked, occurs at both the neural and behavioral levels before the neural maturation or behavioral development of the system in question is complete. Therefore, it is entirely possible that function (''experience'') normally participates in the neural maturation process as well as in behavioral development at early stages, both prenatally and postnatally. In addition to playing its widely acknowledged maintenance role, function may also exert a facilitative and even an inductive, or determinative, influence on early neural maturation and behavioral development [p. 232].

Although the evidence Gottlieb invokes to support his thesis is based primarily on lower-level function, it seems reasonable to suppose although more difficult to prove, that it should apply as well to higher-level functioning, which is on the whole more sensitive than the lower level to experience. Therefore it is possible that immature higher-level systems can be activated by appropriate extrinsic variables and that such activation influences the course of their development. This is not to imply that a single, brief period of activation would be expected to have a marked or permanent effect on the developmental status of the system but rather that prolonged or repeated exposure to such activation, such as might occur in schools, may play an important role, not only in providing information to children but in determining the rate or the ultimate level of development of the neural systems underlying higher-level cognitive processing.

Implication of Results for Theory

Components and Levels Constructs

The results demonstrated that it is useful to (1) analyze discrimination learning into two separate but related components, an encoding component that processes the information and a behavioral regulation component that determines behavioral output; (2) analyze each of these components into two qualitatively different levels of functioning; (3) conceive of cognitive development as a quantitatively increasing tendency for the higher level of function to control problem solution; and (4) conceive of behavior in any given problem situation as jointly determined by developmental status, extrinsic variables, and random factors.

The same results lend support to the suggestion that the continuity–noncontinuity controversy can be resolved by conceiving lower-level function to operate according to continuity-type principles and higher-level function to operate according to noncontinuity-type principles. With regard to different time planes, the results showed that is is possible to consider simultaneously behavioral change on more than one time plane, in this case longitudinal change that occurs over years and performance change that occurs in a matter of minutes.

Modular Function

The notion that each functional level operates in a different mode provides for formulating specific, testable hypotheses about how each module functions. These hypotheses, unlike the broader conceptions about evolutionary and ontogenetic change, can be tested experimentally. The present research, for instance, can be regarded as testing two hypotheses. One hypothesis would be that overtraining and labeling both potentiate selective encoding but the degree of potentiation is inversely related to age. This hypothesis was confirmed. The second hypothesis would be that the combined effects of these variables would be less than the sum of their separate effects, which was disconfirmed. The combined effect was literally additive suggesting the following new, testable hypothesis: The selective encoding module is intermodal or supramodal and may therefore be activated by either visual or linguistic–acoustic input channels and the input from different channels is additive.

Perception and Cognitive Development

If we relate selective encoding to cognition and visual input to perception, the results of this research suggest that repeated perceptual exposure to a given set of relevant cues temporarily enhances their cognition, which is consistent with the Tighe's view of cognitive development (1978). The results also suggest, however, that saying aloud well-learned labels that refer to these cues also temporarily enhances cognition. The fact that the two effects are additive suggest further that the effects of labeling are not readily explained simply as enhancing the perception of the visual cues.[1]

Both effects are, however, performance effects that, by definition, are relatively impermanent, because one can change the relevance of the dimension by merely changing the reinforcement contingencies. Performance effects are not to be confused with developmental effects and demonstrating that perceptual or verbal input can affect performance is not tantamount to demonstrating either that they affect development or that the primary basis for such development is experiential.

The levels formulation assumes that cognitive development is genetically preprogrammed although the course it takes both qualitatively (e.g., what concepts are acquired) and quantitatively (e.g., the rate or ultimate degree of attainment) may be profoundly influenced by experience. There are other researchers in this field (e.g., the Tighe's and the Zeamans both of whom are represented in this volume who believe otherwise). Unfortunately, such a question deals with a time frame that leads to no ready laboratory resolution and such permanent effects that it becomes ethically impossible to experiment with in any case. The evidence that will be brought to bear will of necessity be correlational or incidental. I see the evolutionary and developmental changes in behavior described earlier in this chapter as contributing to the evidence of genetic effects on development but admit this most important question is yet to be resolved.

REFERENCES

Buss, A. H. Reversal and nonreversal shifts in concept formation with partial reinforcement eliminated. *Journal of Experimental Psychology,* 1956, *52,* 162–166.

Campione, J. C. Optional intradimensional and extradimensional shifts in children as a function of age. *Journal of Experimental Psychology,* 1970 *84,* 296–300.

Deese, J., & Hulse, S. H. *The psychology of learning* (3rd ed.). New York: McGraw-Hill, 1967.

Dickerson, D. J., Novik, N., & Gould, S. A. Acquisition and extinction rates as determinants of age

---

[1]The Tighes' performed an optional shift experiment (1970) in which they combined perceptual and label pretraining and found that the combination had no more potentiating effect on reversing than perceptual pretraining taken by itself. At first glance these results would seem inconsistent with ours, but they only required the children to use labels during the brief pretraining. The present research required children to label during the actual training. It will be recalled that even when instructed to label, children tended to stop doing so. It is therefore possible that label pretraining by itself would have had no effect and therefore would not be expected to add to the perceptual pretraining effect. We attempted to resolve this question empirically but, for unknown reasons, were unable to replicate the potentiating effect of perceptual pretraining.

changes in discrimination shift behavior. *Journal of Experimental Psychology*, 1972, *95*, 116–122.

Eimas, P. D. Attentional processes in optional shift behavior. *Journal of Comparative and Physiological Psychology*, 1969, *69*, 166–169.

Fisher, M. A., & Zeaman, D. An attention–retention theory of retardate discrimination learning. In N. R. Ellis (Ed.) *International review of research in mental retardation* (Vol. 6). New York: Academic Press, 1973.

Flechsig, P. Developmental (myelogenetic) localization of the cerebral cortex in the human subject. *Lancet*, 1901, 1027.

Gelman, R. Cognitive development. *Annual Review of Psychology*, 1978, *29*, 297–332.

Gholson, B., Levine, M., & Phillips, S. Hypotheses, strategies and stereotypes in discrimination learning. *Journal of Experimental Child Psychology*, 1972, *13*, 423–446.

Gottlieb, G. Conceptions of prenatal development: Behavioral embryology. *Psychological Review*, 1976, *83*, 215–234.

Harlow, H. F. The formation of learning sets. *Psychological Review*, 1949, *56*, 51–65.

Harlow, H. F. Analysis of discrimination learning by monkeys. *Journal of Experimental Psychology*, 1950, *40*, 26–39.

Harlow, H. F. Early problem learning and early social learning. In M. E. Meyer (Ed.), *Second western symposium on learning: Early learning*. Western Washington State College, 1971.

Kendler, H. H., & D'Amato, M. F. A comparison of reversal shifts and nonreversal shifts in human concept formation behavior. *Journal of Experimental Psychology*, 1955, *49*, 165–174.

Kendler, H. H., & Kendler, T. S. Effect of verbalization on reversal shifts in children. *Science*, 1961, *134*, 1619–1620.

Kendler, H. H., & Kendler, T. S. Vertical and horizontal processes in problem solving. *Psychological Review*, 1962, *69*, 1–16.

Kendler, T. S. Verbalization and optional reversal shifts among kindergarten children. *Journal of Verbal Learning and Verbal Behavior*, 1964, *3*, 428–436.

Kendler, T. S. Continuity theory and cue dominance. In H. H. Kendler & J. T. Spence (Eds.), *Essays in neobehaviorism*. A memorial volume to Kenneth W. Spence. New York: Appleton-Century-Crofts, 1971.

Kendler, T. S. The development of discrimination learning: A levels-of-functioning explanation. In H. W. Reese & L. P. Lipsitt (Eds.), *Advances in child development and behavior* (Vol. 13). New York, Academic Press, 1979. (a)

Kendler, T. S. Cross-sectional research, longitudinal theory, and a discriminative transfer ontogeny. *Human Development*, 1979, *22*, 235–254. (b)

Kendler, T. S., & Kendler, H. H. An ontogeny of optional shift behavior. *Child Development*, 1970, *41*, 1–27.

Krechevsky, I. The genesis of "hypotheses" in rats. *University of California Publications in Psychology*, 1932, *6*, 27–44.

Kuenne, M. R. Experimental investigation of the relation of language to transposition behavior in young children. *Journal of Experimental Psychology*, 1946, *36*, 471–490.

Lashley, K. S. *Brain mechanisms and intelligence*. Chicago: University of Chicago Press, 1929.

Lashley, K. S. The mechanism of vision: XV. Preliminary studies of the rat's capacity for detail vision. *Journal of General Psychology*, 1938, *18*, 123–193.

Lassek, A. M. *The unique legacy of Doctor Hughlings Jackson*. Springfield, Ill.: Thomas, 1970.

Levine, M. A model of hypothesis behavior in discrimination learning set. *Psychological Review*, 1959, *66*, 353–366.

Levine, M. Mediating processes in humans at the outset of discrimination learning. *Psychological Review*, 1963, *70*, 254–276.

Levine, M. Hypothesis behavior in humans during discrimination learning. *Journal of Experimental Psychology*, 1966, *71*, 331–338.

Luria, A. R. *The working brain; An introduction to neuropsychology.* New York: Basic Books, 1973.

Maxwell, A. E. *Analyzing qualitative data.* London: Methuen, 1961.

Medin, D. L. Subproblem analysis of discrimination shift learning. *Behavior Research Methods and Instrumentation,* 1973, *5,* 332–336.

Riley, D. A. *Discrimination learning.* Boston: Allyn & Bacon, 1968.

Riley, D. A., & Leith, C. R. Multidimensional psychophysics and selective attention in animals. *Psychological Bulletin,* 1976, *83,* 138–160.

Schulte, F. J. Structure–function relationships on the spinal cord. In R. J. Robinson (Ed.), *Brain and early behavior.* New York: Academic Press, 1969.

Schusterman, R. J. The use of strategies in the decision behavior of children and chimpanzees. *American Psychologist,* 1961, *16,* 424.

Shepp, B. E., & Adams, M. J. Effects of amount of training on type of solution and breadth of learning in optional shift. *Journal of Experimental Psychology,* 1973, *101,* 63–69.

Silverman, I. W. Effect of verbalization on reversal shifts in children. *Journal of Experimental Child Psychology,* 1966, *4,* 1–8.

Spence, K. W. The nature of discrimination learning in animals. *Psychological Review,* 1936, *43,* 427–449.

Spence, K. W. The differential response in animals to stimuli varying within a single dimension. *Psychological Review,* 1937, *44,* 430–444.

Sutherland, N. S., & Mackintosh, N. J. The learning of an optional extradiminsional reversal shift problem by rats. *Psychonomic Science,* 1966, *5,* 343–344.

Sutherland, N. S., & Mackintosh, N. J. *Mechanisms of animal discrimination learning.* New York: Academic Press, 1971.

Tighe, T. J., Glick, J., & Cole, M. Subproblem analysis of discrimination shift learning. *Psychonomic Science,* 1971, *24,* 159–160.

Tighe, T. J., & Tighe, L. S. Overtraining and optional shift behavior in rats and children. *Journal of Comparative and Physiological Psychology,* 1966, *62,* 49–54.

Tighe, T. J., & Tighe, L. S. Optional shift behavior of children as a function of age, type of pretraining and stimulus salience. *Journal of Experimental Child Psychology,* 1970, *9,* 272–285.

Tighe, T. J., & Tighe, L. S. Stimulus control in children's learning. In A. D. Pick (Ed.), *Minnesota symposium on child development* (Vol. 6). Minneapolis: University of Minnesota Press, 1972.

Tighe, T. J., & Tighe, L. S. A perceptual view of conceptual development. In R. D. Walk & H. L. Pick, Jr. (Eds.), *Perception and experience.* New York: Plenum, 1978.

Trabasso, T., & Bower, G. H. *Attention in learning theory and research.* New York: Wiley, 1968.

Yakovlev, P. I., & Lecours, A. R. The myologenetic cycles of regional maturation of the brain. In A. M. Minkowski (Ed.), *Region-development of the brain in early life.* Oxford, England: Blackwell Scientific Pub. 1967.

Zeaman, D., & House, B. J. The role of attention in retardate discrimination learning. In N. R. Ellis (Ed.), *Handbook of mental deficiency.* New York: McGraw-Hill, 1963.

Zeaman, D., & House, B. J. Interpretations of developmental trends in discriminative transfer effects. In A. D. Pick (Ed.), *Minnesota symposium in child psychology* (Vol. 8). Minneapolis: University of Minnesota Press, 1974.

6
Components in the Hypothesis-Testing Strategies of Young Children

Charles C. Spiker and Joan H. Cantor
University of Iowa

INTRODUCTION

For several decades, research on children's discrimination learning has been a fertile source of both empirical knowledge and theoretical development. Although the specific experimental paradigms have been modified over the years, there has been a remarkable continuity in the theoretical questions that dictated the search for new and better paradigms. One of the enduring theoretical questions concerns the role of mediation in the learning process. Mediational mechanisms have been prominent in various theoretical structures since the early work of Kuenne (1946). During the 1950s and 1960s, the effects of verbal mediation were investigated in experiments concerned with the acquired distinctiveness of cues and mediated generalization (see Cantor, 1965; Spiker, 1956, 1963; for reviews). Some developmental changes in verbal mediation were studied in a variety of learning situations by Kendler (1972) and others. Another persistent theoretical question is concerned with the role that perceptual processes play in extracting the *effective* stimuli from the total stimulus situation in the learning task. Thus, paralleling the search for the effects of verbal mediation in the studies of acquired distinctiveness of cues was the search for the effects of stimulus predifferentiation.

In the 1960s, answers to other closely related theoretical questions were sought in the voluminous literature on children's performance in discrimination-shift tasks. Developmental studies with children in the preschool and early elementary years repeatedly demonstrated the increasing importance of dimension-specific responding as the child matures. Various theoretical mechanisms were suggested to account for these findings. The Kendler and Kendler (1962, 1968)

163

theory was explicit in postulating a developmental shift to a mediational mode of representing the stimuli in dimensional terms. Dimensional mediation was also a feature of our modification of Spence's discrimination-learning theory (Spiker, 1970, 1971; Spiker & Cantor, 1973). The attention theory of Zeaman and House (1963, 1974) placed greater emphasis on perceptual processes, with the assumption that dimension-specific observing responses determine the effective stimuli on each learning trial. The differentiation theory of the Tighes (L. Tighe & T. Tighe, 1966; T. Tighe & L. Tighe, 1972) placed even greater emphasis on the perceptual processes and the emergence of dimensional responding for perceptually experienced subjects. All of these theories have enjoyed a considerable degree of success in explaining the discrimination performance of young children.

Quite independently of these investigations with young children, other theorists in the 1960s conducted intensive investigations of discrimination learning and concept identification in adults. Cognitive theories were developed by Bower and Trabasso (1964), Levine (1963), and Restle (1962) in which assumptions were made about the strategies used by adults in solving these types of problems. The strategies consist of sets of rules (e.g., win–stay, lose–shift) that lead in systematic fashion to the correct solution. Although all the hypothesized strategies involve the systematic planful application of rules, they vary in the efficiency with which solution is achieved. These theories have also enjoyed considerable success in the prediction of performance in the older subject population for which they were developed.

It seems accurate to say, therefore, that we emerged from the 1960s with both theories that focused on the learning of children and theories that focused on the problem solving of adults but without a bridge between these theoretical realms. It is not too surprising, therefore, that theorists at both ends of the age range became increasingly interested in the transitional period. From the perspective of theorists working with younger children, the question takes the form of how and when dimension-specific responses begin to be organized into systematic strategies. For the cognitive theorists the question is how far down the age scale can evidence be found for the use of strategies and which of the strategies are younger subjects likely to use. Early attempts to answer the latter question (Eimas, 1969; Ingalls & Dickerson, 1969; Rieber, 1969) suggested that children as young as first- and second-graders follow systematic rules to some degree in solving discrimination problems. During the past decade, numerous investigators have attempted to determine the conditions under which such hypothesis testing occurs in children and the nature of the strategies used. In addition, initial attempts to bridge the theoretical gap have been made by Gholson and Beilin (1979), Kemler (1978), Kendler (1979), and the present writers (Spiker & Cantor, 1979a).

Our present purpose is to summarize the progress that has been made toward these ends during the past decade in our own and other laboratories. Our goal is to present an overall view of what we know now about the onset of systematic hypothesis testing in young children and the variables that affect the nature and efficiency of the strategies used. We begin with a discussion of methodological issues, because they bear particularly heavily on interpretation of the results. Finally, we discuss some implications of the results to date for modifying existing theories of discimination learning.

METHODOLOGICAL CONSIDERATIONS

The investigation of children's hypothesis-testing behavior has required the development of some rather special techniques. There are two major methods of eliciting and monitoring children's hypotheses, both of which are described in some detail here. The blank-trial probe was developed by Levine (1963) in the study of adult human strategies in problem solving. It was subsequently modified by Gholson, Levine, and Phillips (1972) for their study of hypothesis testing in children. The introtact probe was also developed for the study of adult strategies (Karpf & Levine, 1971) and was later modified for use with younger children (Kemler, 1972; Phillips, 1974, reported in Phillips & Levine, 1975). Each method has some strengths and some weaknesses, and their evaluation continues within the context of studies of factors that affect children's problem-solving performance.

The Blank-Trial Probe

The blank-trial probe has been used most often with discrimination-learning tasks of a more or less conventional sort. A characteristic application of the blank-trial technique may be described as follows. On each trial, two discriminanda are presented and the child is required to choose one of them. The task consists of two types of trials, one in which the child is given feedback concerning the correctness of his choice (feedback trials) and one in which no feedback is provided (blank trials). A block of blank trials is inserted between each pair of feedback trials, with the settings arranged so that a unique pattern of left–right choices is associated with each simple hypothesis. The child's current hypothesis, if any, is then inferred from the pattern of choices made during the block of blank trials (Gholson et al., 1972).

The Introtact Probe

The introtact probe has also been used within the context of more or less conventional discrimination problems although, as seen later, it has also been employed in somewhat different contexts. When this method is employed with adults, the subject is asked to predict, either before or immediately after each trial, what feature (i.e., dimensional value) of the discriminanda is going to be correct on every trial. The predictive value of the blank-trial and introtact probes for the choice behavior of adults has been found to be entirely equivalent (Karpf & Levine, 1971; Phillips & Levine, 1975). For adults, moreover, the introtact probe has proved to be more efficient, both in terms of time required for data collection and in terms of the amount of data lost, than is the more tedious blank-trial procedure. For children as young as second-graders, Phillips and Levine (1975) report the introtact probe to be at least as good as, and perhaps better than, the blank-trial probe in predicting subsequent choice behavior.

Behavioral Indices

Several response measures have been developed to reflect various components of the strategies that subjects employ during problem solving. In addition to the standard measures of discrimination task performance such as proportion of correct choices, number of errors to reach criterion, and trial of last error, a battery of conditional probabilities has been devised, several of which are described briefly now.

The *response consistency* index is a measure of the extent to which the subject chooses in accord with his preceding hypothesis. It is the probability that the subject chooses the discriminandum that exemplifies a certain feature or dimensional value, given that his previous hypothesis named that feature or value. Thus, if the previous probe elicited the hypothesis, "blue," the child manifests response consistency if he chooses the blue discriminandum on the next trial. The *local consistency* index is one of several measures of the extent to which the subject is utilizing feedback appropriately. It is the probability that the subject, following negative feedback on the previous trial, selects as his next hypothesis a feature that was exemplified by the correct discriminandum on the previous trial. Thus, if the subject chose the incorrect discriminandum on Trial n, and if the positive discriminandum on that trial was the large white X with the bar on top, then he is locally consistent if he selects as his hypothesis for Trial $n + 1$ either "large," "white," "X," or "bar on top."

Two other indices provide information about the way in which the subject is utilizing feedback information. The *win–stay* index is the probability that the subject's hypothesis on Trial $n + 1$ was the same as that on Trial n, given that the intervening feedback was positive. The *lose–shift* index is the probability that the subject's hypothesis on Trial $n + 1$ is different from that on Trial n, given that the intervening feedback was negative.

An attempt is often made to assess the degree to which the subject keeps track of which hypotheses have been previously tried and disconfirmed. Kemler (1978) defined an index that she referred to as the *number of repeats per opportunity*. Any hypothesis was counted as a repeat if it referred to a dimension for which either value had been previously tested. The number of opportunities for repeats on a given trial was a count of the number of attributes that had been tested on all prior trials. Spiker and Cantor (1979b) defined the *valid hypothesis* index as the probability that the subject's hypothesis on Trial $n + 1$, given that it is different from that on Trial n, is *not* one that has been specifically proposed and directly disconfirmed by negative feedback on any previous trial. Both of these indices provide some indication of the degree to which the subject is moving toward a solution by reducing the number of incorrect alternatives.

All the indices described here are computed from those trials prior to the criterion run. The restriction of computations to the presolution data prevents the obscuring of trends by the inclusion of a string of correct hypotheses and choices during the criterion run.

Preliminary Training

Preliminary training has been given almost invariably in studies using either blank-trial or introtact probes. Except in studies in which pretraining conditions have been experimentally manipulated, the standard practice has been to give a series of preliminary tasks of the same type as the criterion task in order to acquaint the subject with the general procedures (e.g., blank-trial probes) and the nature of the task solutions. Subjects who have not met criterion in pretraining problems in a set number of trials are generally given the correct solution before a new task is introduced. All the studies to be reported from our own laboratory have included such a learning-to-learn (LTL) condition in which subjects receive three pretraining tasks similar to the criterion task. In each pretraining task, a child who does not solve the task within 10 trials is given the solution and brought to criterion. Thus, each child has experienced the solution to three tasks prior to receiving the criterion task.

VARIABLES RELATED TO HYPOTHESIS TESTING IN CHILDREN

Within the past 10 or 12 years, research has provided considerable information about variables that affect the problem-solving strategies of children. The object of the present section is to review briefly the results of some of the more suggestive of these experiments. Several experiments of a methodological nature have addressed the important problem of assessing the influence of various aspects of the probe itself upon the problem-solving process—the effect of presence or absence of the probe, the effect of different probe types, and the effect of different temporal placement of the probe within the intertrial interval. Other experiments have dealt with various features of the task itself—with the presence of stimulus dimensions and their number, with the presence or absence of memory aids, and with the context within which the problem to be solved is presented.

Developmental changes with age in the various components of problem-solving strategies have been the subject of several experiments. Still other experiments have dealt with the task of isolating some of the molar factors that determine the quality of problem solving exhibited by children, including training in the solvability of discrimination tasks, learning to shift attention among the various stimulus dimensions, and specific training in the systematic testing of hypotheses.

The Problem of Monitoring Children's Hypotheses

There is obviously no direct way to determine the validity of any method of monitoring mental activities in either children or adults. Instead, we construct models, invent or select methods, deduce from the combination of model and method what behavior ought to occur, and compare the predictions with observed behavior. Often when there is disagreement between predictions and observations, it is difficult to decide whether the model is at fault or the method is "invalid." Although it is sometimes unclear as to whether good fortune or perspicacity has provided the larger gains, it appears that there is often general agreement on what constitutes a genuine gain. Hopefully, there will be agreement with respect to the utility of monitoring children's problem-solving strategies by means of the probe.

The Effect of Probing.   The question sometimes arises as to whether a particular scientific phenomenon can be measured, or sometimes even observed, without changing it in some way. This question certainly arises with respect to attempts to monitor a subject's hypothesis testing during problem solving. As is usually the case, the question is not easily resolved. It is conceivable, for example, that the probe would suggest a useful strategy to the subject, particularly to a child, that would not otherwise have developed. It is also conceivable that probing might seriously disrupt normal and useful strategies thereby leading to impaired performance. Moreover, both outcomes might result, although in different individuals. Because there is no alternative method at hand for observing the subject's strategies, the existence of the potential disruption or enhancement of strategy cannot be directly documented.

Several attempts have been made to evaluate the effect of the probes on strategy by observing the quality of problem solving, under the assumption that the strategies of the subjects are reflected more or less directly in solution performance. Thus, if subjects who are probed do not solve problems as well as do those who are not probed, we are inclined to conclude that probing has disrupted the normal processes. If subjects who are probed solve problems better than do those who are not probed, we may wish to conclude either that the probe has facilitated the normal problem-solving process or that it has brought about replacement of the normal process with a superior process. If there are no differences in the problem-solving performances of the two groups, we are tempted to conclude that there is neither a disruptive nor a facilitative effect on the subjects' processes. It must be kept in mind, however, that any one of the three possible outcomes could arise because we facilitated some subjects and interfered with others or even because we facilitated and interfered with the same subjects, but in different degrees. If the investigator's goal is to describe the cognitive strategies of which the children are capable, disruption of the normal processes must be avoided. If the goal is to describe the normal processing, obviously neither interference nor facilitation can be permitted.

The evidence available at the present time indicates that probing children during their problem solving can lead either to interference or to facilitation with their performance. These outcomes seem to be especially likely for the younger children. In a doctoral dissertation, Phillips (1974) compared the blank-trial and introtact probe techniques with each other and with a no-probe condition, using second- and sixth-grade children as subjects. Discrimination-learning problems were employed with four-dimensional discriminanda (letter shapes, letter sizes, letter brightness, and position of bar). No differences were found among the experimental conditions for the sixth-graders. For the second-grade children, however, relative to the no-probe condition, the blank-trial probe resulted in significantly poorer performance, whereas the introtact probe resulted in significantly better performance in solving the problems.

Although we have not used the blank-trial probe in any of our experiments, we have compared the introtact probe with a no-probe condition on two separate occasions. In the first experiment (Cantor & Spiker, 1977), we compared kindergarten children who were given introtact probes with those who were given only a single probe (to assess stimulus preference prior to the first trial). The stimuli for the discrimination task had form and color attributes as irrelevant and size as relevant. Nineteen of the 28 children who received the single probe learned the problem, whereas only 8 of the 28 children who received introtact probes on each trial met criterion. Of the 28 children who received multiple probes, 21 were dimensionally fixated; that is, they restricted their hypotheses to the names of the values of a single irrelevant dimension.

Despite these results, it seemed likely that modifications either in the introtact probing technique or in the nature of the task might lead to a less disruptive impact of the introtact probe. As a result of exploratory research, some of which is described on page 178ff., we modified the nature of the discriminanda. To avoid, or at least to minimize, the dimensional fixation referred to previously, we constructed the discriminanda from a single dimension. For example, we chose four colors (red, green, blue, and yellow) and arranged them to form two artificial bivalued dimensions (pseudodimensions). Pairs of color patches were pasted on each of four black blocks of uniform size and shape in such a way that red and green never appeared on the same block and blue and yellow never appeared together. The two pseudodimensions (red–green and blue–yellow) were arranged to form two different settings of a discrimination problem, red + blue versus green + yellow, and red + yellow versus green + blue. These settings, together with their lateral reversals, produced a four-setting simultaneous discrimination problem with two orthogonal dimensions, one relevant and one irrelevant and varying within trials. A parallel task was also constructed using geometric forms as the components.

An experiment was then designed using such tasks with 78 kindergarten and 72 first-grade children (Cantor & Spiker, 1979). The experiment included a comparison between children within each age level who were given introtact probes prior to each trial and those who received only one probe at the beginning of the task in order to determine dimensional preference. In addition to age and probe factors, we manipulated the amount and type of pretraining that the children received, a factor that need not concern us at the moment (see page 190ff.). For the kindergarten children, there was no difference between the probed and unprobed condition, at any level of pretraining, with respect to either the mean trial of last error or the percentage who reached criterion. The first-grade children who received the introtact probes performed significantly better than those who were not probed, although this superiority held only for those who had received the most extensive pretraining. Kemler (1978) also found no differences between probe and no-probe conditions for kindergarten children (Experiment 3) or for second-, third-, fifth-, and sixth-graders (Experiment 1) (see page 173ff.).

Any attempt to draw firm conclusions from the research reported earlier is probably premature. Nevertheless, for older children and adults, the evidence is consistent with the view that probing during problem solving neither facilitates nor disrupts the cognitive processing. The effect of probing on younger children appears to depend on the nature of the task and the type of probe used, a topic discussed in some detail in the next section.

The Effect of Type of Probe.   It is important to identify any differences in results that might have arisen simply because different types of probe were employed. At first glance, the two probe techniques seem quite disparate. For example, the blank-trial probe requires the omission of feedback on a considerable number of presentations, a condition that could prove quite disconcerting to any subject who failed to understand the associated instructions. The introtact query, coming as it does before each trial, might suggest to any subject who did not understand the associated instructions that the ''correctness'' of the stimulus is controlled by the experimenter's trial-to-trial whim. With the blank-trial method, it is standard practice to eliminate from further analysis patterns of responding to the blank-trial probes that are not identified with simple hypotheses. Moreover, several of the conditional probabilities require that both of two consecutive probes be interpretable, a requirement that significantly increases the amount of data lost. If the response consistency measure is reasonably high, the introtact technique does not result in the elimination of any significant amount of data.

The complete comparability of the two methods seems clearly established for adults (Karpf & Levine, 1971) and for children as young as sixth-graders (Phillips, 1974). Phillips reported no differences between the introtact and blank-trial probes for sixth-grade children, either in discrimination task performance or in the conditional probabilities computed with the probe responses. She reported that second-grade children, however, solved 20% more of their problems under the introtact than under the blank-trial probes.

Direct comparisons of the two probe conditions have not been made for children younger than the second grade, as far as the present writers are aware. Because both methods have been employed in separate experiments with kindergarten and first-grade children, it might seem that an indirect comparison for young children could be made by comparing the outcomes of experiments in which they have been used. Such an effort is fraught with problems, however, because other procedural differences are typically confounded with the probe techniques. The number of feedback trials, for example, has been greater in experiments using introtact probes than in those in which blank-trial probes have been used, probably because the latter must necessarily include a considerable number of blank trials. Moreover, the amount of preliminary training and the number of stimulus dimensions have both been typically greater in experiments in which blank-trial probes have been employed than in those using introtact probes. In spite of these differences, it may be instructive to compare the general performance levels for the two types of probe.

A series of studies in which blank-trial probes were used reveal generally low performance for kindergarten children. On the basis of the results from one of the earlier of these studies, Phillips and Levine (1975) concluded that kindergarten children are "qualitatively different" from adults and elementary school children, because they almost always manifest stereotypic hypotheses that are not altered by feedback. These writers were referring primarily to an experiment by Gholson et al. (1972, Experiment 2) in which the blank-trial probes were used with second-grade and kindergarten children. In this experiment, the stimuli were constructed from four bivalued attributes (brightness, shape, size, and position of a bar). Each child received nine experimental problems, each having 25 trials consisting of five four-trial blank probes and five feedback trials. Although the second-grade children's performance approximated that of older children and adults, the results for kindergarten children provided little evidence for the presence of cognitive strategies. The authors do not report the number of kindergarteners who solved one or more problems, but other reported aspects of their performance suggest that few, if any, did solve any problems. For example, the authors report that only 5% of the kindergarten protocols suggested the presence of a systematic strategy, with the remainder showing the stereotypic patterns associated with position alternation and perseveration and with stimulus preference.

Although some kindergarten children would normally be expected to learn such problems, not many would be expected to do so within five feedback trials. Hence, it is not possible to conclude definitely that the performance of the Gholson et al. (1972) kindergarten children was impaired by the presence of the blank-trial probes. Subsequent research by Gholson and his colleagues (Gholson & McConville, 1974; Gholson, O'Connor, & Stern, 1976) suggested that somewhat better performance can be coaxed from kindergarten children while blank-trial probes are employed. Gholson and McConville (1974) report results for two groups of kindergarten children, differentiated by the type of pretraining they received. Both groups received a series of stimulus differentiation tasks, in an oddity context, in which attributes used in the subsequent discrimination problems were employed. One group received feedback during the oddity tasks whereas the other did not. The children who received feedback during pretraining were reported to have solved 33% of their experimental problems whereas those who did not receive feedback solved only 20% of their problems. Because the authors do not report the number of children who solved one or more problems, it is not clear whether a few children solved all their problems or the majority solved some problems. Nevertheless, kindergarten performance was apparently better than had been reported earlier for kindergarten children (Gholson et al., 1972).

Gholson et al. (1976) reported results for kindergarten children selected by Piagetian conservation tasks to be clearly concrete operational. Half of these children received pretraining on the oddity task with feedback and the other half received the oddity pretraining without feedback. The authors report that the group with feedback solved approximately 33% of their problems whereas the group without feedback solved about 27% of their problems. (For kindergarten children selected to be clearly preoperational and given the same pretraining experiences, the corresponding percentages of problems solved were 8% and 7%.) Once again, the authors do not report the number of children who solved one or more problems, so it cannot be determined unequivocally whether the solved problems were contributed by a small minority or a major portion of each group. Judging from an experiment by Tumblin, Gholson, Rosenthal, and Kelley (1979), who do report data for individual children, although not for the numbers who solved problems, it would be safe to conclude that the solved problems were contributed by a small minority of each group. In this experiment, a maximum of 47% of the children manifested systematic strategies in the best performing of four groups of first-graders who had received different types of pretraining. This high watermark occurred on the last of six four-dimensional preliminary tasks, and the performance of this group dropped to an average of 8.33% on two eight-dimensional experimental problems.

In summary, experiments with kindergarten and first-grade children in which blank-trial probes have been used suggest that children of these ages have considerable difficulty in solving discrimination problems. By contrast, experiments in which introtact probes have been employed indicate that the majority of these children can solve such problems. A fairly typical result is that of Kemler, Shepp, and Foote (1976, Experiment 2), in which 139 kindergarten children were given a discrimination task with five stimulus attributes after having received a relatively brief preliminary task with two stimulus attributes. Both the preliminary and experimental tasks were embedded in a story-and-game context in which the children learned which of two pictures of identical twin girls is Amy by learning which one of several articles of clothing is uniquely Amy's. The attributes were different hats, belts, necklaces, hair ribbons, and eyeglasses. The pretraining attributes were different scarves and vests. One hundred and twenty of the 139 kindergarten children solved the five-attribute task in the 65 feedback trials that were allotted. In the same report, Kemler et al. (1976, Experiment 1) reported that all 50 of the 7-year-old children solved the five-attribute problem. Kemler (1978, Experiment 3) administered a series of four-attribute problems of the same sort, with introtact probes, to 49 kindergarten children after training on a single four-attribute problem. Only one child failed to solve the pretraining problem. Of the 48 who continued in the experiment, 38 solved at least four of the five experimental problems. Every subject solved at least one of the experimental problems.

As indicated on page 169ff., the present writers have also employed the introtact probe in monitoring children's hypotheses during problem solving. In an experiment in which all problems involved two pseudodimensions, constructed from either colors or forms, a group of 24 kindergarten and 16 first-grade children received LTL pretraining (see page 167ff.) on three problems before being shifted to the criterion problem (Cantor & Spiker, 1978, Group LTL). The first introtact probe for each task was administered prior to the first trial and the dimensional value mentioned in the child's probe response was assumed to identify the child's preferred dimension. *For all tasks, the child's preferred dimension, defined in this way, was made irrelevant.* This practice was adopted in all the studies to be reported from our laboratory in order to maximize the amount of information obtained from each subject, and it significantly increases the difficulty of the task. The results showed that performance on the criterion task did not differ significantly for the two age groups. For the combined group, 65% solved the criterion problem within the 40 trials allotted.

In another experiment involving introtact probes (Cantor & Spiker, 1979, Group LTL), we transferred children from tasks with pseudodimensions to tasks with genuine dimensions. The first two pretraining tasks were constructed from pseudodimensions—the first from colors and the second from forms. The third pretraining task, together with the criterion task, had genuine form and color dimensions, although the dimensional values on each discriminandum were spatially separated (partitioned) rather than unitary. These tasks were administered to 26 kindergarten and 24 first-grade children with an introtact probe given prior to each trial. The results showed that 50% of the kindergarten children and 79% of the first-grade children solved the criterion problem in the 40 trials allotted.

In a third application of the introtact probe technique, 30 kindergarten children received pretraining on tasks with pseudodimensions and a criterion task of the same sort on the first of two daily sessions (Spiker & Cantor, 1979b, Group LTL). On the second day, they received pretraining on tasks with two genuine, partitioned dimensions, followed by a criterion task of the same sort. On the first day, 70% of the children solved the criterion problem with pseudodimensions; on the second day, 53% solved the criterion problem with genuine dimensions. These percentages are strikingly similar to those for kindergarten children in the two preceding experiments (65% and 50%, respectively).

To recapitulate, despite the confounding of several factors with the type of probe used in this series of experiments, it would seem that the introtact probe, relative to the blank-trial probe, results in considerably better concommitant learning by children of kindergarten and first-grade ages. The superiority of the introtact method over the blank-trial probes with respect to the learning by second-grade children has been established in a direct comparison.

In general, the use of the blank-trial probe seems to be associated with the choice of stimuli with a large number of dimensions and with the choice of a small number of feedback trials, both of which operate to reduce the number of children who will solve the problems. Moreover, the blank-trial technique requires four consecutive choices in order to determine a single simple hypothesis, a requirement that occasions the loss of large amounts of data from younger children. On the other hand, the argument can be made that some of the verbalizations of many of the younger children, and all the verbalizations of some of the children, do not constitute genuine hypotheses and that the introtact method does not provide a ready means of screening out such instances. For this reason, and others, it may be advisable to continue to collect data with both techniques, ultimately choosing whichever method provides the most useful insights into the cognitive functioning of young children.

The Effect of the Locus of the Probe.   The single blank-trial probe is temporally spread out, because four or more successive trials are required. For each blank trial, however, all dimensional values are in the visual field of the child. Similarly, when the child is asked to respond to the introtact probe, the stimuli are in full view. Kemler (1978) commented on a difference between the blank-trial probe and her own procedures. In her procedure the introtact probe is administered immediately following feedback on each trial except the first, with the positive discrminandum in full view *and clearly identified as correct.* She noted that her unselected kindergarten children had higher win–stay, lose–shift, and local-consistency probabilities than did the kindergarten children selected for being concrete operational by Gholson et al. (1976). She suggested that these differences may have arisen from the fact that the blank-trial procedure, as currently used, requires the child to select a new hypothesis without having perceptual access to the information from the preceding feedback. The children in the blank-trial procedures, in other words, must rely on their memories of the preceding feedback when selecting their new hypotheses.

In all three of our experiments mentioned in the preceding section, the introtact probe was administered immediately before each trial. Thus, although the child had visual access to all attributes of the discrimnanda, the feedback information from the preceding trial was available, if at all, only in memory. A comparison of our conditional probabilities with those of Kemler (1978), for children of the same ages in as nearly comparable conditions as we could find, indicated that her local-consistency, win–stay, and lose–shift probabilities were consistently higher than those we obtained. Only with respect to response consistency were our results superior. For example, all our subjects, including kindergarteners, selected the discriminandum indicated by their hypothesis nearly every time, whereas the second- and fifth-graders of Kemler et al. (1976) made consistent responses only 63% of the time. A subsequent paper by Kemler (1978) reported considerably improved response consistency, at least for the older children in Experiments 1 and 2; however, it was only .73 for the kindergarten children of Experiment 3.

A comparison of the Kemler (1978) experiments with our own indicated that a larger proportion of her kindergarten children solved some criterion problems than was true of our subjects. This fact led us to consider the hypothesis that the Kemler probe technique produces better learning, although the discrepancy might be accounted for by our practice of making the children's preferred dimension irrelevant.

These and other considerations led to the design of an experiment that would test the hypothesis that the locus of the probe has a significant effect on the performance of kindergarten children. For convenience, the Kemler procedure is referred to as a posttrial probe, because the probe is made *after* the choice response and with the stimuli still in place. Our procedure is referred to as a pretrial probe, because the probe is made after the new stimuli have been placed but *prior* to the choice response. The experimental design was a 2 × 2 factorial, with the two types of probes and two types of pretraining. One of the two types of pretraining was the standard LTL condition followed by a single criterion task. The second condition was a control developed for one of our earlier experiments (Spiker & Cantor, 1979b, Group SST). Children in this group received the same number of pretraining problems with introtact probes, but the pretraining problems were simple simultaneous discrimination problems with a single nonspatial dimension relevant and none irrelevant. The SST pretraining was intended to inform the child that the tasks were soluble rather than guessing games but without providing the child with experience in analyzing and shifting attention among two or more nonspatial dimensions.

The pretraining tasks for the LTL groups and the criterion task for all groups included discriminanda constructed from red–green and blue–yellow pseudodimensions. The discriminanda for the pretraining tasks of the SST groups contained a single color dimension, red–green for some tasks and blue–yellow for others. The subjects were 92 kindergarten children, assigned at random in equal numbers to the four groups. All subjects received a minimum of 16 trials on the criterion task and the experiment was terminated for subjects who failed to meet criterion in 40 trials.

A preliminary multivariate analysis of variance that included all dependent measures established that the main effects of type of pretraining and type of probe, as well as their interaction, were statistically reliable. Only the most salient of the results are reported here.

The simplest explication of the results begins with the interaction between probe type and type of pretraining. The effects of probe type were different for the SST and LTL conditions with respect to several of the response measures. The type of probe had no effect on the number of children who learned the criterion task in the SST condition, but there were significantly more learners in the posttrial group than in the pretrial group in the LTL condition. The same pattern held for the proportion of correct choices in the first 16 trials (i.e., there was no difference between the two probe types in the SST condition, whereas the posttrial subjects scored much higher than the pretrial subjects in the LTL condition). Moreover, the valid-hypothesis index did not differ for the two probe types in the SST condition, although there was a large difference in favor of the posttrial probe in the LTL condition.

With respect to the remaining response measures, the effects of type of probe did not differ for the SST and LTL conditions. The response-consistency index was significantly greater for the pretrial probe than for the posttrial probe for both pretraining conditions. The local-consistency, win–stay, and lose–shift indices, however, were all significantly higher for the posttrial probes than for the pretrial probes and the differences were of about the same magnitude for the SST and LTL conditions.

Our interpretation of these results utilizes, and extends, some concepts developed by Kemler (1978). She distinguished between the efficiency of short-term decisions as measured by local-consistency, win–stay, and lose–shift probabilities and the efficiency of long-term decision making that is characterized by, in addition, a low probability of a repeat per opportunity. She concluded that her kindergarten children had quite respectable short-term efficiency but were deficient in regard to the long-term efficiency. Using these concepts to summarize the results of the present experiment, the posttrial probe, relative to the pretrial probe, improved the short-term efficiency of both the SST and LTL children.

Relative to the pretrial probe, the posttrial probe improved the long-term efficiency of the LTL children only.

It is possible to provide a more detailed interpretation of the manner in which these results came about. The pretrial probe, coming immediately prior to the choice response, places a demand on the child to be response consistent. Thus, if the child indicates that the red one might be the one that is always correct, it would be capricious at best to choose the green one immediately afterward. Even if the child viewed the task as a guessing game in which the "correct" value varied from trial to trial, he would be constrained to choose the one designated by his immediately preceding probe response. The same constraint is not placed on the choice of the child who receives a posttrial probe, since the choice response is separated from the preceding probe by a substantial time interval during which the setting for Trial n is removed and that for Trial $n + 1$ is placed. The posttrial probe, coming immediately after the feedback, places a demand on the child to be locally consistent. He is constrained to choose his next hypothesis from the attributes of the stimulus that was just designated as correct. It should also be noted that if a child's choice on Trial n is both incorrect and consistent with his previous hypothesis, he cannot be locally consistent on Trial $n + 1$ without also changing his hypothesis. In brief, children with high local-consistency proba-' bilities will also have high lose–shift probabilities. Moreover, if a child is both correct and consistent with his previous hypothesis on Trial n, and if he is also locally consistent on Trial $n + 1$, then he is more likely to retain his previous hypothesis following the positive feedback than is the child who is not constrained to be locally consistent. In other words, children with high local-consistency probabilities are likely to have high win–stay probabilities.

It should be noted that local consistency does not place the same constraint on the child with respect to repeating a previously disconfirmed hypothesis. In particular, consider the locally consistent child who restricts his hypotheses to the values of an irrelevant dimension. After the first few trials on the task, such a child will not produce a single hypothesis that is valid, but he might still have a perfect win–stay and lose–shift record. It is also important to note that children who are contrained to make locally consistent hypotheses, with the concommitant high win–stay, lose–shift probabilities but with low valid-hypothesis probabilities, can make little progress toward a strategic solution. Such subjects are expected eventually to capture the correct stimulus value by virtue of the win–stay, lose–shift rules, but only if the correct hypothesis becomes available. For children who are perseverating on a single irrelevant dimension, even this outcome is not possible.

The posttrial probes in the present experiment imposed a local consistency constraint on subjects in both the SST and LTL conditions. For the SST children, of whom more than one-third perseverated on the irrelevant pseudodimension, this imposition led to higher win–stay and lose–shift probabilities but without any increase in either the valid-hypothesis probability or in the number of children solving. For the LTL children, however, with only 6.5% perseverating on the irrelevant pseudodimension, the local-consistency constraint resulted in higher valid-hypothesis probabilities and significantly more solvers, in addition to the higher win–stay and lose–shift probabilities. When the imposition of local consistency associated with the posttrial probe was combined with the LTL pretraining on tasks with two pseudodimensions, the result was a substantial increase in the proportion of solvers (from .65 in the LTL pretrial-probe group to .91 in the LTL posttrial-probe group).

Although pretrial probes have not generally produced high local consistency, Mims and Gholson (1977) have reported a variation in feedback procedures that has an effect similar to that of using posttrial probes. Second- and third-graders were given four-dimensional problems under a variety of feedback conditions. Of particular interest here was the verbal–directional–feedback condition in which the experimenter always pointed to the correct stimulus compound while giving verbal feedback for either correct or incorrect choices. Directing the child's attention to the positive compound resulted in a local consistency probability of .87 as compared with only .68 for verbal feedback alone. The fact that the local consistency with directed feedback was not so high as is generally obtained with posttrial probes is probably because the children could not always remember the stimulus information until the pretrial probe was given on the following trial. Whether directed feedback with pretrial probes also improves local consistency for even younger children may depend on the extent to which such memory losses occur.

The Effects of Various Task Features

Different investigators of hypothesis testing in children have developed somewhat different, not to say idiosyncratic, tasks and procedures. It seems worthwhile to consider whether the different methods have arisen as the result of systematic trial and error or are merely superstitions that have developed as the result of fortuitous reinforcement.

The Nature of the Stimuli.   It seems proper to begin with one of our own potential superstitions—the difference between genuine dimensions and pseudodimensions. In our first attempts to teach young children to test hypotheses systematically, we were repeatedly struck with the difficulty of communicating to children the role of dimensions and their values in a discrimination task. We began by using standard stimuli in such tasks for children (e.g., large blue square, small red circle, small blue circle, large red square). Such stimuli have been referred to as unitary (Spiker & Cantor, in press). It seemed that the children had difficulty in separating the dimensions with such stimuli, and we constructed partitioned stimuli in which the dimensional values on each discriminandum were spatially separated. On top of each discriminandum, we placed a color patch (e.g., red or green) and, spatially separated from the patch, a form outline (e.g., circle or square) with colors and forms arranged orthogonally to form a simultaneous discrimination problem with one relevant and one irrelevant dimension and with both varying within trials. The partitioned stimuli greatly simplified the pretraining, because the experimenter could now point to the value of a given dimension without simultaneously pointing to the values of all other dimensions. Unfortunately, it did not alleviate the children's tendencies to restrict their hypotheses to a single dimension (i.e., dimensional perseveration).

In order to reduce the dimensional perseveration, we carried the approach one step further by constructing the stimuli from a single dimension, forming pseudodimensions in the manner described on page 169ff. Subsequent use of the pseudodimensional stimuli strongly suggested that there was a lower incidence of dimensional fixation and a concommitant increase in the proportion of children who solved criterion tasks. These informal observations were supported later in an experiment in which the pseudodimensional stimuli were employed on Day 1 and partitioned stimuli with genuine dimensions were used on Day 2 (Spiker & Cantor, 1979b, Group LTL). In the standard LTL group of this experiment, 70% of the 30 kindergarten children solved the task with two pseudodimensions on Day 1 and only 53% of the same group solved the task with two genuine, partitioned dimensions on Day 2. The finding that Day 2 performance was worse than Day 1 performance, in spite of the greater benefit from learning to learn on Day 2 than on Day 1, clearly indicates that the tasks with genuine dimensions were more difficult than those with pseudodimensions. Moreover, only 13% were dimensionally fixated on Day 1, whereas 43% became fixated on Day 2. There were corresponding differences in the win–stay, lose–shift, and valid-hypothesis conditional probabilities. Examination of the data for the second day by itself would have necessitated much more pessimistic conclusions about the quality of kindergarten children's problem-solving strategies.

It should be noted that some children in the preceding experiment appear to have become dimensionally fixated even when the pseudodimensions were used. This raises the question as to whether the fixation problem has to do with dimensions or simply indicates that some children, for whatever reason, have a restricted sampling of hypotheses. Some light is shed on this problem by one of our recent unpublished experiments in which neither genuine dimensions nor pseudodimensions were used. The problems were constructed by substituting plastic animals for dimensional values, with half the animals placed on the left-hand side and the other half placed on the right-hand side on each trial. The child was asked to predict, following feedback on each trial, which animal he thought was identical to the one that the experimenter had hidden in a box; after the introtact probe, the next setting was presented and the child was required to choose one of the two sides in order to receive the next feedback. The arrangement of the animals in the sequence of trials was such that the formation of pseudodimensions was precluded and the number of viable hypotheses was halved with each feedback, irrespective of where one started in the sequence. Thirty kindergarten children were given three pretraining tasks comparable to those given under the standard LTL condition described earlier. The first task involved only four of the animals and the second used the remaining four. The third pretraining task employed six of the eight animals. The criterion task involved all eight animals, a task that would appear to be comparable to a four-dimensional discrimination problem. Nearly 75% (22) of the children solved the criterion task in the 24 allotted trials. Of the eight who failed to solve, seven used four or fewer hypotheses. These results strongly suggest that the dimensional perseveration phenomenon may not be entirely the result of difficulty in processing dimensional information. It may be in part the result of a general tendency on the part of the child to restrict his hypotheses to a subset of all those available.

Investigators of children's problem-solving strategies have differed with respect to the number of irrelevant stimulus dimensions they have employed in constructing their discriminanda. Although there are exceptions, those who use the blank-trial probe generally use a larger number of dimensions than do those who use the introtact probe. The difficulty of discrimination problems is known to be an increasing function of the number of irrelevant dimensions, but it is not entirely clear what effect this variable might be expected to have on problem-solving strategies. One possibility is that the effect of increasing task complexity in this way would be restricted to an increase in the memory load. In this case, an increase in task complexity should have little or no effect on the short-term efficiency indices of experienced problem solvers, because these indices depend only on information from the immediately preceding trial. Moreover, an increase in the number of irrelevant dimensions would not necessarily affect the long-term efficiency of sophisticated subjects unless the memory capacity were exceeded; in the latter case, the memory overload would manifest itself in the number of repeats of previously rejected hypotheses. There is a second alternative, however, that seems more plausible with respect to inexperienced problem solvers and would lead to the expectation of more widespread consequences. There is the possibility that a large number of irrelevant dimensions would cause a general breakdown in the entire problem-solving process, perhaps because of a general confusion, a state of frustration, or some other distraction. This alternative would anticipate a diminished short-term efficiency as well as poorer long-term efficiency and would especially anticipate such deterioration among younger children.

An experiment by Kemler (1978, Experiment 2) directly addresses the question as to the effects of varying the number of attributes in problems. She used the posttrial introtact probe with second- and sixth-graders. The problems were presented in the "story-and-game" context in which the children were to find the one item of wearing apparel that uniquely identified Amy. Half of the problems consisted of five attributes and the other half contained eight attributes. Kemler found that the eight-attribute problems required a couple of extra trials to solve and that the children had to make one or two extra new hypotheses before solution. All measures of short-term efficiency were at or near unity in both the five- and eight-attribute problems. Although the number of repeats of previously rejected attributes was somewhat higher for the eight-attribute problems than for the five-attribute problems, the number of repeats for both types of tasks was well below that expected by the random-sampling, local-consistency model with which she compared the data. Her conclusion was that there was no evidence, at either age level, that the larger number of attributes produced any deterioration in either the short-term or long-term efficiency.

Kemler (1978) contrasted her findings with those of Gholson and Danziger (1975) who reported the results of an experiment with second- and sixth-graders. Their subjects were given blank-trial probes in the conventional manner and were asked to solve both four-attribute and eight-attribute problems. They found that both age groups had somewhat lower win–stay, lose–shift, and local-consistency probabilities for the eight-attribute problems than for those with only four attributes. Although the long-term efficiency of the sixth-grade children, as indicated by the number who manifested systematic strategies, was about the same for both types of problems, the authors report that, among the second-graders, significantly more of the four-attribute problems manifested systematic strategies than was the case for the eight-attribute problems.

Although we have never compared different numbers of irrelevant attributes within a single experiment, we have unpublished data from two different experiments that bear on this issue. In one of them, 18 first-grade children were administered problems with two partitioned dimensions; in the other, 21 first-graders were given problems with three partitioned dimensions. Both groups received identical LTL pretraining. The stimuli for the first two pretraining tasks involved two pseudodimensions and those for the third problem were constructed from two partitioned dimensions. The stimuli for the two-dimensional criterion task were constructed from color and form and those for the three-dimensional criterion task were color, form, and size (of an arrowhead). The size of the arrowhead was always irrelevant in the three-dimensional task.

Our results resembled those of Gholson and Danziger (1975) rather than those of Kemler (1978). Whereas 89% of the children solved the two-dimensional task, only 52% solved the three-dimensional task in the 40 trials allotted. The win–stay and lose–shift indices for the two-dimensional problem were well above those for the three-dimensional problem. The valid-hypothesis probability for the two-dimensional problem was .71, whereas that for the three-dimensional problem was only .43.

Our attempt to reconcile these different results implicates the posttrial introtact probe that Kemler (1978) employed. As indicated on page 177ff., the administration of the introtact probe immediately after feedback, in the presence of the clearly marked positive discriminandum, constrains the subject to be locally consistent. The local consistency forces a rejection of the disconfirmed previous hypothesis and also increases the probability that the previous hypothesis will be retained if it was not disconfirmed. Hence, Kemler did not find any deterioration of short-term efficiency in her eight-attribute problems. There is still another consequence of the posttrial probe and its concommitant local consistency. The posttrial probe makes it unnecessary for the subject to consider more than half of the total number of possible hypotheses on any one trial, which greatly reduces the memory load as compared to that for the blank-trial or pretrial-probe subject. With the blank-trial probe, or the pretrial introtact probe, the hypothesis is elicited while both discriminanda and all dimensional values are in view, but of course the subject is not informed as to which is correct. In order for the pretrial-probe subject to achieve the same advantage that the posttrial-probe subject has on each trial, he would have to be able to memorize, after feedback on each trial, all the dimensional values of the positive discriminandum. In addition, he would have to be sufficiently planful to remember on each trial to do the memorizing. It is probably unrealistic to expect kindergarten, first-grade, and second-grade children to exhibit the planfulness necessary to *try* to memorize the features of the positive discriminandum following feedback. It also seems quite likely that the smaller number of hypotheses that the posttrial-probe child needs to consider on each trial considerably reduces the level of frustration from that which the blank-trial or pretrial-probe children often endure.

The "Story-and-Game" Context.   The level of performance achieved by the kindergarten children in Kemler's study (1978, Experiment 3) is impressive. After a relatively small amount of pretraining, these 5-year-olds solved problems with four attributes. Nearly 80% of them solved at least four of their five problems and every child solved at least one problem. Although some of the children who solved only one problem may have been fortunate enough to have had a preferred attribute assigned as relevant, the rate of solution is exceptionally good even when this possibility is considered.

Kemler (1978) suggested that the posttrial probe accounted for the superiority of her children, relative to those given blank-trial probes, in the measures of short-term efficiency and presumably in the number of problem solvers. We demonstrated experimentally (page 176ff.) that she was correct in this hypothesis. She also suggested that the "story-and-game" context provided a more effective means of communicating the nature of the task to the children and that this factor might also have improved the children's performance. Although the posttrial probe by itself might be enough to account for the general superiority of the kindergarten children's performance, the present writers are inclined to agree with her surmise about the context.

Kemler's (1978) context for the task may have provided an unusually effective way of explaining to the children that there is one and only one solution to each problem. The notion of the existence of two persons who look very much alike but with each having a proper name is within the experience of most kindergarten children. Letting the children see the pictures transformed before their eyes by an exchange of wearing apparel must surely be an effective way of informing the children that even though appearances change somewhat from trial to trial, there is really only one solution (i.e., finding Amy) and the object of the problem is to find a way to tell which one of the two she is. It would be a significant research contribution to compare that context with the more conventional one, holding constant the attributes themselves.

The Effect of Memory Aids. For present purposes, the term *memory aid* is used to refer to information that is provided to the subject that he would otherwise have to remember from preceding trials. It is useful to distinguish between two classes of such information—information about hypotheses and information about the stimulus settings and their feedback outcomes. Kemler (1978) designated these two classes of information as hypothesis memory and stimulus memory, respectively. When the experimenter provides information that relieves the subject of the need for hypothesis memory, he may provide the subject with information about which hypotheses have been previously disconfirmed, which hypothesis is currently under test, or which hypotheses have not yet been tested. When information is provided to relieve the subject of the need for stimulus memory, the subject may receive information, with respect to one or more preceding trials, concerning which stimulus compound was designated as positive, which compound was designated as negative, or which stimulus was chosen and what the feedback outcome was. The value of such information may well depend on the subject's strategy. For example, a focusing strategy would be facilitated by stimulus memory, whereas a sequential hypothesis-testing strategy would seem to require hypothesis memory (see pages 186ff. and 191ff.).

It is not only likely that the type of strategy employed determines the kind of information needed, but it seems equally likely that the kind of information available affects the type of strategy employed. This fact makes it difficult to determine the effect of memorial aids on problem-solving performance without confounding other factors. An experiment by Eimas (1970) illustrates the nature of the problem. The tasks employed were discrimination problems with three nonspatial dimensions—shape and size of alphabetic letters and color of background on which the letter was displayed. Each problem consisted of 12 blank-probe trials and 4 feedback trials. There were 8 practice and 16 test problems. Let us first consider the conditions arranged for one of his groups of second-grade children (Group M). After each feedback trial, the two discriminanda were left in front of the child throughout the task and, depending on whether the outcome for that trial was positive or negative, a plus or minus sign was placed over the discrimnandum chosen. For this group, then, Eimas provided complete cumulative stimulus information, eliminating any need for the child to have stimulus memory. A control group (Group CON) received the same pretraining and test problems but did not receive the memory aids.

Of the response measures that Eimas reported, the one most relevant here is the percentage of times that the last hypothesis was consistent with the outcome of each of the three preceding feedback trials. The consistency of the last hypothesis with the outcome of the immediately preceding feedback trial was earlier referred to as local consistency. Eimas (1970) found that Group M, relative to Group CON, showed a higher percentage of consistent hypotheses at each of the three degrees of remoteness. Although he does not report the number of children who were globally consistent (i.e., consistent on all three trials), his data indicate that a minimum of about 47% for Group M and 0% for Group CON must have been globally consistent. The maximum percentage that could have been globally consistent is 80% for Group M and 64% for Group CON.

Given such results, it would be tempting indeed to conclude that the memory aids had increased the incidence of focusing in Group M relative to Group CON. Although such a conclusion might be correct, one would be well-advised to be cautious. It is also possible that before the child makes the last hypothesis, he scans the three feedback trials with their attendant outcomes and is able to identify visually the common dimensional value among the positive compounds. For example, he sees that all the positive stimuli are red. Such a strategy would also produce high percentages of third hypotheses that would be consistent with the outcomes of all three feedback trials. Moreover, given what we now know about the incidence of focusing in the early elementary school ages, the scanning strategy seems considerably more likely than the focusing strategy. For any child who used the strategy of concurrently scanning the feedback trials, the memory aids have affected his strategy in an obvious way. As an additional point, it is conceivable that the memory aids might suggest the focusing strategy to children who would not otherwise have thought of such a strategy.

Still another problem with the use of memory aids is that the child may be taught operations with memory aids that mimic strategies in their effects but do not constitute genuine strategies. One of our unpublished experiments conducted several years ago illustrates this problem. We were attempting to increase the number of children who, following pretraining, could test hypotheses systematically. We constructed a set of small, hypothesis cards on each of which was one of the features of the partitioned discriminanda that were used for both pretraining and criterion problems. Thus, one hypothesis card would have an outline of a square, another the outline of a circle, a third one a blob of red color, etc. Forty-eight kindergarten children were given pretraining during which they were taught to test the hypothesis cards, one by one, using the win–stay, lose–shift, and valid-hypothesis rules. The stack of hypothesis cards was placed to the child's right. He would select a card from the stack, place it in full view on the front of the apparatus, and choose from the first pair of blocks the one that had that feature on it. He was taught to continue to select the block with that feature on succeeding trials (win–stay) unless its correctness was disconfirmed by a failure to find a marble inside the block. Then, following the lose–shift rule, he would remove the card, place it to his left, select another (valid) hypothesis card from the stack to his right, and continue the process until the correct feature had been identified. Most children successfully transferred the technique into the second pretraining task; by the third pretraining task, all the children were able to use the procedure flawlessly.

After pretraining was complete, half the children were transferred into the criterion task with the hypothesis cards, and the other half received the same criterion task without the cards. The children who were allowed to use cards during the criterion task performed nearly perfectly, transferring their newly acquired skills with very few errors. Of the 24 children who used cards, 22 learned the criterion task within the 40 trials allotted. Of the 24 children who did not have cards, only 6 met criterion. The children with cards appeared to be performing the task mechanically, although with bureaucratic officiousness and obvious enjoyment. The poor performance of the group for which the cards were removed indicates, however, that there was no grasp of the hypothesis-testing strategy that underlay the use of the hypothesis cards.

We found it difficult to believe that the superior criterion-task performance of the children with hypothesis cards was the result of helping the children to remember the four hypotheses. Our conclusion was that we had taught the children to perform a perceptual motor task with results that mimicked the cognitive strategy of sequential hypothesis testing. When the children were deprived of their mechanical paraphenalia, they had very little idea of how to proceed, performing even more poorly than children of the same age who had received our standard LTL pretraining. One could undoubtedly teach many 5-year-old children to use a calculator successfully to multiply pairs of numbers and read the answers, but it would not be wise to conclude either that they knew the multiplication tables or that they had learned the principle of multiplication.

Parrill-Burnstein (1978) gave one of her four groups of kindergarten children (Group 4) training and memory aids that were quite comparable to those we employed in the preceding experiment. The results were similar to ours with memory aids present—the children who had been trained in the use of the memory aids solved 100% of their problems as compared to 36% for those who had not been trained. The design did not permit an assessment of the children's problem-solving skills after removal of the memory aids.

Kemler (1978, Experiment 1) also made use of memory aids for one of her conditions. Second- and third-graders constituted the younger of her groups and fifth- and sixth-graders were the older group. She provided the children with iconic representations of the values of the stimulus attributes on an orange card and instructed them to place the one that represented the current hypothesis on a silver card. When the child changed hypotheses, he was instructed to put the representation of the previous hypothesis in one of two places—on a black card if he was sure that it was not the secret one or back on the orange card if he was not sure that it was not the secret one. She did not provide the child with criteria for retaining or shifting hypotheses, as Parrill-Burnstein and we did. When the performance on the criterion tasks of children given memory aids was compared with that of children without memory aids, there was no evidence at either age level that the memory aids had facilitated performance on the discrimination problems. Although the children with memory aids had significantly higher levels of response consistency, presumably because the aids helped them to remember the hypothesis under test, there were no differences with respect to any of the other indices of strategy.

The following conclusions seem warranted by the combined results of these experiments. The "memory aids" have facilitated performance, not by aiding memory, but by either suggesting a simple strategy to the children or actually providing the children with a simple strategy. In the experiment by Eimas (1970), the memory aids permitted the children to find the solution by examining the entire set of positive stimuli and finding the value of the attribute that they all had in common. In the experiment of Parrill-Burnstein (1978), as in our own, the children were both instructed in and given practice with the win–stay, lose–shift, and sample-without-replacement principles. Moreover, clear descriptions were provided of the occasions on which these principles were to be applied, thereby relieving the child of the need to make judgments. Kemler (1978) did not provide the children with the win–stay and lose–shift principles, and although her instructions hinted at the principle of sampling without replacement, she did not provide the children with a simple test as to when sampling without replacement should be practiced.

Age-Related Changes in Problem-Solving Strategies

The introduction of the blank-trial probes in the study of children's problem solving made possible some interesting comparisons among children of different age levels. The probes permitted the study of differences among children of different ages, not merely with respect to their rates of solving problems but also with respect to their methods of solving the problems. Although there has been considerable progress in the development of a picture of these age-related changes, it will be seen that the progress has not been without occasional setbacks.

The Definition of Strategy Systems.   In a very influential paper, Gholson et al. (1972) described three different problem-solving stragegies that they reported to occur among adults and children of elementary school age. The first of these strategies, *focusing,* has been mentioned earlier in the present chapter. Focusing is the most efficient solution possible for the problems of concern here. If the stimulus settings for the feedback trials are properly arranged from trial to trial, it is possible for each feedback to halve the number of hypotheses that have not yet been disconfirmed until solution is achieved.

Gholson et al. (1972) described a second strategy, which they called *dimension checking* and which Gregg and Simon (1967) had referred to as local consistency with local nonreplacement of the disconfirmed dimension. Dimension checking, like focusing, requires that the subject be locally consistent. Suppose that a subject who is locally consistent on each trial tests the hypothesis "red" on Trial $n + 1$ and the hypothesis is disconfirmed by negative feedback. Such a subject would know, following feedback on any trial after the first, that he had obtained the hypothesis "red" from the positive discriminandum on Trial n and that "green" cannot be the solution because it was in the negative discriminandum on Trial n. Following disconfirmation of one value on any dimension, this subject would not need to test the complementary value.

The third strategy described by Gholson et al. (1972) is *hypothesis checking*, which also presupposes that the subject is locally consistent. A subject using this strategy system has the two hypotheses corresponding to the two values of each dimension organized in pairs. If the hypothesis corresponding to one value of a dimension is disconfirmed, he next tests the complementary hypothesis and proceeds through the dimensions one by one.

It should be pointed out that all three of the previously described systems presuppose that any subject using them will not only be locally consistent but will also follow the win–stay and lose–shift rules. Gholson et al. (1972) coordinated each type of strategy with specific hypothesis-feedback patterns. Because the hypothesis-checking strategy can produce patterns that mimic dimension-checking patterns and because dimension checking can produce patterns that would be expected from a focusing strategy, rather elaborate corrections for these chance events were worked out (Levine, 1975, pp. 293–299). In addition to these systematic patterns, others were interpreted to represent stereotypic modes of responding that would not lead to solutions (e.g., position alternation, stimulus preference, position preference, and residual patterns that could not be classified).

Developmental Changes in the Strategy Systems.   Differences in the incidence of the strategy systems among children of different age or grade levels have been explored in several experiments by Gholson and his associates (e.g., Gholson et al., 1972; Gholson & Danziger, 1975). In connection with these experiments, which are briefly described below, it should be pointed out that fairly large proportions of the problem protocols were unanalyzable for one reason or another and that the magnitude of these proportions was inversely related to the ages of the children. Two of the criteria that a problem protocol had to meet in order to be appropriate for the strategy-system analysis were that the first three or four probe patterns must have yielded simple hypotheses and that each of these hypotheses must have been locally consistent (Levine, 1975, pp. 293–299). For experiments with younger children, between 60% and 80% of the protocols failed to meet these (and other) criteria. Wherever percentages of problems manifesting strategy systems are reported below, it should be remembered that these percentages pertain only to the *classifiable* problems; these percentages grossly overestimate the incidence of the use of strategies by younger children.

In the first experiment in the series, Gholson et al. (1972) reported the results of two separate experiments in which kindergarteners, second-graders, fourth-graders, sixth-graders, and college students served as subjects. The authors report that college students solved about 45% of their classifiable problems using the focusing strategy, another 45% by dimension checking, and about 10% by hypothesis checking. The differences in performance among the second-, fourth-, and sixth-graders were relatively slight. These children were reported to solve about 10% of their classifiable problems by focusing, between 55% and 65% by dimension checking, and about 15% to 25% by hypothesis checking. Approximately 15% of the protocols either manifested stereotypic responding or were unclassifiable residual patterns. The authors reported that only 5% or 6% of the kindergarten children's problems reflected the use of a strategy system, with stereotypic responding manifested in 94% of the problems. The only strategy reported for any of the kindergarten children was hypothesis checking.

The findings by Gholson et al. (1972) for the kindergarten children were effectively replicated in the control condition of an experiment by Gholson and McConville (1974). The treatment of the children in this group was quite similar to that used by Gholson et al. (1972), and the authors report that none of the problem protocols manifested a strategy system. In an experiment by Gholson et al. (1976), a group of kindergarteners, who were selected for having passed conservation tests on liquid and quantity and who were then given a standard pretraining, were reported to manifest either hypothesis checking or dimension checking on about 45% of their problems. Kindergarten children who failed the conservation tests, however, manifested strategies on less then 10% of their problems.

Richman and Gholson (1978) confirmed the Gholson et al. (1972) findings for second-graders but reported a much higher incidence of focusing for sixth-grade children. One group of second-graders and one group of sixth-graders received pretraining approximating that given by Gholson et al. (1972), except that these children viewed a 10-minute videotape in which a model subject illustrated component skills (i.e., local-consistency, win–stay, lose–shift, and response-consistency rules) by choosing without comment the stimulus complex containing the dimensional value corresponding to the previously stated hypothesis, choosing a new locally consistent hypothesis after disconfirmation, and maintaining a confirmed hypothesis. Although the findings for the second-graders were approximately what they had been in the earlier study, the sixth-grade children were reported to have manifested focusing in 40% of their classifiable problems, whereas only about 10% of the sixth-grade children manifested focusing in the Gholson et al. (1972) experiment.

The developmental picture that appears to emerge from this series of experiments is the following. Unless they have been specifically tutored in testing hypotheses, only a small proportion of even highly selected kindergarten children show a planful, integrated strategy system. Second-graders, however, are reported to use the hypothesis-checking and dimension-checking strategies, as do fourth-graders. By the sixth grade, there is reported to be a substantial incidence of focusing, a strategy that college students are said to use in about 45% of their problems. As indicated in the next section, however, this developmental picture must be viewed in the light of several methodological considerations.

The Strategy-System Analysis Versus the Locally Consistent, Random-Sampling Model.   Kemler (1978) listed the assumptions of a model that describes the information processing of a child who is perfectly efficient on a short-term basis (see page 176ff.). The model assumes that the subject has perfect response consistency and local consistency and that he always follows the win–stay and lose–shift rules. It is also assumed that the subject will choose a new hypothesis following negative feedback by randomly sampling with replacement from the complete set of simple hypotheses. Any child operating from these rules is expected to solve the problem eventually. The only short-term memory requirement is that the current hypothesis must be retained until the next hypothesis is chosen in order to guarantee response consistency and application of the win–stay rule. The trial on which the solution occurs is a random variable. Kemler referred to this model as the random-sampling-with-local-consistency model, although we should remember that it also includes the response-consistency, win–stay, and lose–shift assumptions.

Kemler (1978) noted that the Gholson et al. (1972) system analysis does not allow for the possibility that a child might use a set of rules that yields highly efficient short-term processing of information, without having the planful integration across trials that is implied by each of the three Gholson et al. strategy systems. She also noted that the local-consistency model would predict the occurrence of hypothesis-feedback sequences that would be classified by the systems analysis as dimension checking and hypothesis checking. Finally, she used the local-consistency model to generate the probability of each possible hypothesis-feedback sequence for the three-trial, and sometimes four-trial, blocks that Gholson et al. used in their analyses.

Of the hypothesis-feedback sequences generated by the local-consistency model, Kemler (1978) found that the systems analysis of Gholson et al. (1972) would classify 50% as dimension checking, 30% as hypothesis checking, and 20% as residual patterns and that these percentages do not differ significantly from those obtained by Gholson et al. for second-graders. The local-consistency model therefore clearly provides an alternative explanation for the Gholson et al. results.

Kemler's (1978, Experiment 2) research also raises some question with respect to the accuracy of the incidence of focusing among elementary school children reported by Gholson (1972) and his associates. By definition, the focusing subject's hypothesis following Trial $n + 1$ should not only be locally consistent with the outcome of Trial $n + 1$ but it should also be consistent with the outcome on Trial n. If the subject is not focusing, the probability that the hypothesis following Trial $n + 1$ will be consistent with the outcome of Trial n should be about .5 provided the settings for the trials are randomly selected. Kemler found the mean for eight attribute problems to be .49 for 30 second-graders and .59 for 30 sixth-graders. In neither case was the obtained proportion significantly different from the expected chance value. Thus, she found no evidence that the children were focusing, a result that can be contrasted with a report of Gholson et al. (1972) that from 5% to 12% of second-, fourth-, and sixth-graders' problems were solved by focusing.

Although Kemler's (1978) theoretical considerations and empirical research raise questions about the accuracy of the frequencies Gholson et al. (1972) report for the strategy systems among elementary school children, it seems doubtful that the local-consistency model can account for all the results reported within the context of the systems analysis. For an example, consider an experiment by Richman and Gholson (1978) with second- and sixth-grade children who were given pretraining with videotapes in which focusing, dimension checking, or component rules were modeled. Sixth-grade children who were exposed to the focusing strategy had significantly more problems that manifested the focusing strategy than did children of the same grade who were exposed to the dimension-checking strategy. For both grades, children who were exposed to the dimension-checking strategy manifested the dimension-checking strategy in many more problems than did children of the same ages who had been exposed to the focusing strategy. It is difficult to see how the strategies to which the children were exposed could have had such specific effects if the rules governing the children's behavior were restricted to the set contained in the local-consistency model.

The Effects of Pretraining

Because research on hypothesis testing has usually included training on preliminary problems before administration of the criterion problem(s), it is appropriate to examine the effects of different types of pretraining on the hypothesis-testing behavior.

Training in the Solvability of the Problems.   We noted that many of the kindergarten children in our control groups, who did not receive experience with the problems prior to the criterion task, seemed to approach the discrimination-learning tasks with a guessing set. We thought such children could benefit from a type of pretraining that would teach them to anticipate a correlation between dimensional cues and the kind of feedback that they received, even if no extended experience in shifting attention among the various dimensions or in systematically testing hypotheses were provided for them.

In one of our experiments (Spiker & Cantor, 1979b), we included a group of 30 kindergarten children (Group SST) who were given as pretraining a series of simultaneous discrimination problems with only one (relevant) dimension. This type of pretraining was intended to teach the children to expect an invariant cue–reward relation in the criterion problem. Kindergarten children ordinarily discover the solution to such simple problems within a few trials and, indeed, only one of the 30 children failed to solve the first of the three pretraining problems in 10 trials. All the children solved the second and third pretraining problems within 10 trials. The performance of these children was compared to that of a control group of 60 kindergarten children, half of whom had received no pretraining (Group CON) and the other half of whom had received pretraining in sorting a stack of 40 cards into four piles in terms of which of the four stimulus components was affixed to each card (Group FAM). The criterion task involved two pseudodimensions, one relevant and one irrelevant, constructed from four forms.

The children given pretraining with the simple simultaneous problems performed better than the combined CON and FAM groups in two respects. The mean trial of last error occurred earlier, indicating faster learning than for the controls, and they were better than the control subjects in retaining hypotheses following positive feedback. Both of these outcomes would be expected as a consequence of their having learned that the problems were solvable. Of course, it is also expected that such training would improve the probability of rejecting hypotheses following negative feedback. Detection of any such improvement is not likely, however, when the control condition includes many children who are guessing on a trial-to-trial basis, because these children change hypotheses frequently whether the preceding outcome was positive or negative. The same children received a second criterion problem with genuine dimensions on Day 2, which was preceded by simple simultaneous discrimination problems for Group SST. The advantage for the SST group had been lost, however, presumably in part because the control children had had experience with the criterion problem on Day 1 and also because both groups showed more dimensional fixation in the task with genuine dimensions.

Training in Shifting Attention Among Dimensions.   As indicated in the previous section, pretraining on simple simultaneous discrimination problems probably produces an expectation in at least some of the children that there will be a relation between feedback and stimulus values. It does not, however, teach the child that it may be necessary to shift attention from one attribute to another in order to discover that relation. Because we adopted for all our experiments the practice of assigning the child's preferred dimension as irrelevant, we made certain that a shift of attention would be required for solution. The standard LTL condition was included in each of our experiments in order to provide the attention-shifting experience.

In some of our earlier research on hypothesis testing in children (Cantor & Spiker, 1978, 1979), the LTL condition was compared with a control condition (CON) in which no pretraining was given except for practice in naming the hypotheses and instructions about the nature of the criterion task. In five independent experiments, with children ranging in age from kindergarten to third grade, we found the LTL condition superior to the CON condition in both the win–stay and valid-hypothesis indices. Also, without exception, the LTL group was superior to the CON group with respect to the trial of last error.

In order to assess the effect of learning to shift attention among the stimulus attributes, it is necessary to control for the effect of learning to anticipate a cue–feedback relation. Such a control can be obtained by comparing performance in the LTL condition, in which children learn both to anticipate a cue–feedback relation and to shift attention among the stimulus attributes, with the SST condition, in which children learn to expect a cue–feedback relation but do not have experience in shifting among the stimulus dimensions. This comparison was carried out in a published experiment (Spiker & Cantor, 1979b). For the LTL group in this experiment, the pretraining and criterion tasks on Day 1 were all constructed from two pseudodimensions. The LTL tasks for Day 2 were all constructed from two genuine partitioned dimensions. The pretraining tasks for the SST children were unidimensional and, of course, these children received the same criterion tasks that were given the LTL children. For Day 1, the LTL condition was superior to the SST condition with respect to the trial of last error, the probability of retaining hypotheses following positive feedback, and the probability of making valid hypotheses. There was no difference in the lose–shift index. There was a marked deterioration of the LTL performance from Day 1 to Day 2, not only with respect to discrimination task performance but also with respect to the indices of strategy. Whether the deterioration in performance was the result of the greater difficulty of genuine dimensions or negative transfer resulting from the shift from pseudodimensions to genuine dimensions, the consequence was that Group LTL was superior to Group SST only with respect to the valid-hypothesis index and that comparison was of only borderline significance.

Our research with the LTL condition indicates that the type of pretraining routinely provided children in experiments involving blank-trial probes, as well as in the experiments by Kemler (1978), provides the subjects with at least two critical pieces of information. The first is that there exists in each problem an invariant cue–feedback relation to be discovered, as well as the general nature of that relation. The second is that shifting attention from attribute to attribute may be necessary in order to discover that relation, together with practice in shifting attention. Moreover, our observations across experiments that children consistently perform better in pseudodimensional tasks than in tasks having genuine dimensions lead us to believe that the child learns to shift attention among the attributes more easily if they are constructed from a single dimension such as color or form.

Training in Sequential Hypothesis Testing.   Kemler's (1978) analysis of the Gholson et al. (1972) strategy systems raises a serious question as to whether children of the early elementary school years use the complex strategies that have been claimed for them. The question remained, however, as to whether children of these ages could be taught a simpler strategy. One of our concerns has been with the latter question.

The strategy that seemed most promising was sequential hypothesis testing. As the name suggests, the strategy involves response-consistent, win–stay, lose–shift, and valid-hypothesis rules. By a combination of instructions, demonstrations, and exemplary problems, the child is given a complete list of possible hypotheses. During the pretraining, the child is taught to begin each problem by selecting a hypothesis from the list and to select on the first trial the discriminandum that is consistent with that hypothesis. The child is taught to retain that hypothesis as long as the discriminandum it refers to is designated as correct and to discard the hypothesis and select a new one when the discriminandum it refers to is designated as incorrect. When a new hypothesis is to be selected, emphasis is placed on the selection of a valid one, that is, one that has not been previously tested and disconfirmed. No attempt is made to teach local consistency. The children were not trained until they could perform perfectly; rather they were given three pretraining problems. In the first problem, the experimenter guided the child through testing the entire set of hypotheses, saving the hypothesis that named the negative cue until the penult and the one that named the positive cue until last. The second and third problems were prompted in the sense that the experimenter did not permit the child to violate the win–stay, lose–shift, or valid-hypothesis rules, but the child was otherwise free to choose the hypotheses in any order. We considered the appropriate control for this condition to be the LTL condition. Thus, the controls were children who were given the same number of pretraining problems and were given the solution to any problem that they failed to solve in a set number of trials.

The first comparison of these two conditions was with kindergarten and first-grade children, and it indicated that the special training was reasonably successful (Cantor & Spiker, 1978). The group given the hypothesis-testing pretraining (HYP) was significantly superior in applying the win–stay, lose–shift, and valid-hypothesis rules. Because we used the pretrial introtact probe, both groups were virtually perfect with respect to response consistency (see page 175ff.). Moreover, Group HYP was superior to Group LTL in performance on the criterion discrimination problem with respect to both trial of last error and percentage of children solving. A key indication of the effectiveness of the hypothesis-testing pretraining is the number of children in the two groups who made no strategy errors (i.e., they never failed to win–stay, lose–shift, or give a valid hypothesis). Approximately 58% of the HYP children made no errors in applying the sequential hypothesis-testing strategy, whereas 30% of the LTL children performed without strategy errors. Moreover, 82% of the HYP children and only 48% of LTL subjects made no more than three strategy errors.

The training and criterion problems in the experiment just referred to involved pseudodimensions constructed from forms or colors. Two other experiments with kindergarten and first-grade children have compared the two conditions with tasks that were constructed from genuine, partitioned dimensions (Cantor & Spiker, 1979; Spiker & Cantor, 1979b, Day 2). In both experiments, the HYP condition resulted in somewhat better application of the strategy rules and in somewhat better learning. Altogether, we have nine independent comparisons of the HYP and LTL conditions across experiments. These comparisons contain a total of 231 kindergarten and first-grade children and include both pseudodimensional tasks and tasks with genuine dimensions. Thirty percent of the LTL children, and 40% of the HYP children made no strategy errors. The percentages of children who made three or fewer strategy errors in the LTL and HYP conditions were 46% and 64%, respectively. In none of the nine comparisons was the LTL condition found to be superior to the HYP condition with respect to strategy errors (Spiker & Cantor, in press).

It is clear that the problem-solving strategies of kindergarten and first-grade children can be improved through training. The question immediately arises as to whether children of these ages can be taught more complex strategies such as dimension checking or focusing. It will be recalled that Richman and Gholson (1978) attempted to influence the types of strategy systems used by second- and sixth-grade children by exposing them to the modeling of dimension-checking and focusing strategies on videotape (page 190ff.). The authors reported an increase in the frequency of dimension checking for both grade levels after exposure to the dimension-checking strategy on the videotape. Moreover, the sixth-grade children were reported to have exhibited a larger number of problems solved by the focusing strategy following exposure to the focusing strategy. It remains to be seen whether even younger children can be taught one or more of the complex strategies.

CONCLUSIONS AND IMPLICATIONS

In this final section, we attempt to formulate the major conclusions that are supported by the research reviewed in the preceding sections. Some of these findings point to unresolved empirical issues, and it seems worthwhile to discuss their implications for further research. Finally, we direct attention to some implications for theoretical changes.

Empirical Conclusions

We began by asking what is known about the onset of hypothesis testing in young children. The research that has been reviewed here supports two important clusters of related conclusions. First, most kindergarten children are capable of using simple hypothesis-testing strategies. Some of the most convincing evidence for this evidence for this conclusion comes from the studies in our laboratory in which simplified tasks were employed and the children were specifically pretrained to use the rules of sequential hypothesis testing. For kindergarten children given hypothesis pretraining with pseudodimensions, more than half apply the strategy perfectly, and more than three-fourths make three or fewer strategy errors. The use of pseudodimensions diminishes the pervasive difficulty that children of this age have in shifting attention among the stimulus dimensions. Our contention is that the ability of these children to adopt systematic modes of problem solving is often masked by the dimensional fixation. Although the fixation phenomenon deserves study in its own right, it may lead us to a serious underestimation of the basic problem-solving skills of these younger children if it is not minimized or eliminated in problems. Empirical support for this conclusion can be found in our comparisons of the LTL pretraining with the CON condition. The LTL children are not as efficient hypothesis testers as are the HYP children, but they perform remarkably well compared to the CON children. Our interpretation is that LTL pretraining provides experience in shifting attention among the dimensions, thereby reducing dimensional fixation and permitting the adoption of a systematic strategy by many of the children who did not have the benefit of HYP training.

The central member of our second set of conclusions is that although children as young as 5 years of age (and probably younger) are capable of using systematic strategies, they do not always do so. In this cognitive domain as in several others, including memory, verbal learning, and mediated generalization, there is a general "production deficiency" among younger children. They do not seem to seek out the best strategy for learning, although they can in effect be trapped into adopting such strategies under certain conditions. Our survey of the literature suggests that, for the younger child in particular, the nature of the task, the type and locus of the probe, and the quality of the pretraining are all important determiners of both the occurrence and efficiency of systematic hypothesis testing. For example, given the use of pretrial probes and rather conventional stimuli, we found it necessary to use highly simplified tasks to demonstrate strategies in younger children. Kemler (1978), however, using posttrial probes in the story-and-game context, had good success with considerably more complex tasks.

We are convinced that the locus of the probe is a highly potent variable, because use of the posttrial probe virtually guarantees adherence to the local-consistency and lose–shift rules. Although we found that local consistency does not in turn guarantee the use of a strategy, it does, when combined with learning-to-learn experience, set the stage for the adoption of systematic modes of problem solving.

A final point regarding critical variables concerns the nature of the probe itself. As stated in the introduction, the probe has the potential for dramatically changing the phenomenon under study. We strongly suspect that the blank-trial probe interferes in a variety of ways with the determination of the problem-solving capacities of young children, and we believe that the introtact probe is the best tool so far devised for this purpose. Our results and those from other laboratories (Kemler, 1978; Phillips, 1974) indicate that introtact probes need not interfere with performance, although they may produce some facilitation under certain conditions. It seems likely that the facilitation results from the removal of the production deficiency discussed previously; that is, children who are capable of systematic hypothesis testing are more likely to do so when required to state their hypotheses overtly.

Implications for Future Research

The research that has been reviewed in the foregoing pages has some clear implications with respect to the more fruitful procedures to be used in the study of hypothesis testing of young children. In addition, there are several sets of related research problems that have been broached without having been resolved. In this section, we summarize some procedural recommendations and briefly identify some of the research areas that we consider both promising and in need of further investigation.

Choice of Techniques.   On the basis of our literature review, we would recommend the use of the introtact probe technique, over the blank-trial procedures, for research on problem solving in younger children. If the introtact probe is introduced during the solution of preliminary problems, it seems to become a natural part of the task, especially so when the posttrial probe is used. There are several choices with respect to the type of stimulus materials. If a large number of attributes is needed, the Kemler (1978) materials are probably the best alternative. For smaller numbers of dimensions, pseudodimensions of the type that we have employed would seem to be entirely adequate, although we have never used more than two pseudodimensions. Another attractive alternative, at least to the children, are the plastic animals (page 179ff.) that can also be arranged to form pseudodimensions if desired.

Research on the Interaction of Age and Type of Pretraining.   We are not at all convinced that the lower age limit for teaching the sequential hypothesis-testing technique has been reached. One of the authors, as an exercise in a laboratory class, has used the LTL and HYP pretraining conditions with pseudodimensional tasks with 36 bright 4-year-old preschool children. It is of considerable interest to note that 42% of the HYP children in this experiment were capable of a flawless performance of the sequential hypothesis-testing strategy during the criterion task.

A second research problem is concerned with the teaching of more complex strategies, such as dimension checking or focusing, to children of the younger elementary school ages. With a judicious choice of stimulus materials and a perspicacious selection of instructions and demonstrations, it is possible that second- and third-graders could be taught to focus and that kindergarten and first-grade children could be taught to use the dimension-checking strategy.

Research on the Type of Stimulus Materials.   Our qualitative observations lead us to suspect that the use of pseudodimensional tasks results in better performance, with respect to both hypothesis testing and problem solving, than does the use of tasks constructed from conventional genuine dimensions. Our belief is that pseudodimensions reduce the younger children's tendencies to fixate on a single dimension and thereby increase the probability that the children will eventually arrive at the correct hypothesis. Nevertheless, we know of no studies in which a direct comparison of the two types of stimulus materials has been made.

Comparisons between different experiments also lead us to believe that the partitioned type of stimuli promote better hypothesis testing among younger children than do the unitary stimuli. The only instances in which we found the use of introtacts to interfere with learning were two cases in which unitary stimuli were employed (Cantor & Spiker, 1977; Spiker & Cantor, 1977). This indirect evidence for the superiority of the partitioned stimuli should be validated against a direct comparison.

We think that direct comparisons in both cases will support the indirect evidence. We also suspect that the superiority of one type of stimulus over the other is in both cases due to the same factor—reduction in the incidence of dimensional fixation. In any event, the dimensional-fixation phenomenon warrants further investigation.

Research on Memory Aids.   An important unresolved issue is whether memory aids can be used to supplement the presumably deficient memorial capabilities of young children, thereby improving their problem-solving strategies. In those applications in which the memory aids have been demonstrated to be effective, the memory aids may also have suggested a strategy to the children that would not have arisen without the aids. One way in which the memorial function of the memory aids can be unconfounded from their function as an instigator of strategies is to compare the performance of two groups, both of which have been taught the same strategy and both of which have identical memory aids, but only one of which has been taught to use the memory aids in implementing the strategy. Since both groups would be in possession of the strategy, the role of the memory aids in reducing the memory requirements of the task could be determined. It would seem that memory aids must surely facilitate the focusing strategy, even for adults, when the discriminanda consist of a large number of attributes.

Implications for Theory

The research reviewed in the preceding sections has two major implications for theorizing over the next several years. The first is that neither the incremental theories of learning nor the cognitive theories of problem solving describe very accurately the problem-solving behavior of children between the ages of about 3 or 4 years and approximately 10 or 12 years. The second implication is that there is an urgent need to address theoretically the *acquisition* of problem-solving strategies.

Saltatory Learning Versus Incremental Problem Solving. The empirical research of the last 10 years indicates that both the incremental associative theories and the cognitive hypothesis-testing theories are in need of modification. Children between 3 and 10 years of age are far more planful than is consistent with the incremental theories in their present form. Even with such notions as response-produced stimulation and mediating mechanisms, the changes in associative processes that were generally conceivable in such theories would be too slow and unsystematic to account for the hypothesis-testing behavior actually observed. Appropriate modification of the classical associative theories is not out of the question, however. The associative theory proposed nearly 20 years ago by Zeaman and House (1963), and reaffirmed more recently (Zeaman & House, 1974), contains parameters with permissible ranges that could accommodate very rapid shifts in attention from dimension to dimension, as well as rapid conditioning of instrumental behavior. The present authors have also offered a tentative associative schema that was specifically designed to address the facts of experiments on hypothesis testing (Spiker & Cantor, 1979a). In this schema, too, the associative processes are speeded up by means of one-trial acquisition and extinction. One of the more innovative and promising theoretical ventures is that recently described by Kendler (1979), in which she proposes a gradual incremental model of learning for younger children, a cognitive saltatory model for older children and adults, and a probabilistic choice of models for children of intermediate chronological ages.

At the other end of the continuum, the cognitive hypothesis-testing theories have generally assumed perfect processing of information according to one or more sets of rules, with each set defining a specific strategy. Our research, as well as that of others, however, indicates that no matter what strategy the younger child may be following, he is likely to make errors, and he may not even use the same strategy across successive problems of the same type. The errorless use of a strategy, of course, is not a necessary assumption in cognitive theorizing. Formulations such as that of Trabasso and Bower (1968) predict that the subject will make sequences of choices that would in other frames of reference be interpreted as "strategy errors." One of the main difficulties of the Tra-basso–Bower model, at least as far as young children are concerned, is that it fails to predict that large numbers of subjects may fail to learn despite extensive training. Kendler's (1979) two-level theory would accommodate such an event in the incremental mode.

The Acquisition of Strategies.   In studying adults, the task of the cognitive theorists has been to identify and describe fully developed strategies. With young children, the problem is different and much more complex—describing the *acquisition* of strategies in theoretical terms. The acquisition process is undoubtedly a gradual one, easily influenced by the variables discussed in earlier sections of this chapter, as well as by memory factors and general motivational variables such as boredom, fatigue, and distractibility. For any theory to be successful at these ages, it must permit variability in the application of the rules of strategy.

The production deficiency, mentioned previously, also has implications for theory in this respect. Our research indicates that certain critical variables may determine whether or not a given child will even attempt to use a strategy in a given situation. Any successful theory must, therefore, deal with the fact that the same child may apply a strategy perfectly under one set of conditions (e.g., with posttrial probes) and then show no evidence of using that same strategy, or indeed any other discernible strategy, under another set of conditions (e.g., pretrial probe).

REFERENCES

Bower, G. H., & Trabasso, T. Concept identification. In R. C. Atkinson (Ed.), *Studies in mathematical psychology*. Stanford, Calif.: Stanford University Press, 1964.

Cantor, J. H. Transfer of stimulus pretraining in motor paired-associate and discrimination learning tasks. In L. P. Lipsitt & C. C. Spiker (Eds.), *Advances in child development and behavior* (Vol. 2). New York: Academic Press, 1965.

Cantor, J. H., & Spiker, C. C. Dimensional fixation with introtacts in kindergarten children. *Bulletin of the Psychonomic Society*, 1977, *10*, 169–171.

Cantor, J. H., & Spiker, C. C. The problem-solving strategies of kindergarten and first-grade children during discrimination learning. *Journal of Experimental Child Psychology*, 1978, *26*, 341–358.

Cantor, J. H., & Spiker, C. C. The effects of introtacts on hypothesis testing in kindergarten and first-grade children. *Child Development*, 1979, *50*, 1110–1120.

Eimas, P. D. A developmental study of hypothesis behavior and focusing. *Journal of Experimental Child Psychology*, 1969, *8*, 160–172.

Eimas, P. D. Effects of memory aids on hypothesis behavior and focusing in young children and adults. *Journal of Experimental Child Psychology,* 1970, *10,* 319–326.

Gholson, B., & Beilin, H. A. A developmental model of human learning. In H. W. Reese & L. P. Lipsitt (Eds.), *Advances in child development and behavior* (Vol. 13). New York: Academic Press, 1979.

Gholson, B., & Danziger, S. Effects of two levels of stimulus complexity upon hypothesis sampling systems among second and sixth grade children. *Journal of Experimental Child Psychology,* 1975, *20,* 105–118.

Gholson, B., Levine, M., & Phillips, S. Hypotheses, strategies, and stereotypes in discrimination learning. *Journal of Experimental Child Psychology,* 1972, *13,* 423–446.

Gholson, B., & McConville, K. Effects of stimulus differentiation training upon hypotheses, strategies, and sterotypes in discrimination learning among kindergarten children. *Journal of Experimental Child Psychology,* 1974, *18,* 81–97.

Gholson, B., O'Connor, J., & Stern, I. Hypothesis sampling systems among preoperational and concrete operational kindergarten children. *Journal of Experimental Child Psychology,* 1976, *21,* 61–76.

Gregg, L. W., & Simon, H. A. Process models and stochastic theories of simple concept formation. *Journal of Mathematical Psychology,* 1967, *4,* 246–276.

Ingalls, R. P., & Dickerson, D. J. Development of hypothesis behavior in human concept identification. *Development Psychology,* 1969, *1,* 707–716.

Karpf, D., & Levine, M. Blank-trial probes and introtacts in human discrimination learning. *Journal of Experimental Psychology,* 1971, *90,* 51–55.

Kemler, D. G. *A developmental study of hypothesis testing in discriminative learning tasks.* Unpublished doctoral dissertation, Brown University, 1972.

Kemler, D. G. Patterns of hypothesis testing in children's discriminative learning: A study of the development of problem-solving strategies. *Developmental Psychology,* 1978, *14,* 653–673.

Kemler, D. G., Shepp, B. E., & Foote, K. E. The sources of developmental differences in children's incidental processing during discrimination trials. *Journal of Experimental Child Psychology,* 1976, *21,* 226–240.

Kendler, H. H., & Kendler, T. S. Vertical and horizontal processes in problem solving. *Psychological Review,* 1962, *69,* 1–16.

Kendler, H. H., & Kendler, T. S. Mediation and conceptual behavior. In J. T. Spence (Ed.), *The psychology of learning and motivation* (Vol. 2). New York: Academic Press, 1968.

Kendler, T. S. An ontogeny of mediational deficiency. *Child Development,* 1972, *43,* 1–17.

Kendler, T. S. The development of discrimination learning: A levels-of-functioning explanation. In H. W. Reese & L. P. Lipsitt (Eds.), *Advances in child development and behavior* (Vol. 13). New York: Academic Press, 1979.

Kuenne, M. R. Experimental investigation of the relation of language to the transposition behavior in young children. *Journal of Experimental Psychology,* 1946, *36,* 471–490.

Levine, M. Mediating processes in humans at the outset of discrimination learning. *Psychological Review,* 1963, *70,* 254–276.

Levine, M. (Ed.). *A cognitive theory of learning.* Hillsdale, N.J.: Lawrence Erlbaum Associates, 1975.

Mims, R. M., & Gholson, B. Effects of type and amount of feedback upon hypothesis sampling systems among seven- and eight-year-old children. *Journal of Experimental Child Psychology,* 1977, *24,* 358–371.

Parrill-Burnstein, M. Teaching kindergarten children to solve problems: An information-processing approach. *Child Development,* 1978, *49,* 700–706.

Phillips, S. *Introtacts in children's discrimination learning.* Unpublished doctoral dissertation, State University of New York at Stony Brook, 1974.

Phillips, S., & Levine, M. Probing for hypotheses with adults and children: Blank trials and introtacts. *Journal of Experimental Psychology: General,* 1975, *104,* 327–354.

Restle, F. The selection of strategies in cue learning. *Psychological Review,* 1962, *69,* 329–343.

Richman, S., & Gholson, B. Strategy modeling, age, and information-processing efficiency. *Journal of Experimental Child Psychology,* 1978, *26,* 58–70.

Rieber, M. Hypothesis testing in children as a function of age. *Developmental Psychology,* 1969, *1,* 389–395.

Spiker, C. C. Experiments with children on the hypothesis of acquired distinctiveness and equivalence of cues. *Child Development,* 1956, 27, 253–263.

Spiker, C. C. Verbal factors in the discrimination learning of children. In J. C. Wright & J. Kagen (Eds.), Basic cognitive processes in children, *Monographs of the Society for Research in Child Development,* 1963, *28,* 53–69.

Spiker, C. C. An extension of Hull–Spence discrimination learning theory. *Psychological Review,* 1970, *77,* 496–515.

Spiker, C. C. Application of Hull–Spence theory to the discrimination learning of children. In H. W. Reese (Ed.), *Advances in child development and behavior* (Vol. 6). New York: Academic Press, 1971.

Spiker, C. C., & Cantor, J. H. Applications of Hull–Spence theory to the transfer of discrimination learning in children. In H. W. Reese (Ed.), *Advances in child development and behavior* (Vol. 8). New York: Academic Press, 1973.

Spiker, C. C., & Cantor, J. H. Introtacts as predictors of discrimination performance in kindergarten children. *Journal of Experimental Child Psychology,* 1977, *23,* 520–538.

Spiker, C. C., & Cantor, J. H. The Kendler levels-of-functioning theory: Comments and an alternative schema. In H. W. Reese & L. P. Lipsitt (Eds.), *Advances in child development and behavior* (Vol. 13). New York: Academic Press, 1979. (a)

Spiker, C. C., & Cantor, J. H. Factors affecting hypothesis testing in kindergarten children. *Journal of Experimental Child Psychology,* 1979, *28,* 230–248. (b)

Spiker, C. C., & Cantor, J. H. Cognitive strategies in the discrimination learning of young children. In D. K. Routh (Ed.), *Learning, speech, and the complex effects of punishment.* New York: Plenum, in press.

Tighe, L. S., & Tighe, T. J. Discrimination learning: Two views in historical perspective. *Psychological Bulletin,* 1966, *66,* 353–370.

Tighe, T. J., & Tighe, L. S. Stimulus control in children's learning. In A. D. Pick (Ed.), *Minnesota symposia on child psychology* (Vol. 6). Minneapolis: University of Minnesota Press, 1972.

Trabasso, T., & Bower, G. *Attention in learning.* New York: Wiley, 1968.

Tumblin, A., Gholson, B., Rosenthal, T. L., & Kelley, J. E. The effects of gestural demonstration, verbal narration, and their combination on the acquisition of hypothesis-testing behaviors by first-grade children. *Child Development,* 1979, *50,* 254–256.

Zeaman, D., & House, B. J. The role of attention in retardate discrimination learning. In N. R. Ellis (Ed.), *Handbook of mental deficiency.* New York: McGraw-Hill, 1963.

Zeaman, D., & House, B. J. Interpretations of developmental trends in discriminative transfer effects. In A. D. Pick (Ed.), *Minnesota symposia on child development* (Vol. 8). Minneapolis: University of Minnesota Press, 1974.

7 Structural Principles in Categorization

Douglas L. Medin
University of Illinois

INTRODUCTION

What Holds a Category Together?

What makes a category a category, and why are some categories better than others? Most people would agree that robin, sparrow, and eagle form a sensible grouping whereas elephant, rocket, and shoestring do not. And it seems obvious why—the members of the first set are fairly similar to each other, but those of the second set are not. Yet this example is quite deceptive—canary, banana, and the moon do not comprise a ''good'' category even though they share an attribute in common (yellowness). Questions concerning principles of category structure are nontrivial, and many of the ''obvious'' answers to these issues may not hold up well under closer scrutiny.

One way of addressing the issue of constraints on categories is to ask what makes a category sensible and what function is served by categorization. In laboratory studies involving artificially constructed categories, the answer is easy. The purpose of categorization (from the subjects' point of view) is to produce a correct response and a category is whatever the experimenter decides is going to be a category. The latter decision is usually based on the theories under consideration.

In real-world situations, categorization may serve multiple functions (as numerous people have suggested, among them Bruner, Gibson, and Rosch). First of all, categorization allows one to relate new experiences to old. We don't perceive, remember, and talk about each object and event as unique but rather as an instance of a class or concept that we already know something about. When we find ourselves in a new situation, we are confronted not with an array of unique entities but rather objects that are members of classes like chairs, desks, and telephones. Once we have assigned an entity to a category on the basis of its perceptible attributes, we can infer some of its nonperceptible attributes. For example, having used perceptible properties like color, size, and shape to decide an object is an apple, we can infer that it is edible and that it has a core containing seeds. In short, a basic cognitive task is a segmentation of the environment by which nonidentical stimuli are treated as equivalent.

Because experiences might be partitioned in a limitless variety of ways, we are again led to ask what makes a good or useful category. Given that natural concepts evolve out of human experience, answers about the structure of categories may contain hints concerning fundamental cognitive processes operating on those categories. It is hard to credit the possibility that human culture has passed on categories having a structure not at all coordinated with constraints of human information processing.

Organization of this Paper

Other than intuition, what may be used to educe principles of category structure? Can we predict how people will organize categories naturally, or, given some organization, can we say what structural principles went into it? The present chapter draws on two sources of observations: categorization theories and (seemingly) atheoretical maxims. To varying degrees, categorization theories imply constraints on category structures, constraints that have rarely been evaluated experimentally. The maxims to be considered are aphorisms such as the idea that categories are well-structured to the extent that they maximize cue validity. These statements bear closer scrutiny in their own right, and there are some interesting links between them and particular classification theories.

This chapter is organized into four main sections. In the first section, I consider several maxims or guidelines for category structure. My aim is to flesh out these ideas and to point out some of their shortcomings and strengths. Then I examine relationships between category constraints and particular classification theories. Thirdly, I intend to combine observations from both the theories and the maxims to argue for one particular view of category structure. I conclude with some reservations and speculations concerning developmental changes in classification learning.

It should be noted from the outset that this discussion should be amply sprinkled with hedges. Doubtless the functions of categorization differ from person to person and from situation to situation. In some contexts, a large category such as *vegetables* may be efficient for some purpose. In other settings, much more refined categories such as *poisonous mushrooms* may act as fundamental. Although similarity will be treated as a fixed entity, it must be acknowledged that selective attention can serve to either increase or decrease the effective similarity between any two stimuli. Having hinted at these hedges, in what follows we largely ignore them, mainly because they seem to be refinements that await a better overall picture.

MAXIMS FOR CATEGORY STRUCTURE

The idea of this section is not so much to review research relevant to these maxims as it is to examine just what they imply about category structure. I argue that many of these implications are implausible and, therefore, that these maxims are unlikely to provide useful constraints. Nonetheless, many of these implications are testable and it is always possible that some cogent experimental evidence will provide support for one or more of these maxims, despite my reservations.

Maximizing Cue Validity

One has only to look at concepts reflected in our language such as poodle, dog, pet, mammal, and animal to verify that people use multiple, overlapping categories that may differ in their level of abstraction. Rosch and her associates (Rosch, Mervis, Gray, Johnson & Boyes-Braem, 1976) found that one level of abstraction, which they call the basic level, is more fundamental than either the associated superordinate or subordinate level. For example, by their criteria, *chair* would be a basic level concept, but *furniture* and *rocking chair* would not be. Their claims are reinforced by a variety of empirical results (see Mervis & Rosch, 1981, for an up-to-date review).

It has been argued that the basic level is the level at which cue validity is maximized. Although there is an entire set of issues associated with determining the attributes or features of concepts that would be needed to compute cue validity, it would be convenient if cue validity could be used to determine the basic level. But, as we soon see, it cannot.

Cue validity of some feature i can be defined as the probability that an entity belongs to category j, given that feature i is present; that is,

$$\text{cue validity} = \frac{P(\text{category } j \text{ and feature } i)}{P(\text{category } j \text{ and feature } i) + \sum_{k \neq j} P(\text{category } k \text{ and feature } l)} \quad (1)$$

The denominator is equal to the probability of the feature.

Now consider the following levels of concepts: sparrow, bird, warm-blooded, and animal. It can be shown that cue validity will increase monotonically with the level of abstraction. For example, the cue validity for the attribute *egg laying* associated with sparrow will be fairly low because other birds, fish, reptiles, insects, and some mammals also lay eggs. Cue validity will be increased with respect to the category bird, because other birds will be included in the numerator of Equation 1. Moving the level to warm-blooded will further increase cue validity (anteaters would be added) and cue validity would be highest for the category animal (which includes *all* egg layers).

The core of the matter is this: Cue validity at worst will stay the same and can never decrease as one moves to higher levels of abstraction. Consequently, cue validity cannot be used to determine basic level nor can it be used as a measure of category goodness, unless it should turn out that the best and most useful categories are the most abstract categories. This is counter to both common sense and a large body of experimental literature. This is not to say that cue validity is not important in categorization, only that it is unlikely to stand by itself as the basis for category structure.[1]

Maximizing Differentiation

Another approach to categorization is to argue that it is analogous to discrimination learning and that categories are most sensible and easiest to learn when categories are most differentiated. Maximizing differentiation is equivalent to minimizing average between category similarity. Although this idea initially seems plausible, it almost surely will not work. Minimizing average between category similarity will not work because one is always led by this formulation to prefer two contrasting categories to any other number.

That minimizing average between categories implies that subjects will always sort stimuli into exactly two categories is not intuitively obvious, but it is fairly easy to demonstrate. For example, suppose a subject is given a choice between partitioning a set of stimuli into three categories, A, B, and C, or lumping A and B of the categories together. Let $\bar{S}_{ij}$ be the average between category similarity of category i and category j. Then we can always change the labels on the categories such that A and B have greater between-category similarity than do either A and C or B and C ($\bar{S}_{ab} > \bar{S}_{ac}$, and $\bar{S}_{ab} > \bar{S}_{bc}$). According to our criterion we should lump A and B if

$$(\bar{S}_{ac} + \bar{S}_{bc})/2 < (\bar{S}_{ab} + \bar{S}_{bc} + \bar{S}_{ac})/3.$$

On can quickly determine that this will be true whenever $\bar{S}_{ac} + \bar{S}_{bc} < 2\bar{S}_{ab}$, which is equivalent to our initial assumption. This implies that subjects would always put two of the categories together (A and B) and never partition the stimuli into three distinct categories. It is extremely doubtful that this generally

---

[1]Murphy (1982) has independently developed this and related arguments against cue validity as the sole basis of category organization.

would be true, and, therefore, maximizing differentiation cannot be the sole principle of category organization.

Maximizing Inferences from Category Membership

This guideline is consistent with the idea that categorization allows us to go beyond the information given to draw inferences (e.g., this object, an apple, has a core). With total number of features held constant, maximizing inferences is equivalent to maximizing the probability of a feature given a category, in some sense the converse of cue validity.

There are at least two problems with the criterion of maximizing the probability a feature is present given the category. The most glaring difficulty is that it implies that the most specific categories will provide the best categories. For example, singing, building nests in trees, and eating worms can be predicted more accurately from the knowledge that the animal in question is a robin than that the animal in question is a bird. Maximizing inferences is equivalent to maximizing within category similarity and the latter is maximized for the most specific categories. And the problem only becomes worse if number of features is taken into account, because more specific categories will have all the features of more general categories plus their own characteristic features. In its extreme form, the idea of having the most specific categories has the problem that they will rarely, if ever, be used. If every patient a doctor saw was totally unique, then the doctor's medical knowledge could never be brought to bear. At a minimum there must be some tradeoff between the frequency that a category can be applied and maximizing the probability that a feature is present given the category.

A second question that can be raised is why one should focus on inferring features from category membership to the exclusion of inferring features from other features. The features used to determine category membership could also be used to infer other features directly, without going through the two-step process of inferring membership and then drawing further inferences from membership. I would not want to go so far as to say that categorization serves no function in drawing inferences, only that, in some formal sense, inferences from features to features would serve as well as inferences from features to membership to other features.

Moreover, inferences from features to features might not have the same category structure as inferences from category membership to features and might permit a somewhat different category organization. Consider a situation where stimuli are comprised of binary-valued attributes from four stimulus dimensions. For example, color might be one dimension and we might use the value 1 to denote red and the value 0 to denote blue. Suppose we have two potential categories, X and X', each having four members as shown in Fig. 7.1.

In both cases the value 1 is typical for each of the dimensions and the probability of a feature given the category is the same for X and X'. Note,

EXEMPLARS	CATEGORY X DIMENSIONS				EXEMPLARS	CATEGORY X' DIMENSIONS			
	A	B	C	D		A	B	C	D
1	I	I	I	O	1	I	I	I	I
2	I	I	O	I	2	I	I	O	I
3	I	O	I	I	3	I	I	I	O
4	O	I	I	I	4	O	O	I	I

FIG. 7.1.   Two hypothetical categories having four members, each comprised of values on each of four dimensions.

however, that dimensions *A* and *B* for category *X'* have correlated attributes such that, knowing the value on one dimension, one could be certain of the value on the other dimension.

Considering only the criterion of maximizing inferences from category membership, there is no basis for claiming that one of these categories is better organized than the other. But there may be important structural differences between the two categories that are being ignored. Rosch and Mervis have argued that real-world categories are organized to take advantage of correlated attribute clusters (Mervis & Rosch, 1981; Rosch, 1975, 1978; Rosch & Mervis, 1975), a claim that is consistent with the idea that relations between features play an important role in categorization processes.

Maximizing Within Category Similarity and Minimizing Between Category Similarity

A plausible conjecture at this point is that neither within-category similarity nor between-category similarity by itself determines category membership, but some joint function does (Mervis & Rosch, 1981). Although it is intuitively appealing, there are good reasons to be cautious in endorsing this view.

First of all, one should remember that in general one cannot simultaneously maximize within-category similarity and minimize between-category similarity. Maximizing within-category similarity calls for the most specific categories and minimizing between-category similarity calls for the most general categories (this point is not original with me—see, e.g., Tversky, 1977). It seems then that one can only maximize some function of within- and between-category similarity.

To my knowledge the only attempts to be specific about this function have used either a difference or a ratio of average similarity (Homa, Rhoads, & Chambliss, 1979; Rosch & Mervis, 1975). The conjecture to be evaluated is that categories are good to the extent that they maximize within-category similarity relative to between-category similarity.

Because maximizing within-category similarity and minimizing between category similarity is the most popular aphorism for category structure, it is considered in some detail. First, we take up the case of a preexisting category to which one might add members or set up a new category and then we turn to situations where contrasting categories are already present.

Single-Category Case

To Add, Not to Add, or to Delete.   Suppose that we are given a category comprised of n members and then are presented with one or more candidates and asked to either accept or reject them as members of a category. According to the principle of maximizing within-category similarity, we should accept a candidate if it increases the average within-category similarity.

If $n = 1$, this algorithm will never get off the ground because any new member will decrease average within-category similarity. If $n = 2$, then a candidate could be accepted but a new issue would be raised, as pointed out to me by a University of Illinois graduate student, Gerald Dewey. The new issue is this: If one can add members to categories when they increase within-category similarity, it seems that one also might delete members from a category when that would increase within-category similarity. Were deletions allowed, the category would remain at size 2 because there would always be one of three members whose deletion would lead to increased within-category similarity (except in the trivial case where all members were equally similar to each other).

Lumping Versus Setting up a New Category.   Consider a modification of the task such that we start with a category of n members having an average similarity $\bar{S}_W$ and present two new stimuli having similarity to each other of $\bar{S}_H$ and similarity $\bar{S}_B$ to the preexisting category. The instructions are either to create a new category with these two new stimuli or to lump them into the old category. The potential situations are summarized in Table 7.1 where the different possibilities for within- and between-category similarity are laid out.

If one were maximizing the ratio of within- to between-category similarity, one would never set up a new category, because the ratio is always highest when the between-category similarity is zero. Using the difference in within- and between-category similarity, one would set a second category whenever

$$\frac{\binom{n}{2} \bar{S}_W + \bar{S}_H}{\binom{n}{2} + 1} - \bar{S}_B > \frac{\binom{n}{2} \bar{S}_W + 2n\bar{S}_B}{\binom{n}{2} + 2n} - 0.$$

Some algebraic readjustments lead to the only slightly less complicated inequality, implying that one would set up a new category when

$$2 [\bar{S}_W(2n^2 - 3n + 1) + \bar{S}_H)n + 3)] > \bar{S}_B(n^3 + 6n^2 - 5n + 14).$$

What does this inequality tell us? It suggests a problem. If n is very large, one would almost never set up a new category even if $\bar{S}_H$ were much larger than $\bar{S}_W$ and $\bar{S}_B$ were quite small. To see this, assume for the moment that similarity can

TABLE 7.1
Patterns of Similarity When either a New Category Is Developed or a
Single Category Remains[a]

	Within-Category Similarity	Between-Category Similarity
Single category (size $n + 2$)	$\dfrac{\binom{n}{2}\, \bar{S}_W + 2n\bar{S}_B}{\binom{n}{2} + 2n}$	0
Two categories	$\dfrac{\binom{n}{2}\, \bar{S}_W + \bar{S}_H}{\binom{n}{2} + 1}$	$\bar{S}_B$

[a]The notation, ( ), refers to combinations that is, $\binom{n}{2}$ is n items taken two at a time.

range between 0 and 1 with 0 representing no similarity and 1 representing maximal similarity. Then if $\bar{S}_W = .80$, $\bar{S}_H = .99$, and n were 20, $\bar{S}_B$ would have to be approximately .10 or less before a new category would be set up. For what it's worth, my intuition is that, to the contrary, new categories should be more likely to be set up when n is large (and one has some idea of within-category variability) than when n is small.

Contrasting Categories

Adding Members. Assume that two categories each of size n have been set up and that their average between-category similarity is $\bar{S}_B$ and in both cases the average within-category similarity is $\bar{S}_W$. A stimulus X is presented that has similarity $\bar{S}_1$ to the first category and similarity $\bar{S}_2$ to the alternative category. Suppose further that the stimulus is more similar to the first category than the second ($\bar{S}_1 > \bar{S}_2$) and that the subjects' task is to either assign X to category 1 or put it in neither category (reject it).

According to the rule under consideration, X will be placed into category 1 whenever

$$\frac{\binom{n}{2}\, \bar{S}_W + \binom{n}{2}\bar{S}_W + n\bar{S}_1}{\binom{n}{2} + \binom{n}{2} + n} - \frac{n^2\bar{S}_B + n\bar{S}_2}{n^2 + n} > \bar{S}_W - \bar{S}_B.$$

This inequality can be reduced to

$$\bar{S}_1 + n(\bar{S}_1 - \bar{S}_2) > \bar{S}_W + n(\bar{S}_W - \bar{S}_B).$$

This inequality is comprehensible in that it implies roughly that X will be accepted into category 1 if the difference between its similarity to category 1 and category 2 is as large as the difference between the within-category and the between-category similarity. Even so, there are some concerns that can be raised. If $\bar{S}_1 - \bar{S}_2 = \bar{S}_W - \bar{S}_B$, then X will be accepted if $\bar{S}_1 > \bar{S}_W$ and rejected if $\bar{S}_1 < \bar{S}_W$. One might have thought that the decision should be based only on $\bar{S}_1 - \bar{S}_2$ versus $\bar{S}_W - \bar{S}_B$. Related to this is the observation that if $\bar{S}_1 > \bar{S}_W$ but $\bar{S}_1 - \bar{S}_2 <$

$\bar{S}_W - \bar{S}_B$, then whether or not X is accepted will depend on category size (n). When n is small, X will be accepted; but, for larger values of n, X will be rejected. Conversely, if $\bar{S}_1 < \bar{S}_W$ but $\bar{S}_1 - \bar{S}_2 > \bar{S}_W - \bar{S}_B$, then X will be rejected for small n and accepted for large n. This may be a minor problem but I can see no rationale for why the judgment should depend on category size in the manner predicted.

Forced-Choice Categorization.   If we force subjects to put a new item into one of two preexisting categories, then maximizing within-category similarity relative to between-category similarity boils down to putting the item into the category to which it has the greater average similarity. I mention this primarily because a large set of categorization models, such as prototype models, would have precisely this expectation. But even here there may be a problem. Suppose that an item falls exactly in between two categories but that one of the two categories has much higher within-category variability (smaller average within-category similarity) than the other. Intuition suggests that the new item would be sorted into the high variability category; the choice rule under discussion predicts no preferences. Indeed, if one were to apply an analysis in terms of likelihood ratios, an item closer to the low variance category actually might be much more likely to have been drawn from the high variance category. (See Fried, 1979, for related evidence.)

Lumping Versus Setting up a Third Category.   Again suppose we have two categories of size n with average within-category similarity $\bar{S}_W$ and average between-category similarity $\bar{S}_B$. Two new stimuli are presented with similarity $\bar{S}_H$ to each other, similarity $\bar{S}_{W'}$ to category 1, and similarity $\bar{S}_{B'}$ to category 2 (we use two prospective members to avoid the issue of whether or not a category can have only one member). The task is either to put the new stimuli in category 1 or to set up a new category.

The algebra associated with the given situation is tedious and largely unilluminating. Suffice to say that for some cases lumping is predicted to increase with n, and for others lumping is predicted to decrease with n. There is no clear rationale for why this should be so.

Summary

I have been trying to make two points concerning the stratagem of maximizing within-category similarity and minimizing between-category similarity. One is that, because it is based on *average* similarity, it is far from theoretically neutral. Rather it is a natural extension of what Medin and Schaffer (1978) refer to as independent cue models. Specifically, these models assume that categorization judgments are based on an additive, independent summation of component information. Data inconsistent with independent cue models (Medin & Smith, 1981) indirectly undermine this maxim.

The other point is that when examined in detail, this maxim has certain implications that are far from obvious. It is conceivable that these counter-intuitive predictions are correct. Without empirical support, however, their intuitive implausibility suggests that the criterion itself is incorrect. The idea that categories are cohesive to the extent that they maximize within-category similarity and minimize between-category similarity, by itself, does not seem to constitute or resolve the issue of structural principles in categorization.[2] We turn now to specific categorization theories to see what implications they have for category structure.

CLASSIFICATION THEORIES AND CATEGORY STRUCTURE

The Classical View and Defining Features

One view of category structure is that natural concepts are characterized by simple sets of defining features that are singly necessary and jointly sufficient to determine category membership (Katz & Postal, 1964). A candidate exemplar either does or does not possess these defining features and thereby either is or is not a member of the category. The idea that categories are comprised of these defining features is considered in detail by Smith and Medin (1981), who dubbed this idea the ''classical view.''

The classical view has a lot to say about category structure. Defining features are what make a category a category and the difficulty of learning a category will depend on the difficulty in discovering these defining features and the extent to which the defining features of contrasting categories overlap with the category in question.

Despite its precise statements concerning category structure, the classical view will not be given further consideration. The major problem is that the classical view may be appropriate for only a small set of categories. The scholarly consensus (see Mervis & Rosch, 1981; Rosch & Lloyd, 1978; Smith & Medin, 1981, for reviews) has it that most natural concepts are not well-defined but rather are based on relationships that are only on the average true. Features are said to be characteristic rather than defining. Members of a category may vary in the number of characteristic features they possess and correspondingly vary in the degree to which they are judged to be good examples (typical) of a

---

[2]Larry Barsalou (personal communication, 1981) pointed out that this discussion proceeds as if a given exemplar can only belong to one category. In fact, however, items may belong to a variety of categories, and which category is employed may depend on an organism's plans and goals. This underlines the difficulty of using any single factor such as similarity as the sole determinant of category structure. At a minimum one would need a theory for how plans and goals modify similarity.

category (Mervis & Rosch, 1981; Rosch, 1973; Rosch & Mervis, 1975; Smith, Shoben, & Rips, 1974). For example, cows are rated to be better exemplars of the concept *mammal* than are whales (McCloskey & Glucksberg, 1978). In this view, instances are neither arbitrarily associated with categories nor strictly linked by defining features but rather reflect more nearly a "family resemblance" structure (Rosch & Mervis, 1975).

The Probabilistic View and Linear Separability

The Probabilistic View

If many natural categories do not have defining features, how do people acquire and use them? Posner and Keele (1968) proposed that people form an impression of the central tendency of a category as a result of experience with exemplars and that categorical judgments come to be based on this central tendency, or prototype. An eagle, for example, would be judged to be a bird and not a mammal because it is more similar to the bird prototype than to the mammal prototype.

What does prototype theory imply about the structure of categories? The main constraint is that categorizing on the basis of similarity to a prototype has to work in the sense that all members will be accepted and all nonmembers will be rejected. If, by some quirk of fate, sparrow were mammals rather than birds, a prototype process would not work, because sparrows have many characteristic features of birds and few characteristic features of mammals.

The idea that category representations are based on characteristic attributes and that classification decisions are based on how closely an examplar matches the summary representation of a category is known as the *probabilistic view*. Prototype theory is one instance of a class of models conforming to the probabilistic view. Because what is said about prototype theory applies as well to the other models, we use prototype theory as a shorthand way of referring to the probabilistic view.

One way of thinking about classifying stimuli on the basis of similarity to prototypes is that it involves a summing of evidence (e.g., characteristic features) against some criterion. The more typical the category member, the more quickly the summing of evidence should exceed the criterion. Therefore, it would not be surprising to find that people categorize robins as birds more rapidly than they categorize penguins as birds (see Mervis & Rosch, 1981, for a review). The key constraint is that this summing of evidence (or, alternatively, similarity to prototype) accepts members and excludes nonmembers of a category.

The formal term for the constraint just given is that categories be *linearly* separable or separable by a linear discriminant function (Sebestyen, 1962). Linearly separable categories are categories that can be partitioned on the basis of a weighted, additive combination of component information. If two categories are linearly separable, then their members could be classified correctly on the basis of similarity to the respective prototypes, that is, every member of a category will be more similar to the prototype for its category than to the prototype for any contrasting categories.

Prototype, average distance, and versions of cue validity and frequency models fall under this domain (see Medin & Schaffer, 1978, for a more complete description of these models); all imply that categories should be linearly separable. Linear separability is also of interest because it has received important consideration in the closely allied area of pattern recognition and classification by machines (Nilsson, 1965).

Because linear separability is such an important constraint in formal models of classification, one might expect considerable interest in determining whether linear separability is a basic constraint in human information processing. Surprisingly little attention has been paid to this issue.

One way of evaluating the importance of linear separability to human categorization is to set up two categorization tasks similar in major respects, except that in one task the categories would be linearly separable and in the other categorization task they would not. A clear implication of independent cue models is that the task involving linearly separable categories should be easier to master than the task not conforming to this constraint; that is, the idea is to see if it is important that categories be separable by an additive combination of component information. Paula Schwanenflugel and I have recently completed a series of studies examining linear separability (Medin & Schwanenflugel, 1981), which I shall briefly summarize.

Is Linear Separability an Important Structural Principle?

The design of one experiment is shown in Fig. 7.2. In this example, stimuli are comprised of values on four component dimensions, described in terms of a binary notation. The number 1 represents the typical or characteristic value for members of category A and the value 0 is typical for category B members. No defining features exist to partition categories A and B, but the categories in the top half of the figure are linearly separable. Each category A member has three values typical of category A and no B member has more than two values typical of category A. Although the overall average similarity of the two categories in the bottom of Fig. 7.2 is the same as for the top of Fig. 7.2, the stimuli in the bottom half do not constitute linearly separable categories. Exemplar B_3 has more values typical of category A than either exemplar A_1 or A_2. If linear separability is important in classification, then the classification problem in the top half of Fig. 7.2 should be easier than that shown in the bottom half.

Not all categorization models share this prediction. According to the context model of Medin and Schaffer (1978), similarity of exemplars to each other is the major factor controlling classification difficulty. Specifically, high similarity of

LINEARLY SEPARABLE CATEGORIES

| CATEGORY A | | | | | CATEGORY B | | | | |
EXEMPLAR	D_1	D_2	D_3	D_4	EXEMPLAR	D_1	D_2	D_3	D_4
A_1	1	1	1	0	B_1	1	0	1	0
A_2	1	0	1	1	B_2	0	1	1	0
A_3	1	1	0	1	B_3	0	0	0	1
A_4	0	1	1	1	B_4	1	1	0	0

CATEGORIES NOT LINEARLY SEPARABLE

| CATEGORY A | | | | | CATEGORY B | | | | |
EXEMPLAR	D_1	D_2	D_3	D_4	EXEMPLAR	D_1	D_2	D_3	D_4
A_1	1	0	0	0	B_1	0	0	0	1
A_2	1	0	1	0	B_2	0	1	0	0
A_3	1	1	1	1	B_3	1	0	1	1
A_4	0	1	1	1	B_4	0	0	0	0

FIG. 7.2   Abstract representation of the alternative categorization tasks. Each task involved eight stimuli varying along four dimensions.

exemplars within categories facilitates categorization and high similarity of exemplars between categories impairs performance.

The context model is just one of a number of alternative classification models that do not imply that linear separability is an important constraint. These alternative models, which we refer to collectively as *relational coding models,* have in common the assumption that classification involves in one way or another combinations of attributes or features (Anderson, Kline, & Beasley, 1979; Hayes-Roth & Hayes-Roth, 1977; Neumann, 1974; Reitman & Bower, 1973). Because this use of combinations implies something other than an independent summation of component information, relational coding models do not require that categories be linearly separable. Although the models vary in their assumed underlying processes, they share the prediction of the context model that high similarity of exemplars within categories facilitates performance and high similarity of exemplars between categories impairs it.

If instances of high similarity are an important variable in classification, the task where the categories are not linearly separable (NLS) might be easier than the linearly separable (LS) task. According to this principle, instances of high similarity within a category should facilitate learning and high similarity across categories should impair it. We define the stimuli as highly similar if they differ in value along only one dimension. Inspection of Fig. 7.2 reveals no cases of high within-category similarity and six cases of high between-category similarity (A_1 and B_1, A_1 and B_2, A_1 and B_4, A_2 and B_1, A_3 and B_4, A_4 and B_2) for the LS task. In contrast, for the NLS task there are four cases of high similarity within categories (A_1 and A_2, A_3 and A_4, B_1 and B_4, B_2 and B_4) and only three cases of high between-category similarity (A_1 and B_4, A_2 and B_3, A_3 and B_3). Therefore, on the basis of similarity relationships, the NLS categorization task is predicted to be easier to master than the LS. In other words, with overall similarity held constant, the experiment pits high similarity of exemplars against linear separability.

The basic procedure was straightforward. The stimuli were geometric shapes differing in color, form, size, and number. Stimuli were presented one at a time in a random order to participants. They assigned it to either category A or category B and then were told whether they were correct or incorrect. Subjects were told that their task was to learn to classify the stimuli correctly, that categorization could not be based on any one feature alone, and that the task was difficult but eventually they should be able to be correct all the time. Thirty-two subjects were given the linearly separable categorization task and an equal number were given the other task. Training continued until a participant met the learning criterion or until each exemplar had been presented 16 times.

Type of instruction was an additional variable. Subjects given *inference* instructions were told to think of the task as being analogous to learning two artistic styles. They were asked to focus on abstracting out general characteristics of each category (style) so that they could correctly classify new examples that would be presented later. They were told that the specific stimuli to be seen during learning were important only as aides to abstracting out general style.

Subjects given *facts* instructions were also told to think of the stimuli as being analogous to artistic styles, but they were also reminded that Picasso and other artists often change their style. They were further informed that the stimuli in their task might not be representative of the category and that they should perform the task by focusing on individual stimuli rather than be attempting to abstract out the general style.

Altogether the combinations of classification tasks and subjects created four distinct groups; the instructional manipulation was designed to see if the relative difficulty of the LS and NLS tasks would interact with the type of strategy used by subject. The *inferences* instructions were designed to maximize higher level abstraction and the *facts* instructions aimed to minimize abstraction.

The results were clear-cut. For both types of instructions the NLS task proved to be easier than the LS task, contrary to prototype theory but consistent with theories that emphasize the similarity of exemplars to other exemplars. The *facts* instructions were associated with fewer errors than the *inferences* instructions.

One can argue that the classification task in the previous experiment is not representative of categorization in general. There are three ways in which the geometric stimuli may not have been optimal for studying classification performance. First it might be argued that the stimuli used in the previous study were not as complex as those found in natural categories, that is, the geometric forms that were used differed solely on four dimensions, whereas instances of natural categories differ on many dimensions. The fact that instances of natural categories differ on many dimensions means that a person is required to ignore certain dimensions of an instance and attend to others when making a categorization decision.

Second, it might be argued that natural categories usually consist of many instances, whereas in the previous study only a few instances of each category were used. The small stimulus set used may have permitted the subjects to use the equivalent of a paired-associate learning strategy.

Finally, the attributes of the geometric stimuli in the study just described were binary valued and a given value (e.g., red) was identical wherever it appeared. For natural categories, attributes such as *feathered* are themselves an abstraction, and the exact realization of an attribute varies from instance to instance (e.g., feathers of a peacock versus feathers of a crow).

The stimuli for the next experiment were selected to address all three of these possibilities. The categorization stimuli consisted of a potentially infinite set of photographs of faces. These faces varied systematically along four dimensions (hair color, hair length, smile type, and shirt color), while varying freely on all other dimensions. Although attributes of the faces were encoded as binary values (e.g., light hair versus dark hair), the realization of some value (light hair) could vary considerably from face to face. If the factors of stimulus set size, presence of irrelevant features, and variability within a given attribute value, either alone or in conjunction, elicit or constrain the process of summing evidence from component dimensions, then linear separability should now become important. The actual stimuli used, taken from old college yearbooks, were faces of women that varied in hair color, shirt color, smile type, and hair length, as well as in other numerous, irrelevant, attributes. The structure of the linearly separable and nonlinearly separable categories is shown in Fig. 7.3. There are several aspects of note for these structures: First, both the linearly separable and nonlinearly separable categories show the same overall similarity (that is, the frequency of the values on the component dimensions is the same for the LS as for the NLS categories). Second, the two category types differ with respect to between-category similarity. Although *average* between-category similarity is equated, the LS categories show more instances of high between-category similarity of types (four) than the nonlinearly separable categories (no instances of high between-category similarity). Therefore, relational coding models predict that the linearly separable categories will be more difficult to learn than the nonlinearly separable categories.

Although both the LS and the NLS classification task proved to be fairly difficult, performance improved steadily with practice, as seen in Fig. 7.4. Figure 7.4 also shows an advantage for the NLS condition, which developed quickly and did not change with practice. The error data also do not support the idea that linear separability is important in classification. Subjects in the LS task averaged 34.0 errors, whereas subjects in the NLS task averaged 28.8 errors, a

LINEARLY SEPARABLE CATEGORIES

TYPE	CATEGORY A DIMENSION				TYPE	CATEGORY B DIMENSION			
	D_1	D_2	D_3	D_4		D_1	D_2	D_3	D_4
A_1	O	I	I	I	B_1	I	O	O	O
A_2	I	I	I	O	B_2	O	O	O	I
A_3	I	O	O	I	B_3	O	I	I	O

CATEGORIES NOT LINEARLY SEPARABLE

TYPE	CATEGORY A DIMENSION				TYPE	CATEGORY B DIMENSION			
	D_1	D_2	D_3	D_4		D_1	D_2	D_3	D_4
A_1	I	I	O	O	B_1	O	O	O	O
A_2	O	O	I	I	B_2	O	I	O	I
A_3	I	I	I	I	B_3	I	O	I	O

FIG. 7.3   Abstract representation of the alternative categorization tasks. Note that individual stimulus *types* rather than individual stimuli are represented. Each task involved six stimulus types and a potentially infinite set of individual stimuli representing these types.

difference in the direction predicted by relational coding models but short of statistical reliability ($t[62] = 1.35, p < .10$).

In a final attempt to find evidence for the importance of linear separability, the category strucutres were simplified. Specifically, the number of relevant dimensions was reduced from four to three. Independent cue models, such as prototype theory, assume that classification is equivalent to a summing of evidence and our

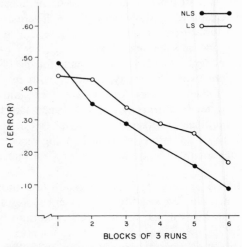

FIG. 7.4   Proportion of errors as a function of practice for the linearly separable (LS) and not linearly separable (NLS) tasks involving an unlimited set of stimuli.

intent was to examine the simplest case of summation. There were only three relevant dimensions, and in the linearly separable task subjects could correctly classify all stimuli by looking at the three attributes and using a two out of three rule; that is, if two of the three values were typical of category A, then that stimulus belonged to category A.

To accomplish this simplification, the second dimension from the structures used in the last experiment was eliminated (held constant). Because the LS task remains separable and the NLS task remains nonseparable, independent cue models predict that the LS task should be easier.

Although performance consistently improved with practice, less than half the subjects in either group met the learning criterion. Mean errors during learning were virtually identical—NLS subjects averaged 38 errors and LS subjects averaged 39.5 errors. The LS task was no easier to learn than the NLS task, contrary to the prediction of independent cue models.

Despite our varied attempts, we have been unable to find any evidence that linear separability is a factor in classification learning. To my knowledge, these studies represent the first direct comparison of learning of LS and NLS categories. Therefore, cautions concerning the generality of these results are even more pertinent than is usually the case.

One reaction to these experiments is that they are not a fair test of the importance of linear separability because the difficulty of the tasks (there were many nonlearners in the last two experiments) is clear evidence that the categories were unnatural. Weird categories produce weird results supporting weird theories. Although this claim has merit, it is not truly applicable to these experiments. The category structure for the LS task was dictated by theories that imply linear separability is important, and from the perspective of these theories it is hard to imagine an easier task than using a two out of three rule. If such a simple rule can be associated with such a difficult classification task, then perhaps linear separability is not the key to category structure.

The Exemplar View

The exemplar view accepts the idea that many concepts may not have defining features but differs from the probabilistic view in that it assumes that category judgments may be based on the retrieval of specific-item information rather than category-level information (e.g., by reference to a prototype).

Do exemplar-based theories provide meaningful constraints on category structure? The most optimistic answer is a hedge. To begin with, this class of models is somewhat diffuse. Smith and Medin's (1981) review lumped into this class all models that either do not rely on an abstract summary representation or are not based on an additive summation of component information. For example, the context model is neither tied to the assumption that a distinct representation is set up for each exemplar nor does it assume an additive summation rule. An average distance model does assume that every exemplar is represented and does use an additive combination rule (and thus implies that linear separability is an important constraint). Both are considered exemplar models.

Exemplar models seem to imply that something belongs in a category if you have learned that it does. A lamprey is a fish because you have been told that lampreys are fish. But this is totally unconstrained and provides no guidelines at all concerning category structure.

At this point one may despair of any likelihood that theories will have anything useful to say concerning what makes a category cohesive. In the remainder of this chapter we pursue an alternative approach to these questions. Although many models do not say anything direct about category structure, they do imply that some categorization tasks should be easier than others. If these predictions are generally supported, then we may obtain some hints as to the structural principles that these theories are exploiting, by looking at the basis of these predictions.

CONTEXT THEORY AND CORRELATED ATTRIBUTES

Context Model

Although the context model often has been presented as an exemplar view model and contrasted with probabilistic view models, it can be argued that the key aspect of the model is not that it assumes exemplar storage but rather that it assumes components are treated in a nonindependent manner.

The context model assumes that when some stimulus or cue is presented in some experimental context and some event occurs (e.g., the classification assignment), information concerning the cue, the context, and the event are stored together in memory and that both cue and context must be activated simultaneously in order for information about the event to be retrieved. A change in either the cue or the context can impair the accessibility of information associated with both. It is further assumed that a particular stimulus component serves a cue function *and* acts as context for other cues. This means that components will combine in an interactive rather than independent manner.

This formulation is closely related to the assumptions of the Estes hierarchical association model (Estes, 1972, 1973, 1975). Estes employs the notion of a "control element" and assumes (1) that neither cue nor context is directly associated with an event or outcome; and (2) that inputs from both the cue and context are needed to activate the node and provide access to the representation of an event.

As applied to classification, the context model proposes that when an item is presented to be classified, that item acts as a retrieval cue to access information associated with similar stored exemplars. The various cue dimensions comprising stimuli in some context are assumed to be combined in an interactive, specifically multiplicative, manner to determine the similarity of two stimuli.

The multiplicative rule has the implication that an exemplar may be classified more efficiently if it is highly similar to one instance and dissimilar to a second than if it has medium similarity to two instances of a category. Hence the context model predicts that categorization performance will vary with the number of stored exemplars that are highly similar to the test item. Independent-cue models are insensitive to such density effects. In a series of four experiments, Medin and Schaffer (1978) obtained clear support for the context model. Data from original learning, transfer, and speeded classification were in each case more in line with the context model than with a generalized independent-cue model. In addition, a mathematical version of the context model gave an excellent quantitative account of classification performance on transfer tests involving new and old instances. A follow-up study varied the strategies subjects employed and although strategy variations produced large differences in performance, certain relationships were invariant over strategy, relationships that were captured by the context model and not by independent-cue models (Medin & Smith, 1981).

The fact that high similarity to one instance and low similarity to another instance will outweigh medium similarity to two instances in some sense makes the context theory a configural model. Correlated attributes represent one type of configural information. If people are sensitive to correlated attributes, then it would be very convenient if natural categories were organized around correlated attributes. In the next section, this rationale is slightly expanded and then the application of the context model to some recent experiments on correlated attributes are described.

Correlated Attributes

Rosch and her associates have recently argued persuasively that real-world categories are formed to take advantage of correlated attribute clusters (Mervis & Rosch, 1981; Rosch, 1975, 1978; Rosch & Mervis, 1975). The perceived world of objects is not a total set (in Garner's, 1974, sense) but rather is a subset. In other words, certain attributes tend to co-occur. For example, animals with feathers are very likely to have wings and beaks, whereas animals with fur are very unlikely to have wings and beaks. There are two very important advantages to being sensitive to correlated attribute clusters. First, this allows an organism to predict attributes of an object from knowledge of other attributes (as noted on page 207). Second, those categories that best follow the natural correlation of attributes are likely to be maximally differentiated from each other. When combined, these two ideas remind one of the principle of maximizing within category similarity and minimizing between category similarity. The analogy, however, is not quite correct. It is incorrect in the sense that there may be correlated attributes *within* a category that provide further internal structure. Correlated attributes within a category could provide clusters of exemplars that might act as subcategories at a more refined level of analysis. There is evidence that natural categories do have correlated attributes within categories (Malt & Smith, 1981; Smith & Medin, 1981).

People also seem to use correlated attributes as a basis of classification when categories are ill-defined. In one set of studies designed to evaluate correlated attributes, we (Medin, Altom, Freko, & Edelson, 1982) used a simulated medical diagnosis task. Subjects learned about a fictitious disease, burlosis, from hypothetical case studies of patients having the disease. The case studies included descriptions of symptoms that tend to be characteristic of burlosis. Some symptoms were correlated with each other, whereas others were independent. After subjects studied the descriptions, they were presented with pairs of new cases and asked to judge which was more likely to have the disease, based on what they had learned from the earlier case studies.

During an initial training phase, subjects were presented with nine different case studies of the fictitious disease burlosis. The basic design of the learning cases is depicted in Fig. 7.5. For each subject, two symptoms were completely correlated in that a given patient either had both symptoms or neither symptom. For example, in Fig. 7.5, eye condition and weight condition were perfectly correlated symptoms. Each description involved five symptom dimensions: blood pressure (high or low), skin condition (splotches or rash), muscle condition (stiffness or loss of control), eye condition (puffy or sunken), and weight condition (loss or gain). One symptom of each pair was selected to be typical (notation 1 in Fig. 7.5) and the other was selected to be atypical (notation 0).

The transfer tests of primary interest are shown in Fig. 7.6. For one type of test, both new case descriptions broke the correlation between the symptom dimensions, eye condition and weight condition. On these tests virtually all

SYMPTOMS OF BURLOSIS

CASE STUDY	BLOOD PRESSURE	SKIN CONDITION	MUSCLE CONDITION	CONDITION OF EYES	WEIGHT CONDITION
1. R.L.	0	1	0	1	1
2. L.F.	1	1	0	1	1
3. J.J.	0	0	1	1	1
4. R.M.	1	0	1	1	1
5. A.M.	1	1	1	1	1
6. J.S.	1	1	1	1	1
7. S.T.	1	0	0	0	0
8. S.E.	0	1	1	0	0
9. E.M.	1	1	1	0	0

FIG. 7.5   Case studies presented during learning according to the binary notation. The fourth- and fifth-symptom dimensions are perfectly correlated.

TEST TYPES

UNCORRELATED vs UNCORRELATED   UNCORRELATED vs CORRELATED

01110 vs 11101   11100 vs 11101
11001 vs 11110   01111 vs 11101
01010 vs 11010   01011 vs 11110
10001 vs 10101   10000 vs 10010

FIG. 7.6   Transfer tests evaluating the effects of number of typical symptoms and the presence or absence of correlated symptoms in the burlosis experiment.

classification models would expect people to choose the description having the greater number of typical symptoms to be more likely to have burlosis. The other type of test pitted number of typical symptoms against whether or not the symptom correlation was broken. For example, the pattern 10010 has two typical symptoms, whereas the pattern 10000 has only one, but the latter pattern preserves the correlated attribute structure. The context model predicts that people will select descriptions involving correlated attributes as more likely to have burlosis. Independent-cue models predict that number of typical symptoms will continue to govern choices.

The results were clear. For the tests where pattern of symptom correlations was broken in both descriptions, the description having the greater number of typical symptoms was judged more likely to be associated with burlosis. In the tests where the descriptions with fewer number of typical symptoms preserved the pattern of symptom correlations and the description with more typical symptoms did not, the pattern of choices was reserved; that is, the description with fewer typical symptoms but preserving the correlations was judged to be more likely to have burlosis, as predicted by configural-cue models such as the context model.

The task used in the previous experiment may seem strange in that only a single category was used. Although no subject complained about the oddness of the task, we ran an additional experiment using two contrasting categories.

The design of the follow-up experiment is shown in Fig. 7.7. Case studies involved one of two diseases, terrigitis or midosis, and as in the earlier studies the values along the last two symptom dimensions were perfectly correlated. For the first two symptom dimensions the value 1 was typical of terrigitis and the value 0 typical of midosis. Following original training, subjects were presented with new case studies and asked to classify them as having terrigitis or midosis. All 16 possible combinations of symptom patterns were presented on these transfer tests. Of these new patterns, 8 exactly matched one of the original case studies, but the other 8 did not. The context model predicts that classification is based on similarity to case studies but does not assume that only exact matches influence performance. The multiplicative similarity function also implies a sensitivity to correlated symptoms for both exact matches and nonexact matches that

TERRIGITIS					MIDOSIS				
DIMENSIONS					DIMENSIONS				
CASE	D_1	D_2	D_3	D_4	CASE	D_1	D_2	D_3	D_4
E.M.	I	I	I	I	R.L.	I	O	I	O
S.T.	O	I	I	I	A.M.	O	O	I	O
R.M.	I	I	O	O	S.E.	O	I	O	I
L.F.	I	O	O	O	J.J.	O	O	O	I

FIG. 7.7   Abstract representation of the contrasting categories for the terrigitis/midosis experiment. The third- and fourth-symptom dimensions are perfectly correlated.

preserve symptom correlations. The success of the context model's predictions can be assessed by how well it fits the transfer data quantitatively.

The main results are shown in Table 7.2. Subjects performed quite accurately on symptom patterns that exactly matched a case study from the training phase. There was also a systematic effect of the first two symptom dimensions—subjects were 12% to 16% more accurate on matching patterns if the first and second symptoms were typical of the disease than if one of the two symptoms was atypical.

TABLE 7.2
Transfer Tests and Response Proportions Associated with Fig. 7.7

Test Description		Observed (Predicted) Proportion of Terrigitis Responses	
Exact match to old terrigitis patterns	1111	.88	(.85)
	0111	.73	(.76)
	1100	.89	(.86)
	1000	.77	(.73)
Exact match to old midosis patterns	1010	.25	(.24)
	0010	.12	(.15)
	0101	.33	(.27)
	0001	.17	(.14)
New patterns	0000	.53	(.56)
	0100	.75	(.73)
	0110	.36	(.34)
	1110	.45	(.46)
	0011	.53	(.54)
	0100	.67	(.66)
	1001	.28	(.27)
	1101	.38	(.44)

Predicted values derived from the context model are shown in parentheses.

Exactly the same pattern held for new transfer patterns. In general, new patterns were placed in the category associated with the symptom correlation that the new pattern manifested, but there were also clear effects of the first two symptom values. Thus it appears that, for both exact matches to old case studies and for new combinations of symptoms, subjects used correlated symptoms *and* typical symptoms in making their classifications. This is the pattern of performance predicted by the context model.

Quantitative Fits to Context Model.   According to the context model, when new items are presented on a transfer test, they will act as retrieval cues to access stored information associated with similar case studies. Similarity along a symptom dimension is assumed to vary between 0 and 1, with 1 representing identity or maximum similarity. Overall similarity of a transfer item is assumed to be a multiplicative function of individual symptom similarities. If we represent the similarity on the four symptom dimensions in Fig. 7.7 by a, b, c, and d, respectively, then transfer description 0110 would have an overall similarity to case study R.L. (1010) of $a \cdot b \cdot 1 \cdot 1$, or $a \cdot b$; that is, matching symptoms have a similarity of 1 whereas mismatches are represented by a corresponding similarity parameter. By the same system, the new item would have similarity b to case study A.M., $c \cdot d$ to case study S.E., and so on. Small values for similarity along a symptom dimension imply that a mismatch on that dimension would be salient.

The similarity parameters were estimated by a grid search designed to minimize the difference between predicted and observed transfer performance, according to a least-squares criterion. The probability of classifying a transfer description as terrigitis was assumed to be equal to the sum of similarities of the description to the terrigitis case studies divided by that sum plus the sum of the similarities of the description to the four midosis case studies. The resulting estimates for a, b, c, and d were .52, .40, .32, and .06, respectively, and the predictions associated with these parameters are shown in parenthesis in Table 7.2. The parameter estimates suggest that the correlated dimensions, c and d, tended to be more salient than the first two dimensions. The fit to the data shown in Table 7.2 is excellent—the average absolute deviation of predicted and observed proportions is less than .03, the root mean squared deviation is .03, and 98% of the variance is accounted for by the model.[3]

Overall, the idea that correlated attributes have a critical role in categorization appears to have considerable promise. Sensitivity to correlations, first, is consistent with the principle of being able to infer the presence of other attributes from known attributes. And sensitivity, moreover, may be an indirect property of memory retrieval processes (at least according to the context model).

---

[3]More recent research in our laboratory by William Wattenmaker shows that the correlation between symptoms need not be perfect for people to use them on transfer tests.

CONTEXT THEORY, STRATEGIES, AND DEVELOPMENT

Ill-Defined Concepts and Hypothesis Testing

Much of this chapter has been concerned with the structure of ill-defined categories, that is, categories that do not have defining features. Earlier work on concepts used well-defined categories and focused on such issues as the relative difficulty of acquiring different rules, strategies for formulating and testing alternative hypotheses, and the transfer of behavior to new stimulus sets (Levine, 1975; Trabasso & Bower, 1968). It may be worth pointing out that current hypothesis-testing models would have difficulty in predicting that ill-defined concepts would be learned at all, because there may be no "correct" hypothesis to describe category membership of fuzzy concepts like *furniture*. A child learning about birds might entertain the hypothesis that birds fly, only to discard this conjecture when encountering either a nonflying bird (e.g., an ostrich) or a flying nonbird (e.g., a bat). A hypothesis-testing process that discarded hypotheses whenever contradictory information was encountered would throw out important information about concepts (i.e., their characteristic features).

The further evidence that young children are less likely than older children to use strategies suggests a moral here, but it takes the form of a speculation. Instead of viewing the tendency of young children to be nonstrategic as a shortcoming, it may be more accurate to view nonstrategic behavior as precisely the means by which children are able to learn ill-defined concepts. Strategies may get in the way.

There is some evidence to support this speculation. Kossan (1981) tested second- and fifth-grade children on different types of category structures and encouraged children either to attack the problem conceptually or to be nonstrategic (i.e., to use a paired-associate learning strategy). Although fifth-grade children performed better than second-grade children overall, for the ill-defined category structures second-grade children given paired-associate instructions outperformed fifth-grade children given conceptual instructions (see also Farah & Kosslyn, 1981, for a more extensive discussion of children's learning of ill-defined concepts).

One reason why strategic behavior may not always be efficient is that the set of possible hypotheses is very large. Consider correlated attributes. Suppose that in some domain the entities could be characterized in terms of eight binary-valued attributes (this is, of course, an oversimplification). Then there would be 28 possible pairwise correlations to be examined. A child might take a long time to hit on the correct hypothesis. In contrast, consider what nonstrategic behavior might accomplish. The context model is based on storing exemplar information and, as we have seen, is sensitive to correlated attributes. If children store information in the nonindependent manner implied by the context model, then learning a few examples will allow the child's classification to reflect correlated attributes in the absence of any higher level abstraction.

Selective Attention and Context

So far the context model has been presented as if it had no strategic component. Actually, in both its original application to discrimination-learning phenomena (Medin, 1975) and more recent applications to classification performance (Medin & Schaffer, 1978), selective attention has been an integral part of the model. In some attention theories (Zeaman & House, 1963) it is assumed that learning is confined to the dimension to which a subject attends. The context model makes the less stringent assumption that the similarity parameter of two cues along a dimension is less when that dimension is attended than when it is not attended; that is, differences on a dimension are more salient when attention is directed toward that dimension. Only as a special case, however, would the similarity parameter be zero for an attended dimension and one for a nonattended dimension (for related evidence, see Kellogg, 1980).

In the original presentation of the context model (Medin, 1975), I offered the not entirely original suggestion that developmental shifts in discrimination performance might involve an increased ability to overcome the effects of particularized contexts; that is, older children may be more efficient at attending to relevant information and ignoring irrelevant information. Several years earlier, Tighe and Tighe (1972) similarly had argued that whereas all subjects can and usually do learn something about instance–reward relations and the category–reward relations of simple concept tasks, the contribution of each type of solution varies with age. Younger subjects are relatively more likely to learn and remember instance properties (Tighe, Tighe, & Schechter, 1975).

Recently there has been accumulating evidence that there is a fundamental developmental shift in childrens' processing of multidimensional stimuli. Specifically, young children are more likely to process stimulus dimensions as integral (and less likely to process them as separable) than older children (see chapters by Kemler and by Shepp, this volume). The operational definitions of integral and separable dimensions suggest that this change represents an increased ability to attend selectively. This is consistent with the Tighes' theory.

In light of the preceding discussion and analysis of ill-defined concepts, however, it may be erroneous to view the younger child's attentional behavior as a limitation. The same process that is associated with highly specific learning and limited transfer may also be associated with learning correlations among attributes that give structure to many categories. Abstraction is an efficient process when one knows what information should be discarded. In many discrimination-learning tasks it may be clear which information is irrelevant but relevancy would be difficult to judge in the broader set of classification tasks where the potential contrast categories are not always present. For example, in learning to tell the difference between cats and dogs, size is a good cue whereas domesticity is not. But ignoring domesticity and learning only about size could prove costly later when one might want to distinguish dogs and wolves or dogs and coyotes.

SUMMARY AND A RESIDUAL PROBLEM

Probably very few readers will come away with the conviction that they know just what makes a category a category and what makes one task easy and another hard. I have tried to undermine both the viability of "atheoretical" guidelines for category structure and any residual confidence that categorization theories themselves place psychologically valid constraints on what may be a category. In their stead, the idea that correlated attributes may provide an organizing principle in categorization was briefly touted, but its main attraction may turn out to be that it has not yet been subject to stringent tests.

It remains to be seen just how category representations that exploit correlated attributes relate to the maxims with which we began this chapter. For example, both sensitivity to correlated attributes and cue validity can be thought of as facilitating inferences from attributes and category membership to allow organisms to "go beyond the information given." These inferences will also tend to be more accurate to the extent that within-category similarity is maximized and between-category similarity is minimized. But the main point is not that these maxims have no value; rather they seem more to be *consequences* rather than the *cause* of what makes a category good or sensible. To use a somewhat overdrawn analogy, the maxims may be like stating that good football teams score a lot of touchdowns and give up few touchdowns. Presumably, points scored or given up are by-products of more basic principles of skill. The maxims for category structure may best be thought of as byproducts or as acting in the service of more basic principles. To some extent the same criticisms can be leveled at the principle of correlated attributes.

Some different approaches may be in order, and I mention only one. Within the category bird, there is probably a correlation between the type of feather and whether or not the feet are webbed. But this is not a raw correlation that just happens to emerge. For example, adjusting to an aquatic environment may bring about a number of adaptations (e.g., webbed feet, water-repellent feathers) that would manifest themselves as correlated attributes. Likewise, correlated symptoms in medical diangosis may arise from a common underlying source. I find it intriguing that many of the subjects in our burlosis experiments not only noticed that certain symptoms were correlated but they also offered numerous explanations as to why. It may be that "relatedness" acts as a conceptual glue holding correlated attributes together directly and categories together indirectly.

ACKNOWLEDGMENTS

This research was supported by U.S. Public Health Service Grant MH32370. Ed Shoben, Elissa Newport, Gerald Dewey, Jerry Busemeyer, Carolyn Mervis, and Larry Barsalou provided helpful comments on earlier drafts of this chapter.

REFERENCES

Anderson, J. R., Kline, P. J., & Beasley, C. M. A general learning theory and its application to schema abstraction. In G. H. Bower (Ed.), *The psychology of learning and motivation* (Vol. 13). New York: Academic Press, 1979.

Estes, W. K. An associative basis for coding and organization in memory. In A. W. Melton & E. Martin (Eds.), *Coding processes in human memory.* Washington, D.C.: Winston, 1972.

Estes, W. K. *Memory and conditioning.* In F. J. McGuigan & D. B. Lumsden (Eds.), *Contemporary approaches to conditioning and learning.* New York: Wiley, 1973.

Estes, W. K. Structural aspects of associative models for memory. In C. N. Cofer (Ed.), *The structure of human memory.* New York: Freeman, 1976.

Farah, M. J., & Kosslyn, S. M. Learning concepts. In H. Reese & L. P. Lipsett (Eds.), *Advances in child development and behavior* (Vol. 16). New York: Academic Press, 1981.

Fried, L. S. *Perceptual learning and classification with ill-defined categories.* Michigan Mathematical Psychology Program technical report, 1979.

Garner, W. R. *The processing of information and structure.* New York: Wiley, 1974.

Hayes-Roth, B., & Hayes-Roth, F. Concept learning and the recognition and classification of exemplars. *Journal of Verbal Learning and Verbal Behavior, 1977, 16,* 321–338.

Homa, D., Rhoads, D., & Chambliss, P. The evolution of conceptual structure. *Journal of Experimental Psychology: Human Learning and Memory, 1979, 5,* 11–23.

Katz, J. J., & Postal, P. M. *An integrated theory of linguistic descriptions.* Caudbridge, Mass.: MIT Press, 1964.

Kellogg, R. T. Is conscious attention necessary for long-term storage? *Journal of Experimental Psychology: Human Learning and Memory, 1980, 6,* 379–390.

Kosan, N. E. Developmental differences in concept acquisition strategies. *Child Development, 1981, 52,* 290–298.

Levine, M. *A cognitive theory of learning: Research on hypothesis testing.* Hillsdale, N.J.: Lawrence Erlbaum Associates, 1975.

Malt, B. C., & Smith, E. E. *Correlational structure in semantic categories.* Unpublished manuscript. Stanford University, 1981.

McCloskey, M. E., & Glucksberg, S. Natural categories: Well-defined or fuzzy sets? *Memory & Cognition, 1978, 6,* 562–572.

Medin, D. L. A theory of context in discrimination learning. In G. H. Bower (Ed.), *The Psychology of learning and motivation* (Vol. 9). New York: Academic Press, 1975.

Medin, D. L., Altom, M. W., Edelson, S. M., & Freko, D. Correlated symptoms and simulated medical classification. *Journal of Experimental Psychology: Learning, Memory and Cognition,* 1982.

Medin, D. L., & Schaffer, M. M. Context theory of classification learning. *Psychological Review, 1978, 85,* 207–238.

Medin, D. L., & Schwanenflugel, P. L. Linear separability in classification learning. *Journal of Experimental Psychology: Human Learning and Memory, 1981, 7,* 355–368.

Medin, D. L., & Smith, E. E. Strategies in classification learning. *Journal of Experimental Psychology: Human Learning and Memory, 1981, 7,* 241–253.

Mervis, C. B., & Rosch, E. Categorization of natural objects. In M. R. Rosenzweig & L. W. Porter (Eds.), *Annual review of psychology,* 1981, *32,* 89–115.

Murphy, G. L. Cue validity and basic levels in categorization. *Psychological Bulletin,* 1982.

Neumann, P. G. An attribute frequency model for the abstraction of prototypes. *Memory & Cognition,* 1974, *2,* 241–248.

Nilsson, N. J. *Learning machines.* New York: McGraw-Hill, 1965.

Posner, M. I., & Keele, S. W. On the genesis of abstract ideas. *Journal of Experimental Psychology,* 1968, *77,* 353–363.

Reitman, J. S., & Bower, G. H. Storage and later recognition of exemplars of concepts. *Cognitive Psychology,* 1973, *4,* 194–206.

Rosch, E. On the internal structure of perceptual and semantic categories. In T. E. Moore (Ed.), *Cognitive development and the acquisition of language.* New York: Academic Press, 1973.

Rosch, E. Universals and cultural specifics in human categorization. In R. Breslin, S. Bochner, & W. Lonner (Eds.), *Cross-cultural perspectives on learning.* New York: Halsted Press, 1975.

Rosch, E. Principles of categorization. In E. Rosch & B. B. Lloyd (Eds.), *Cognition and categorization.* Hillsdale, N.J.: Lawrence Erlbaum Associates, 1978.

Rosch, E., & Lloyd, B. B. *Cognition and categorization.* Hillsdale, N.J.: Lawrence Erlbaum Associates, 1978.

Rosch, E., & Mervis, C. B. Family resemblances: Studies in the internal structure of categories. *Cognitive Psychology,* 1975, *7,* 573–605.

Rosch, E., Mervis, C. B., Gray, W. D., Johnson, D. M., & Boyes-Braem, P. Basic objects in natural categories. *Cognitive Psychology,* 1976, *8,* 382–439.

Sebestyn, G. S. *Decision-making processes in pattern recognition.* New York: Macmillan, 1962.

Smith, E. E., & Medin, D. L. *Categories and concepts.* Cambridge, Mass.: Harvard University Press, 1981.

Smith, E. E., Shoben, E. J., & Rips, L. J. Structure and processes in semantic memory: A featural model for semantic decisions. *Psychological Review,* 1974, *81,* 214–241.

Tighe, T. J., & Tighe, L. S. Stimulus control in children's learning. In A. D. Pick (Ed.), *Minnesota symposia on child psychology* (Vol. 6). Minneapolis: University of Minnesota Press, 1972.

Tighe, T. J., Tighe, L. S., & Schechter, J. Memory for instances and categories in children and adults. *Journal of Experimental Child Psychology,* 1975, *20,* 22–37.

Trabasso, T., & Bower, G. H. *Attention in learnings theory and research.* New York: Wiley, 1968.

Tversky, A. Features of similarity. *Psychological Review,* 1977, *84,* 327–352.

Zeaman, D., & House, B. J. The role of attention in retardate discrimination learning. In N. R. Ellis (Ed.), *Handbook of mental deficiency: Psychological theory and research.* New York: McGraw-Hill, 1963.

8 Intuitive Physics: Understanding and Learning of Physical Relations

Norman H. Anderson
University of California, San Diego

Introduction

Intuitive physics refers to our commonsense reactions about the physical events in the world around us. When we see a billiard ball in motion, for example, we have certain expectations about its trajectory, including possible collisions with other balls and rebounds from the cushions. When we throw a ball or prepare to catch a ball, we also have certain expectations and behaviors. Much of our daily life is spent in manipulating objects: cups and spoons, papers and pencils, hands and feet, . . . Such problems of intuitive physics are the concern of this chapter.

Intuitive physics is a blend of perception, cognition, and action. Perception has obvious relevance, and many studies in classical perception bear on intuitive physics. However, the cognitive component of intuitive physics is not less important. In the example of the billiard ball, extrapolation of a free trajectory may be largely perceptual, but prediction of postcollision behavior is largely cognitive. The action component appears in motor behavior, as in preparing to catch a ball. Because of this threefold blend of perception, cognition, and action, intuitive physics provides an interesting domain for psychological analysis.

Two simple tasks of intuitive physics are shown in Fig. 8.1. The left panel shows a collision task: If the pendulum is released, it will strike the ball, driving it up the inclined plane. As a subject, your task would be to predict how far up it will roll. The inclined plane in the right panel is even simpler: If the ball is released, it will roll down. Here your task would be to predict its travel time.

These two tasks were studied in the experiments reported later in this chapter and so the following theoretical discussion centers on them. Intuitive physics is much broader and richer than appears in these two tasks, of course, and some

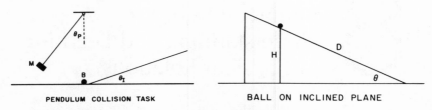

PENDULUM COLLISION TASK   BALL ON INCLINED PLANE

FIG. 8.1   Two tasks of intuitive physics. Left panel shows pendulum–ball collision task: Subjects predict how far the struck ball will travel up the inclined plane.
Right panel shows Galileo's inclined plane: Subjects predict travel time for ball to
roll down the inclined plane.

other tasks will be considered in the final section on developmental problems.
However, the simple structure of the two tasks in Fig. 8.1 helps focus attention
on some basic problems of understanding and learning. These problems are
outlined in the following section, which relates them to the present theoretical
approach.

INTUITIVE PHYSICS AS INFORMATION INTEGRATION

Multiple Causation

The present approach to intuitive physics is through a theory of information
integration (Anderson, 1974, 1981, 1982). The guiding idea is that intuitive
physics typically depends on multiple stimulus cues; these cues are integrated to
determine the response. Predicting what happens when the pendulum strikes the
ball, for example, involves an integration of information about the release angle
of the pendulum, its mass, the mass of the ball, and the slope of the incline. Even
in the simpler task of the inclined plane, predicted travel time depends on an
integration of the angle of incline and the travel distance of the ball. Subjects
readily make such predictions; understanding how subjects do this is not so easy.

Multiple causation in intuitive physics, as in perception, involves the twin
problems of *analysis*—ascertaining the effective stimulus cues—and *synthesis*—
determining how these cues are integrated. The primary focus of the present
approach is on the problem of synthesis, especially the form and nature of the
rules that govern the integration of disparate cues into a unitary response. These
integration rules can also provide useful tools for analysis, especially for measuring psychological values and for defining cognitive units.

Function Knowledge

The cognitive unit in many tasks of intuitive physics may be viewed as a function
in a mathematical sense. The physical relations in the tasks illustrated in Fig. 8.1

are mathematical functions, of course, and presumably the same is true of the corresponding psychological relations. A mundane but notable characteristic of civilization is the steady increase in density and velocity of moving objects in our environment. An organism able to survive in and indeed construct such an environment presumably has high ability with functional relations.

If you predict the ball's behavior in either task of Fig. 8.1, your predictive scheme generates a functional relation between the prescribed judgment response and the stimulus variables. We cannot assume, however, that your predictive scheme mimics nature's physics. Instead, it is necessary to develop methods for determining the function knowledge of intuitive physics.

Function knowledge differs from the traditional outlook that knowledge is categorical or classificational. The cognitive unit corresponds to the functional relation or its generator. A concept need not be "a category of things," as the common definition has it, but a functional relation. This difference in the structure of knowledge leads to different problems and to different theoretical perspective than arises from the view that knowledge is categorical or classificational.

Function Learning

Representation of knowledge as functional relations raises a variety of questions about learning, two of which may be noted here. The first is how these functions are learned. One possibility is that a few basic curve shapes develop in early childhood and that later learning consists largely of selecting a curve shape or pattern and calibrating its parameters to the given task. This view may have considerable truth and it will suffice for the time being. However, it may be more appropriate for one-dimensional valuation functions than for many-variable integration functions.

The second question concerns the effectiveness of various kinds of information for function learning. When the cognitive unit is a function, traditional trial-by-trial accuracy information may not be too useful; a single trial cannot say anything about function shape. Different kinds of learning information, especially information that is relevant to curve shape and function pattern, need to be explored.

Background Knowledge

A primary characteristic of intuitive physics is its dependence on previous experience. We learn about motions and collisions of objects from earliest infancy. Adult performance requires selecting from a mass of background knowledge and applying that to the task at hand.

This basic role of background knowledge contrasts with the *tabula rasa* approach that appears in studies with nonsense syllables or conditioned reflexes.

The *tabula rasa* approach seeks to minimize the role of background knowledge, an attractive and useful tactic for investigation. That tactic is not appropriate for intuitive physics, however, which requires conceptual analysis of the nature and operation of background knowledge.

Schema Analysis

Much of intuitive physics may be represented in terms of schemas. Integration functions, for example, are schemas that organize the information in a multiple-stimulus field. Valuation functions are schemas that retrieve and utilize background information for the operative task.

The idea of schemas has long been popular as one reaction to the need to allow for organization and structure in knowledge. Schema concepts appear in the many interesting tasks of intuitive physics studied by Inhelder and Piaget (1958). More immediately relevant is the study by Björkman (1965), who considered the task of the inclined plane and gave a thoughtful discussion of some problems of functional relations in intuitive physics. In recent years, schema concepts have become increasingly popular but experimental analysis has lagged. One attraction of intuitive physics is that certain operative schemas appear amenable to quantitative analysis. A more detailed discussion of the integration-theoretical approach to schemas is given in Anderson (1982, Section 7.16).

KNOWLEDGE FUNCTIONS

Several kinds of knowledge functions are involved in the experimental tasks that are considered later. This section discusses some of their properties, treating them as mathematical functions that represent certain psychological operations. The following integration diagram gives an overview of three primary functions, namely, valuation, integration, and action.

Integration Diagram

The integration diagram in Fig. 8.2 shows physical stimuli, $\{S_1, S_2, S_3, \ldots\}$, that impinge on the organism and are transformed by the perceptual cognitive apparatus into their psychological counterparts, $s_1, s_2, s_3, \ldots\}$. These psychological stimuli are integrated to produce an implicit, psychological response r that is externalized to become the observable response R. This notation follows the convention of capital letters for observable, physical quantities, and lowercase letters for unobservable, psychological quantities.

This processing chain involves three operations or functions, **V, I**, and **A**. The *valuation function* **V** transforms the physical stimuli S_i into psychological stimuli s_i. The *integration function* **I** transforms the field $\{s_i\}$ of psychological stimuli

STIMULUS   INTEGRATION   DIAGRAM

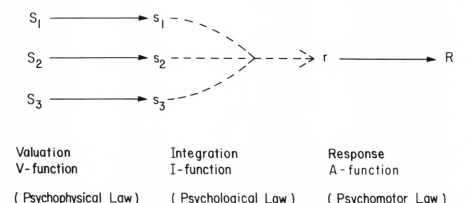

Valuation	Integration	Response
V- function	I-function	A - function
(Psychophysical Law)	(Psychological Law)	(Psychomotor Law)

FIG. 8.2   Stimulus integration diagram.

into a psychological response *r*. Finally, the *action function* **A** transforms the implicit response *r* into the observable response *R*.

This diagram is simplistic but it serves to bring out a central property of integration theory, namely, the dual focus on integration and on psychological values. The integration function is concerned with multiple causation at the psychological level. Stimulus input and response output must both be represented as psychological values.

Valuation: A Constructive Operation

The valuation operation processes the physical stimulus information to determine its psychological values. The foremost characteristic of valuation is its constructive nature (Anderson, 1981, 1982). Stimulus values are not givens; neither are they properties of the physical situation. Instead the person must assess the physical situation and infer its relevance and implications for the task at hand.

This constructive nature of valuation may be emphasized by the dependence of value on task: The same physical stimulus may have different values in different tasks. In the collision situation, for example, subjects could be asked to predict postcollision motion of the pendulum rather than the ball. This instruction sets a different task or goal, one in which the incline angle of the plane has minimal relevance.

This view that values are constructed within the specific task situation entails some difficult theoretical problems that are taken up in the later discussion of molar unitization. For present purposes, the valuation function is considered as a cognitive unit characterized by function shape and function parameters. Although a sharp line cannot be drawn between shapes and parameters, there is a real distinction. One may be clear that the shape is straight line, for example, without any clear idea about its slope.

Integration Functions: Cognitive Algebra

Shape principles for the integration operation must be multidimensional because integration involves joint operation of two or more variables. One two-dimensional shape principle that is likely to be prominent in intuitive physics is the linear fan shape that reflects the operation of a multiplication rule. Many physical laws involve multiplication of variables and so exhibit the linear fan shape (see, e.g., Fig. 8.3). Some examples from psychology are taken up in the experimental studies considered at a later point. Other important shape principles are the parallelism pattern, which reflects an adding-type integration rule, and the barrel pattern, which reflects a ratio rule.

These two-dimensional shape principles may, in some tasks, correspond to cognitive units in a simple visual way. Like the one-dimensional shape principles for valuation, they may be manipulable in the mind's eye. An example appears in the graphic response mode discussed in connection with the inclined plane experiment of Fig. 8.4. More often, however, the shape principle will be implicit in the rule that generates the responses.

A different aspect of integration rules concerns their role as knowledge functions. From the present theoretical view, integration functions are considered to embody general-purpose skills. They are available for use in coping with diverse tasks according to the person's sizing up of the task situation. Two theoretical questions thus concern the nature of the task analysis performed by the person and the nature of the available integration rules.

The question of what task characteristics control the integration function has not received much explicit study. In some cases, the physical task itself obeys an algebraic rule. The inclined plane of Fig. 8.1 is famous for Galileo's discovery of perhaps the first law of physical dynamics. However, the person's judgments presumably do not proceed from knowledge of this physical law, at least in any verbal form, and indeed the data in the later experiments show certain deviations from the physical law. What task cues elicit the observed response patterns is unknown.

In contrast, quite a bit is known about the form of the integration rules. Numerous experiments across many areas of psychology have revealed the operation of a fairly general *cognitive algebra* (Anderson, 1981). Even in young children, information integration often follows algebraic rules such as averaging and multiplying (Anderson, 1980). Because cognitive algebra is bound up with psychological measurement, further discussion is deferred to the next main section.

Action

Two aspects of the action function, **A,** which relates the implicit response to the observable response, require brief discussion. These are function shape and motor skill. A third aspect, concerned with a graphing response mode, is considered later.

The shape of the action function characterizes the relation between R and r. This is conceptually different from the other functions. It may not seem that any question should arise about the shape of the **A** function. The pendulum collision task, for example, does not seem to require any distinction between implicit and overt response. The subject points to where the ball is expected to roll and that would seem to be that.

For the inclined plane, of course, the shape of **A** is clearly important because the judgment of travel time is a number-word. The question is whether this number-word is a faithful representation of the unobservable response or whether the response language introduces a distortion. This question, it should be noted, may be pertinent even with the pointing response. Mathematically, the question is whether **A** is a linear or nonlinear function. This is the classical measurement question of the linear (equal interval) scale that is taken up in the next main section.

An important feature of the action function, emphasized in its name, is its skill aspects. The motor skills in catching a ball, for example, require much more than a prediction of its trajectory. Such motor skills are important in sports and present many interesting problems for psychological analysis. Even simple tasks of pitching pennies and rolling balls require a cognitive analysis that relates motor behavior to perceptual–cognitive skills of stimulus integration. Although motor skills are outside the scope of this discussion, they deserve mention because of their importance for more general problems of intuitive physics.

COGNITIVE ALGEBRA AND PSYCHOLOGICAL MEASUREMENT

Functional Measurement

Cognitive algebra depends on psychological measurement. Each stimulus variable must be measured in its subjective metric, which is not generally equivalent to its objective, physical metric. The necessity for psychological measurement is obvious; an adding rule, for example, would not add up if the wrong values were added. Study of cognitive algebra thus depends on obtaining linear (equal-interval) or ratio scales of subjective value.

Psychological measurement has been a source of controversy since the time of Fechner. This controversy has been dramatized by Stevens (1974), who emphasized that two plausible methods of numerical responding, namely, the common method of rating and his own method of magnitude estimation, yielded quite different results. Both response measures could not be true linear scales, therefore, but Stevens provided no way to determine which, if either, was valid.

Functional measurement provided a way out of this controversy. The essential idea is to use the integration rule as a base and frame for measurement. This reverses the traditional approach and makes measurement derivative from, not prior to, substantive investigation (Anderson, 1981, Chapter 5).

Linear Fan Theorem

One result from functional measurement is used in the present experiments, namely, the linear fan theorem (Anderson, 1981, 1982). Consider two stimulus variables combined in factorial design and suppose we wish to test the hypothesis that the subject integrates these variables by a multiplying rule. The linear fan theorem says that the multiplying rule will, under specified conditions, yield a factorial graph that exhibits the pattern of a linear fan. The linear fan pattern is thus a diagnostic sign of a multiplying rule.

Examples may be seen in the experimental data of Fig. 8.4, which plots travel time judgments for the inclined plane as a function of travel distance (horizontal axis) and angle of incline (curve parameter). The center panel shows a nearly pure form of the linear fan pattern; this data pattern suggests that subjects multiply the two stimulus variables.

The left panel of Fig. 8.4 shows the linear fan pattern in a slightly disguised form. The diminishing returns shape of each curve stems from the use of the objective, physical distance measure on the horizontal axis. If the subjective, psychological distance scale is used instead, the curves will straighten out and form a pure linear fan pattern.

The linear fan pattern in Fig. 8.4 has three consequences. First, the fan pattern implies that the two stimulus variables are integrated by a multiplying rule. In addition, success of this integration rule solves two problems of measurement. On the response side, the multiplying rule implies that the rating response that was used in this experiment is a valid linear scale. On the stimulus side, linear scales of both stimulus variables can readily be obtained. Thus, the linear fan theorem provides a method to determine the integration rule and to solve the two associated problems of psychological measurement (Anderson, 1981, Section 1.4, 1982, Section 2.2).

Background Knowledge and Molar Unitization

The constructive nature of the valuation operation reflects the pervasive role of background knowledge. To illustrate, suppose a bit of gum is stuck to the ball on the inclined plane. Few subjects will have had any experience with partly sticky balls rolling down slopes. Instead, they will recollect gum stuck to their shoes, syrup on their hands at breakfast, and other such distantly relevant experiences.

It is this diverse aggregate of background knowledge that is processed by the valuation operation to judge how the bit of gum will influence the rolling of the ball. This valuation will indeed be a guess, uncertain and possibly quite inaccurate. Our main concern, however, is not with the accuracy of this inference but with its existence and nature.

Similar constructive processes are involved for all stimulus variables in the physical field. Rarely is direct transfer of knowledge possible. Instead, the valuation process is a web of thought that utilizes an ill-defined aggregate of background knowledge. This background knowledge is largely unknown, indeed largely unknowable to the investigator. Values might seem undeterminable, therefore, and the prospects of cognitive algebra hopeless.

Fortunately, exact theory is possible by virtue of the unitization principle (Anderson, 1981, 1982). No matter how intricate the valuation operation, the resultant value can be treated as a molar unit with respect to the integration operation. Under certain conditions, functional measurement can measure this value. Regardless of the complexity of the molecular processes involved in valuation, their effects are all precisely and completely summarized in the functional values. This allows exact theory at the molar task level.

No less important, this approach provides a window into the subterranean workings of the valuation processes. These molar values are measured in the psychological metrics that functioned in the subject's reactions. Hence these molar values are boundary conditions that any molecular theory of processing must obey.

EXPERIMENTAL STUDIES

Two tasks of intuitive physics are taken up in this section. Both have already been illustrated in Fig. 8.1. One derives from Galileo's famous experiments about the motion of a ball on an inclined plane. The other involves collisions, in which a pendulum mass strikes a ball or train, driving it up an incline. Subjects predicted travel time or travel distance for the rolling ball.

These tasks obey physical laws; these laws constitute nature's standard of correct response. One main question concerns subjects' preexperimental knowledge and its relation to physical law. This experiential background is extensive but it cannot be assumed that subjects' knowledge has similar structure to the physical law.

A second main question concerns problems of learning and transfer. Nature sets a standard of correctness that subjects can, in principle, determine by just observing the actual physical events in each task. It cannot be taken for granted, however, how subjects will utilize such observations.

The present approach, it should be emphasized, is mainly concerned with knowledge structure rather than with accuracy of prediction. Primary focus is thus on the shapes of the valuation functions and especially of the integration functions. The present methods allow these functions to be determined in their own right, thereby contributing to the mapping of the subjects' knowledge structures.

Method and Procedure

The experiments reported here have not previously been published except for Fig. 8.4, which appears as Fig. 4.22 in Anderson (1981, Note 4.5.3a). Task and procedure were fairly simple, however, so only a brief outline is needed.

In the standard response mode, subjects made predictions for one stimulus condition at a time. An absolute response was used in the collision task: subjects predicted travel distance of the ball by pointing to a location on the actual incline. A graphic rating response was used in the inclined plane experiment: subjects predicted travel time of the ball down the plane by pointing to a location on a 20-cm rod. This graphic rating scale was calibrated during the instruction–practice period with stimulus end anchors in the usual way to ensure a linear (equal-interval) response measure (Anderson, 1982, Section 1.1).

A novel graphing response was also used. Subjects sketched complete curves and complete factorial graphs on a sheet of quadrille paper. In contrast to the single-stimulus predictions, the graphing response makes visible to the subjects the structure or pattern of their predictions. This graphing procedure, which requires care to ensure that subjects understand their graphs, is described later for the collision experiment of Fig. 8.7.

Each experiment varied two stimulus variables in factorial design. These designs are explicit in the graphs of the various experiments. Additional details are in the figure legends.

These experiments were exploratory but each one represents considerable pilot work on instructions and choice of stimulus levels. All subjects were college students. General procedure, including practice and instructions, followed the guidelines in Anderson (1982, Chapter 1).

Galileo's Inclined Plane

In the task illustrated in the right panel of Fig. 8.3, subjects predicted the time required for the ball to roll down the inclined plane. Under ideal conditions, the physical travel time is

$$\text{Travel time} = cD/\sqrt{H} = c\sqrt{D}/\sqrt{\sin \theta}.$$

The distances D and H are defined in the figure; the constant c depends on the gravitational force and the moment of inertia of the ball. This famous equation is

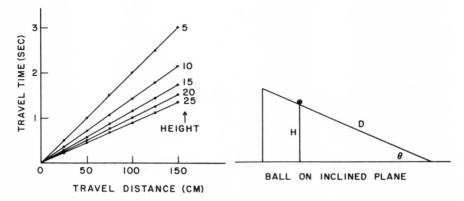

FIG. 8.3 Galileo's experiment of the inclined plane. Right panel shows task schematic. Left panel plots physical travel times as a function of travel distance (horizontal axis) and initial elevation (curve parameter).

perhaps the first discovered mathematical law of dynamics (Galileo, 1638/1974, Proposition V, p. 177).

If D and H are varied in factorial design, the factorial graph of the physical clock times will exhibit a linear fan pattern. This is illustrated in the left panel of Fig. 8.3. By virtue of the linear fan theorem, this fan pattern reflects the algebraic structure of Galileo's law, namely, a multiplying rule or strictly speaking, a dividing rule. Thus, it is easy to verify Galileo's law—if a clock is available (Anderson, 1981, Section 5.6.4). It is a tribute to Galileo's experimental ingenuity that he was able to discover this law without a clock capable of measuring the short time intervals involved (see Drake, 1978, pp. 85–90).

In the present experiments, subjects were not asked to rediscover Galileo's law. Their task was quite different, namely, to make intuitive guesses about the travel times. These intuitive judgments were readily made without benefit of any book learning. Among the experimental questions, however, is whether these intuitive judgments will exhibit a pattern similar to that found in nature.

Background Knowledge: Schematic Inclined Plane

One purpose of this experiment was to study preexperimental knowledge. Accordingly, a schematic plane was used and no actual ball rolling ever occurred. A second purpose was to test the graphing response mode.

The left panel of Fig. 8.4 shows the initial set of predictions for the single stimulus conditions. Each curve represents one angle of inclination; the points on each curve represent the five distances of the ball from the foot of the incline. Two features of these data deserve comment. First, the curves form a diverging fan that is somewhat similar to the actual physical pattern, already shown in Fig.

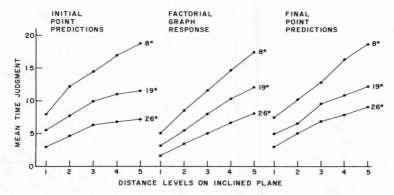

FIG. 8.4 Predictions of travel time for ball on schematic inclined plane. Left panel shows predictions for each of the 15 combinations of travel distance and angle of incline presented one at a time. Center panel shows mean of the factorial graph response. Right panel shows subsequent replication of the single-stimulus predictions. Sixteen college students served as subjects in all three conditions in the listed order and rated travel time on a graphic response scale. After Anderson (1981).

8.3. Second, the curves bow downward, as though subjects followed a law of diminishing returns. Each unit increase in distance produces progressively less increase in travel time. This curvature does not mar the linear fan shape, however, for it represents a nonlinearity in the valuation function for distance, not a deviation from the multiplying rule of integration. If this functional scale of distance is used on the horizontal, the curves will form a linear fan (Anderson, 1981, Section 1.4). Thus, the integration of the two stimulus variables follows a multiplying rule.

The factorial graph response mode was used in the second part of the experiment. Each subject sketched a set of three curves on a sheet of graph paper, and the mean of these factorial graphs is shown in the center panel of Fig. 8.4.

The main feature of this graphing response mode is the near-perfect linear fan pattern. The curvature in the single stimulus predictions in the left panel has disappeared; all three curves are virtually straight. This pattern of curves is more like the physically correct pattern seen in Fig. 8.3. There is a temptation to suggest that the graphing response mode helped subjects clarify and firm up their preexperimental knowledge. Perhaps a better interpretation is that subjects have a tendency to assume and impose linear relations that is facilitated by the graphing response.

The last part of the experiment repeated the first part, with subjects making single-stimulus predictions for each of the 15 angle–distance combinations. The main new feature of these data, shown in the right panel of Fig. 8.4, is that the linearity found with the graphing response transfers to these single-stimulus predictions. Statistical tests of the quadratic component of distance showed significant curvature in the left panel of Fig. 8.4, a significant decrease in curvature between left and right panels, and nonsignificant curvature in the right panel itself. The graphing response procedure can thus induce substantial transfer to the single-stimulus predictions.

Inclined Plane: Effect of Observation

The purpose of this experiment was to assess how observations of the physical events might alter subjects' preexperimental knowledge. A rigid, plastic plane was used with a V-groove for rolling a steel ball. Travel times for this apparatus follow Galileo's law very closely. Accordingly, the incline angles were changed from the previous experiment to allow a reasonable range of physical travel times.

Preexperimental knowledge is shown in the left panel of Fig. 8.5. These are single-stimulus judgments, prior to any actual ball rolling, but with the ball located on the plane at specified distances and given angles. In the main, the pattern is similar to the corresponding graph for the schematic plane in the left panel of Fig. 8.4. The angle variable has less effect and the 6° and 11° curves show mild curvature. Overall, however, the curves form a near-linear fan.

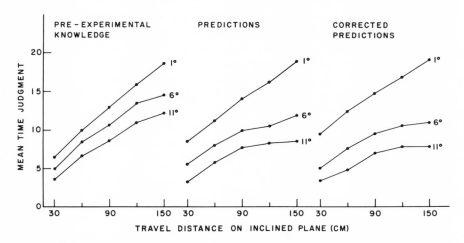

FIG. 8.5 Predictions of travel time for ball on actual inclined plane. Left panel shows preexperimental knowledge, prior to ball rolling, in the form of single-stimulus predictions for the 15 combinations of travel time and angle of incline. Right panel shows judgments of actual travel time observed by the subjects. Center panel represents predictions followed by actual ball rolling. Twelve college students served as subjects in all three conditions.

In the second part of the experiment, subjects made predictions just as in the first part, but then the ball was released so they could observe the actual travel time. Following this, a corrected prediction was also made, that is, a direct judgment of the actual travel time for that trial.

These predictions and the corrected predictions are shown in the center and right panels of Fig. 8.5, respectively. Comparing these two panels with the preexperimental knowledge already noted in the left panel shows that observation of the events had two consequences. First, the angle variable now exhibits much larger effects than was recognized in preexperimental knowledge—in agreement with the physical facts. Second, the near-linear fan shape has disappeared and the two lower curves show strong curvature—contrary to the physical facts. Observation of the actual events has increased overall accuracy but has caused the psychological law to deviate in structure from the physical law.

Also noteworthy is the close similarity between the center and the right panels of Fig. 8.5. This implies that learning was both rapid and effective. Rapid learning may be characteristic of certain tasks of intuitive physics. The main component of learning in the present task was the calibration of the valuation function for angle. Calibration requires only a few trials and so shows up early in the predictions.

Pendulum–Ball Collision

In this experiment, a weighted pendulum bob was drawn back and released to strike a ball, driving it up an inclined trough. A single actual trial was included casually in the instructions to induce an approximate calibration of the response. Subjects pointed to a location on the incline to indicate their predictions.

Preexperimental knowledge is shown for the two experimental conditions in the upper half of Fig. 8.6. Each curve in the right panel is steeper and higher than the corresponding curve in the left panel: The heavy pendulum is expected to propel the light ball farther than the light pendulum propels the heavy ball. The three curves in each panel show the effect of number of weights inserted into the pendulum bob. Both conditions exhibit a linear fan form, with significant divergence in both panels.

In the next part, subjects observed all 12 collisions used in the experimental design, plus an additional 6 collisions of their own selection. Following these observations, the first part was repeated.

These observations had marked effects, as shown by comparing the dotted curves in the upper and lower panels. On the left, the effect of pendulum release angle has increased, as shown in the steeper slopes of the lower dotted curves; the effect of the pendulum mass has also increased, as shown by the greater separation of the three lower dotted curves. The right panel shows a similar effect of pendulum release angle, together with a disappearance of the effect of pendulum mass.

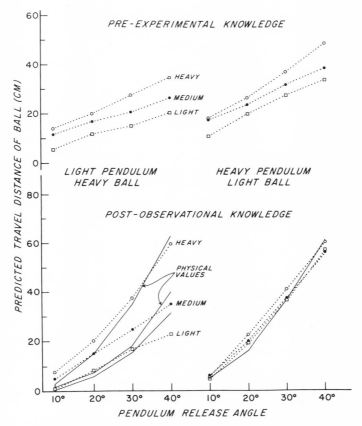

FIG. 8.6   Predictions of travel distance for ball driven up inclined plane by
pendulum impact. Upper panels show preexperimental knowledge for each of two
conditions, prior to observing actual collisions. Lower panels show predictions
following the observations; dotted curves represent actual physical distances.
Eight college students served as subjects in each condition.

Accuracy has also increased substantially. Accuracy may be assessed in the
lower panels of Fig. 8.6 by comparing the dotted curves of subjects' predictions
with the distances that the ball actually rolled, shown by the solid curves. This
increase in accuracy is clearest in the lower right panel. Here the three physical
curves were so close together that they could not be plotted separately and the
subjects' predictions also show near-identity.

Some systematic inaccuracy still remains that is consistent with the hypothesis
of a general linearization tendency mentioned previously. In every case, the
predicted curves are straighter than the actual physical curves. A similar linearization tendency can be detected in the effect of pendulum weight. In the left

panel, the three curves for pendulum weight are more equally spaced than the physical curves, and this pattern also appears in the preexperimental knowledge.

More extensive study would be needed to verify this linearization hypothesis. It may be noted, incidentally, that this hypothesis entails two stages in the valuation operation: a first stage that yields perceptual values; and a second stage that transforms the perceptual values into the values functional in the task at hand. It is the relation between the functional and perceptual values to which the linearization hypothesis refers. Linearity or lack thereof between the functional values and the physical values has marginal cognitive relevance because physical values are not themselves perceived. The diminishing returns previously seen in the lower curves of Fig. 8.5 does not have its locus in the psychophysical law for perceptual distance. Quite the contrary; this nonlinearity is of interest because the perceptual value of the distance variable is approximately a linear function of physical distance over this range.

Pendulum–Train Collision

In this experiment, a weighted pendulum struck a toy train, driving it up an inclined track. Weight and release angle of the pendulum were varied and subjects predicted how far the train would roll up the track. A buffer strip was fixed behind the resting location of the train at the bottom of the track to prevent impact damage and derailment. Subjects hefted the weights several times during practice to gain an appreciation of their potential effect, a procedure also followed in the preceding experiment. To lend reality to the task and to allow an approximate response calibration, a single collision was casually included as part of the instructions. No further collisions were observed until Part 4. In Parts 1, 2, and 3, the experimenter drew back the pendulum to the specified release angle and told the subject how many weights it would contain. However, the pendulum was not actually released to strike the train.

Part 1 studied single stimulus predictions based on preexperimental knowledge. These results are shown in the left panel of Fig. 8.7. Both stimulus factors have substantial effects: The effect of pendulum release angle appears in the slope of the curves; the effect of pendulum weight appears in their vertical separation. The overall pattern is roughly a diverging fan, which happens to be physically correct.

In Part 2, subjects drew their own factorial graphs. This part began with an instruction period to make the graphing task clear. Distance along the train track was transposed to vertical distance on the graph paper and single curves were drawn for each stimulus variable. Subjects began by placing points on the graph paper for each pendulum angle, assuming a fixed mass, connecting these four points with a curve, and then adjusting the curve with a colored pencil as they saw fit. This same process was repeated with a second sheet of graph paper to encourage subjects to adjust their initial curves. The experimenter then in-

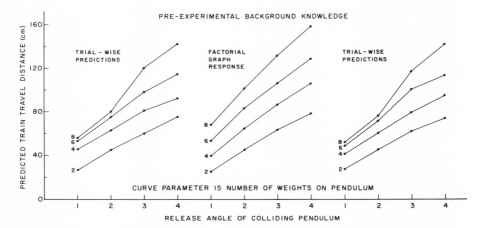

FIG. 8.7 Predictions of travel distance for train driven up inclined track by pendulum impact. All three panels represent preexperimental knowledge, prior to actual observations. Left panel presents single-stimulus predictions for the 16 combinations of pendulum release angle and pendulum weight. Center panel shows factorial graph response of same 16 combinations, and right panel shows subsequent replication of the single-stimulus predictions.

terpreted this graph nondirectively in terms of conformity with or deviations from a proportional relation, asked subjects if that was how they wanted it, and had them make a third graph. This same procedure was then employed for the mass variable, assuming a fixed release angle.

Finally, subjects made a complete graph with four curves, one for each mass. The mean of these graphs is shown in the center panel of Fig. 8.7. These factorial responses are visibly more regular than the trial-wise predictions and exhibit a neat linear fan pattern.

Part 3 was a replication of Part 1 and the results, shown in the right panel of Fig. 8.7, are virtually identical with those of Part 1 in the left panel. The graphing responses of the intervening part did not induce much visible change in the knowledge structure. Variability decreased; the mean squares for the three- and four-way interactions involving subjects and replications were about half as large in Part 3 as in Part 1. However, decreased variability could result from general practice as well as from the graphing exercise.

In Part 4, subjects observed and graphed effects of eight actual collisions. The first four collisions varied pendulum distance from low to high, using the second level of mass. The last four collisions varied the mass from low to high, using the second level of distance. This procedure provides complete information on each valuation function with minimal information on the integration function. These two graphs were then collected and the subject made a final set of single-stimulus predictions.

These postobservational predictions are shown in Fig. 8.8, together with the actual physical values. The main outcome is that the observations had surprisingly little effect. In fact, the response pattern is not greatly different from the preobservational judgments (right panel of Fig. 8.7), whereas it is substantially different from the correct physical pattern shown by the dotted curves in Fig. 8.8. The failure to utilize the observations can be best appreciated by looking at the second level of pendulum distance in Fig. 8.8. These four physical values were actually observed by the subjects, yet their actual predictions are nowhere near. This outcome probably results from specifics of task and procedure rather than any general difficulty in utilizing event observations. Nevertheless, this outcome shows that it cannot be taken for granted that subjects will utilize event observations effectively, even in such simple physical situations.

General Discussion

These experiments had two main goals: to determine knowledge structures in some tasks of intuitive physics and to see how these knowledge structures change under certain informer–reinforcer conditions. The main working assumption was that functional relations are basic components of many knowledge structures.

One notable result is that preexperimental knowledge in every experiment approximated the linear fan pattern that characterized the prevailing physical law. In these particular tasks, at least, the psychological integration function has similar form to nature's integration function.

Correct form was less frequent in the psychological valuation functions. In one case, they were bowed down instead of linear; in another case, they were linear instead of bowed up. Such deviations are not surprising because the physical form is itself sensitive to task details. The bowed-up physical curves in the lower part of Fig. 8.6, for example, depend on such apparatus peculiarities. However, the results did suggest a general linearization tendency associated with valuation operations.

Results on informer–reinforcer effects do not provide a simple picture. Intuitive physics has interest because the correct response is not arbitrary, as in typical learning experiments, but open to observation in the task itself. Direct observation would be expected to improve prediction, therefore, and that was mainly true. Nevertheless, significant exceptions were also found. In the inclined plane of Fig. 8.5, observation improved the calibration for the angle function but introduced a nonlinearity into the valuation function for distance. Again, in the train-collision experiment of Fig. 8.8, marked inaccuracies remained despite direct observation of travel distance. The present experiments were explanatory and hence tried out a variety of conditions; more systematic work is needed to determine what factors do and do not make event observation effective.

One final implication of these experiments deserves emphasis: Accuracy criteria are not adequate for cognitive analysis. Traditional learning theory has

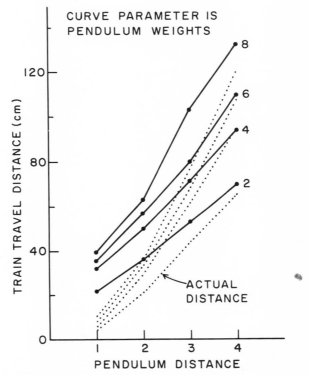

FIG. 8.8 Predictions of travel distance for train driven up inclined plane by pendulum impact. Dotted curves represent actual travel distances, selected values of which were observed by the subjects. Solid curves represent postobservational predictions.

centered on correct response, largely in terms of trial-wise accuracy. Accuracy might seem even more basic in intuitive physics because nature herself sets the standard and provides automatic, often harsh punishment for inaccuracy. The present experiments suggest that trial-wise information–reinforcement is not adequate because the cognitive units are function shapes. Hence it is necessary to develop informer–reinforcers that embody shape principles. On the stimulus side, subjects could be shown graphs of correct shapes of the valuation and integration functions. On the response side, they could be shown similar graphs of their own predictions. But even accuracy criteria based on function shape are not sufficient; to use such criteria is to continue the normative approach of evaluating behavior by reference to objective standards. However useful the normative approach may be, cognitive analysis must be able to operate at a descriptive level that can analyze psychological processes in their own right (Anderson, 1981, Section 1.8.1).

LEARNING

This section comments on four aspects of learning in intuitive physics. One main theme is that intuitive physics leads to a perspective somewhat different from traditional learning theory. Although the difference between these two perspectives has been recognized, both implicitly and explicitly, by diverse other writers, it deserves emphasis. To a person educated in traditional learning theory, intuitive physics provides a beneficial balance to some limitations and narrowness of the traditional approach.

Functions and Categories

Knowledge in intuitive physics involves functional relations. This view of knowledge is clear in the foregoing experiments, especially with respect to valuation functions. This function view of knowledge bears on the general problem of what is learned and on specific procedures for inducing learning.

Traditional learning theory embodies a conception of knowledge as association and classification in categories. In the associationistic view, learning is a matter of discrete S–R associations, epitomized by Thorndike's "trial-and-error" approach. Functions do arise—by generalization—but the function is not the cognitive unit of learning. This outlook may be recognized even in Tolman, as in his claim that all psychology, except language processes, could be studied in the white rat. In fact, the rat's intuitive physics hardly compares with higher mammals or even birds. The best of these, moreover, are at a perceptual-motor level that is at most a carrier of human intuitive physics of the inclined plane.

The dominance of categorical thinking appears also in concept formation. The definition, "a concept is a category of things," is well illustrated in the work of Hull, Hovland, and Gibson. The attempts to represent knowledge organization by Tulving and Mandler are in terms of categories and hierarchical classifications. Even modern information processing theories have largely fixated on discrete propositional representations and have neglected problems of quantification, which are essential to function knowledge (see Anderson, 1981, Section 1.8).

The importance of categorical thought goes without saying; the importance of function thinking does not. Function thinking entails many differences in experimental inquiry, some of which are taken up in the following three subsections.

Calibration

Calibration operations are one main locus of learning effects. The most obvious calibration concerns the unit on the response scale. The subject may possess correct function shapes and yet be very inaccurate. Specifically, the subject's factorial graph and the correct factorial graph may have the same shape but differ by a proportionality scale factor.

When the function shapes are correct, a single trial can suffice to calibrate the response scale. In terms of an accuracy criterion, learning can be extremely rapid. But this requires preexistence of the basic knowledge structure. What is learned pertains to applying this knowledge structure.

This utility of single-trial information contrasts with its disutility when the basic knowledge structure is incorrect. To illustrate, suppose that subjects employ an adding rule in a task that embodies a multiplying operation. Children, for example, judge area of rectangles by the adding rule, height + width, instead of the physically correct height × width rule (Anderson & Cuneo, 1978a; Wilkening, 1979). Suppose also that this adding rule is already calibrated to minimize mean inaccuracy. Any single response will typically be in error, of course, because the function shape is incorrect. If subjects react to this error by recalibrating the response unit, inaccuracy will increase. Single-trial accuracy information may thus harm, not help.

That single-trial information may be harmful emphasizes the need for different kinds of informer–reinforcers. This point can be emphasized further by noting that single-trial accuracy information in principle cannot lead to correct integration functions. Single-trial accuracy information may work in practice if subjects aggregate shape and relation information across a number of trials. It seems clear, however, that better results can be expected from informers directed at structure of knowledge.

Calibration is not merely a matter of the response scale. Calibration also appears in parameters of valuation functions. One aspect of learning in the pendulum collision experiment of Fig. 8.6, for example, was that pendulum mass had greater importance than had been recognized in preexperimental knowledge. Such valuation processes, however, require different informational reinforcement than needed to calibrate the response unit.

Information and Reinforcement

A function view of knowledge suggests a corresponding approach to information–reinforcement schedules. If function shapes are cognitive units, learning may be more effective with information related to function shape. Two issues of function learning are noted here.

The first issue concerns the kinds of information that can be given. Standard single-trial information about correct response can, as already noted, be very effective for response calibration. Single-trial accuracy information can also be used to determine function shape if subjects can aggregate this information across trials.

A related kind of information is available from paired trial comparisons. Galileo's experiment comparing the descent times of light and heavy balls dropped from the leaning tower of Pisa provides an apt illustration. Such paired comparisons can provide convincing evidence for null effect of a variable. This approach can also be used in reverse, as in Galileo's demonstration that air has weight: He pumped a bladder full of air and compared its weight before and after. Such comparative information can help determine parameters of valuation functions.

Different kinds of information seem necessary to determine shape itself. Both verbal and visual informers could be used. Subjects could be told, directly or indirectly, that a given valuation function followed a law of diminishing returns, for example, or had an ogival shape. This approach was used by Brehmer and Slovic (1980) in a study of value invariance in information integration. Integration functions could be described analogously. Alternatively, shape information could be presented in a visual display. One such picture could easily be worth a thousand of Thorndike's trials and errors.

The second issue concerns what may be called *function thinking,* in which the cognitive units are mathematical functions or function generators. Function thinking appears in the use of patterned stimulus information, already mentioned, and in the graphing response mode illustrated in the Galileo experiment. Function thinking is common in scientific research and is a basic conceptual tool for understanding the world around us.

Learning theory has not given much attention to function thinking. There are a number of experiments on mathematical models of function learning, for example, but nearly all use point response and single-trial accuracy feedback (Anderson, 1964; Birnbaum, 1976; Björkman, 1965; Brehmer, 1976; Carroll & Rosenberg, 1976; Lopes, 1976; Norman, 1974; Svenson, 1971). Oddly enough, an analogous situation seems to prevail in mathematics education, which emphasizes discrete algorithms that arise in arithmetic and combinatorial problems, at the expense of graphics and function thinking. Function responses and feedback seem more appropriate for function thinking.

The preceding discussion has been concerned with learning at the descriptive level of the functions themselves. Underlying these function shapes, however, is a body of background knowledge that tends to be overlooked in an abstract treatment of learning but whose importance becomes clear in analysis of specific tasks. This matter may conveniently be taken up in the following discussion of transfer.

Background Knowledge and Transfer

Learning of intuitive physics starts in the cradle, as the infant begins its lifelong interaction with objects and movements in its environment. By the time we can conveniently begin to study intuitive physics, our subjects already know a lot about it. The study of intuitive physics must pay attention to this preexperimental background knowledge.

The importance of preexperimental knowledge was apparent in the foregoing experiments. In the Galileo experiment, for example, the left panel of Fig. 8.4 shows that preexperimental knowledge had much the same pattern as the physically correct response. In many tasks, learning of intuitive physics is more a transfer of old knowledge than learning of new knowledge.

Two kinds of transfer deserve comment. One concerns principles that govern function shapes. Most obvious is the monotonicity principle, that the response is an increasing or decreasing function of the stimulus. There may also be a general principle of diminishing returns that can be applied to various specific situations. For integration functions, similarly, there presumably are general principles that yield linear fan and other patterns.

A second kind of transfer concerns function parameters. In the pendulum collision task, for example, the motion imparted to the ball will depend on numerous situational specifics, especially those associated with the collision coupling of pendulum and ball. If a rubber strip is glued to the front of the pendulum, subjects will expect less imparted motion. Formally, such effects may be represented as a molar collision parameter, perhaps conceptualized as an initial, subjective *vis viva* of the ball. Present concern, however, is mainly with the valuation process that yields the value of the collision parameter.

It is easy to imagine the valuation process associated with the rubber strip. The visual elements serve as retrieval cues for memory traces that have more or less relevance to the collision. These might include hammering experiences with soft and hard material or pressing soft and hard materials with the fingers. Such experiences suggest that the rubber wedge will cushion the collision and decrease the value of the collision parameter. The task also calls for a more difficult judgment, in effect the assignment of a specific value to the collision parameter, which requires consideration of the thickness and elasticity of the rubber strip as well as its shape.

The key idea in this view of transfer is *goal-directed adaptability*. Transfer is not a matter of plugging in previously learned habits. Transfer is a constructive process that is guided by the task goal of the moment. It involves memory retrieval of diverse bits and pieces of knowledge that may have only distant or analogical relevance to the task at hand. It involves evaluation of this retrieved information as well as an integration into a unitary response.

Transfer is thus complicated. The background knowledge is as variegated as it is ill-defined. Beyond general principles of the kind already discussed, therefore, exact theory might seem out of the question. However, exact theory is possible by virtue of the unitization principle for background knowledge that was discussed previously. Within its limitations, this approach takes complete account of the transfer and provides a molar encapsulation of the operative background. Accordingly, this approach may also provide a basis for experimental analysis of schemas and related forms of knowledge structure (Anderson, 1982, Section 7.16).

DEVELOPMENTAL PROBLEMS

Intuitive physics begins in the cradle and is a prominent part of our early existence. Developmental studies are important, therefore, and some selected issues are considered in this section. These relate generally to pioneering investigations by Piaget, who has studied children's behavior in many tasks of intuitive physics (Inhelder & Piaget, 1958).

Application of integration theory involves two key changes from Piaget. First, the tasks are studied as problems of stimulus integration. Second, functional measurement methodology is employed. This approach has shown that children have much higher cognitive abilities at much earlier ages than had been found with Piagetian methods. Moreover, these abilities reflect cognitive structures quite different from those of Piagetian theory. Integration theory thus leads to a theoretical position substantially different from that of Piaget.

Problem of Centration

Piaget's major conclusion about how young children integrate information is that they don't. Children in the preoperational stage, up to 6 or 7 years of age, are considered to *center* on one dimension of the stimulus as a basis for their response. This centration tendency is treated as a primary characteristic of preoperational thinking.

One illustration arises in studies of liquid conservation. Children who see liquid poured from a narrow glass into a wide glass think there is less liquid in the wide glass. They appear to center on the height, ignoring the diameter of the glass.

Similar centration is claimed in the moral realm. Children asked to judge badness of certain acts are claimed to center either on the damage caused by the act or else on the intention behind the act. Up to the age of 10 years, according to Piaget, they do not integrate the two dimensions. Piaget and his associates concluded that centration is a pervasive characteristic of preoperational thinking, and this view has been widely accepted (see, e.g., Flavell, 1970, p. 1013).

Unfortunately, the Piagetian doctrine of centration rests on inadequate methodology. Piaget presented children a choice between two conditions that may be represented as corner cells in a 2×2 design. In the liquid task, for example, the two factors are liquid height and glass diameter. Each occurs at two levels, which yields a 2×2 design. In Piaget's choice task, however, the child chooses between the two diagonal cells, which is logically insufficient to demonstrate centration. Similar choice tasks were used in other areas, such as moral judgment, and the same criticism applies.

It may seem surprising that such inadequate methodology has been the mainstay for some 40 or 50 years, not only of the Piagetian group but also in the United States. However, Piaget himself relied heavily on verbal protocols and questioned the children about the basis for their choice. It is perhaps these verbal justifications, rather than the choice data, that gave rise to the centration doctrine. But the verbal protocols are also subject to objection: A child asked to justify a choice of the glass with the higher level of liquid is unlikely to refer to the small diameter.

When integration theory was applied to the liquid quantity task, it seemed at first to support Piaget's centration interpretation. This outcome is illustrated in the left panel of Fig. 8.9 for 5-year-olds. In this experiment, children saw single glasses of liquid varied in height and diameter and made a numerical judgment of amount of liquid (Anderson & Cuneo, 1978a). Liquid height has substantial effect, as shown by the slopes of the curves; glass diameter has negligible effect, as shown by the near identity of the curves. This method gives a clear, convincing demonstration of centration.

This centration result seemed odd, however, because no centration had appeared in related experiments on judgments of desirability of toys (Butzin & Anderson, 1973) or even in Piaget's own task of moral judgment (Leon, 1976, 1980; see also Butzin, 1978). Indeed, the very same children who centered in the liquid quantity task showed no centering in a parallel task of judging area of rectangles. This array of results is contrary to the doctrine that centration is a pervasive characteristic of preoperational thought.

It took some time to pin down the reasons for this discrepancy but the final finding is illustrated in the comparison of the two panels of Fig. 8.10. This particular experiment was identical to the liquid experiment already described

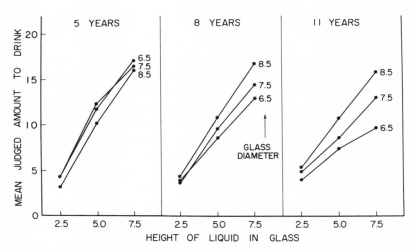

FIG. 8.9   Judgments of liquid quantity as a function of height of liquid in glass and glass diameter for three age groups. From Anderson and Cuneo (1978a). Copyright © 1978 by the American Psychological Association. Reprinted by permission.

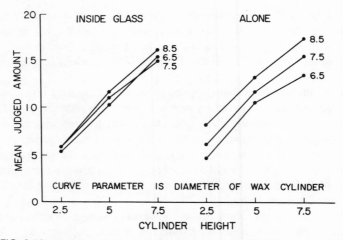

FIG. 8.10 Judgments by 5-year-olds of amount of wax in cylinder as a function of height and diameter of cylinder. Left panel: wax cylinders inside of glasses; right panel; wax cylinders stand alone. From Anderson and Cuneo (1978a). Copyright © 1978 by the American Psychological Association. Reprinted by permission.

except that it used frozen liquid in the form of wax cylinders. When these wax cylinders were placed inside glasses, the centration results of the left panel were obtained, exactly as with the proper liquids in Fig. 8.9.

The critical result appears in the right panel of Fig. 8.10. Here the wax cylinders were taken out of the glasses to stand alone. Here diameter has an effect; eliminating the glass container, which is irrelevant to judging quantity of contents, eliminates the centration effect.

To sum up, centration is not a pervasive characteristic of preoperational thought. Instead, it appears to be a peculiarity of glassware. This centration has a plausible rationale, which in fact was the original hypothesis in this experiment. To drink from glasses and cups is an important perceptual-motor skill that children must learn. Liquid height is an essential stimulus cue in this skill. At the daily table, moreover, glasses and cups have a small range of diameters, whereas the height of the contents varies from full to empty. These factors focus daily attention on the height cue. The glass container triggers off this particular habit.

Three implications follow from this series of experiments. First, the centration doctrine should be replaced by systematic studies of the development of integrational abilities and skills. Indeed, children as young as 3–4 years have shown impressive integrational capacities (Anderson & Butzin, 1978; Cuneo, 1980, 1982).

Second, the centration that was observed for liquids in glasses points to the importance of long-term experiential learning of intuitive physics. Behavior may not have a direct relation to the logical structure of the task. It may reflect operation of a melange of situational cues and learning experiences. The cited results thus reinforce the earlier discussions of the importance of background information.

Third, the detailed analyses pointed to the operation of a cognitive algebra in children's perceptual judgments. Not only are young children proficient integrators, but their integrations may follow algebraic rules. This implication is taken up in the next subsection.

General-Purpose Adding Rule

The curves in the right panel of Fig. 8.10 have an unnatural pattern: They are parallel. According to the parallelism theorem (Anderson, 1981), this pattern suggests that the children are adding height and diameter of the cylinder to arrive at their judgment. This is contrary to nature because the actual quantity obeys a multiplying rule: the height times the squared diameter. Nature's rule would yield a linear fan in the factorial graph, not parallelism.

This unnatural integration pattern appears even with the simplest stimuli, namely, rectangles. The 5-year-olds judge area by a height + width rule, whereas nature follows the height × width rule. This is surprising; the child need only look to see how much is there. Even if young children were not very good at judging area, or even if they used the rating scale in a clumsy way, some semblance of the linear fan should appear. The observed parallelism therefore comes under suspicion.

However, a series of eight experiments by Anderson and Cuneo (1978a) supported the height + width rule against a variety of alternative interpretations. Moreover, the height + width rule was discovered independently in Germany by Wilkening (1979), who carried the analysis to the level of individual child. The height + width rule seems real, therefore, and the problem is to determine what it means.

The present hypothesis is that the height + width rule reflects the operation of a general-purpose adding rule. Children do not possess adult concepts of perceptual quantities such as area. They understand that a quantity judgment is required, however, and they are sensitive to pertinent one-dimensional cues. These one-dimensional cues are fed into the general-purpose adder to yield the observed response.

If this hypothesis is correct, then similar results should be obtained in other perceptual tasks with young children. Striking support has been obtained by Cuneo (1978, 1982) for judgments of numerosity of a row of beads. These judgments obeyed the length + density rule, whereas physical number obeys the length × density rule. Related results are discussed later for Wilkening's (1981, in press) studies of the time–distance–velocity trinity.

Cognitive Units

Cognitive algebra can provide information about cognitive units. The essential idea is that success of an algebraic rule tends to confer construct validity on the conceptual terms of the model.

An illustration is provided by the height + width rule for 5-year-old's judgments of rectangle area. The success of this adding rule implies that height and width are cognitive units to the child—and that area is not a cognitive unit. If the child responded to the area, or to the shape, the adding rule would fail.

Success of an algebraic rule is not definite proof that the terms of the model correspond to cognitive units; the underlying process does not necessarily have the same form. In the case of the height + width rule, in particular, the child could be judging in terms of the perimeter or boundary, with no concept of height or width as separate entities. However, this perimeter interpretation was ruled out by the evidence for the general-purpose adding rule already cited.

Shepp, Burns, and McDonough (1980) have questioned the height + width rule on the basis of similarity and classification data that suggest that rectangles are integral stimuli that are perceived in a holistic way. However, the integration theory analysis is not predicated on any assumption that height and width are cognitive units; that is an implication of the data. The quantitative precision of the parallelism theorem in the tasks studied by Anderson and Cuneo (1978a), Cuneo (1980), and Wilkening (1979, 1980) provides strong evidence against the holistic view and for the height–width representation.

Shepp et al. (1980) consider their results to be inconsistent with the results obtained from the present integration studies. Their position appears to reflect a belief that perceived stimulus structure is basic and prior to constraints imposed by specific judgment tasks. Hence the integration tasks should reflect the same perceived stimulus structure that they infer from their tasks of classification and similarity judgments.

In the present view, by contrast, these differences in result may reasonably be attributed to specific task requirements. Similarity–classification judgments of rectangles may well involve their shape, which is a relative function of height and width. Present methods may be helpful for quantitative analysis of classification (Anderson, 1982, Section 3.10) and of similarity (Anderson, 1981, Section 5.6.5).

Perceptual Rule Development

Older children obey the height × width rule for judgments of liquid quantity, as shown by the linear fan pattern in the right panel of Fig. 8.9, and also for rectangle area (Anderson & Cuneo, 1978a). This rule development is slow for rectangles, being incomplete even at 11 years (see also, Leon, 1982).

It is a mystery, however, where these integration rules come from and how they develop. Nature ordinarily gives no more than single-trial accuracy information and has even less concern than society for effective instruction about how to integrate. As previously emphasized, single-trial accuracy information is not well suited for learning integration rules. Yet the work of Cuneo (1980, 1982) shows the adding rule to be present already at 3-plus years, and some evidence for a true multiplying rule at 5 years has also been found (Anderson, 1980, Figure 1.11). These and other considerations suggest that cognitive algebra arises more as natural development than as reinforced learning.

Also unknown is the nature of the transition between the adding and multiplying rules. According to an all-or-none hypothesis, the response on each trial is governed by just one rule, with the transition characterized by increasing frequency of the multiplying rule. An alternative is that both rules act jointly, with the transition characterized by increasing weight for the multiplying rule. Study of this question at the individual level becomes possible with functional measurement methodology (Anderson, 1982, Section 2.2.3; Wilkening, 1980). Further study of these questions would be facilitated if informer–reinforcer conditions could be found that would hasten or retard rule development.

Distance, Time, and Velocity

The importance of moving objects in the life of the child suggests a corresponding importance for concepts of velocity, travel time, and travel distance. For uniform motion, these three quantities are interlocked by the physical relation: Distance = time × velocity. Given two, the third is mathematically determined. Psychologically, however, these three concepts are rather different. Distance may be apprehended perceptually, for example, but not time. Accordingly, the development of the psychological interrelations among these three concepts deserves study.

This problem has been investigated by Wilkening (1981, in press), who obtained judgments about an animal fleeing from a barking dog. Three tasks were used; each gave information about two of the terms and asked for judgments about the third. The given information pertained to how long the dog barked, the speediness of the fleeing animal, and how far the animal traveled.

One main result was the operation of cognitive algebra. The specific results may be briefly summarized. Judgments of distance, given time and velocity, followed an adding rule in 5-year-olds (when an eye-movement strategy was eliminated) and a multiplying rule for 10-year-olds and adults. Judgments of time, given distance and velocity, followed a subtracting rule for 5-year-olds and a dividing rule for 10-year-olds and adults. Judgments of velocity, given distance and time, followed a distance-only rule for 5-year-olds and a subtracting rule for 10-year-olds and adults. This last result was replicated when the task was simplified to include a visible memory aid for the time variable.

These judgments thus follow algebraic rules, but this cognitive algebra is not consistent with the physical algebra, which imposes mathematical consistency on the three tasks. In intuitive physics, as in social judgment, cognitive algebra is not a mere reflection of mathematical algebra (Anderson, 1981, Section 1.5.6).

Rule Assessment Methodologies

Functional measurement provides a general methodology for diagnosing what rules children and adults use to process multiple-stimulus fields. Algebraic rules have been the main concern in the preceding discussion, but other integration rules have also been studied.

An alternative, binary-decision methodology has been introduced by Siegler (1978) for certain tasks of intuitive physics such as a two-arm balance scale. In this task, varied numbers of unit weights are placed on each arm at varied distances from the fulcrum; the child's task is to say which arm will go down or whether they balance. To study preexperimental knowledge, blocks are placed under each arm to keep the balance level, thereby eliminating learning experiences. Siegler has developed a battery of weight–distance configurations that are supposed to diagnose what rule the child used to process the given information.

The basic assumption in Siegler's (1978) approach is that younger children consider only one variable at a time and do not integrate the information. This represents an interesting advance over the Piagetian centration doctrine, however, because it allows both stimulus variables to have an effect. For example, in Siegler's Rule III, which is the most frequent teen-age rule, the child is assumed to make a sequence of binary, equal–different comparisons, first of weight and then of distance, across the two arms. This leads to the correct answer except when the lesser weight is at the greater distance from the fulcrum.

These two rule assessment methodologies have been compared by Wilkening and Anderson (1980, 1982), who show that Siegler's binary-decision methodology is severely limited in diagnostic power. For example, suppose that younger children actually integrated the stimulus information according to the general-purpose adding rule previously discussed. The binary-decision methodology cannot diagnose this integration rule. It does not generally fail safe, however, but erroneously concludes that one or another of the nonintegration, binary-decision rules is operative.

The task used by Siegler (1978) embodies a paired choice, and choice may well elicit a binary-decision strategy. Even so, the choice task may misrepresent knowledge structures in intuitive physics that can be observed in nonchoice versions of the same tasks. Although Siegler's approach may be found to represent the choice processing, it may still misrepresent the development and structure of knowledge.

The Problem of Conservation

Younger children do not understand that the amount of liquid in a glass does not change when it is poured into another glass. As Fig. 8.9 shows, they judge amount by the height of the liquid. If the contents of the glass are poured into a glass of greater or lesser diameter, they judge the amount to be less or more, respectively. Older children recognize that quantity is conserved but the origin of this knowledge is a mystery.

Piaget (1941/1965), who focused attention on the problem of conservation, assumed that it depends on certain operations, especially compensation and extensive quantification. For present purposes, the main implication is that preoperational children, up to 6 or 7 years, cannot conserve owing to lack of the necessary operations.

An alternative view, based on perceptual judgment and learning, was presented by Anderson and Cuneo (1978a, 1978b; see also Bogartz, 1978). This view of conservation involves the three concepts of *object invariance, quantitative properties,* and *property invariance.* Conservation itself is defined somewhat differently from Piaget as an expectation of invariance, especially of some quantitative property.

Some form of object invariance is present in the first year of life. The conservation experiments do not refer to object identity, however, but to one or another quantitative property of the object. Such quantitative properties must of course be developed before they can be conserved (Gibson, 1969, p. 357). Development of these diverse property concepts depends on perceptual processes and experiential factors, especially comparative judgment, that vary with the property in question.

Development of property concepts is necessary for conservation but not sufficient. Two sources of property conservation may be discerned. The first is by transfer from object invariance. An expectation of property invariance may derive from the primitive concept of object invariance by a process of association or classical conditioning.

The second source of conservation is in variegated specific experiences. The importance of specific experience is indicated by the disappearance of the diameter effect when the wax cylinders were inserted into glasses (Fig. 8.10). One specific experience that would seem conducive to development of conservation concepts is consumption. Drinking and eating causes things to disappear; they can be used up; there is only so much.

The present view of the development of conservation differs from that of Piaget in a number of ways. Foremost, of course, is that conservation is considered to derive from the primitive concept of object invariance by simple associative learning and from perceptual learning, not from concrete or logical operations. Conservation can thus be expected in preoperational children.

A second difference concerns the developmental relation between quantity judgments and conservation. Extensive quantification, as the term is used by Piaget (1941/1965, pp. 9–24, 244), must mirror the physical quantity and so judgments based on extensive quantification will exhibit the physically correct integration rule. Piaget's theory thus implies that the physically correct rule will appear at least as soon as conservation because extensive quantification is prerequisite to conservation. In the present view, in contrast, conservation does not depend on extensive quantification (Anderson & Cuneo, 1978a, p. 371). Hence children who judge by the physically incorrect adding rule may in principle exhibit conservation.

Once the concept of conservation has reached some level of solidity, especially once it becomes verbalizable, it may be able to function as an operating idea. This form of conservation differs from the perceptually based concepts just discussed; it also differs from Piaget's (1941/1965, pp. 9–24) view, which requires conservation to depend on and embody extensive quantification. The present view of conservation as a general idea treats it as qualitative, no longer dependent on quantification. An incidental implication is that it may be possible to obtain conservation responses even though the physical quantity is not conserved. A more important implication is that the development of conservation for simpler quantitites, such as length, provides a potential basis to facilitate learning of conservation of more difficult quantities, such as area and volume.

Concept Development

Developmental studies have a tendency to focus on questions of ages at which concepts first appear and on questions of which concepts develop earlier. This tendency is treacherous and leads too readily to simplistic research and theory. All the foregoing results point to the importance of situational specifics on the one hand and background knowledge and skills on the other. Many concepts originate in and perhaps are never completely divorced from a diffuse perceptual–cognitive background.

The idea of eliminating all collateral knowledge so as to study a concept in its pure form certainly sounds attractive. It represents a frequent, if largely implicit, line of thought and experimental procedure. This approach is predicated, however, on an implicit assumption that the concept under study exists as an autonomous entity.

An alternative, almost opposite view, is possible. In this view, concepts begin as tenuous aspects of particular skills. Only gradually and only partially do they evolve into autonomous existence. Proper concepts may not be able to function separated from situational support. Indeed, some concepts might better be considered less as cognitive entities and more as common properties of a battery of skills.

This view suggests a corresponding experimental strategy. Instead of trying to eliminate attention and memory requirements, for example, they would be systematically manipulated as integral components of the operative concepts. Such systematic manipulation provides one way to separate the focal concept from its support.

To illustrate, consider conservation. As is well known, children's judgments in the conservation tasks are also influenced by perceptual cues, such as the height of the liquid in the glass. The standard conservation tests pit the conservation tendency against the perceptual cues. Perceptual cues are part of the task, of course, and cannot all be eliminated. Consequently, the conservation tendency cannot be observed until it is strong enough to overcome the perceptual cues. Until then, its development is masked from view.

The alternative approach is to construct tasks in which the perceptual cues and the conservation tendency are integrated to provide the observed response. If this integration obeys an algebraic rule, then functional measurement methodology can be used to dissect the relative effect of the conservation tendency from the integrated response. This analysis allows measurement of even very weak conservation tendencies and thus provides a sensitive method for studying their development (Anderson, 1980; Anderson & Cuneo, 1978a). Although no empirical applications have been made, the frequent success of cognitive algebra in integration tasks with children suggest that this approach will be useful for quantitative analysis of concept development.

ACKNOWLEDGMENTS

This work was supported by Grants BNS-7904675 and BNS-8004845 from the National Science Foundation and by grants from the National Institute of Mental Health to the Center for Human Information Processing, University of California, San Diego. I wish to thank Alan Anderson, Suzan Heglin, and Scott Prussing for their assistance. I am especially indebted to Tom Tighe for many cogent comments and criticisms on the drafts of this chapter.

REFERENCES

Anderson, N. H. Linear models for responses measured on a continuous scale. *Journal of Mathematical Psychology,* 1964, *1,* 121–142.

Anderson, N. H. Information integration theory: A brief survey. In D. H. Krantz, R. C. Atkinson, R. D. Luce, & P. Suppes (Eds.), *Contemporary developments in mathematical psychology* (Vol. 2). San Francisco: Freeman, 1974.

Anderson, N. H. Information integration theory in developmental psychology. In F. Wilkening, J. Becker, & T. Trabasso (Eds.), *Information integration by children.* Hillsdale, N.J.: Lawrence Erlbaum Associates, 1980.

Anderson, N. H. *Foundations of information integration theory.* New York: Academic Press, 1981.

Anderson, N. H. *Methods of information integration theory.* New York: Academic Press, 1982.

Anderson N. H., & Butzin, C. A. Integration theory applied to children's judgments of equity. *Developmental Psychology,* 1978, *14,* 593–606.

Anderson, N. H., & Cuneo, D. O. The height + width rule in children's judgments of quantity. *Journal of Experimental Psychology: General,* 1978, *107,* 335–378. (a)

Anderson, N. H., & Cuneo, D. O. The height + width rule seems solid: Reply to Bogartz. *Journal of Experimental Psychology: General,* 1978, *107,* 388–392. (b)

Birnbaum, M. H. Intuitive numerical prediction. *American Journal of Psychology*, 1976, *89*, 417–429.

Björkman, M. Studies in predictive behavior. *Scandinavian Journal of Psychology*, 1965, *6*, 129–156.

Bogartz, R. S. Comments on Anderson and Cuneo's "The height + width rule in children's judgments of quantity." *Journal of Experimental Psychology: General*, 1978, *107*, 379–387.

Brehmer, B. Subject's ability to find the parameters of functional rules in probabilistic inference tasks. *Organizational Behavior and Human Performance*, 1976, *17*, 388–397.

Brehmer, B., & Slovic, P. Information integration in multiple-cue judgments. *Journal of Experimental Psychology: Human Perception and Performance*, 1980, *6*, 302–308.

Butzin, C. A. *The effect of ulterior motive information on children's moral judgments.* Unpublished doctoral dissertation, University of California, San Diego, 1978.

Butzin, C. A., & Anderson, N. H. Functional measurement of children's judgments. *Child Development*, 1973, *44*, 529–537.

Carroll, J. D., & Rosenberg, S. Learning on a response continuum: Comparison of a linear change and a functional learning model. *Journal of Mathematical Psychology*, 1976, *13*, 101–118.

Cuneo, D. O. *Children's judgments of numerical quantity: The role of length, density, and number cues.* Unpublished doctoral dissertation, University of California, San Diego, 1978.

Cuneo, D. O. A general strategy for judgments of quantity: The height + width rule. *Child Development*, 1980, *51*, 299–301.

Cuneo, D. O. Children's judgments of numerical quantity: A new view of early quantification. *Cognitive Psychology*, 1982, *14*, 13–44.

Drake, S. *Galileo at work.* Chicago: University of Chicago Press, 1978.

Flavell, J. H. Concept development. In P. H. Mussen (Ed.), *Carmichael's manual of child psychology* (Vol. 1, 3rd ed.). New York: Wiley, 1970.

Galilei, G. [*Two new sciences*] (S. Drake, trans.). Madison: University of Wisconsin Press, 1974. (Originally published, 1638.)

Gibson, E. J. *Principles of perceptual learning and development.* New York: Appleton-Century-Crofts, 1969.

Inhelder, B., & Piaget, J. [*The growth of logical thinking*] (A. Parsons & S. Milgram, trans.). New York: Basic Books, 1958. (Originally published 1955.)

Leon, M. *Coordination of intent and consequence information in children's moral judgments.* Unpublished doctoral dissertation, University of California, San Diego, 1976.

Leon, M. Integration of intent and consequence information in children's moral judgments. In F. Wilkening, J. Becker, & T. Trabasso (Eds.), *Information integration by children.* Hillsdale, N.J.: Lawrence Erlbaum Associates, 1980.

Leon, M. Extent, multiplying, and proportionality rules in children's judgments of area. *Journal of Experimental Child Psychology*, 1982, *33*, 124–141.

Lopes, L. L. Individual strategies in goal-setting. *Organizational Behavior and Human Performance*, 1976, *15*, 268–277.

Norman, K. L. Rule learning in a stimulus integration task. *Journal of Experimental Psychology*, 1974, *103*, 941–947.

Piaget, J. [*The child's conception of number*]. New York: Norton, 1965. (Originally published, 1941.)

Shepp, B. E., Burns, B., & McDonough, D. The relation of stimulus structure to perceptual and cognitive development: Further tests of a separability hypothesis. In F. Wilkening, J. Becker, & T. Trabasso (Eds.), *Information integration by children.* Hillsdale, N.J.: Lawrence Erlbaum Associates, 1980.

Siegler, R. S. The origins of scientific reasoning. In R. S. Siegler (Ed.), *Children's thinking: What develops?* Hillsdale, N.J.: Lawrence Erlbaum Associates, 1978.

Stevens, S. S. Perceptual magnitude and its measurement. In E. C. Carterette & M. P. Friedman (Eds.), *Handbook of perception* (Vol. 2). New York: Academic Press, 1974.

Svenson, O. Changing the structure of intuitive estimates of time-savings. *Scandinavian Journal of Psychology*, 1971, *12*, 131–134.

Wilkening, F. Combining of stimulus dimensions in children's and adult's judgments of area. *Developmental Psychology*, 1979, *15*, 25–33.

Wilkening, F. Development of dimensional integration in children's perceptual judgment: Experiments with area, volume, and velocity. In F. Wilkening, J. Becker, & T. Trabasso (Eds.), *Information integration by children*. Hillsdale, N.J.: Lawrence Erlbaum Associates, 1980.

Wilkening, F. Integrating velocity, time, and distance information: A developmental study. *Cognitive Psychology*, 1981, *13*, 231–247.

Wilkening, F. Children's knowledge about time, distance, and velocity interrelations. In W. J. Friedman (Ed.), *The developmental psychology of time*. New York: Academic Press, in press.

Wilkening, F., & Anderson, N. H. *Comparison of two rule assessment methodologies for studying cognitive development* (Tech. Rep. CHIP 94). La Jolla, Calif.: University of California, San Diego, Center for Human Information Processing, June 1980.

Wilkening, F., & Anderson, N. H. Comparison of two rule-assessment methodologies for studying cognitive development and knowledge structure. *Psychological Bulletin*, 1982, *92*, 215–237.

9 The Perception and Use of Information by Good and Poor Readers

George Wolford
Carol A. Fowler*
Dartmouth College, Hanover, N.H.

Introduction

Many children who do not experience particular difficulty in academic domains such as math (Yule, 1973) have considerable difficulty learning to read. Investigators have tried to identify the kinds of skills that are deficient or that have failed to develop in those poor readers. Based on an examination of the literature and on a series of experiments that we have conducted, we have identified a deficit consistent with many of the observed differences between good and poor readers. That deficit concerns the way poor readers perceive and use information, and it bears interesting similarities to the relationships between perceived stimulus structure and cognitive performance reported elsewhere in this volume.

CONFUSION ANALYSIS

A number of investigators have proposed particular deficiencies that distinguish poor from good readers. Vellutino (1979) in a review of the literature suggested that the proposed sources of reading problems can be classified into four categories: (1) visuo-spatial; (2) intersensory integration; (3) serial-order recall; and (4) verbal processing. Vellutino argued that the bulk of the evidence favors the final candidate, verbal processing.

Within the category of deficits in verbal processing, considerable attention has been directed to the possibility that poor readers are particularly deficient in

---

(Also at Haskins Laboratories, New Haven, Conn.)

the degree to which they rely on a phonetic code during reading-related tasks (Shankweiler & Liberman, 1976). Support for this hypothesis is based, in part, on a series of experiments showing that good readers are more influenced by manipulations of the phonetic properties of stimuli than poor readers are.

An example of these findings is described in Shankweiler, Liberman, Mark, Fowler, and Fischer (1979). They presented second-grade children with five-letter consonant strings for either immediate or delayed recall. Half of the strings was chosen from a set of rhyming consonants and the other half was chosen from a set of nonrhyming consonants. They found that good readers were superior to poor readers in performance on the nonrhyming strings. Switching to rhyming strings had little effect on the poor readers but was quite damaging to the good readers, reducing their performance nearly to the level of the poor readers. The investigators' interpretation of the pattern of results was that good readers were relying heavily upon a phonetic code and that the rhyming strings (which are highly confusable phonetically) make the use of a phonetic code disadvantageous. Poor readers, placing less reliance on the phonetic code, are less troubled by the phonetic confusability. The final ingredient in the interpretation is the assumption that a phonetic code will generally lead to superior performance in readinglike tasks unless phonetic confusability is deliberately maximized.

Much of the impetus to our investigations stemmed from a reanalysis of the Shankweiler et al. (1979) experiment. We were interested in examining the kinds of errors that the subjects made in their experiment. We used a technique developed by Wolford and Hollingsworth (1974), which allowed us to classify each error as a phonetic confusion, a visual confusion, or neither. In addition the technique permitted the calculation of a chance value for each error category.

The mean percentages of phonetic confusion errors for each reader group in each condition are shown in Table 9.1. Due to the choice of the character sets in the experiment by Shankweiler et al. (1979), only the phonetic confusions could be reliably computed. The chance value of a phonetic confusion was 57.5% for each of the conditions. The high value of chance arises from the inclusion of the rhyming character set.

Consistent with the interpretation of Shankweiler et al. (1979), the good readers made significantly more phonetic confusions than the poor readers. In fact, the good readers made significantly more than chance phonetic confusions in every cell. No other group differed from chance in any cell.

Although these data seemed to support the phonetic deficit hypothesis, we were quite surprised that the poor readers appeared to be making exactly chance numbers of phonetic confusions in every cell. To understand our concern, it helps to consider why adults or good young readers make confusion errors in the first place. A plausible hypothesis is that the letters are stored as a set of features or attributes (Gibson, 1969). At the time of response, some of those features have been lost, so good readers base their responses on the remaining features. Sometimes this response will be correct and sometimes not. When an error is

TABLE 9.1
Percentage of Errors that Are Phonetic Confusions (Chance = 57.5)

	Nondelay Mean	N	Delay Mean
Auditory Presentation			
Poor readers	56.7	11	58.6
Marginal readers	63.4	16	59.9
Superior readers	81.1*	17	80.1*
Visual Presentation			
Poor readers	59.9	11	64.1
Marginal readers	60.7	16	62.5
Superior readers	72.8*	17	72.8*

*Significantly different from the chance value of 57.5 according to a matched pairs t test.

made, it will be related to the correct response (i.e., a confusion error). The type of relationship will depend on the nature of the code used to store the information.

There are at least three possibilities why poor readers do not make phonetic confusion errors. The first possibility is that all the information has been lost at the time of the response. This is contradicted by the fact that poor readers are significantly above chance on the probability of a *correct* response in every cell. The second possibility is that poor readers are using some code other than phonetic (possibly visual) for the task. Although this is a plausible alternative, it is somewhat discounted by the fact that poor readers were at chance even when the characters were presented auditorily. The third alternative, and the focus of our work, is that poor readers might be deficient in their ability to make use of partial information. Their performance, then, would be fine as long as the information concerning the correct answer was reasonably complete. If decay or other degradation occurred, however, the poor readers might fail to incorporate the remaining information in their response. We refer to this hypothesis as the "partial-information hypothesis" and continue to use the same name for it even as our understanding of *why* poor readers fail to use partial information undergoes some revision as outlined in the following.

We undertook a series of experiments with good- and poor-reading children to investigate the partial-information hypothesis. In all the studies that we report, the children averaged just over 8 years of age. They were tested either in the summer before they entered the third grade or in the following fall or winter. Children in the two reading groups were matched for age and for IQ as measured by the Peabody Picture Vocabulary Test (Dunn, 1965) but differed significantly on the word attack and word identification subtests of the Woodcock Reading Mastery Test (1973). Poor readers were children whose performance was lowest among those tested on the Woodcock test; good readers were children who exceeded the grade-level norms on the Woodcock subtests and best matched the poor readers on age and IQ. In the letter memory and similarity studies, described in the following, the poor readers averaged only 2 months behind the grade-level norms. In the other studies, they lagged by more than one-half year. In the letter memory and similarity studies, good readers read at the fifth- to sixth-grade level.

LETTER MEMORY STUDIES

We carried out an experiment (Wolford & Fowler, in press) to compare the partial-information hypothesis against a phonetic or visual deficit hypothesis. The logic of the experiment required a comparison of the performance of good and poor readers on a visual and on a phonetic task. According to the partial-information hypothesis, good readers should make primarily visual confusions on the visual task and phonetic confusions on the phonetic task. Poor readers should make essentially random errors on the two tasks. A phonetic-deficit hypothesis would predict a similar outcome on the phonetic task but would have no basis for expecting a difference between good and poor readers on the visual task.

For the visual task we chose tachistoscopic whole report of letter strings. Wolford and Hollingsworth (1974) found that adults made substantial and only visual confusions among letters on that task. For the phonetic task we chose short-term memory for letters, using a paradigm modeled after Conrad (1967) and similar to the one used by Shankweiler et al. (1979). We had ample evidence from our reanalysis described earlier and from Conrad (1967) that subjects make predominantly phonetic confusions on that task.

In both tasks, strings of four consonants were presented visually on each trial; they were presented simultaneously and briefly in the whole-report task but successively and for a longer duration in the short-term memory task. In addition, in the latter task, children were asked to name the letters as they appeared and then to name some interfering digits before recalling the letter strings. In both tests, children recalled the letter strings by writing them on an answer sheet.

The confusion data for the 12 good and 12 poor readers are presented in Table 9.2. The numbers in the table represent the probabilities of visual and phonetic confusions on the two tasks converted to Z-scores. A value of zero indicates chance responding.

The confusion data support the partial-information hypothesis. Good readers made significant numbers of phonetic confusions on the short-term memory task and significant numbers of visual confusions on the whole-report task. Poor readers made random errors on both tasks.

Using partial information effectively should improve overall accuracy on many tasks. Constraining a response to be consistent with available partial cues

TABLE 9.2
Index of Phonetic and Visual Confusions for Letter-Memory
Experiment Based on Z Scores (Chance = 0.00)

	Task			
	Conrad		Whole Report	
Group	Phonetic	Visual	Phonetic	Visual
Good	1.52*	−.57	−.33	1.33*
Poor	.67	.20	.17	.66

*Significantly different from chance using t tests ($p < .01$). All other values $>.05$.

will generally reduce the number of possible responses to well below the number of possible responses in the entire set. Consistent with this expectation, the good readers achieved a significantly higher probability correct on both tasks. On the short-term memory task, the good readers' probability of a correct response was .32; that of the poor readers was .18. On the whole-report task, the corresponding values were .42 and .35. All of these values significantly exceed a chance level of performance.

Although the experiment just described offers support for the partial-information hypothesis, there remains substantial evidence in the literature in favor of a phonetic-deficit hypothesis or against a visual-deficit hypothesis. We believe that many investigators have confounded their manipulations with the usefulness of partial information, finding differences between good and poor readers in just those cases where partial information is useful and failing to find differences where partial information is not useful.

We consider two studies to illustrate this point. Shankweiler et al. (1979) found that poor readers performed at a similar level on rhyming versus nonrhyming strings. Good readers were superior to the poor readers on the nonrhyming strings but their performance suffered on the rhyming strings, dropping nearly to the level of the poor readers. We would argue that one effect of the rhyming manipulation would be to reduce the usefulness of partial information. Remembering part of a letter does not help much if all the letters share that part.

Several studies were carried out by Vellutino and his colleagues showing no difference between good and poor readers on visual tasks (see Vellutino, 1979, for a review). In many of those experiments, subjects were shown a sequence of forms (e.g., Hebrew characters in Vellutino, Steger, Kaman, & DeSetto, 1975) and then were asked to reproduce those forms from memory. Responses were scored as correct only if they were fairly accurate reproductions of the correct form. With this scoring technique, and using the unfamiliar Hebrew characters, partial information is of limited value. Recalling a part of the figure would generally not lead to a complete reproduction, because the children would not know how to fill in the missing information based on the parts that they could recall.

CHINESE CHARACTER STUDY

In order to test our hypothesis further, we carried out an experiment (Wolford & Fowler, in press) that attempted to manipulate the relative performance levels of good and poor readers by varying the usefulness of partial information. We hoped to create three situations: one in which using partial information would not affect performance, and hence good and poor readers should perform alike; a second one in which using partial information would aid performance, and hence good readers should perform better than poor readers; and a final one in which using partial information might impair performance, and hence good readers should perform *worse* than poor readers.

To accomplish these objectives, we presented 19 good and 21 poor readers with a set of 21 Chinese characters to memorize. The acquisition set appears as the first three columns of Fig. 9.1.

After a delay of about 20 minutes, we asked the subjects to reproduce as many of the characters as possible. Note that on this *reproduction* task, partial information is not useful to the subject; correct reproduction requires the subject to have *all* the necessary information. These data were scored in three ways: number of attempts, number of exact reproductions, and number of essentially correct reproductions. There were few, if any, perfect reproductions, so we focused on the other two measures. The good readers made 3.84 attempts compared with 3.73 attempts by the poor readers. The good readers averaged 1.45 essentially correct reproductions, whereas the poor readers averaged 1.00 reproduction. On neither of these measures was the difference between good and poor readers significant. According to the partial-information hypothesis, one would not expect a difference between good and poor readers because partial information is of limited utility on this recall task. One could presumably manipulate the difference between good and poor readers by making the scoring procedure more or less stringent.

The last two conditions, in which partial information was useful and misleading, respectively, were created by administering an old/new recognition test about an hour after the recall test. On the recognition test, we presented 14 of the items from the acquisition list plus 14 new items ("foils"). As shown in Fig. 9.1, 7 of those foils were chosen to be visually similar to particular items on the acquisition list and 7 were chosen to be visually dissimilar to any item on the acquisition list.

According to the partial-information hypothesis, good readers should make a higher percentage of hits (correctly identifying old items as old) than poor readers. Unlike the recall test, remembering part of a character might well lead a

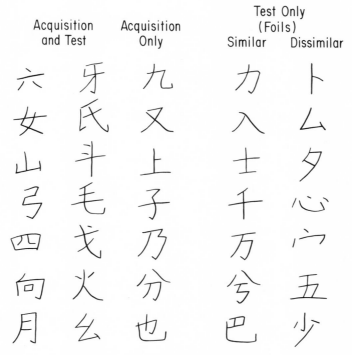

| Acquisition and Test | Acquisition Only | Test Only (Foils) Similar | Dissimilar |

FIG. 9.1.   The set of Chinese characters used for the acquisition and test phases.

subject to identify an item as old correctly. The percentage of hits is also affected by a subject's criterion so we used the percentage of hits minus the percentage of false alarms to unrelated foils as our performance measure. (We lacked sufficient data to compute reliable d's.) The good readers were superior to poor readers on this measure 0.53 versus 0.43, but the difference did not achieve significance [$t(39) = 1.66$, $P = .10$].

The final condition in this experiment (misleading partial information) was realized by comparing the number of false alarms made by good and poor readers to the two foil types. If good readers are using partial information, they should be affected by foil type, making more false alarms to the related foils than to the unrelated foils. Poor readers should not be affected by the foil type. The false alarm data are shown in Fig. 9.2. An interaction in the predicted direction between foil type and reader group was significant [$F(1, 39) = 4.56$, $p = .036$).

We were successful, then, in manipulating the relative performances of good and poor readers by manipulating the relative usefulness of partial information. In the recall test, partial information was of limited value and good and poor readers performed similarly. Identifying old items on a recognition test should profit from the use of partial information and good readers were superior to poor

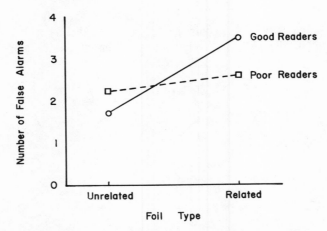

FIG. 9.2   Mean numbers of false alarms for good and poor readers as as a function of foil relatedness.

readers (though not significantly). Finally, the use of partial information could lead a child astray in trying to reject foils similar to acquisition items, and in fact good readers made more errors (false alarms) on the related foils than poor readers.

PART LETTER STUDY

In the first two experiments the information was assumed to be incomplete due either to a failure to extract all the necessary information or to a loss of necessary information by forgetting. We next asked (Wolford & Fowler, in press) what would happen if, instead of relying on these assumptions, we presented the readers with partial information in the first place.

We attempted to answer this question by presenting good and poor readers with 12 complete and 12 incomplete letters. The incomplete letters are presented in Fig. 9.3. We asked the children to name the letters as rapidly as possible and we recorded both their accuracy and latency to name.

According to the partial-information hypothesis, good and poor readers should perform at similar levels on the complete letters, but the good readers should be superior to the poor readers on the incomplete letters. We anticipated near-ceiling performance on the whole letters and included the latency data to distinguish between a true lack of difference and a lack of difference due to a ceiling effect. On the whole letters, the good readers did not differ from the poor readers either on accuracy or on reaction time. The two groups were very accurate in this condition, the good readers averaging 99% accurate and the poor

FIG. 9.3   The set of partial letters used in the part letter study.

readers 98.5%. The corresponding response latencies were 1.71 sec and 1.55 sec, respectively. On the partial letters, poor readers were significantly less accurate than good readers, averaging 58.3% accurate as compared to 69.3% for the good readers. It is interesting to note that they were as fast as good readers, averaging 4.31 sec per response as compared to 4.51 sec for the good readers.

So in the case where completeness is manipulated directly, poor readers are shown to be deficient only when the information is incomplete. We should mention that poor readers are able to make some use of partial information as they were far above chance in performance on the part letters. They were just not as efficient as good readers in using the partial information.

SIMILARITY EXPERIMENTS

A pair of scaling studies was designed as an addendum to the whole-report and short-term memory paradigms described earlier. We were concerned that the confusion analyses performed in those studies might not be accurate for children because we were using similarity spaces based on adult scaling data. For instance, the lack of confusion errors by poor readers might have resulted from a difference in what is considered similar rather than a failure by poor readers in the use of partial information.

In order to find some idea of how our children viewed letter similarity, we had them engage in two scaling tasks. After completing the whole-report and Conrad tasks, we had the 12 good readers and the 12 poor readers sort the consonants we had used in that study twice, once based on visual similarity and once based on acoustic or auditory similarity. The stimuli for the sorts were decks of index cards; in the center of each card was a single rub-on letter.

The children were instructed to place the letters in piles so that all the letters in a pile looked (sounded) like one another. They were permitted to use as many or

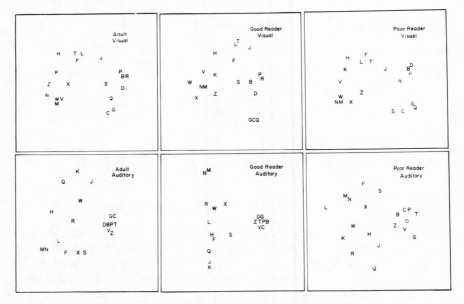

FIG. 9.4 The two-dimensional scaling solutions for adults, good readers, and poor readers for the visual and phonetic similarity of letters.

as few piles as they chose. In addition, for the auditory sort, we asked them to base their judgments on the letter names (i.e., how they sound when saying the alphabet).[1] The purpose of the last instruction was to control for the fact that many letters have multiple pronunciations when used in words. In addition, we had a group of 12 adults carry out the two sorting tasks using the same instructions and stimuli as the children. These latter data are referred to as the *adult* sorts.

We examined the similarity judgments for the different groups in several ways. We first subjected the sorting data for the adult and the good- and poor-reading groups to a nonmetric multidimensional scaling analysis (McGee, 1966). The results of those analyses are summarized in Fig. 9.4.

A visual inspection of the scaling figures indicates that, in general, the three groups view letter relationships in similar fashions. The location and labeling of the axes in these scaling solutions are arbitrary. For all three visual solutions, it appears that a good choice for the axes would be approximately the two diago-

---

[1] We refer to these sorts as acoustic or auditory rather than phonetic. "Acoustic" refers to the properties of the acoustic energy pattern that serves as stimulus to a listener; "auditory" refers to the same stimulus transduced by the auditory system, and "phonetic" refers to the stimulus' linguistic description as a set of features. Either of the first two descriptors, but not the third, readily rationalizes the consistent tendency of our subjects to weight the vowel more heavily than the consonant in judging similarity.

TABLE 9.3
Quality of Letter and Character Sorts

| | Replication 1 Letters | | | |
| | Visual | | Auditory | |
	Overlap	Work (2)	Overlap	Work (2)
Adults	−1.33	1.58	6.17	1.41
Good	3.08	1.37	1.33	3.94
Poor	−8.16	3.56	−1.67	5.44

	Replication 2						
	Letters				Chinese Characters		
	Visual		Auditory				
	Overlap	Work (2)	Overlap	Work (2)	Overlap	Work (2)	Work (3)
Good	−5.42	2.01	3.89	4.35	−8.84	9.75	2.4
Poor	−8.33	2.90	−6.33	9.25	−20.52	10.06	3.5

nals. One diagonal could be labeled "straight versus round" and the other "perpendicular versus oblique." The choice of axes for the acoustic solution is less clear although it appears that the letters are grouped primarily by the vowel sound in the letter name. It does not appear, then, that poor readers view letter similarity in radically different ways from adults or good readers.

Although the overall appearance of the scaling solutions is similar across groups, a higher value of work[2] was required to achieve a two-dimensional solution for the poor readers than for the other two groups. The values of work obtained for the different groups are presented in Table 9.3 under Replication 1. We interpret the higher values of work as indicating that whereas the poor readers are using the same dimensions as adults and good readers in judging similarity, there is more noise in their judgments, that is, poor readers simply are not very good in judging similarity.

To evaluate this hypothesis more carefully, we needed a measure of the quality of a letter sort that could be evaluated statistically. Values of work were not available for individual subjects and could not be interpreted statistically. We began by constructing an ideal visual alphabet and an ideal acoustic alphabet (see

---

[2]Work is a quantity used by McGee (1966) to measure the goodness of a solution. Lower values indicate a better solution. Work is conceptually similar to the quantity called stress in other scaling programs.

TABLE 9.4
The Ideal Alphabets for Letters and Chinese Characters

	Ideal Alphabets	
Visual Letters	Auditory Letters	Chinese Characters
CGQ	GJ	万 カ 乃 九
FH	HKR	分 勺
JLT	MN XFSL	上 士 十
BDPR	QW	子 牙
MN XKW	BDP CT VZ	也 巴 毛
V		又 入 火
SZ		幺 女
		四

Wolford & Hollingsworth, 1974, for details). These alphabets were constructed by first carrying out a hierarchical clustering analysis of pairwise similarity ratings. These ratings were collected by Wolford and Porter (1976). They had a large group of college students rate all possible consonant pairs for visual and auditory similarity. Those data are referred to as the *ideal* judgments. We then constructed an "ideal alphabet" from the clustering analysis of these judgments by choosing an arbitrary diameter in the clustering solution, the same diameter for both the visual and acoustic analyses. Any letters that clustered together above that diameter were placed on the same row of the appropriate ideal alphabet. Therefore, all the letters that appear on one row of the ideal visual alphabet were judged by our criterion to be visually similar. Those ideal alphabets appear in Table 9.4.

Our measure for the quality of an individual sort consisted of the overlap between that individual sort and the ideal alphabet. If a subject placed two letters in the same pile of a sort, that pair received a +1 if both members of that pair appeared on the same row of the appropriate ideal alphabet and a −1 otherwise. Those overlap scores appear in Table 9.3 under Replication 1 for each group and each type of sort.

We carried out an analysis of variance on those scores, beginning only with the good and poor readers. The good readers were significantly superior to the poor readers overall $[F(1, 22) = 7.04, p = .014]$. The effect of sort type was not significant. Although the difference between the good and the poor readers was especially large on the visual sort, the interaction was not significant $[F(1, 22) = 3.31, p = .07]$. When the adults were included, they were found not to differ from the good readers, but both the adults and the good readers had significantly higher overlap scores than the poor readers.

Poor readers, then, appear to have some difficulty in making similarity judgments. This deficit may be related to the partial-information hypothesis. Similarity judgments may require the subjects to decompose the characters into parts or features and then base their judgments on the number of overlapping features. These sorting data also are *inconsistent* with the phonetic-deficit hypothesis. The poor readers were at least as deficient in carrying out a visual sort as they were in carrying out an acoustic sort.

We wondered, however, whether the problem experienced by poor readers might be confined to linguistic material. Perhaps the superiority of good readers is the result of their greater familiarity with letters rather than a greater ability to deal with partial information.

To test this possibility we had a new group of 19 good readers, 21 poor readers, and 20 college students sort a set of 20 Chinese characters on the basis of visual similarity. The Chinese characters were selected from among those appearing in Fig. 9.1. In addition we asked the children to sort the 20 consonants used in the letter memory studies. The letters were sorted twice, once based on visual similarity and once based on auditory similarity, as a check on our previous results.

We carried out the same analyses as before. The ideal Chinese alphabet was constructed from a hierarchical clustering of the adult data. The ideal Chinese alphabet appears in Table 9.4, and the overlap and work socres in Table 9.3 under Replication 2. Using the overlap scores, the good readers were significantly superior to the poor readers on all three sorts. Looking first at the letter data, the good readers were significantly superior overall $[F(1, 38) = 7.70, p = .008]$. Although in this experiment the difference between good and poor readers appeared larger on the auditory sort than on the visual sort, once again the interaction was not significant $[F(1, 38) = 1.79, p = .19]$. On the Chinese sort, the good readers were also significantly superior to the poor readers $[F(1, 38) = 5.19, p = .027]$. The adults were not included in the analyses as their data were used in constructing the ideal alphabet.

Once again, then, the poor readers were deficient in judging similarity. That difficulty is not limited to a particular modality nor is it limited to linguistic stimuli. The deficit cannot be explained by familarity because the good and poor readers are presumed to be equally unfamiliar with the Chinese characters. We argue, then, that the deficit is a general one, having to do with the ability, or lack of ability, to treat a stimulus as a set of parts or attributes.

In all the studies preceding the scaling studies, the information for subjects was partial or degraded in some fashion, either explicitly as in the part letter study or due to assumed memory loss as in the character memory studies. On the basis of the scaling experiments, we believe that the problem experienced by the poor readers is not restricted to situations in which information is incomplete. Instead, we believe that poor readers may have difficulty even when the stimuli are complete if optimal performance requires that the stimuli be perceived as sets of attributes or component parts so that judgment can be based on those component parts.

WORD MEMORY

We have reviewed some observations suggesting that poor readers fail to make effective use of partial information in a variety of settings. We turn now to a new line of investigation that we hope eventually will allow us to embed our findings in a broader interpretative context than the partial-information hypothesis affords.

We find provocative the false alarm profiles of good and poor readers suggested by a triad of recognition memory studies. Our own study, described earlier, compared the recognition memory of good and poor readers for unfamiliar Chinese characters. In that study, good but not poor readers made disproportionate false alarms to visually related as compared to neutral foils. An earlier study by Mark, Shankweiler, Liberman, & Fowler (1977) reported comparable findings when acquisition items were written words and foils were rhymes of acquisition items or were unrelated to them. Here, good but not poor readers were more susceptible to rhyming than to neutral foils. These latter findings were replicated by Byrne and Shea (1979) who, in addition, reported *no* difference as a function of reading skill in relative false alarm rate to neutral foils and foils related semantically to acquisition items. In that study, both reading groups were susceptible to semantic similarity. Across the triad of studies, then, good and poor readers performed similarly when foils related semantically to old items and differently when foils related to acquisition items in their graphic or phonetic properties.

There is evidence that this pattern of difference and similarity among good and poor readers generalizes beyond the recognition memory task to other tasks in which the use of partial information can affect performance. Findings that poor readers are deficient in their use of phonetic information is very well documented across a variety of tasks (Liberman, Shankweiler, Liberman, Fowler, & Fischer, 1977; Mann, Liberman, & Shankweiler, 1980; Mark et al., 1977). Deficient use of graphic or visual information by poor readers is less consistently reported, but it has been observed by Morrison, Giordani, and Nagy, 1977, and by Wolford and Fowler (in press). Moreover, as we indicated earlier, we believe that the partial-information hypothesis can predict the conditions under which the deficiency is and is not observed. In intersting contrast to these studies is evidence that poor readers are not particularly impaired in their use of semantic information in speech or reading-related tasks (Cole & Perfetti, 1980; Perfetti, Goldman, & Hogaboam, 1979; Schvaneveldt, Ackerman, & Semlear, 1977). For example, Cole and Perfetti reported that poor readers are just as benefited by a preceding sentence context as are good readers in listening for mispronunciations in spoken stories. Similarly, Mann et al. (1980) find the expected difference between good and poor beginning readers in the effects of phonetic confusability in recall of spoken sentences; that is, good readers show more impairment than poor readers due to the confusability manipulation. However, the investigators found no differences between the reading groups in the effects on recall of manipulations of the meaningfulness of sentences. The reading groups showed equal impairment to recall performance when sentences were semantically anomalous.

Despite this evidence substantiating the false alarm profile that we extracted from three separate studies, we considered it important to observe the uses of phonetic, visual, and semantic information within a single study. We have conducted two experiments designed with this purpose in mind, and we describe them shortly. First, however, we describe a perspective on the response profile that motivated our inclusion of a fourth condition in our studies.

The perspective was provided by some observations of recognition memory performance among adults and children reported by Tighe, Tighe, and Schecter (1975). They observed a developmental difference in the tendency to abstract or, more likely, to use information about the category membership of words or concepts. In their studies, young children (7 years of age) and adults learned to make one instrumental response to half of the words in a list and to make a different instrumental response to the remaining words. The category membership of the words (animals, body parts) was redundant with the instrumental response so that subjects had the option of learning to discriminate the critical settings for the responses based on the words' category memberships or based on their token identities. In a later forced-choice test of recognition memory for these words, adults made many more false alarms than children to words sharing category membership with words on the acquisition list. This suggested that adults had learned to discriminate the settings for each response based primarily on the category memberships of the words but that children had attended primarily to token identity. Despite that difference, however, children evidenced a sensitivity to the category membership of the words. In some trials of the recognition memory test, none of the forced-choice options was in fact an old item; all were foils. Of the foils, one shared category membership with half of the old items and the other two foils were from categories not represented on the acquisition list. Here children chose the word from the familiar category more than one-third of the time (although still less frequently than the adults). These findings suggest that children abstract, but do not always use, information that attributes are shared among items to which they are exposed. The findings by Tighe et al. (1975) reported here are buttressed by analogous ones in other tasks. In studies of concept formation (see Tighe & Tighe, 1978, for a review of their work), findings indicate that young children focus on reinforced *instances* (e.g., black and small, and black and large when black items of any size are always reinforced). In contrast to children, adults attend to individual levels of dimensions (e.g., black). Compatibly, Shepp (1978) reports that, in sorting tasks, young children treat as integral dimensions of stimuli that adults may treat as separable.

The interpretations by Tighe and his colleagues (1975) of their findings and by Shepp (1978) of his bear an obvious similarity to the partial-information hypothesis. The partial-information hypothesis in its original formulation ascribed the performance differences between good and poor readers to a difference in response strategy whereby poor readers are less likely than good readers to guess the identity of a whole from some of its parts. However, the scaling studies suggested a more general disinclination of poor readers to treat complex stimuli as a constellation of attributes, whether or not the stimuli are degraded. This disinclination is similar to that found by Tighe et al. and by Shepp to be characteristic of young children. The similarity among these interpretations led us to consider the possibility that the poor readers' impairment in using partial information might be understandable as retardation relative to good readers in developing a tendency to extract or use component attributes, which may be shared with other stimuli. (Quite possibly, of course, what is critical for developing attention to shared attributes is *experience* in tasks that promote such attention. If reading is a major source of such experience, then poor readers may be retarded in partial-information use because they have had less experience in reading or in reading-related tasks than good readers. Therefore, inefficient partial-information use may be a consequence rather than a cause of poor reading.) This interpretation would account for the differential performances by good and poor readers in the studies by Mark et al. (1977) and by Wolford and Fowler (in press). In both studies, good readers were more susceptible than poor readers to phonetic or visual attributes shared by foils and acquisition items. This is expected if poor readers are more likely than good readers to focus on token identity of stimuli and, correspondingly, are less likely to attend to shared attributes.

The hypothesis that poor readers are deficient in response to features or dimensions of stimuli in a set does not readily explain the absence of a difference between the reading groups in susceptibility to semantic foils in the study by Byrne and Shea (1979) described earlier. If false alarms to semantic foils are made because subjects recognize semantic features shared by foils and acquisition items, then according to the partial-information hypothesis poor readers should have made fewer false alarms to semantic foils than good readers, but they did not. Several ways to modify the hypothesis can be imagined that would allow it to handle this outcome. For example, possibly, a tendency to extract information about the shared attributes of words develops at different times or rates for their formal attributes (their graphic and phonetic properties) than for their substantive (semantic) attributes. By hypothesis, then, poor readers at the ages tested by Byrne and Shea (age 7.6) are not delayed relative to good readers in their tendency to recognize shared attributes of the concepts named by words (although both groups may differ from adults in this respect) but are delayed in their tendency to recognize shared phonetic or graphic attributes of the words themselves.

Our next study had two major aims. One was to determine whether the false alarm profiles for good and poor readers suggested by the combined outcomes of the studies by Byrne and Shea (1979), Mark et al. (1977), and Wolford and Fowler (in press) are stable. The second was to discover whether a bridge might be established between the interpretations by Tighe et al. (1975) of their findings with children and adults and our findings relating to good- and poor-reader differences.

Test of Recognition Memory

To determine whether the differences between good and poor readers reported by Wolford and Fowler (in press), by Mark et al. (1977) and by Byrne and Shea (1979) are general, we included all the confusability conditions examined separately in those studies in a comprehensive test of recognition memory. Foils were unrelated, graphically related, phonetically related, and related in meaning to acquisition items. To compare any differences that we might find between good and poor readers with the developmental differences found by Tighe et al. (1975), we also included foils related in category to acquisition items.

The acquisition list of items consisted of 63 words. Of these 63, eight were names of body parts, and the remaining words did not group into categories. Forty-four of the acquisition words, including four names of body parts, recurred during the test phase of the experiment and were therefore the "old" items. The test list also included 64 new items (foils). Four were names of body parts. These were confusable with the four names of body parts on the acquisition list that did not recur as old items in the recognition test. Fifteen were neutral foils unrelated to any acquisition items. The remaining 45 new words were confusable with the remaining 15 acquisition items that did not reappear on the test list. For each of these 15 acquisition items, three confusable foils were selected. One was graphically similar to the target acquisition word but was phonetically dissimilar to it. A second resembled the acquisition word phonetically but not graphically. A third foil was a synonym or close associate of the acquisition word. An example of a target item and its matched foils is "white" (acquisition item) "whole" (visual foil), "right" (phonetic foil) and "black" (semantic foil; following Bryne and Shea, 1979, many of the semantic foils were antonyms to acquisition items). Examples of body-part acquisition items are "nose," "foot"; category foils for these are "arm," "head." All the words in the experiment are listed in Carroll, Davies, and Richman's (1971) list of words appearing with some frequency in third-grade textbooks. Across the critical acquisition items, their confusable and neutral foils, and the "old" test items, words were matched in length and frequency.

The experimental procedures for the adults and children differed somewhat one from the other. Among the adults, the acquisition list was introduced as a test of vocal reaction time for word naming. On each trial, one of the words in the acquisition list appeared on the screen of a CRT. Students read the word as quickly as they could, and their vocal response time was printed on the terminal screen after every trial. Following the 63 acquisition items and a short delay, the test trials were presented. During each of these trials, subjects saw one of the test items printed on the CRT. They responded "old" and "new" by hitting one of two labeled keys on the terminal keyboard.

In the children's version of the experiment, words were printed on file cards. The experimenter showed each word to the child and read it aloud to him or her. The child was then asked to find the word he or she had just seen on a matrix of words that included the target word and six others on the acquisition list. This was to ensure attention to the graphic properties of the words. The experimenter's reading the word provided the phonetic properties, and we assumed that the word's familiarity would ensure access to its meaning. Following the acquisition trials and a delay, the test trials were presented. In these trials, the experimenter presented a test word printed on a file card and the child indicated whether the word was "old" or "new."

The recognition memory study was run twice with different subjects and with minor changes in materials and procedure. The two runs of the experiment differed in several ways. First, because the phonetic manipulation appeared weak in the first run, particularly among the children, some new phonetic foils replaced others in the second run. In a second effort to boost phonetic false alarms, the delay between acquisition and test was reduced from about 30–45 minutes to 15–20 minutes. Third, in the initial version of the experiment, the experimenter did not read the test words aloud to the children; in the second run, she did. These changes in fact had no differential effect on false alarm rates to phonetic foils. The only consequences of the modifications was to *reduce* the number of false alarms overall in the experiment. (Presumably this was a consequence of having reduced the time between acquisition and test.) Comparing the two runs in an analysis of variance, there was a main effect of run on false alarms; however, that variable did not interact with any other. Consequently the results of the two studies are combined here.

The subjects were 31 college students and 86 third-grade children, 45 reading below grade level and 41 reading above grade level.

The measure of major interest in this study is the false alarm rate for each group in each condition of foil relatedness. We first looked at each of the three groups separately and considered only the foil types that replicate the conditions in the studies of Wolford and Fowler (in press), Mark et al. (1977), and Byrne and Shea (1979)—that is, neutral foils and foils graphically, phonetically, and semantically similar to acquisition items. For all three groups, the main effect of foil type was highly significant [adults: $F(3, 90) = 5.6, p = .002$; good readers: $F(3, 120) = 3.47, p = .02$; poor readers: $F(3, 132) = 6.3, p < .001$]. Collapsing across the three levels of foil relatedness, among the adults and good readers, planned comparisons reveal a significantly greater number of false alarms to related as opposed to neutral foils [adults: $F(1, 90) = 11.62, p = .001$; good readers: $F(1, 120) = 4.76, p < .03$]. Among the poor readers, this difference is not significant [$F(1, 132) = 1.91, p = .17$]. Paired t tests comparing false alarms to neutral and related foils among adults show significantly more false alarms to graphically related [$t (30) = 3.91, p < .001$] and semantically related foils [$t(30) = 3.99, p < .001$] than to neutral foils. False alarm errors to phonetically related foils are only marginally more frequent than to neutral foils [$t(30) = 1.83, p = .07$]. Among good readers, likewise, false alarms to graphically confusable foils and semantically confusable foils exceed those to neutral foils [$t(40) = 2.37, p = .02$ and $t(40) = 2.39, p = .02$, respectively]; false alarms to phonetic foils do not. Among poor readers only false alarms to semantically confusable foils exceed those to neutral foils [$t(44) = 3.91, p < .001$].

With the single exception of the phonetic condition, these findings confirm those of earlier recognition memory studies. Poor readers do not make false alarms due to foils that are graphically confusable with acquisition items, but they do make confusions errors when foils are semantically confusable with acquisition items. Good readers make confusion errors in both conditions. Whereas two earlier studies had shown phonetic confusions among the good but not poor readers, the present study gives little evidence of phonetic confusions by either group. However, it is plausible to attribute this failure to confirm earlier findings to the weakness of our own phonetic manipulations and not to flaws in earlier studies. In our study, even the adults made few false alarms to phonetic foils.

In respect to the first aim of our study, then, we were partially successful. We reconfirmed that good but not poor readers attend to and use graphic properties of words and that both are sensitive to their semantic properties; however we did not confirm differences in their attention to phonetic properties.

Turning now to the second aim of our study, we compared our findings to those of Tighe et al. (1975). We first examined the false alarm rate to foils related in category membership to acquisition words. Adults and good and poor readers all made substantially more errors to foils sharing category membership with acquisition items than to neutral foils [adults $t(30) = 5.38, p{\sim}0$; good readers: $t(40) = 3.07, p = .004$; poor readers: $t(44) = 3.07, p = .004$]. However, the three groups are distinguishable in their relative susceptibility to category and neutral foils. To show this difference, false alarms to category and neutral foils were transformed into difference scores. A one-way analysis of variance comparing differences among the groups of subjects on these scores yields a significant effect [$F(2, 114) = 3.70, p = .03$]. There are different ways in which this significant effect may be assessed. First, if the differences in performance are related to differences in age, as the findings of Tighe et al. suggest, then a linear trend test (Winer, 1971) in which false alarm rates for each group are weighted according to the group's deviation from the mean age of the three groups should account for most of the variance in the analysis. In fact, it does [$F(1, 114) = 6.47, p = .011$]; 87% of the variance in the main effect of group is accounted for in this analysis. Adults make significantly more false alarms to foils sharing category membership with target items than do 8-year-old children. In a second analysis of these data, the groups were compared by weighting their false alarm rates according to their reading levels; that is, the false alarm score for each group of subjects was weighted according to the deviation of the group's reading score from the mean of the reading scores. (Adults were assigned a score of 13.0) A trend test using these weights yields a highly significant result $[F(1, 114) = 6.79, p = .01]$, which in fact accounts for most of the variance in the main effect of group and somewhat more of the variance (92%) than did the analysis by age. This shows that level of reading achievement rationalizes the differences among the groups in overall false alarm rate to foils sharing category membership with acquisition-list items.

We next broadened our statistical comparison of adults and good and poor readers to include the remaining foil types. For the purposes of this comparison, false alarms to neutral foils were subtracted from false alarms to graphic, phonetic, semantic, and category foils for each subject. These difference scores, averaged across the members of each group, are displayed in Fig. 9.5.

A two-way analysis of variance compared false alarms to the four confusion categories among the three reading groups. In the analysis, there was a main effect of group $[F(2, 114) = 3.67, p < .03]$ and of foil type $[F(3, 342) = 24.93, p \sim 0]$ but no interaction. Post hoc tests attribute the effect of foil type primarily to the relatively large number of false alarms in the category condition as compared to the other three conditions. False alarm rates among the graphic, phonetic, and semantic conditions did not differ significantly, although the difference between the phonetic condition and the other two approached significance. The absence

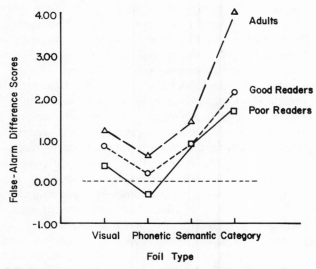

FIG. 9.5   False alarm differences scores for adults, good readers, and poor readers in the word recognition study.

of an interaction of group and foil type suggests among other things that the category condition, which we included to enable a comparison of our good- and poor-reader differences with differences between adults and children reported by Tighe et al. (1975), led to performance differences among the groups similar in kind to those caused by the other manipulations of foil relatedness. In turn, this suggests that however we explain performance differences among the groups in the category-relatedness condition, the same explanation should apply to performance differences in the other conditions. Despite the absence of a significant interaction, however, the figure does show that good and poor readers, though different in the graphic, phonetic, and category conditions, are not different in false alarm rates to semantic foils. This convergence in performance is worth noting because it replicates the findings of Byrne and Shea (1979), who report differences between good and poor readers in false alarm rate to phonetically confusable foils but not to semantically confusable foils.

A planned comparison of the significant group effect with false alarms weighted according to the age differences among the groups is highly significant $[F(1, 114) = 6.22, p = .01]$ accounting for 85% of the variance in the main effect. As before, a trend test with weights assigned according to reading level is also significant $[F(1, 114) = 6.83, p < .01]$ accounting for 93% of the variance in the main effect.

Overall, these findings reveal a relationship between reading skill and false alarms rate to confusable foils that is somewhat stronger than the relationship between age and false alarm rate. The differences among the groups would seem to reflect differential tendencies to attend to the token identities of words as opposed to their component dimensions or features. Extrapolating from the studies by Tighe et al. (1975), we can interpret the poor readers' performance as characteristic of relatively younger children as compared to that of the good readers. The results do not demand this interpretation of course; we could conclude at this point simply that false alarm rate is related to reading skill (or, compatibly with both interpretations, to reading and other relevant experience). But our study does establish that the developmental differences observed by Tighe et al. (1975) are similar to the good- and poor-reader differences that we and others have found.

Generation Study

The outcome of the recognition study, although informative, was disappointing in some respects. First, one manipulation of major interest to us—that of phonetic confusability—was not strong enough to produce significant phonetic confusions in any group. Additionally, the differences between good and poor readers in false alarm rate to confusable foils generally were quite small as the figure shows. Indeed, overall, the average difference between the difference scores of these two groups was just .30 false alarms—not a very striking difference given the large difference between the groups in reading achievement.

Our final study sought converging evidence with the recognition study of differential attention by good and poor readers to the various attributes of written and spoken words. Whereas in the recognition study the *tendency* to use partial information is assessed, our final study assessed the *ability* to use partial information effectively when its use is enforced by an experimental task. This was accomplished by employing a word-generation task in which subjects were given a target word and a class of attributes (graphic ones, for example), and their task was to list as many words as they could that share the specified attributes with the target word. Thus, attention to attributes of the words is enforced by the nature of the task.

The generation study, like the recognition study, was run twice on different groups of children with some changes in procedure and materials. In this case, some of the changes affected the groups differentially and therefore the results of the two studies are presented separately.

In the first version of the study, children were shown 16 words in all, four in each of the conditions of graphic, phonetic, semantic and category similarity. Words were blocked by condition. On each trial, children were shown a word, which was also spoken aloud by the experimenter, and were asked to generate (by saying them) words which resembled the cue word on some dimension: graphic, phonetic, semantic or category. (For example, the children were asked to think of and say words that "look like" or "sound like" the cue word.) The experimenter transcribed the children's responses.

In the second version of the study, the number of cue words in each condition was reduced from four to three, an explicit criterion was established for terminating a trial (i.e., a trial was ended when 20 seconds had elapsed since the child's last response), and some changes were made in introducing the child to each condition and in collecting his or her responses. In introducing each task, the experimenter not only told the children what the relevant similarity dimension was (look alike, sound alike, etc.) but in addition provided two forced-choice pretraining trials in which of three words both shown and read to the child, two resembled each other on the critical dimension and one was distinctive. (For example, in the graphic similarity condition, children saw "boy," "surprise," and "bag"). Children were asked to point to the related words. They were told that the kind of resemblance shared by the related words on the card was the resemblance they were to provide in subsequent trials. A final change in procedure was for the children to write their responses rather than say them in the graphic similarity condition. The total number of responses in each condition and the rated quality of each response were scored. Quality was assessed by three raters in the first version of the study and two in the second, and scoring was blind with respect to the reading level of the child who had produced each word. Words were rated on a 5-point scale with 5 signifying a high degree of resemblance between cue and response on the specified dimension. The final score for each child in each condition was obtained by multiplying the child's total number of responses in a condition by his or her average rating. We used this

TABLE 9.5
Scores (Rating × Frequency) of Good and Poor Readers in (a) First-
and (b) Second-Generation Study

	Visual	Phonetic	Semantic	Category
(a) Good	57.8	81.1	96.5	220.2
Poor	50.7	61.3	84.1	193.7
t (39)	1.02	2.56	1.31	1.91
P	.32	.01	.19	.06
(b) Good	34.9	65.1	59.2	163.4
Poor	26.8	42.3	49.0	145.4
t (43)	2.04	4.40	1.59	2.26
P	.05	.001	$>.10$	.05

score because we considered it likely that average rating alone would penalize children who produced many responses.

The scores for the first-generation study are given in Table 9.5a. High scores in the table show a close resemblance between subjects' responses and the cue word, and this indicates use of the relevant attributes in word generation. In all conditions, the good readers' scores were higher than those of the poor readers. t tests comparing the groups separately in the four conditions (see Table 9.5a) reveal highly significant differences between the groups in the phonetic similarity condition and marginally significant differences in the category condition but no differences in the graphic and semantic conditions.

The scores for children in the second-generation study are given in Table 9.5b. t tests (see Table 9.5b) revealed significant differences in the graphic, phonetic, and category conditions but not in the semantic condition.

The response pattern in the second-generation study is quite similar to that in the first. In both studies, the good- and poor-reader differences are largest in the phonetic condition and least in the semantic. In the second study, relative to the first, the differences between the reading groups were large in all conditions— large enough for statistical significance in the visual condition but not in the semantic condition.

The response patterns in the generation studies not only resemble each other, they also resemble that in the recognition study. In both sets of studies, good and poor readers perform similarly in conditions involving semantic attributes of words but differently in graphic and category conditions. The major difference between the recognition and recall studies is in the phonetic condition; but we attribute this difference to our failure in the recognition study to manipulate phonetic confusability successfully.

GENERAL DISCUSSION

These studies and those of other investigators that suggested them give us some confidence that the response pattern we have observed across several tests of recognition memory is stable in tasks where use of partial information affects performance. The general pattern is that poor readers are not distinguished from good readers in their use of semantic attributes of words but differ from good readers, sometimes markedly, in the use of graphic, phonetic, and category attributes. In particular, in tests of recognition memory, both good and poor readers make disproportionate false alarm responses to foils related semantically to acquisition items. Similarly, in generation studies, good and poor readers produce similar qualities and quantities of words related semantically to cue words. In contrast to their similar performances when semantic attributes of words are manipulated, good and poor readers differ in performance when use of other attributes of words is assessed. In tests of recognition memory, good readers, but not poor readers (or, to a lesser extent, poor readers), make more false alarms to foils related graphically, phonetically or in category to acquisition items than they make to neutral foils. Similarly, in generation studies, good readers tend to produce words of greater graphic, phonetic, and category resemblance to cue words than do poor readers.

We interpret the performance differences between the reading groups as reflecting differences in the tendency to extract or use stimulus attributes. This is most likely to affect performance when the information available for correct response is incomplete (e.g., due to loss from memory). However, it reveals itself also in some situations where all the information necessary for correct response is made available in the stimulation to the child and loss from memory is not a factor. These are situations (e.g., the scaling studies and the generation studies), in which performance is optimized if stimulus attributes are extracted and used.

Our interpretation of the response pattern when the relevant stimulus attributes are graphic, phonetic, or categorical does not immediately explain the absence of a difference between the groups when the critical attributes are semantic. Further investigation is necessary to resolve this outcome. Here, we mention two interpretations that we have considered.

Byrne and Shea (1979) offer one interpretation. In their study, both good and poor readers made false alarms to semantic foils but only good readers made phonetic confusion errors. Byrne and Shea propose that for the young child, and for the poor reader more than for the good reader, words and the concepts they label are inseparable, and consequently he or she finds it difficult to focus on a word's form.

A second interpretation derives from the observation that many of the foils in our recognition study (and also in Byrne and Shea's, 1979) are high associates of their corresponding acquisition items. Conceivably when an acquisition item is presented to a subject, its high associates are automatically accessed along with the acquisition item itself. On a later test of recognition memory, then, a high associate of an acquisition word seems familiar itself, not because it shares semantic features with the acquisition item but because it *is* familiar, having been accessed during the acquisition phase of the experiment. This effect is the same for poor and good readers because it does not depend on recognition of the semantic features shared by acquisition items and semantic foils. A similar proposal can explain good- and poor-reader performance in the semantic-generation condition. Here acceptable responses to the cue word may be generated by producing words that are associated to the cue word in memory.

By this hypothesis, good and poor readers differ in responses to category foils even though they do not differ in response to semantic foils because pairs of acquisition items and category foils (e.g., "eye"–"foot") tend not to be as high associates as pairs of acquisition items and semantic foils (e.g., "more"–"less"). Unfortunately our word lists were not well designed for an appropriate item analysis to be done because many acquisition item–foil pairs in the experiment are not listed in tables of word associations. Therefore, we cannot test the hypothesis without devising new word lists.

For the present then we are left with some fairly clear indications that good and poor readers differ in their use of component attributes. This difference will be particularly likely to affect performance under conditions of partial-information availability but will also affect performance when information is complete and the subjects' task requires focus on individual attributes of stimuli. In addition, we have suggestions that the poor readers' processing mode may be characteristic of relatively younger children as compared to that of the good readers. Our data suggest that the deficit of poor readers may be continuous with fundamental developmental processes relating to the perception and use of stimuli.

ACKNOWLEDGMENTS

This research was supported by NIMH Grant MH 33179 awarded to the first author and by NIH Grant HD 01994 to Haskins Laboratories. We wish to thank Mandy Murphy and Robin Shrier for their assistance in collecting the data and the children and parents in the region for volunteering their time. We would also like to thank Kit Shum for constructing the Chinese characters.

REFERENCES

Byrne, B., & Shea, P. Semantic and phonetic memory codes in beginning readers. *Memory & Cognition,* 1979, *7*, 333–338.

Carroll, J. B., Davies, P., & Richman, B. *Word frequency book.* New York: American Heritage Pub., 1971.

Cole, R., & Perfetti, C. Listening for mispronunciations in a children's story: The use of context by children and adults. *Journal of Verbal Learning and Verbal Behavior,* 1980, *19*, 297–315.

Conrad, R. Interference or decay over short retention intervals? *Journal of Verbal Learning and Verbal Behavior,* 1967, *6*, 49–54.

Dunn, L. M. *Peabody picture vocabulary test.* Circle Pines, Minn.: American Guidance Service, 1965.

Gibson, E. J. *Principles of perceptual learning and development.* Englewood Cliffs, N.J.: Prentice-Hall, 1969.

Liberman, I. Y., Shankweiler, D., Liberman, A. M., Fowler, C. A., & Fischer, F. W. Phonetic segmentation and recoding in the beginning reader. In A. S. Reber & D. Scarborough (Eds.), *Toward a psychology of reading: The proceedings of the CUNY conference.* Hillsdale, N.J.: Lawrence Erlbaum Associates, 1977.

McGee, V. Multidimensional scaling of "elastic" distances. *British Journal of Mathematical and Statistical Psychology,* 1966, *19,* 181–196.

Mann, V., Liberman, I. Y., & Shankweiler, D. Chidren's memory for sentences and word strings in relation to reading ability. *Memory & Cognition,* 1980, *8,* 329–335.

Mark, L. S., Shankweiler, D., Liberman, I. Y., & Fowler, C. A. Phonetic recoding and reading difficulty in beginning readers. *Memory & Cognition,* 1977, *5,* 623–629.

Morrison, F. J., Giordani, B., & Nagy, J. Reading disability: An information-processing analysis. *Science,* 1977, *196,* 77–79.

Perfetti, C., Goldman, S., & Hogaboam, T. Reading skill and the identification of words in context. *Memory & Cognition,* 1979, *7,* 273–282.

Schvaneveldt, R., Ackerman, B., & Semlear, T. The effect of context on children's word recognition. *Child Development,* 1977, *48,* 612–616.

Shankweiler, D., & Liberman, I. Y. Exploring the relations between reading and speech. In R. M. Knights & D. K. Bakker (Eds.), *The neuropsychology of learning disorders: Theoretical approaches.* Baltimore: University Park Press, 1976.

Shankweiler, D., Liberman, I. Y., Mark, L. S., Fowler, C. A., & Fischer, F. W. The speech code and learning to read. *Journal of Experimental Psychology: Human Learning and Memory,* 1979, *5,* 531–545.

Shepp, B. From perceived similarity to dimensional structure: A new hypothesis about perceptual development. In E. Rosch & B. Lloyd (Eds.), *Cognition and categorization.* Hillsdale, N.J.: Lawrence Erlbaum Associates, 1978.

Tighe, T. J., & Tighe, L. S. A perceptual view of conceptual development. In R. D. Walk & H. L. Pick, Jr. (Eds.), *Perception and experience.* New York: Plenum Press, 1978.

Tighe, T. J., Tighe, L. S., & Schechter, J. Memory for instances and categories in children and adults. *Journal of Experimental Child Psychology,* 1975, *20,* 22–37.

Vellutino, F. R. *Dyslexia: Theory and research.* Cambridge, Mass.: MIT Press, 1979.

Vellutino, F. R., Steger, J. A., Kaman, M., & DeSetto, L. Visual form perception in deficient and normal readers as a function of age and orthographic linguistic familiarity. *Cortex,* 1975, *11,* 22–30.

Winer, B. J. *Statistical principles in experimental design*(2nd. ed.). New York: McGraw-Hill, 1971.

Wolford, G., & Fowler, C. A. Differential use of partial information by good and poor readers. *Developmental Review,* in press.

Wolford, G., & Hollingsworth, S. Evidence that short-term memory is not the limiting factor in the tachistoscopic full-report procedure. *Memory & Cognition,* 1974, *2,* 796–800.

Wolford, G., & Porter, G. *Simultaneous and sequential presentation of visual arrays.* Paper read at the annual meeting of the Psychonomic Society, St. Louis, 1976.

Woodcock, R. W. *Woodcock reading mastery tests.* Circle Pines, Minn.: American Guidance Service, 1973.

Yule, W. Differential prognosis of reading backwardness and specific reading retardation. *British Journal of Educational Psychology,* 1973, *43,* 244–248.

10 Some Issues on the Relation between Perceptual and Cognitive Development

Herbert L. Pick, Jr.
University of Minnesota

Introduction

What is the relation between perceptual and cognitive development? Classically, there has been a two-sided answer to this question. On the one hand, perception itself is considered to depend on higher-order cognitive processes. On the other hand, perception is considered to be a very primitive process that, although, supplanted in mature human behavior by more sophisticated cognitive processes, may nevertheless supply the elements or building blocks for cognition. The chapters of Shepp, of Anderson, and of Zeamen and Hanley (this volume) bear on these two answers by dealing both with the elements that perception may supply for cognition (especially Shepp and Zeaman and Hanley) and with operations for combining these elements (especially Anderson). Let us breifly consider each of the classical views.

The traditional theory of perception to which a large number of psychologists still subscribe held that perception was to a large extent based on some kind of cognitive (i.e., inferential) process. This view is the one handed down from Berkeley and Helmholtz and exists in modern form in the ideas of Brunswik (1944) and Gregory (1966). It is well known that this conceptualization of perception starts with the perceiver having sensations mediated by built-in receptor organs. Historically that idea was championed by Johannes Muller but its modern proponents have the more sophisticated physiology of complex feature detectors. The basic sensations are then processed with an inferential-like process. The inferences can involve integration of simultaneous sensations and/or they can involve integration of current sensations with past associations. In the latter case, memory is obviously implicated so perception not only is based on a

293

cognitive inferential operation but also uses the cognitive memorial function and whatever integrating operation is involved. Traditionally this view has been most generally applied to three types of perceptual problems: depth perception, constancy, and illusions.

Most early perceptual theorists did not directly deal with perceptual development but this classical theory was, in fact, a theory of perceptual development in the sense that mature perception could not occur without sophisticated cognition. Taking the developmental implications of this classical empiricist theory seriously led to a number of paradoxes. One of these is how animals and little children, both with seemingly limited cognitive capacities, could have relatively good depth perception and perceptual constancy. Related to this was the fact that mentally retarded persons by and large also have good depth perception and constancy. A second paradox is the fact that adults often have a great deal of difficulty getting back to the basic sensations. They primarily experience the results of the cognitively processed sensations, that is, the percepts. This paradox appears again in modern information processing views. An amusing characterization of it is made by Neisser (1976) who presents a figure of the chain of processing that runs from the image through several stages of processing and more processing until finally consciousness is reached. The standard resolution has been, and is, an appeal to overlearning (now automatization) of the cognitive processing. This combined with contemporary views about the very brief storage of the sensory information explains why we, as adults, can't recover the sensations on which the percepts are based. Although this resolution seems reasonable, the classical theory has never done well in resolving the first paradox of the perceptual precocity of cognitively naive organisms.

Notwithstanding the paradoxes in applying this theory to development of perception, it is vital to know the basic sensory elements faced by the young child that become the building blocks of the cognitive process resulting in perception. From the perspective of the classical theory, in order to understand how a child comes to see depth from the two-dimensional display on his retina, in order to understand how a child comes to see a meaningful persistent object in the world when receiving essentially meaningless sensory stimulation, we have to know what the initial sensations are. This is one motivation for current application to children's perception of very sophisticated types of stimulus analysis and sensory measurement.

The other side of the answer to the question of the relation of perceptual and cognitive development takes perception as the primitive or primary process on which cognition is based. This is exemplified by Piaget's cognitive theory (but not his theory of perception). According to his cognitive theory, perception is a very primitive process that at best informs more sophisticated, intellective processes and at worst misleads them. For example, the earliest, most primitive stage of cognitive development is the sensory motor stage in which the only thing an infant knows about an object is the way he or she interacts with it, initially simply reflexive interaction. Even at its height of development, perception is similar to preoperational thought (Flavell, 1963), and perception at best gives probabilistic and variable, rather than absolute, knowledge. If that is not bad enough, when faced with conservation tasks, the preoperational child is misled by her perception and has a terrible time realizing that one has to overrule the perceptual appearance of something with a cognitive rule about whether something has been added or subtracted. Perception can become more veridical through perceptual activity that overcomes distortion attributable to fixation on restricted aspects of a stimulus. While lack of conservation (e.g., of volume) may be attributable to fixation of *perception* on the dimension of height, say, in detriment to registering both the height and width of a column of fluid, one resolution of this error is the *perception* that nothing has been added or subtracted. Thus perception can't be all bad. Indeed, for Piaget, it is a mode of adaptation, just one not so sophisticated as cognition. For such a theory, it is of course also important to know what the units and dimensions of perception are so that one can predict when perception will be veridical and when it will provide distorted information. It is also vital to understand the operations by which these elements are combined. In short, it is important from both the traditional empiricist point of view about the relation of perceptual and cognitive development and from the cognitive approaches such as Piaget's to know what the basic perceptual dimensions are and how they are related to more complex cognitive units.

CONCEPT FORMATION AND PERCEPTUAL AND COGNITIVE DEVELOPMENT

One important arena where cognitive and perceptual explanations of behavior have confronted one another is that of categorization and concept formation. (See Medin, this volume, for an excellent analytic treatment of the nature of categories. The present brief discussion is to relate categories to perception.) Psychologists have taken a number of approaches to the study of concepts. In one approach, concepts are thought of as categories of objects or physical stimuli. An early example of this view is Hull's analysis of concept formation in terms of finding a common element among a series of figures (Hull, 1920). Hull's analysis was generalized by Bruner, Goodnow, and Austin (1956) to the task of finding particular values of particular stimulus dimensions among a set of stimuli, although there might be no common element or common stimulus. The recent work of Rosch and her colleagues (Rosch, 1973; Rosch, Mervis, Gray, Johnson, & Boyes-Braem, 1976) represents a somewhat different approach to the study of concepts but one that is still concerned with categories of objects; in her case, categories of natural objects. Her work is concerned with the structure of the organization of people's categories of real-world objects. A "basic-level" category is defined by commonalities in people's descriptions of objects and how they act on the objects, by the ease with which objects can be imagined, and by the overlap in their shape, etc. Then these categories and subordinate and super-ordinate categories help define the structural organization of the world's objects.

Many psychologists interested in concept formation have felt the study and analysis of stimulus dimensions might provide a link between perception and cognition. Although concepts seem to be a higher-order cognitive entity, it may be the case that concepts in the sense of categories based upon common stimulus elements or common values of stimulus dimensions reflect a not-so-high level perceptual process. If this is true, then Rosch's (1973) real-world categories may be the first level where concepts are not based entirely on perceptual analysis but require a constructive cognitive process. At first glance, there seems to be no obvious physical variable for perception of all the members of the basic-level categories. (A penguin is a bird, albeit an atypical one.) In a recent discussion, however, Jones and Pick (1981) have suggested that Rosch's categories also may have a perceptual basis but one differeing from simple similarity of shape. They argue that a better description of basic-level categories is in terms of what Gibson (1979) calls affordances (see cf. also E. J. Gibson, 1982). Essentially the idea is that objects of a class may afford a common action and this affordance is specified in the information in the optical array when an object is seen. It is possible that the natural adaptive correlations of attributes discussed by Medin (this volume) are combinations of properties that provide affordances for organisms.

A still different level of concept and conceptualization is the focus of Ander-son's concern (this volume). He is interested in concepts as functional relation-ships between variables of the physical world. Thus, he is no longer dealing with physically present stimulus objects and their elements and dimensions but, rather, constructive processes based on these. According to Anderson's analysis, people still register stimuli and stimulus dimensions, but he takes these as more or less given and is more concerned with how one psychological dimension is related to another and how psychological values along two or more dimensions are integrated.

It seems fairly compelling that concepts at the level of functional relationships must be cognitive and cannot be explained by perception alone. Nevertheless, we must recognize the possibility that there is information directly available for the perception of such relationships. One difficulty in entertaining this possibility stems from the fact that the information may be dynamic and is presumably registered over time; whereas our naive view of perception is that it depends on static information and is instantaneous. However, good examples of sensitivity to such relationships defined by dynamic information include Johansson's vector displays (Johansson, 1964), resulting in perceptual events and Lee's work (Lee, 1974), showing that subjects seem to respond to time to contact in guiding their locomotion. Time to contact is mathematically specified by a complex ratio of rather simple physical stimulus dimensions but one that includes velocity vectors as well as constant scalar values.

A still more abstract level of concepts is that of most interest to Piaget. As is well known, he considered the development of such concepts as space, causality, and the idea of object itself. Again, one would think, as Piaget did, that these abstract concepts are clearly constructive; there is apparently no information for the perception of such properties as object rigidity, object permanence, and one object causing another to move. Yet there is considerable recent evidence that there is information available for the perception of such properties and that even young children are sensitive to that information (Gibson, 1982; Harris, in press; Olum, 1958). For example, in one of her experiments, Gibson habituated young infants to several different rigid transformations and found that the habituation did *not* generalize to a subsequent nonrigid transformation but did generalize to a novel rigid transformation. The implication of such experiments is that there is some aspect of stimulation that is informative about this important property of the environment.

STIMULUS ANALYSIS AND PERCEPTUAL AND COGNITIVE DEVELOPMENT

Dimensions of stimulation have also traditionally been of considerable interest to perceptual and learning theorists concerned with changes in perception as a function of experience. Obviously such changes in perception are closely related to the issues of perceptual and cognitive development raised previously. Shifts in the effectiveness of stimulus dimensions can provide a way for understanding the role of learning in perception as well as the role of perception in learning (Gibson & Gibson, 1955; Gibson, 1969; Wohlwill, 1960). As Zeaman and Hanley (this volume) point out in their chapter, a number of learning theorists have viewed the effectiveness or salience of stimulus dimensions as being largely determined by experiential factors. Zeaman and Hanley are quite convincing in summarizing considerable evidence for the possible biological determinance of at least some stimulus dimension preferences. A very plausible case can be made for such a structural basis, relying on converging indirect evidence.

What could underlie structural bases of stimulus-dimension preference? One obvious possibility is the relative discriminability of the stimuli along the different dimensions. Thus, if children prefer to use color as a basis for grouping stimuli at one age and form at a later age, it might be that the colors are more discriminable than the forms at the early age and vice versa later on. In the extreme case it wouldn't be surprising if subjects used one dimension when the stimuli were not discriminable at all along the other dimension. In most of the instances Zeaman and Hanley described, it seemed quite obvious that the extreme case did not obtain. The children would have been able to discriminate the stimuli along the less preferred dimension if that were the only one varying. However, even in less extreme cases it may well be that the stimulus dimensions with the larger perceptual differences would be preferred. Very few studies have tried to equate the discriminability of the stimuli across the different dimensions to see if the same preference held up. Gliner, Pick, Pick, and Hales (1969) tried to do just this in a study of stimulus-dimension preference between form and texture. They found in a visual task that, with equal discriminability of form and texture differences (as determined by a psychophysical procedure), form was the preferred dimension across the entire age range studied. In the same task performed tactually there was a preference shift with age from texture to form. A reasonable interpretation but still not logical proof would attribute dimension preferences correlated with discriminability differences to structural factors and dimension preferences when discriminability is equated to control processes in Zeaman and Hanley's use of these terms.

Besides these theoretical reasons, it is, of course, very useful for practical purposes to know what the units and dimensions of perception are. Thus, if we know the dimensions involved in the perception of spatial layout, for example, we can structure the environment in such a way that people, especially children, won't become lost or we can perhaps train them better how to find their way around. Or, for example, knowing the dimensions or features involved in the discrimination of letters, we could train children better how to start to perceive letters or we could perhaps design a better alphabet. The recognition of objects, in general, is an important aspect of children's percpetion but we have no way of describing what the dimensions of object perception are. In fact, we don't really know how to describe any systematic dimensional structure of objects themselves. Only for delimited sets of objects, such as letters, are we able to define a set of features or dimensions that are reasonable (Garner, 1979; Gibson, Schapiro, & Yonas, 1968).

Given all the previous theoretical and practical concerns implicating dimensions of perception, the recent systematic work of Shepp (1978, this volume) and of Smith and Kemler (1977) applying the concepts of separable and integral dimensions to children's perception has been a welcome and exciting contribution. In the work that Shepp (this volume) reviewed for us, an important trend he identified was the shift with age from perception based on integral dimensions to perception based on separable dimensions. The elegant converging evidence that he adduces in the support of this trend is very convincing. However, that trend should be considered in the context of other, seemingly related changes that occur during development. I am thinking of the changes during infancy in sensitivity to external and internal features of stimuli, to part–whole relations, and to compound–component aspects of stimuli.

Researchers such as Bushnell (1979), Milewski (1976), and Gannon and Swartz (1980) have shown that infants up to about 2 months of age will not register an internal figure embedded in a surrounding form. The typical experiment is to habituate infants to such a compound stimulus and then to change the internal or surrounding figure. Up to 2 months of age, infants only detect changes in the surrounding form; after this age, changes in either feature are detected. Control experiments indicate that the internal form can be perceived when presented in isolation.

Perception by infants of part–whole relations have been investigated in a number of studies (Bower, 1966; Cornell & Strauss, 1973; Miller, 1972; Miller Ryan, Sinnor, & Wilson, 1976). Here, typically an infant is habituated to a compound stimulus (e.g., two dots and an x within a circle) and is tested for generalization to the elements of the compound or, alternatively, is habituated to the elements presented in isolation and then tested for generalization to the compound. The logic of the experiment is that if the amount of responding to the compound equals the sum of responding to the elements individually, the baby is not responding to the unique configuration of the whole. If the responding to the compound and the sum of the responding to the elements differ, it suggests that the configuration of elements is indeed psychologically more than the sum of the parts. The results suggest that, up to 4 months, the whole is equivalent to the sum of the parts, but after this age the whole does constitute a unique configuration.

In studies of perception of stimulus dimensions by infants (Cohen & Gelber, 1975; Fagan, 1977) exactly analogous to the compound–component studies described by Zeaman and Hanley (this volume), infants have been habituated to compound color–form stimuli (e.g., a red traingle). They are then shwon a pair of stimuli such as a red square and a green square. Preference for the green square in this novelty test would indicate that the infant had isolated, at least to some extent, the color dimension because there was no identical compound stimulus in the choice. (Interestingly, this procedure capitalizes on the reliable preference for novelty discussed by Zeaman and Hanley (this volume) to show attention to the color dimension.) Infants shown another pair such as a red triangle and a green triangle could also indicate sensitivity to the color dimension by preferring to look at the green triangle, but this could also indicate sensitivity to the difference between the original and the new compound stimuli. However, if the degree of preference were greater in the second novelty test than in the first, it would suggest that both the compound and stimulus dimension were being discriminated. The results suggest that up to about 5 months perception was based on stimulus dimensions of form and color, but after this age the compound stimulus was also being perceived as a compound.

The external–internal results suggest that young babies are responding to isolated elements and not to holistic patterns. The part–whole results suggest again that young infants are responding to parts or elements and that only after 4 months of age do they begin to respond to holistic properties of the stimuli. This seems like a reverse trend to that described by Shepp (this volume), going from integral to separable dimensions in older children. Although these elements in the external–internal and part–whole experiments are not the same sorts of stimulus dimensions as Shepp and his colleagues had derived from Garner's (1974) analysis, the stimulus dimensions of form and color used by Cohen and Gelber (1975) are much like the kind that Shepp has been studying with older children. Of course, the operations for identifying separable and integral dimensions, as defined by Garner and used by Shepp with children, are very specific and not at all like the habituation–dishabituation operations used in infant experiments. This might account for the difference in direction of the trends and the age at which they occur. Nevertheless, in discussing such dimensions it is not uncommon for researchers to speak more generally about the implications of the separable–integral distinction and use terms like *configurational* or *holistic characteristics* and *analyzability* of stimulus dimensions (Kemler, this volume). If the distinction is, in fact, very narrowly defined, it would suggest a disappointing lack of generality of its application. A more interesting possibility would be that these different trends at different ages reflect fundamentally different processes and that some sort of early primitive integration or synthesis is followed later by a more sophisticated differentiation or analysis.

In order to realize the full value of the extension of the separable-integral distinction to perceptual development, the number of stimulus dimensions examined should be increased. The distinction has been formally worked out for relatively few dimensions and has been applied to development in even fewer cases. Of course, the demonstration of the defining operations for separable and integral dimensions requires considerable work, and verifying their applicability or nonapplicability to children is even more demanding.

No doubt when other dimensions are examined, it is quite likely that a more complex developmental picture will emerge. For example, it is quite possible to imagine other changes in sensitivity that will probably go from separable to integral—early responding on the basis of relatively simple physical dimensions and later responding on the basis of integral combinations of these dimensions. Perhaps something like this happens when we become sensitive to more complex units in reading (as mentioned by Zeaman and Hanley) and speech perception. What is the status of such higher-order stimulus dimensions? They may presumably serve as the basis for organizing sets of stimuli or objects. To take a case in point, consider the experiment of Smith and Kemler (1978) described in Shepp, this volume. (Kemler, this volume, also describes an experiment similar in principle.) They had five values of each of two stimulus dimensions (X and Y). In one case, the stimuli were to be sorted with $x_1, y_1; x_1, y_2; x_1, y_3; x_1, y_4$ going into one group and $x_2, y_1; x_2, y_2; x_2, y_3; x_2, y_4$ going into another group. In a second problem, the stimuli had to be sorted with $x_2, y_1; x_3, y_2; x_4, y_3; x_5, y_4$ going into one group and $x_1, y_2; x_2, y_3; x_3, y_4; x_4, y_5$ going into another group. Shepp considers two possibilities. The first problem should be easier than the second if the subjects can respond in terms of the simple and separate physical dimensions and values, x_1 and x_2. If not, the two should be about equal difficulty. Smith and Kemler (1978) found the first task either easier or of no greater difficulty than the second with dimensions such as hue and saturation and size and brightness. But, consider what would happen if the stimuli were concentric rings with the x_1 stimulus being various brightness values of the inner ring and the y_1 stimuli being various brightness values of the outer ring. Now the second problem would consist of a principle that stimuli with a brighter inner ring than outer would belong to one group, whereas stimuli with a brighter outer ring than inner would belong to the other group. Relative intensity or brightness contrast is generally a more informative variable than absolute intensity, because conditions of illumination constantly change in the world. Thus, it is not surprising that we are considerably more sensitive to this variable; it is quite likely that the second problem would be easier. *Formally,* the structure of the stimulus domain is the same, but with contrast, a more informative integral or higher-order stimulus dimension, the second problem is not only not likely to be *more* difficult than the first but in fact is likely to be considerably easier. This higher-order dimension is very much like Zeaman and Hanley's (this volume) compound dimensions.

Kemler (this volume) has a nice discussion of discrimination in relation to similarity structure. Responding in terms of integral dimensions is typically considered developmentally more primitive. The present argument is that responding in terms of integral dimensions could also be a developmental achievement. Consider, for example, spatial layout. We would expect that children learning their way around their city neighborhood would learn first in terms of a city block metric and, indeed, have difficulty making Euclidean distance judgments. Adults, on the other hand, probably automatically respond in euclidean terms when making distance judgments. As Zeaman and Hanley point out in their discussion of whether or not compounds are dimensional in nature, overall similarity may be different than ordering on the basis of a specific higher-order stimulus dimension. Operationally, these possibilities seem very difficult to separate. Kemler has pointed out that people tend to take an analytic dimensional approach when confronted with a problem-solving situation and this tendency could be used for distinguishing between these theoretical possibilities. If a problem-solving set induced subjects to respond to a compound, maybe we could infer that they were treating it as a dimension. Perhaps the most sophisticated ability would be to respond on either basis depending on the task.

A variable such as contrast used in the previous hypothetical example is probably not a particularly interesting developmental one. Although there is some recent evidence, e.g., Salapatek & Banks (1978), of changes in contrast sensitivity in early infancy, it is quite likely that these can be attributed to physiological maturation of the mechanisms involved in lateral neural inhibition and of course are a candidate for Zeaman and Hanley's (this volume) biologically determined preference. Can we find developmental changes toward more integrality occurring with stimulus variables closer to the interface or perception and cognition? Perhaps the development of face perception is such an example.

Current literature suggests that in the perception of faces there may be a developmental trend from holistic perception to perception on the basis of elements at an early age and then from elemental to more holistic perception at a later age. Research with infants (Fagan, 1976; 1977; Fagan & Singer, 1979) suggests that, at 5 to 6 months of age, faces are discriminated on the basis of global variables such as age and sex and not on the basis of specific features such as length, texture, and shade of hair, nose profile, eye separation, or width of mouth. By 7 months of age, however, different specific features do aid discrimination of same-sex faces. This change seems analogous to the shift from integral to separable dimensions. With older children there is some evidence for an opposite kind of trend. Diamond and Carey (1977) have suggested that there is a shift in the basis of recognition of faces about the age of 10 years, with younger children relying on relatively specific and isolated features and older children using more configurational properties. Although they summarize considerable evidence in favor of this point of view, their main experiment consists of facial recognition study with various kinds of distracting cues. Subjects were asked to recognize in a pair of photographs of faces a previously seen target face. The same face in the pair might differ from the original target in terms of incidental (paraphernalia) cues such as earrings, or eye glasses, or in facial expression. Sometimes the foil in the pair would have the same paraphernalia or facial expression as the original target. The pattern of results generally supported their hypothesis. The younger children were misled by changes in paraphernalia and superficial changes in facial expression.

Another possible example of a developmental trend toward increasing sensitivity to more informative higher-order properties of stimuli could possibly be the trend toward overconstancy with age in size perception. Traditionally, this has been attributed to young subjects basing their size judgments more on the simple "separable" dimension of retinal image size, whereas older subjects' size judgments were thought to be based on some complex "integral" combination of image size and distance information. (Actually, it seems very unlikely to me that children are responding to image size as a stimulus dimension. This is a very difficult thing to do. If children are given the explicit task of matching objects on the basis of size of retinal image, they perform very poorly in comparison with adults, and even adults don't do very well on an absolute basis. A more likely cnadidate for the basis of size-constance judgments is Sedgewick's [Sedgewick, 1980] horizon ratio principle. He has shown that the horizon line cuts all equal-size objects at the same height, in fact, at eye-level height. Thus, people could use this as a basis for comparing the size of objects. If there is no horizon line in view, people might use a distant line such as the edge of a field as an approximation to the horizon in making their size judgments. This would introduce an error in the direction of over-constancy, which is often found for adults. If children were doing the same thing, the fact that they were shorter would lead to less of a tendency in the direction of over-constancy).

INTEGRATION, ACTION AND FUNCTIONS IN PERCEPTUAL AND COGNITIVE DEVELOPMENT

The examples of face perception and size constancy, possibly involving the use of higher-order stimulus دmension, implies the importance of task variables determining our perception. ‏It has been suggested that this can happen in a very general way when there is a shift in general "mode" of perception (e.g., from object perception to picture perception, from social perception to inanimate object percpetion, from sound perception to speech perception) (Pick & Saltzman, 1978). This can presumably also happen in a more restricted way when the task influences what stimulus variable is being detected within a mode. The possibility of assessing task effects on perceptual judgments is just one of a number of very interesting properties of Anderson's (this volume) model. Judgment task is one of a number of factors recently receiving considerable attention as context variables (Jenkins, 1977; Rogoff, in press). Other variables include background and tacit knowledge that one brings to a task. Anderson's scheme with his unitization principle provides a way of at least taking into account this background knowledge in the input to the integration operation. By focusing on the results of integration, Anderson is able to validate hypotheses about the inputs and, as he says, make "measurement derivative from, not prior to, substantive investigation."

It is difficult to comment comprehensively on Anderson's (this volume) model because of its theoretical breadth and the variety of empirical research conducted within its framework. However, there are a few additional remarks I would like to make on two aspects of the model. The first aspect again concerns the input to the integration operation. Anderson's model implies that the physical-stimulus dimensions (S_i) are evaluated to form corresponding psychological dimensions (s_i) and that these are then integrated. This seems to reject, or at least ignore, the possible importance of a variety of higher-order or integral dimensions such as perceptual contrast as illustrated previously and Zeaman and Hanley's (this volume) compound-stimulus dimensions. As is argued from those examples, it may well be the case that we can be very sensitive to the resultant higher-order variables and insensitive to the component variables because, in fact, they are not components. A mechanical analog for this possibility has been suggested by Runeson (1977), comparing a polar planimeter and a perceiver. The polar planimeter is a mechanical device consisting of arms and bearings and rollers used for measuring the area of ‏irregular plane figures by moving an index point on an arm around the perimeter of the shape. Although the measurement procedure involves moving the index along a line, the device cannot be used very conveniently for measuring length and would, in fact, only be able to give linear measures by calculating back from area. Similarly, the perception of size under Sedgewick's hypothesis as described previously would constitute an analogous case in human perception. In Anderson's intuitive physics, if subjects' judgments agreed with nature in producing, for example, a graph of linear fan form, it would not necessarily imply that the component S_i variables were detected and the consequent s_i variables were then integrated in the way the model implies; there is the possibility of direct sensitivity to a valid higher-order dimension.

Part of the comprehensiveness of Anderson's (this volume) model is the fact that it implicates action. Theoretically, action is implicated in how the subjective or phenomenal response function is transformed into overt response functions, whether they be conceptual functions such as numerical scales or performance skills. Empirically, action is implicated in his experiments involving a graphic response mode where subjects were able to see the relationships among their predictions and perhaps become more attentive to the functional relations among the variables. This result demonstrates, over a somewhat extended period of time, something that must be happening in ongoing perception all the time, namely, our action itself is producing some of the important stimulus information that is guiding our perception and action. Separating these as most of us are wont to do is very artificial and distorts the processes we are trying to understand. This observation has been made very cogently by Gibson (1979) and by Neisser (1976), but few of us really understand yet how to use that idea in thinking about perception, cognition, and action.

A final, most interesting aspect of Anderson's chapter concerns the implications of the type of knowledge he is dealing with (i.e., function knowledge). In thinking about the development of sensitivity to functional relationships, one wonders whether there might not be an order in which this occurs in children. For example, might we not detect monotonic direct functions first, then monotonic inverse functions, then perhaps curvilinear functions, and subsequently become sensitive to more subtle aspects of function shape, like accelerating or decelerating functions? Also related to the fact that he is dealing with this type of knowledge, Anderson is able to make the very interesting observation that when the correct function is known by the subject, information from a single trial may suffice for calibration. However, if the functional relation being considered is not correct, a single trial's information not only may not be adequate but may be deleterious to performance.

Conclusion

The observations made and the questions raised in the foregoing comments are attempts to help analyze the relationship between perceptual and cognitive development. They are only possible because of the systematic empirical work and the careful theoretical analyses as exemplified in the chapters by Anderson, Shepp, and Zeaman and Hanley.

ACKNOWLEDGMENTS

Work on this chapter was supported by Program Project Grant HD-050207 from the National Institute of Health to the Institute of Child Development of the University of Minnesota and by the Center for Research in Human Learning of the University of Minnesota. The work of the Center is supported by research grants from the National Science Foundation and from the National Institute of Child Health and Human Development.

REFERENCES

Bower, T. G. R. Heterogeneous summation in human infants. *Animal Behavior,* 1966, *14,* 395–398.

Bruner, J. S., Goodnow, J. J., & Austin, G. A. *A study of thinking.* New York: Wiley, 1956.

Brunswick, E. Distal focusing of perception: Size constancy in a representative sampling of situations. *Psychological Monographs,* 1944, *56*(1), Whole No. 254.

Bushnell, I. W. R. Modification of the externality effect in young infants. *Journal of Experimental Child Psychology,* 1979, *28,* 211–229.

Cohen, L. B., & Gelber, E. R. Infant visual memory. In L. Cohen & P. Salapatek (Eds.), *Infant perception: Form sensation to cognition: Basic visual processes* (Vol. I). New York: Academic Press, 1975.

Cornell, E. H., & Strauss, M. S. Infants' responsiveness to compounds of habituated visual stimuli. *Developmental Psychology,* 1973, *9,* 73–78.

Diamond, R., & Carey, S. Developmental changes in the representation of faces. *Journal of Experimental Child Psychology,* 1977, *23,* 1–22.

Fagan, J. F. Infants recognition of invariant faces. *Child Development,* 1976, *47,* 627–638.

Fagan, J. F. An attentional model of infant recognition. *Child Development,* 1977, *48,* 345–359.

Fagan, J. F. & Singer, L. T. The role of simple feature differences in infants' recognition of faces. *Infant Behavior and Development* 1979, *2,* 39–45.

Flavell, J. H. *The developmental psychology of Jean Piaget.* Princeton, N.J.: D. Van Nostrand, 1963.

Ganon, E. C., & Swartz, K. B. Perception of internal elements of compound figures by one-month-old infants. *Journal of Experimental Child Psychology,* 1980, *30,* 159–170.

Garner, W. R. *The Processing of Information and Structure.* Hillsdale, N.J.: Lawrence Erlbaum Associates, 1974.

Garner, W. R. Letter discrimination and identification. In A. D. Pick (Ed.), *Perception and its development.* Hillsdale, N.J.: Lawrence Erlbaum Associates, 1979.

Gibson, E. J. *Principles of perceptual learning and development.* New York: Appleton-Century-Crofts, 1969.

Gibson, E. J. The concept of affordances in development: The renaiscaence of functionalism. In W. A. Collins (Ed.), *Minnesota symposia on child psychology* (Vol. 15): *The concept of development.* Hillsdale, N.J.: Lawrence Erlbaum Associates, 1982.

Gibson, E. J., Schapiro, F., & Yonas, A. Confusion matrices for graphic patterns obtained with a latency measure. In *The analysis of reading skill: A program of basic and applied research.* (Final Report, Project No. 5-1213). Cornell University and U.S. Office of Education, 1968, 76–96.

Gibson, J. J. *The ecological approach to visual perception.* Boston: Houghton-Mifflin, 1979.

Gibson, J. J., & Gibson, E. J. Perceptual learning: Differentiation or enrichment? *Psychological Review,* 1955, *62,* 32–41.

Gliner, C. R., Pick, A. D., Pick, H. L., Jr., & Hales, J. J. A developmental investigation of visual and haptic preferences for shape and texture. *Monographs of the Society for Research in Child Development*, 1969, *34*(6), Serial No. 130.

Gregory, R. L. *Eye and brain*. New York: World University Library, 1966.

Harris, P. Cognitive development in infancy. In J. Flavell & E. Markman (Eds.), *Carmichael's manual of child psychology*. New York: Wiley, in press.

Hull, C. L. Quantitative aspects of the evolution of concepts; an experimental study. *Psychological Monographs*, 1920, *28*(1), Whole No. 123.

Jenkins, J. J. Remember that old theory of memory? Well, forget it! In R. Shaw & J. Bransford (Eds.), *Perceiving, acting, and knowing*. Hillsdale, N.J.: Lawrence Erlbaum Associates, 1977.

Johansson, G. Perception of motor and changing form. *Scandinavian Journal of Psychology*, 1964, *5*, 181–208.

Jones, R. K., & Pick, A. D. Categorization and affordances. *The Behavioral and Brain Sciences*, 1981, *4*, 292–293.

Lee, D. N. Visual information during locomotion. In R. B. MacLeod & H. L. Pick, Jr. (Eds.), *Perception: Essays in honor of James J. Gibson*. Ithaca, N.Y.: Cornell University Press, 1974.

Milewski, A. E. Infants discrimination of internal and external pattern elements. *Journal of Experimental Child Psychology*, 1976, *22*, 229–246.

Miller, D. J. Visual habituation in the human infant. *Child Development*, 1972, *43*, 481–493.

Miller, D. J., Ryan, E. B., Sinnott, J. P., & Wilson, M. A. Serial habituation in two-, three-, and four-month-old infants. *Child Development*, 1976, *47*, 341–349.

Neisser, U. *Cognition and reality*. San Francisco: Freeman, 1976.

Olum, V. Developmental differences in the perception of causality under conditions of specific instructions. *Vita Humana*, 1958, *1*, 191–203.

Pick, H. L., Jr., & Saltzman, E. Modes of perceiving and processing information. In H. L. Pick, Jr., & E. Saltzman (Eds.), *Modes of perceiving and processing information*. Hillsdale, N.J.: Lawrence Erlbaum Associates, 1978.

Rogoff, B. Approaches to integrating context and cognitive development. In M. E. Lamb & A. L. Brown (Eds.), *Advances in developmental psychology* (Vol. 2). Hillsdale, N.J.: Lawrence Erlbaum Associates, in press.

Rosch, E. On the internal structure of perceptual and semantic categories. In T. E. Moore (Ed.), *Cognitive development and the acquisition of language*. New York: Academic Press, 1973.

Rosch, E., Mervis, C. B., Gray, W. D., Johnson, D., & Boyes-Braem, P. Basic objects in natural categories. *Cognitive Psychology*, 1976, *8*, 382–349.

Runeson, S. On the possibility of "smart" perceptual mechanisms. *Scandinavian Journal of Psychology*, 1977, *18*, 172–179.

Salapatek, P., & Banks, M. S. Sensory assessment: Vision. In F. D. Minifie & L. L. Lloyd (Eds.), *Communicative and cognitive abilities—early behavioral assessment*. Baltimore: University Park Press, 1978.

Sedgewick, H. A. *Perceiving spatial layout: The ecological approach*. Paper presented at the meetings of the American Psychological Association, Montreal, Quebec, Canada, September 1980.

Shepp, B. E. From perceived similarity to dimensional structure: A new hypothesis about perceptual development. In E. Rosch & B. B. Lloyd (Eds.), *Cognition and Categorization*. Hillsdale, N.J.: Lawrence Erlbaum Associates, 1978.

Smith, L. B., & Kemler, D. G. Developmental trends in free classification: Evidence for a new conceptualization of perceptual development. *Journal of Experimental Child Psychology* 1977, *24*, 279–298.

Smith, L. B., & Kemler, D. G. Levels of experienced dimensionality in children and adults. *Cognitive Psychology* 1978, *10*, 502–532.

Wohlwill, J. F. Developmental studies of perception. *Psychological Bulletin*, 1960, *57*, 249–288.

11 Commentary on the Development of Perception and Cognition

Eleanor J. Gibson
Cornell University

Introduction

My comments on the chapters and discussion of the Conference are divided into three parts, organized as follows: (1) my own views on perception and how it develops; (2) comments on the three chapters I was invited to review specifically; and (3) a more general comment on views expressed by more than one participant and the way I would characterize the conference as a whole. A brief statement of my views on perception and how it develops is essential because they differ considerably from all of those expressed in the conference; what I have to say about the chapters can only be understood in the light of them.

AN ECOLOGICAL APPROACH TO PERCEPTUAL DEVELOPMENT

In my view, *perception* is obtaining information about the environment and oneself in it; the function of perception is keeping in touch with the environment and guiding action in it.[1] This involves a continuous monitoring of what is happening and how we are doing. Perception begins with exploration, that is, a search for invariants and order in events and for affordance of objects and places.

---

[1]These ideas follow closely from *The Ecological Approach to Visual Perception* by James J. Gibson (1979). They are necessarily abbreviated here. The application to development and developmental research has been described in detail by E. J. Gibson and E. Spelke in "Development of Perception," a chapter in the revised *Carmichael's Manual of Child Psychology* (Ed. by P. Mussen) in press.

There is information for these invariants and affordances in the ambient array of stimulation, and the information at any given time specifies its sources—the events and places and objects in the environment. Perception of these places, events, and so on is direct, because the sources are specified by the information in the array that is available to the perceiver, who need not invent or construct them. An active perceiver may (or may not) discover the invariants and affordances that are available; as they are acted on new information is provided to be explored and to guide further action. This is a theory of an active perceiver in a world of ongoing events that are continuously monitored, rather than a theory of static snapshots that must be integrated.

What is to be perceived in this environment are the surfaces and layout of the world and events in it (changes in the surface layout). There are also, in our world, representations of places and things and events, and characters that stand for them and properties of them. These last, when perceived, do not constitute a case of direct perception of the world. The perception is mediated by pictures or printed symbols like letters and words. There is first-hand (direct) perception of some affordances in this case (writing affords reading) but second-hand perception, too—the meaning the writer was trying to portray, or the order he or she was trying to embody in the display. It is important to mention this distinction, because most of the material presented in the tasks discussed at this conference is of this latter kind. The fact that they are "tasks" is important, too. In everyday life we observe what goes on around us spontaneously and in accord with our plans and intentions. In the tasks given subjects in the research presented in the chapters of this volume, very specific constraints are imposed by the experimenter, including the actions to be executed by the subject—normally a yes or no decision.

Perceptual development is characterized by exploration and a search for invariants and affordances. As they are discovered, perception is differentiated and increasingly distinguished by embedded and superordinate structure. The developmental change can be described not only as increasingly differentiated but also an increasingly economical, as perceptual learning goes on in particular situations or specific tasks. Economy applies to the use of embedded structure at a superordinate level or of any order in the array that has utility for adaptive action.

Perceptual learning does not require reinforcement as learning theories of the forties demanded; detecting the invariant, the order, the affordance in the event is itself reinforcing and the differentiation thus achieved is not lost. "Differentiated perception" is not a "mode of perceiving" but a change in what is perceived. It does not mean perceiving parts but perceiving embedded relations in the array. It is whole and unified (as perception under normal conditions always is). The caricature of "the smoker" is useful for illustrating this point (see Fig. 11.1). When first viewed, it looks to most people like a collection of bits of Chinese characters, but as we explore it, we quickly discover order and

FIG. 11.1 From E. G. Boring, H. S. Langfeld, and H. P. Weld. *Psychology*. New York: Wiley, 1935.

structure in the array and perceive its affordances as a face. Our perception of it has not become less unified or whole, if anything more so—but it has become differentiated at the same time. Furthermore, once the affordance and embedded relations have been detected, they are instantly perceived on a later exposure, not forgotten or overlooked. Perception has become more selective, one might say. But neither is it true to say that at some stage perception is nonselective. It seems to be selective in some ways at least, in even the youngest subjects we have studied. Consider E. Spelke's experiments (1979) in which infants observe movies of two events presented simultaneously before them, equally available to look at. When the sound track for one of them is played in a central location, the infant does not look equally back and forth but looks first and longer at the one specified in sound. Perception is exploratory, but the tendency to search for order results, whenever possible, in unification and economy. What is selected, perceptually, depends on what has utility for the task, if there is a set task, and on what brings order, unity, and perceived affordances in everyday perception.

COMMENTS ON CHAPTERS BY GARNER, KEMLER, AND WOLFORD AND FOWLER

Garner

Garner's theme (Chapter 1, this volume), as the title states, is conceived from the information processing view of perception. This view, prominent in today's experimental literature, is in many ways opposed to the view that I have expressed, especially in seeking to define processing levels or stages, and in the displays and highly constrained tasks that characterize the research. As Garner explicitly says, the "research has been focused on the nature of the dimensions that generate the stimuli we use in our experiments [p. 1]." Dimensions are assumed from the start. They derive from a kind of order in the array that we are equipped to perceive. The dimensions considered are all ones that can be displayed on paper or a television screen.

The tasks are very constrained as to what the subject must do. He or she may be asked to classify according to a small number of alternatives or to respond *same* or *different*. He or she is not going anywhere or performing anything. This is a kind of microcosm, a segment cut off from the everyday stream of behavior; an elegant kind of research that may or may not tell us about perceiving under natural conditions.

The question Garner is asking is whether the dimensions he and other information processors have chosen to study are treated differently by a human adult perceiver, some of them having a kind of privileged status or priority role with respect to others. He considers two types of interaction involving stimulus dimensions: (1) those involving asymmetry of a process without any necessary asymmetry in the logical structure of the stimuli; and (2) those involving asymmetry in the logical structure of the stimulus set without any necessary expectation of processing asymmetry. Because he is looking for an interaction, this is a very difficult distinction for the reader to comprehend. Surely, the interaction must implicate both dimensional relations and whatever processes are going on. The processes chosen as headings for the first type are selective attention, response interference, and name encoding. Why these processes? I assumed at first that they were considered different levels of process, presumably separate and independent, going on in stages like a flow chart and that they were presumed to account for the various asymmetries, which would be shown to be uniquely related to them as varying levels. As I read on, this idea did not work out. The three processes refer to task parameters, used as criteria for determining asymmetry in an experiment.

For example, when certain dimensions are combined, selective attention is sometimes possible for one but not for the other. Experiments are described with pitch and consonant sounds; one can attend to pitch and ignore variations in consonant sounds but not vice versa. Pitch is thus presumably processed at a lower level. Other pairs of dimensions are considered, like color and form and location and orientation, and evidence is cited for asymmetric selective attention. There is little speculation about why it should occur or what the processes at different levels actually are.

Asymmetries may also show up as interference, for example, when number value and numerosity occur in conflicting combinations, or position (up–down) and direction of an arrow. Absolute position wins over words and thus "seems to play a more basic or fundamental role than those dimensions whose meaning is derived and arbitrary [p. 12]." Physical structure versus name results in asymmetries when physical identity, length, name, and number system (Roman or Arabic) are compared in a same–different task, leading to the conclusion that physical dimensions interfere with arbitrarily defined symbolic ones and are processed at a lower level. I find it difficult to see what purpose it serves to type these results as due to asymmetries in processing rather than to structure of the stimulus set, especially because I do not know what processes are meant when levels of them are referred to. Perhaps I am missing the point of the processing—stimulus-structure distinction.

The second part of Garner's chapter has to do with asymmetries in stimulus structure and takes up two types, part–whole asymmetry and contingent dimensions. I was glad to find that "there is no single principle about wholes being processed before parts or parts being processed before wholes [p. 22]." The conclusion fits my own understanding: that perception is always of something unitary, but there is usually embedded structure there to be differentiated. Differentiation is relational; the whole is not lost by perceiving structural relations. If there is a "processing" difference, it is not one of "which comes first." But it seems obvious that instructions for the tasks used in the experiments described could easily be altered so as to yield a priority for either whole or part. For that matter, the parts are themselves perfectly good wholes in the sense of being meaningful entities, and I doubt that their relationship to other parts would be totally unperceived, whatever the instructions.

The work on contingent dimensions is very interesting, quite aside from Garner's original question. Order imposed by contingent relations in a task provides a structure that offers the opportunity for more economical processing, if it is picked up. Nested dimensions or potential "rule-giving" dimensions can reduce uncertainty; detection of such relations is of great utility. Whether some dimensions are inherently better, in the sense of being more effective in a primary or a rule-giving role, seems to me less important than the fact that the subjects in these experiments were able to perform the rather esoteric tasks efficiently, making use of conditional structure in accordance with task demands. It seems, too, that the demands of a given task would interact with the dimensional structure, so that status of a dimension would be at least to some extent task-dependent. But perhaps certain dimensions (e.g., color and location) are favored channels for pickup of structural relations in a display, as Garner would like to conclude. If that be the case, it seems as though developmental research would be a good place to look for evidence and certainly relevant experiments exist, as pointed out in Chapter 4.

It seems to me quite possible that some aspects of stimulus information have a privileged, built-in status as the perceiver searches for order in the world, but is it right to pick out "dimensions" like color, form, and pitch when looking for primitives of this kind? Should we not consider what has most utility to the organism for acting effectively and adaptively? Properties like rigidity of surfaces, palpability of fruits, stampeding vibrations and thunderous noises, and sharpness of edges have affordances for behaving adaptively. The human species might well have evolved perceptual systems that are effective for picking up these multimodally specified properties, whereas properties like "form" and spots on the top or bottom of a paper are so abstract in themselves that it seems intuitively unlikely that constraints of survival in the human habitat could have singled them out.

The research Garner cites impressed me most, in the end, by the striking economy of perceptual processing presented. I think a major trend in perceptual development is increasing economy of perception—the discovery and use of invariants and nested structure—and it is a revelation to see how adaptive perceiving can be in even the most artifical and complex laboratory task.

Kemler

Kemler (Chapter 3, this volume) contrasts with Garner in being primarily concerned with development but, like Garner, she is concerned with dimensions, particularly dimensional learning tasks that involve partitioning an array. The tasks given the children in her experiments require classification. She is asking on what the children base their classifications and whether the basis for classifying changes developmentally. Her answer, generally speaking, is that young children classify on the basis of overall similarity, treating stimuli as undifferentiated wholes, whereas older children treat stimuli as "analyzed sets of dimensional components." They divide up the array, looking for differences that will partition it, basing the division on abstract dimensions with criterial attributes.

Sometimes there is the implication that it is perception that is differentiated, as when she says that younger children perceive holistically but adults and older children do not. Early perception is presumably global and nonselective, whereas adult perception is analytic and dimensional. Masters (1981), in an *Annual Review* article, comments on Kemler's hypothesis that there is a trend from perceived similarity to perceived dimensional structure, that "children would need to perceive dimensional structure in stimuli before being able to acquire the skill of selective attention [p. 112]." I am not sure that Kemler would accept this addendum to her hypothesis, but it evidently is likely to be interpreted this way, that little children must somehow do dimensional learning before selective attention will be available. This proposition is not only logically indefensible, as I see it, but is in any case wrong, because there is now excellent evidence that quite young infants attend selectively (Bahrick, Walker, & Neisser, 1981).

I am also bothered by the implication, perhaps not intended, that adult perception is not of wholes. I return again to the point that perception is not of wholes or parts but is typically unified. Perception that is differentiated is no less whole and unified (cf. the example of the "smoker"). Differentiation does not mean perceiving parts but implies perceiving embedded relations, a structured whole. Differentiated and undifferentiated perceiving are not "modes of processing" that can be learned as skills and turned on or off as strategies. The difference is a difference in what is perceived. I do not believe that young children perceive via an undifferentiated mode but rather that there are a lot of things they have not yet learned to perceive. Perhaps dimensions are one of them, because they are, as I think of them, abstracted over a number of items, potentially quantifiable, and exhibit relations of transitivity, as do for example weight, height, volume, or brightness. I doubt that they are often directly perceived as such in daily life. I think what we perceive directly are meanings—what my husband (Gibson, 1979) called affordances. We perceive that a car is coming toward us and we had better not pass or that a cookie looks good to eat. We don't often analyze the car's speed and distance or the cookie's dimensions of thickness, color, etc., although these properties enter into the perceived affordances.

Kemler points out that young children are indeed sensitive to differences between two objects, like a big cookie and a little one, but she says that is distinct from the issue of whether children appreciate the nature of the differences they perceive. In my sense, I don't think so; let children choose between the cookies and they will take the big one every time. But that is not what Kemler means: she says that "When differentiation is complete in Gibson's sense, . . . it may still be incomplete in the current sense that analysis does not occur . . .[p. 83]." I think we can resolve this apparent difference of opinion peaceably. Young children's perceptions are differentiated in the sense of being meaningful and guiding behavior one way or another, but classifying by dimensions, when no action except finishing a task assigned by an experimenter is involved, is something else again.

Most of the research cited by Kemler is not about perception but about classifying things according to some kind of rule. And I think there is the tacit assumption that bases of classifications must be verbalizable by the child if differentiation in her sense is to be possible. Consider her example of a pseudo-conservation task: The experimenter shows a child two squares of paper of the same size, asking the child if they are the same size; then one paper is colored black and the child is asked if they are still the same size. Many say no. This is a verbal task presenting no affordances for action. She says that young children have a tendency to interpret any difference as evidence of the difference that is queried. Why not? The query may seem to the child to prompt the answer. I doubt that this tells us anything about what the child perceives. She says again, that "a child might look to see that this particular act of cutting did not change color without knowing the general rule that cutting always leaves color intact [p. 86]" and thus answer correctly. It may be, she says, elicited by the question rather than being a "spontaneous tendency derived from everyday activity [p. 86]." But observing the color is surely as spontaneous as knowing a rule about cutting.

Conceptual knowledge is involved here when the rule is known. To prevent the child from simply perceiving the result, Kemler performs the cutting in such a way that the effects of the cutting were out of view of the child and asks him to guess "What does my piece of paper look like now? [p. 87]." I am not sure where this leaves us. Differentiated perception, as Kemler distinguishes it from so-called holistic perception, is based on knowledge of component property relations referred to as dimension, but are we talking about perception?

Developmentally, what accounts for the change toward more "analytic processing"? Kemler suggests that higher-order control processes are involved. More analysis occurs when the task calls for deliberate problem-solving activities. Experiments with rule-learning tasks are cited to bear this out. It does seem to be the case that children in our culture, at least, learn very early to conform to rules and to classify by dimensions. When they know that there are categories to be learned and proceed to do so intentionally, they use criterial attributes in a very rulelike fashion. "The requirement to discover a rule (or even the implicit requirement to apply a rule) prods individuals to be analytic [p. 98]." I am reminded of the cross-cultural research of Michael Cole and his colleagues (Cole & Scribner, 1974), and I wonder how much of this is culture-specific. Many adults in other cultures cannot perform "concrete operations" like those called for in the conservation task (Dasen, 1975, 1977). I also wonder if this training affects children's perception at all as they develop. I suppose it does, because it presumably biases them toward discovery of some invariants rather than others.

The conclusion that "in the course of normal perceptual and cognitive development the balance shifts from holistic to analytic [p. 101]" seems to me deceptively simple. I cannot accept it as true for perception without some amendment. And if we are to understand the development of classification, I believe that the tasks and requirements presented and the expectations of the culture need to be given a larger share of the story.

I have often stressed that as perception develops, it becomes more differentiated, a point on which Kemler and I are agreed. What is perceived changes as embedded structure is detected. The tasks given children and the values stressed by their culture play a role in this change and so, I think, children's own inherent cognitive motivation as they search for order and invariance in the world. This search may result in the discovery of dimensions useful for performing a classification task, but as Smith (1981) says, "Specifically, the apparent developmental trend from the apprehension of overall similarity to the apprehension of separate dimensional relations may be restricted to the simple stimulus variation prevalent in most laboratory tasks [p. 812]." The task and its context surely have a profound influence in determining whether and what kind of dimensional analysis takes place, as Kemler makes clear. But there are other kinds of differentiated structure and embedded relations that we develop the ability to perceive, in speech and music, for instance, and in events like games. Dimensional analysis does not seem relevant for understanding how they come to be perceived.

Wolford and Fowler

Chapter 9 (this volume) is concerned with accounting for the difference between good and poor readers (poor readers who are not impaired in some overall fashion). After comparing their performance on a number of tasks, Wolford and Fowler propose a "partial-information hypothesis"—that good and poor readers are differentially impaired in performance when the information needed to respond is incomplete. For example, poor readers are less able to name letters when they are incompletely presented. Their errors on recognition tasks are apt to be random, whereas those of good readers are based on use of similar attributes. The partial-information hypothesis is further refined by Wolford and Fowler, and I would like to refine it still further by making explicit what I think are four separate hypotheses.

The first is stated quite explicitly: Poor readers have difficulty in perceiving a stimulus as a set of attributes of component parts. This hypothesis is defended by letter-sorting studies for which scaling analyses showed that good readers made superior similarity sorts. The idea seems closely related to Kemler's developmental hypothesis that younger children tend to perceive unanalyzed wholes rather than differentiated dimensions.

A second hypothesis, distinct from the first, is that good readers are better able to use partial information when it is useful for the task, that is, to detect its utility and put it to use. Wolford and Fowler cite an experiment by Tighe, Tighe, and Schecter in which category membership of words is redundant with an instrumental discriminatory response required of their subjects, so that discrimination could be made more economically on the basis of the category rather than the word's identity. Children knew the categories but did not use them, whereas adults did. This task is reminiscent of some of Garner's where contingent relations (conditional structure) within a task were potentially facilitative. Adults performing in his experiments did make effective use of conditional structure. Perceiving attributes is not the same thing as perceiving that they have a particular utility, what they afford for performing an assigned new task.

Both good and poor readers are aware of the semantic attributes of words even though the poor readers seem to be less able to abstract them in the further sense of perceiving the utility of a shared semantic attribute. But poor readers, Wolford and Fowler suggest, may become aware of shared semantic attributes of concepts named by words earlier than they recognize shared phonetic and graphic attributes of the words (the third hypothesis). In a study of recognition memory, they included foils in the recognition test that were confusable with target items in meaning, or phonetic or graphic features. Adults and children who were good readers made errors attributable to semantic and graphic confusability (though not phonetic); children who were poor readers made errors due to semantic confusability but not graphic. These results bear out their hypothesis that the poor readers are more sensitive to semantic attributes than to graphic. Reading achievement did appear to be associated, however, with errors due to shared category membership of targets and foils. The results are interpreted as reflecting different tendencies to attend either to "token" identities of words or on the other hand to their component features.

Although this interpretation is reasonable, it seems wise to observe caution in generalizing it, because there is evidence that attention to different features of words may be to some degree task specific (Gibson, 1971). I am introducing this as a fourth hypothesis. A developmental experiment by Condry, McMahon-Rideout, and Levy (1979) using a tachistoscopic matching task found that second-graders were easily able to attend selectively, upon demand, to varied features of words (graphic, phonetic, and semantic). The graphic task was the easiest for them and graphic distractors were highly effective when the task was selective for sound. Selecting for rhyme and meaning were more difficult in that order, for second-graders, but leveled out developmentally. Generalizing from experiments to the normal reading situation is not a straightforward matter. Young children and possibly even poor readers are able to attend to all features of words so far discussed when they are told to, though they may not do so spontaneously or may be susceptible to interference from other features.

Task dependency in the use of attributes is not in conflict with Wolford and Fowler's hypotheses, and indeed ease of shifting attention to different attributes of words might differentiate good and poor readers. Their study requiring good and poor readers to generate words that resemble a sample word in graphic, phonetic, semantic, or categorical features showed the poor readers inferior to the good readers overall, although less in the graphic and semantic conditions. It is notable, however, that the poor readers could perform the task and generate a number of words even on the more difficult phonetic and categorical dimensions.

The hypothesis is suggested that high association might account for the poor readers' better performance when semantic rather than graphic, phonetic, or categorical attributes of words were the appropriate feature to be attended to. I would favor a different explanation. The principal affordance of words is for communication, where meaning is all that matters. This is how children learn about words from the start, in a context where the word's meaning is obvious. There is every reason why this attribute of a word should be privileged and accessed easily by young and less proficient readers. A majority of the reading errors of children in the early first grade are meaningful and acceptable in context before they show the influence of graphic similarity (Biemiller, 1970). (One might wonder, now, how "physical" dimensions like graphic attributes have come to be more privileged dimensions than so-called name codes for Garner's more sophisticated subjects. Is it the result of task constraints or of years of education in a special kind of culture?) Generating an appropriately restricted word in Wolford and Fowler category condition and selecting a synonym in the Condry et al. (1979) experiment seem to impose a more abstract requirement on the young reader than does the simple awareness of the word's affordance. Perhaps this is the same point that Wolford and Fowler are making.

The final, favored hypothesis of Wolford and Fowler is that good and poor readers differ when the task requires focusing on "individual attributes of stimuli," a strategy that is thought to be attained developmentally. The hypothesis is consistent with Kemler's and Shepp's views. Applying it to individual differences in a skill like reading recalls to me the distinction between "reflective" and "impulsive" cognitive styles (Kagan, 1965; Kagan, Rossman, Day, Albert, and Phillips, 1964), although the authors do not mention it.

Now, a crucial question: Do individual differences in focusing on attributes or dimensions of words have a possible causal role in determining who the good and poor readers are going to be? Does use of partial information, because the child detects a word's attributes, explain superior reading performance? Or, as Wolford and Fowler themselves ask, is detection and use of a word's features in laboratory tasks of the kind we have been discussing a result of being a good reader? I find the second alternative as plausible as the first.

SOME GENERAL COMMENTS

In the end, what was this conference about? It was certainly more narrowly focused than the title *Development of Perception and Cognition* suggests. Looking over the chapters, it seems to have centered on dimensional learning (learning to attend to dimensions?) and learning of categories. The theory is based not on a theory of perception but on learning theory, though not a new learning theory, so far as I can see. It refers back, rather, to what Sheldon White called the "Learning Theory Tradition and Child Psychology" in the 1970 edition of Carmichael's *Manual of Child Psychology*. White said then, "The most significant programmatic approach of American psychology, the stimulus–response tradition, still remains an identifiable approach among psychologists who study children [p. 657]." He described it as a waning tradition, saying that we were in the midst of the second American revolution. The learning theory tradition at that time was characterized by the use of paradigms embodying regularized techniques for basic research and by application of theories derived from Hull and

Spence that were conceived during the 1930's and 1940's. The targets for research were discrimination problems, transposition problems, and reversal–nonreversal shift problems. Innovations in the theory were visible mainly as the introduction of mediation theories and dimension-selecting mechanisms. Response-produced cues, verbal mediation, and attentional responses were permissible within this system, but no one ever talked about perception. Now it appears to be possible to talk about perception. but otherwise I see little change in the work stemming from this tradition, as I think most of these chapters do.

The developmental chapters are bracketed on the one hand by Garner's, which is concerned with perception but within a very specialized laboratory environment; and on the other by Medin's, which is concerned entirely with categories. Both chapters are very interesting but they say nothing about development and it is not obvious how they fit into a developmental theory of perception or cognition. It will be clear to anyone who has read this far in my comments that I want to see a true revolution. I want to see developmental studies of perception in real, everyday settings. I do not by any means want to rule out experiment, but I do not want the experiments or the theories to derive mainly from paradigms and models taken over from a psychology based on adults. I see that happening in the current literature on attention in children; paradigms from adult information-processing experiments are simply carried over and performed on school-age children. Our understanding of development and our developmental theories are advanced not one jot.

How is development thought to occur in the chapters we have been discussing? Kemler, Shepp, and Kendler all agree that there is progression to a more abstract categorical level of performance, presumed to be based on ability to use ordered dimensions for an increasingly economical classification or problem solution. Explanatory devices suggested by Kendler to underlie this change include selective encoding or attention, and hypothesis testing, which supplant nonselective encoding and incremental learning in younger children, incremental learning being an accumulation of quanta of reinforcement, as I understand it. I do not find these ideas attractive, because there is ample evidence available to show that selective attention is operating in very young infants; and because I do not believe that accumulations of reinforcement are the means of early learning, nor do I see how they lead to change. Outcomes are critical in learning, but not as increments of reinforcement. Yet there is developmental change. How does it happen? Perception does become more differentiated and cognitive functioning becomes more economical. I think there is an inherent motive to seek invariants and order in the world, even a world designed by schools and laboratory psychologists. Finding order that describes the array and links up to task demands becomes more and more effective because order in the world is embedded to different degrees and differentiation has to proceed within the hierarchical or conditional structure presented, from simple orders (perhaps mere segregation of items to start with) to deeply embedded ones; and because access within any given task to properties of order (similarities, conditionalities, etc.) becomes wider and easier as task-related affordances become generalized. In the Tighe, Tighe and Schecter experiment cited by Wolford and Fowler, the children know a lot about categories of the terms they are dealing with, but they don't as yet perceive the usefulness of this knowledge for the task as given. Affordances seem to generalize from task to task (like use of makeshift tools by adults when standard ones are not available), even as order is being differentiated and perhaps afterward.

Kemler asks explicitly, what prompts the changing balance from holistic to analytic modes of processing in the normal course of development? I would not agree with her use of holistic in this description of what develops, but dependence on dimensions and categories certainly increases; partly, she says, because analysis into properties simply becomes easier for the child. But also, the explanation is to be found at "the level of higher-order control processes." She points out, in this connection, that the nature of the task has a powerful effect on how analytic the performance will be. A deliberate task demand for use of rules, for example, results in increased analytic performance and classification by dimensions even in kindergarten children. I believe our culture (school environments especially) often makes such demands. Kemler suggests that spontaneous analysis and dimensional classification is prompted by "self-conscious, reflective modes of processing elicited by a rule-learning situation [p. 95]"—maybe a kind of metacognition characteristic of our culture, fostered especially during the early school years. The idea is very plausible and a valuable insight, but it does not account for all development. Kemler comments that analysis into properties affords flexibility because classes can be differently constituted for different purposes. I agree. Different classes or categories have different affordances and they can be related in different ways to different tasks. Learning affordances is an important aspect of perceptual development and I expect the study of it to give us insights about development.

It may be that the tasks used in the experiments cited in these chapters show up a kind of developmental lag in attention as compared with attending to directly perceptible properties and events in the world, because they all require what I referred to earlier as mediated perception of printed characters and figures inscribed or depicted on a two-dimensional surface. Their affordances are not so obvious and a second phase of attentional development may ensue as children are given school experience. Because our culture is heavily oriented toward the printed word and toward following instructions, it could well be argued that studying selective attention to words in instructed tasks is of equal importance to understanding development of spontaneous selective attention to real events and objects.

It is inelegant to wind up with a definitional criticism, but I am going to make one that may be considered so. All of these chapters seem to me to use the term *stimulus* in an inexcusably loose and careless way. What is a stimulus, anyhow?

What in the world is a "multidimensional stimulus"? Houses, people, and chairs, I am sure everyone would agree, are not stimuli. Surely, neither are drawings on paper and black circles and triangles of different sizes on white cardboard. According to Osgood (1953), "A stimulus may be defined as that form of physical energy that activates a receptor [p. 12]"; or for a more recent but longer definition, see the *Handbook of Perception* (Vol. 1) (Carterette & Friedman, 1974, p. 111). These are commonly accepted definitions, I believe, although they can be quarreled with in some respects (Gibson, 1960). I think there is something contradictory in talking about analyzing a stimulus into dimensions; and accepting contradictions is bad for straight thinking. In thinking about perception, we need to distinguish three levels of description: the world to be perceived, its objects, surfaces, events, and layout; the ambient array in a medium that provides information for our perceptual systems; and finally what is perceived—describable sometimes in terms of properties and dimensions, but most directly as what something affords for behavior.

REFERENCES

Bahrick, L. E., Walker, A. S., & Neisser, U. Selective looking by infants. *Cognitive Psychology,* 1981, *13,* 377–390.

Biemiller, A. J. The development of the use of graphic and contextual information as children learn to read. *Reading Research Quarterly,* 1970, *6,* 75–96.

Boring, E. G., Langfeld, H. S., & Weld, H. P. *Psychology: A factual textbook.* New York: Wiley, 1935.

Carterette, E. C., & Friedman, M. P. (Eds.). *Handbook of perception* (Vol. I). New York: Academic Press, 1974.

Cole, M., & Scribner, S. *Culture and thought: A Psychological introduction.* New York: Wiley, 1974.

Condry, S. M., McMahon-Rideout, M., & Levy, A. A. A developmental investigation of selective attention to graphic, phonetic, and semantic information in words. *Perception & Psychophysics,* 1979, *25,* 88–94.

Dasen, P. R. Concrete operational development in three cultures. *Journal of Cross-Cultural Psychology,* 1975, *6,* 156–172.

Dasen, P. R. Are cognitive processes universal? A contribution to cross-cultural Piagetian psychology. In N. Warren (Ed.), *Studies in cross-cultural psychology* (Vol. 1). London: Academic Press, 1977.

Gibson, E. J. Perceptual learning and the theory of word perception. *Cognitive Psychology,* 1971, *2,* 351–368.

Gibson, E. J., & Spelke, E. The development of perception. In P. H. Mussen (Ed.), *Carmichael's Manual of Child Psychology,* Vol. 3, Third Edition. New York: Wiley, in press.

Gibson, J. J. The concept of the stimulus in psychology. *The American Psychologist,* 1960, *15,* 694–703.

Gibson, J. J. *The ecological approach to visual perception.* Boston: Houghton-Mifflin, 1979.

Kagan, J. Reflection-impulsivity and reading ability in primary grade children. *Child Development,* 1965, *36,* 609–628.

Kagan, J., Rossman, B. L., Day, D., Albert, J., & Phillips, W. Information processing in the child: Significance of analytic and reflective attitudes. *Psychological Monographs,* 1964, *78,* (Whole No. 578).

Masters, J. A. Developmental psychology. In M. R. Rosenzweig & L. W. Porter (Eds.), *Annual review of psychology, 1981* (Vol. 32). Palo Alto, Calif.: Annual Reviews, Inc., 1981.

Osgood, C. E. *Method and theory in experimental psychology.* New York: Oxford University Press, 1953.

Smith, L. B. Importance of the overall similarity of objects for adults' and children's classifications. *Journal of Experimental Psychology: Human Perception and Performance,* 1981, *7,* 811–824.

Spelke, E. S. Perceiving bimodally specified events in infancy. *Developmental Psychology,* 1979, *15,* 626–636.

White, S. H. The learning theory tradition and child psychology. Pp. 657-701 In P. H. Mussen (Ed.), *Carmichael's Manual of Child Psychology* (Vol. 1). New York: Wiley, 1970.

12

Categorization, Perception, and Learning

William K. Estes
Harvard University

Introduction

Like many other contributors to this volume, I am concerned with the way the three terms in my title enter into an account of the way we learn to classify objects or events on the basis of sensory evidence. The long-term goal of research bearing on this question is presumably to help us understand how, for example, people come to recognize samples of speech sounds as instances of linguistic categories (phoneme, syllable, word) or to identify objects as exemplars of familiar categories.

Both relevant experimental research and efforts toward theory construction have turned on four questions: (1) What sensory evidence is used as a basis for natural categories? (2) How is the sensory input processed to yield units susceptible to cognitive operations? (3) What determines the character of natural categories that prove to have broad generality across individuals and even cultures? (4) Given the existence of functionally significant categories in an individual's environment, how does the individual learn to distinguish members of different categories and associate them with different appropriate actions?

All of these questions and the phenomena they refer to are intricately interrelated in theory and doubtless also in practice, but nonetheless they are associated with relatively distinct bodies of research. The interrelationships of categorization, perception, and learning are perhaps most clearly at issue in relation to question 4—the focus of this chapter, as it has been for a number of other chapters in this volume, including, in particular, those of Kemler, Kendler, Medin, and Spiker and Cantor.

Looking back over some 50 years of research on this question, one can identify three principal paradigms that have been used to study learning relative to perceptual categories. In the early part of that period, nearly all research was conducted in the first of these paradigms, which may be termed classical discrimination learning. From the experimenter's standpoint, just two stimuli are to be discriminated, for example, a high versus a low tone, a dark versus a light gray stimulus card, and the learner is differentially reinforced for assigning two alternative responses correctly to the two stimuli or for responding to one and withholding response to the other. Thus what is to be learned is defined by a rule that is entirely unambiguous from the standpoint of the experimenter but that may be ambiguous from the standpoint of the subject.

The second paradigm, associated with the literature on concept identification and hypothesis selection, includes two sets or classes of stimuli that are to be mapped onto two alternative responses (typically category labels). The correct mapping is unambiguously defined by a rule that is initially known to the experimenter and can be discovered by the learner.

The third category, and one of special interest in contemporary cognitive psychology, is associated with natural categories and prototype formation. Typically the learning situation involves the categorical assignment of stimuli, in some cases indefinitely large in number, belonging to two classes or collections with the property that family resemblance is greater within than between the classes but class membership is not definable in terms of any explicit rules specified by the experimenter or discoverable by the learner.

In the following pages I first sketch an outline of the history of research and theoretical development with regard to each of these three paradigms and then discuss some current issues and research directions.

DEVELOPMENT OF THE THREE MAJOR PARADIGMS

Classical Discrimination Learning

Basic Phenomena. The initial problems for theoretical interpretation are a set of phenomena observed in both classical conditioning and trial-and-error learning. In the former case, exemplified by some of the experiments of Pavlov (1927), a dog might be conditioned by pairing an unconditioned stimulus with a particular tone and withholding the unconditioned stimulus upon presentation of its semitone. The typical result was that the animal would first begin to salivate upon presentation of either tone, the magnitude of response to both increasing over early trials; then, as reinforced and unreinforced trials continued in a haphazard sequence, the magnitude of the conditioned response would continue to increase in the presence of the conditioned stimulus (the tone) and decline in the presence of the other stimulus (the semitone). The speed and final accuracy of discrimination typically depend on the similarity of the stimuli, perfect discrimination not being achievable with very similar stimuli.

In the trial-and-error situation, an animal, most often a laboratory rat, might obtain reward in the form of food or relief from an electric shock by jumping through a stimulus card imprinted with one stimulus and fail to obtain a reward upon jumping through a simultaneously displayed card imprinted with another stimulus (the stimuli being, e.g., a large and a small circle). Properties of learning are similar to those of classical conditioning except that in the trial-and-error situation it often proves possible to train animals to virtually perfect discriminations even between stimuli so similar that initially generalization is almost complete.

Discrimination as a Growth Process: Excitation–Inhibition Theory.   The theory that set the standard of rigor for the analysis of discrimination learning was that of Spence (1936, 1937). In Spence's theory a stimulus present on rewarded trials accrues an increasing excitatory tendency to evoke the rewarded response, whereas a stimulus present on nonrewarded trials increasingly tends to inhibit the nonrewarded response. Both excitation and inhibition generalize in an orderly fashion to similar stimuli, the extent of generalization being a smooth decreasing function of similarity. The formation of a discrimination is the essentially mechanistic result of a series of differentially reinforced trials on which both excitation and inhibition generalize from each of the positive and negative stimuli to the other but in such a way that the net excitatory strength of the positive stimulus gradually exceeds that of the negative stimulus until the corresponding response tendencies are sufficiently different to yield behavioral evidence of the discrimination.

Spence's (1936, 1937) theory was regarded by some of his contemporaries, notably Lashley (1942), as unrealistically mechanical and passive, but nonetheless it achieved some impressive successes. One of these was an account of the characteristic way in which animals tend to persevere in position habits for many trials during the early training of a discrimination and then break the position habit abruptly and begin to show progress toward mastering the discrimination. Another success was an account of transposition. An example of transposition is the observation that an animal trained under a routine in which a dark gray stimulus, G_1, is rewarded and a lighter gray stimulus, G_2, is unrewarded tends, on a final test in which the lighter stimulus, G_2, is paired with a still lighter one, G_3, to approach G_2 and avoid G_3, indicating that it has, in effect, learned a relative discrimination between darker and lighter shades of gray.

The dominance of Spence's (1936, 1937) theory for some 20 years is understandable in view of its specific successes in accounting for classical laboratory findings on discrimination together with the fact that its basic conception of discrimination learning as a growth process that is, the gradual accrual of excitatory and inhibitory tendencies over trials, fit well with experimenters' intuitions regarding the learning process in simple classical and instrumental conditioning situations typified by very slow development of discriminations, often extending over hundreds of trials.

Discrimination as a Categorizing Process.   By the early 1950s the center of gravity of research on discrimination began to shift toward higher organisms, first monkeys in the extremely influential work of Harlow (1949) and then human subjects (reviewed in Neimark & Estes, 1967, and Trabasso & Bower, 1968). Concurrently there appeared a new variant of stimulus–response learning theory based on the conception of learning as sampling and categorizing rather than a simple growth process (Estes, 1950, 1959). This ''statistical'' model seemed in some respects better attuned to the task of representing the characteristically more rapid and insightful processes of discrimination and classification in human learners.

In the statistical model it is assumed that each of the stimuli to be discriminated in the given situation, together with its background context, presents to the learner a population of aspects or constituents only a portion of which is sampled and available to enter into learning on any one trial. During learning, each of these aspects or constituents, termed *stimulus elements,* generates in the learner's memory system a corresponding unit that may be termed a *memory element.* A typical discrimination learning situation, thus, takes the form shown in Fig. 12.1. The two stimuli to be discriminated, *A* and *B,* are represented as two sets of elements, some of which are common to the two stimuli. At the beginning of learning, as shown at the top of the diagram, the corresponding memory elements are in a null state, that is, unassociated with either of the categories. However, as learning proceeds, elements sampled on trials when *A* is the correct categorization are tagged as belonging to the *A* category and those occurring on *B* trials as members of the *B* category, as shown at the bottom of the diagram.

The reason why difficulty with discrimination is related to similarity is that elements in the overlap of the two sets necessarily constitute a mixture of elements tagged for *A* and for *B* even at the asymptote of learning. Thus when one of the stimuli, say *A,* is presented, and the individual samples its available elements, the sample will include a mixture with most of the elements tagged for *A* but some also tagged for *B*. Because, in the model, the probability of the learner's categorizing the *A* stimulus correctly is proportional to the fraction of sampled elements tagged for *A* rather than *B,* this original form of the model accounts for a number of facts concerning rates of discrimination learning as a function of proportions of *A* and *B* trials, and degree of similarity of the stimuli, but does not allow the prediction of ultimately perfect discrimination that is often observed in human learning and sometimes even in animal learning situations (Burke & Estes, 1957).

Several modifications of the original model were proposed to enable it to accommodate findings of perfect discrimination of similar stimuli. One of these was simply to modify the assumptions as to the relationship between the state of

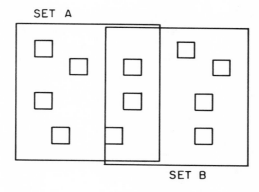

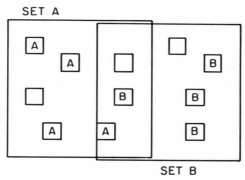

FIG. 12.1   Discrimination learning in a stimulus-sampling model. The stimuli, *A* and *B*, to be discriminated are represented by sets of aspects, or elements, that overlap in part. Initially the elements are unassociated with either stimulus in the learner's memory (signified by the small empty cells in the upper diagram), but, after some training, elements come to be categorized in memory as associated with *A* or *B* (lower diagram).

memory and the individual's choice responses (Bower, 1959; Estes, 1960; La-Berge, 1962). The common assumption of all these proposals is that, in effect, a learner when consulting memory at a point of choice engages in a "vicarious trial and error" or, in mathematical terms, "random walk" process in order to arrive at a choice. This idea has become generally accepted but goes only part way toward solving the "overlap problem" together with other phenomena that were arising in the course of concurrent research.

The Overlearning Reversal Effect.   Among the new phenomena prominent in the research of the early 1960s, one in particular proved of special theoretical importance—the so called "overlearning reversal effect" (Mackintosh, 1964;

Shepp & Turrisi, 1966). The basic observation was that when a learner is given training on a discrimination between two stimuli, A and B, with, say A positive and B negative, and then at some point undergoes a switch of conditions so that A becomes negative and B positive, learning of the new discrimination after the reversal proves under some circumstances to be faster the greater the amount of preshift training on the original A+ versus B− discrimination. This finding was of special interest for learning theorists of the period because Spence's (1936, 1937) discrimination model and its variants predicted the opposite—that is, more training on the original discrimination should yield a slower shift (because a larger differential between excitatory and inhibitory strength would have to be overcome in the postshift training). The original statistical model is not much better off, implying either no effect of degree of preshift training on speed of reversal (Burke & Estes, 1957) or a small speedup on the first reversal (LaBerge, 1959).

Dual-Process models.   In order to handle both the overlap problem and the overlearning reversal effect, investigators in both theoretical traditions found it necessary to go from the relatively simple models assuming a single basic learning process to more complex ones incorporating at least two processes operating either on different levels of organization or at successive stages of learning. In the case of statistical learning theory, the new development was introduction of an assumption of patterning or unitization (Estes, 1959) and a "mixed model" incorporating learning at the levels both of elementary memory units and higher-order units (Atkinson & Estes, 1963). The basic idea was that memory elements activated on a particular learning trial, whether they arise from the unique aspects of the stimulus presented or the aspects it has in common with the alternative stimulus, form a higher-order unit or patterned memory trace. The unit formed on a trial on which, say, A is the correct categorization will be associated only with A even though some of the constituents are common to stimuli A and B. This model provided a way of handling both the overlap problem and the overlearning reversal effect, and it also found support in some novel experiments generated in efforts to provide the model with rigorous tests (Estes & Hopkins, 1961; Estes, 1972).

It might be mentioned further that the idea that higher-order patterned or "configured" memory traces are formed under some circumstances has been independently rediscovered by more recent investigators of human verbal memory (e.g., Foss & Harwood, 1975; Ross & Bower, 1981). At the present stage of development the obvious merits of the mixed statistical model are accompanied by two important limitations. One of these is that there has yet been proposed no principled account of the way in which higher units take form. The second is that the model at present offers no explicit way of accounting for some phenomena of discrimination learning relative to stimulus dimensions that are discussed in the following.

A way of modifying the statistical model that does not involve unitization or patterning has been suggested from time to time (Bush & Mosteller, 1951; Restle, 1955), the idea in essentials being that the elements common to two stimuli to be discriminated become adapted in the course of discrimination learning so that following adaptation they simply carry a low weight in response determination. This concept does help handle the overlap problem, but experiments that test directly the idea that common cues become adapted have generally yielded negative results (Binder, 1963; Binder & Estes, 1966; Robbins, 1972). The weight of evidence seems to be that discrimination learning is not a passive process of adapting ambiguous cues but rather an active one in which advantage is taken of the most unambiguous cues available in the situation, either by a process of unitization, as in the pattern model, or by other processes of selective attention, assumed in the class of models to be considered next.

In the tradition of the excitation–inhibition model, the response to the overlearning reversal effect and related phenomena was to preserve the essentials of Spence's (1936, 1937) model but add to it the assumption that a learner's choice responses become associated with the output of stimulus analyzers (Sutherland, 1959) or with mediating or selective attentional responses (Kendler & Kendler, 1962; Lovejoy, 1968; Zeaman & House, 1963). In all of these variants, discrimination becomes a two-level process with two relatively distinct stages. At the outset of learning, the tendencies of the discriminative stimuli to evoke the choice responses are strengthened or weakened as in Spence's model, but at the same time the learner's tendency to observe relevant dimensions selectively (in the Zeaman & House model) or to label them by means of some mediating response (in Kendler and Kendler's version) is modified similarly by the effects of reward and nonreward. Consequently, over a series of trials, the learner comes to base choice responses not directly on the discriminative stimuli but only on the mediating response or the aspects to which he or she has learned to attend. Further, in all of these models except that of Kendler and Kendler (1962), it is assumed that stimulus processing is a more complex affair than conceived in the earlier theories. Rather than responding to a stimulus either as a whole or as a composite of constituent elements, the learner is conceived to analyze the stimulus in terms of attributes or dimensions, learning to confine attention to the dimensions that are relevant in the particular situation and then associating choice responses with the values on these dimensions that provide the basis for a correct categorization.

Dimensional Shifts.   A major triumph for the models based on an assumption of selective attention to stimulus dimensions was their ability to account for a cluster of findings on what were termed extradimensional versus intradimensional shifts (House & Zeaman, 1962). The essentials of the shift phenomena can be illustrated as follows. Suppose that, in an original training series, learners were required to assign an *A* response to stimulus cards containing either red triangles or red circles and a *B* response to cards containing blue triangles or blue circles, with size of the stimuli varying randomly. We would speak of an intradimensional shift, if on the achievement of some criterion of learning, conditions were switched so that the subjects were now required to assign an *A* response to yellow circles or yellow triangles and a *B* response to green circles or green triangles, with size again varying randomly. New associations would have to be formed, but the relevant dimension is color in the case of both preshift and postshift problems, so that, in terms of the two-process models, the subject need not learn a new attentional response following the shift; and thus postshift learning should be faster than preshift learning.

We would speak of an extradimensional shift if, following the same criterion of original learning, the subjects were shifted to new contingencies in which the *A* category was to be assigned to all large stimuli regardless of color or form and the *B* response to all small stimuli. In this case the subjects who had previously learned to attend selectively to color as a relevant dimension would now have to learn to attend selectively to size and thus, on the average, postshift learning would be no faster than preshift learning. This predicted difference between the two kinds of shifts was abundantly confirmed experimentally and has provided a major source of support for the models assuming a process of selective attention to dimensions (Estes, 1970).

Assessment of Models.   By way of evaluation, it may be said that, for the broad range of experiments exemplifying the classical discrimination paradigm, substantial progress can be claimed both for the class of theories assuming discrimination learning to be basically an incremental growth process and for the class assuming it to be basically a process of categorization and unitization. Models developed in both traditions have not only proved able to account for most of the classical phenomena in the field but also have led to a substantial accumulation of genuinely new findings. Neither type of model seems fully sufficient to handle the whole range of robust phenomena, the statistical (mixed) model in its present form not accommodating the results on dimensional shifts and the selective attentional models not having been addressed to phenomena of patterning. One might hope that some way could be found to make a decisive choice between the two types of models, but I can see no a priori basis for judging that such an outcome is to be expected. It may be, rather, that discrimination learning is a more complex process than we yet fully appreciate and that all its aspects cannot be captured in any one type of model that has yet been developed.

Developmental Trends.   The dual-process structure characterizing most of the current models has received additional support from some developmental observations suggesting that young children learn discriminations between novel stimuli in essentially the manner conceived in the original Spence (1936, 1937) model or the statistical model but, with increasing age, exhibit a transition to the mode described by the dual-process models. Kendler and Kendler (1962) hypothesized that the higher-order component of the dual-process model depends on implicit responses and implicit response-produced stimuli, which are instigated by the observable stimuli and mediate choice responses. The implicit responses may represent verbal labels for the relevant cues in a discrimination problem, and this interpretation has been commonly assumed by other investigators. However, Kendler and Kendler emphasized that the mediators are purely hypothetical constructs, not necessarily related to any classes of observable behavior. In support of the mediational hypothesis, they observed that instructions to label the stimuli increased the tendency to perform in the way expected on the dual-process model in the case of kindergarten children (Kendler, 1964) and that the proportion of children performing in this fashion increased in a regular manner from kindergarten to college-grade levels (Kendler & Kendler, 1970). Other investigators, although confirming the age trend, have obtained evidence indicating that training of the kind that would promote verbal labeling is inessential. Tighe (1965) conducted a study similar in design to that of Kendler (1964) and found that pretraining designed simply to increase the children's attentiveness to the stimulus dimensions produced a tendency to manifest the apparently dimensional-based responding predicted by the dual-process model.

Subproblem analyses of the type introduced by Tighe, Glick, and Cole (1971) seem especially diagnostic. Their analyses dealt with the changed as compared to the unchanged stimulus—category pairs in extradimensional shifts. The comparison can be illustrated in terms of the example used previously. Suppose that after children have learned a discrimination problem with choices of red circles or triangles rewarded and blue circles or triangles nonrewarded, the assignments are switched so that all the triangles, say, are positive regardless of color and all circles negative. A special prediction of the dual-process type of model concerns a stimulus such as a blue triangle, which was negative before the shift but positive afterward (a changed stimulus) as compared to a red triangle that was positive before the shift but also positive afterward (an unchanged stimulus). If the children were learning to associate the correct response categories with the individual stimuli as wholes, then changed and unchanged pairs should show different courses of learning following the shift. In the example, the children would initially continue choosing the red triangle but would have to learn to choose the blue triangle. If, however, the children were attending to dimensions, so that before the shift they learned that color was relevant and all red stimuli positive, then following the shift they would have to learn that form was relevant and all triangles positive. Thus, in this case, the children should be expected to pass through a phase in which they avoid both red triangles and blue triangles at the beginning of postshift training and to exhibit similar courses of acquisition of the new discrimination on both the changed and the unchanged stimuli.

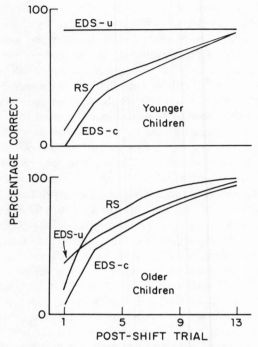

FIG. 12.2   Schematization of typical course of postshift learning relative to specific stimuli: EDS-u and EDS-c represent performance on stimuli whose assignments were unchanged and changed, respectively, in an extra dimensional shift;
RS represents performance on a reversal shift. The younger children continue to
respond correctly to unchanged stimuli while having to learn new responses to
changed ones, indicating that they had learned only associations to specific stimuli
during preshift training. Older children have to relearn on both types of stimuli,
indicating that they had learned to respond in terms of stimulus dimensions.

The expected picture, illustrated in Fig. 12.2, was nicely confirmed in studies
reported by Tighe, Glick, and Cole (1971) and Tighe (1973). In both cases, 4-
year old children showed the pattern expected on the assumption that learning
was solely a matter of associating stimuli with responses, as in the original
Spence (1936, 1937) model, whereas 10-year old children exhibited the pattern
expected on the basis of the dual-process model. Whether the shift with age from
the single-process to the dual-process model should be interpreted in terms of
maturation, learning, or some combination is an open question.

Hypothesis Testing

Though the theories reviewed in the previous section were developed to account
for the learning of discriminations between particular stimuli, it was recognized

from a very early time (Hull, 1920) that, at both the empirical and theoretical levels, this kind of learning shades imperceptibly into simple concept formation. This point is especially clear in the case of the models derived from statistical learning theory and in the dual-process model based on an assumption of selective attention to dimensions. In terms of the latter, for example, an individual presented the task of discriminating a red from a blue triangle would be conceived to learn first to attend selectively to color and then to make appropriate differential responses to the values red versus blue on this dimension. But once this learning had occurred, the individual would be expected to respond appropriately to red or blue forms other than triangles, and one might say that a simple concept had been formed.

In all the models considered, both discrimination and simple concept formation are conceived to be processes of forming appropriate associations between stimulus attributes and categories. Indeed, in the minds of many investigators associated with the tradition of stimulus–response learning theories, the natural question has seemed to be, "what other kind of theory would be possible?" An answer contributed from time to time by investigators more interested in human cognition than basic learning processes has been that an individual does not have a concept unless he or she not only proves able to respond appropriately to instances but can also give a rule characterizing all possible instances. No mechanism has been proposed whereby general rules could be generated from limited experiences, so the type of theory that has been favored by investigators holding that rules are essential ingredients of concepts is one in which the learning process is not one of storing information but rather one of selecting from among a preexisting repertoire of rules or hypotheses.

Actual theories based on the primacy of rule selection developed only slowly. In connection with some of the early experiments on rats that were part of the basis for Spence's (1936, 1937) theories, Krechevsky (1932) observed that an animal's behavior could often be described in terms of the notion that its choices over sequences of trials were governed by hypotheses of the form "the reward is always on the left" or "the reward is always behind the black card," or the like. Further, he presented analyses showing that error patterns during the early part of learning were often less haphazard than seemed to be called for by the stimulus–response model and, rather, fit quite well the conception of responding in accord with hypotheses. The force of such proposals was weakened, however, by the demonstration that Spence's model could actually account for some of the observed nonrandom response patterns, and no further significant developments with regard to concept learning by rules and hypotheses appeared until the mid-1950s.

At that point an extensive study of human problem solving in simple concept learning situations (Bruner, Goodnow, & Austin, 1956) gave new impetus to the rule-oriented approach. Bruner et al. contrived new experimental procedures in which subjects were not simply exposed to programmed series of experimental trials, as in the classical experiments, but rather were permitted to request information they wished to observe in order to progress toward solution of a problem. With these procedures, they adduced both behavioral and introspective information supporting the conception of concept learning in terms of the systematic testing of hypotheses.

This work did not lead immediately to any very formal theorizing, but the ideas were picked up by Restle (1962) who revised his earlier theory based on stimulus sampling and adaptation of common cues so that the sampling process referred to hypotheses rather than cues. The learning mechanism, formerly one of forming or adapting associations, became one of comparing hypotheses with feedback and retaining only hypotheses that yield consistently correct categorizations. This approach was further extended and elaborated by Trabasso and Bower (1968) and Millward and Wickens (1974) into a rather elaborate framework providing a systematic account of the strategies characteristically employed by relatively sophisticated human learners to sample and select within populations of potentially relevant hypotheses and arrive at rules characterizing concepts. This development of formal models for hypothesis testing was complemented during the period by the approach of Levine (1959, 1966) who first developed a systematic description of performance by monkeys on discrimination problems in terms of hypotheses that could be identified with specific response patterns, and then extended the same approach to human learning.

The family of hypothesis-selection models has provided instructive interpretations of aspects of conceptual learning by human beings and other higher primates that seem, for the present at least, to be beyond the reach of the learning models. On the other hand, the hypothesis-selection approach has some definite limitations. One is that the models are applicable only to relatively sophisticated learners who may be conceived to approach a problem with a repertoire of relatively well-formed hypothesis from which to choose. This condition may be quite well met in the case of much human learning in academic situations and even by experienced monkeys, but it seems unlikely to be appropriate for the learning of less sophisticated animals or young children, or perhaps even for human adults in less structured situations.

Natural Categories and Family Resemblance

It has been recognized since the earliest days of experimental psychology that not all concept formation can be described in terms of the learning or discovery of explicit rules of the kind that suffice for correct performance as defined in classical discrimination learning or hypothesis-selection experiments. We find it easy, for example, to assign nearly all the people we meet to categories *child* and *adult;* however we have available no specific rule for the category assignment, except for legal definitions that vary from place to place, and some assignments would doubtless vary across individuals or even for the same individual from time to time. Similarly we appear to deal with many other categories, *optimist, neurotic, slang, tool,* and so on, on the basis of greater family resemblance between exemplars of a category than between exemplars and nonexemplars, rather than on the basis of any specific set of defining properties.

Sir Francis Galton (1879) proposed that we form mental representations of such "ill-defined categories" (the term being due, I believe, to Neisser, 1967, rather than Galton) having much the properties of composite photographs that could be formed by stacking the negatives of a number of snapshots of the same object or type of object and passing light through the stack. The resulting image would lose much of the detail of each of the single snapshots, or exemplars, but would preserve some of the commonalities. And one might say, in modern terminology, that the composite image would serve as a prototype of the category.

Experimental Approaches.   Methods for investigating the possible formation of such mental representations were lacking in early experimental psychology and in fact did not become available until after the appearance of a seminal study by Attneave (1957). Attneave produced families of randomly shaped geometrical forms by starting with arbitrarily defined prototypes for each of the categories and then generating exemplars by making limited variations on the shapes of the prototypes. He found that experimental subjects proved able to learn to categorize shapes into the families more accurately if they had prior experience with the prototypes.

Systematic investigation of this type of learning began with a series of studies by Posner and Keele (1968, 1970) who used haphazard dot patterns as stimuli and generated families of these, corresponding to categories of objects, by producing small perturbations in the positions of individual dots from their positions in the prototypes. In a typical experimental design, subjects would be presented with limited sets of exemplars of two categories, not including the prototype of either, on a series of training trials on each of which the subject attempted to categorize an exemplar and then received informative feedback. Following this training, tests would be given, including training stimuli and new exemplars of each category, including the prototypes. A burst of studies using this design and various sets of materials, both verbal and nonverbal, generated in accordance with the same ideas as those of Posner and Keele, yielded a number of robust findings. One of these was that on test trials subjects typically classify newly experienced prototypes as fast and accurately as old training stimuli (Homa & Chambliss, 1975; Posner & Keele, 1970). Forgetting of learned categorizations over a retention interval proceeds more rapidly as measured by performance on categorizing previously experienced exemplars than as measured by performance on categorizing previously unexperienced prototypes (Homa & Vosburgh, 1976; Posner & Keele, 1970). And performance on transfer tests is better predicted by the similarity of transfer stimuli to the prototypes of the categories than by the frequencies with which features of the transfer stimuli have been experienced during training (Franks & Bransford, 1971).

These findings arising from the laboratory analysis of learning relative to ill-defined or "fuzzy" categories exhibit striking complementarity to those of an essentially contemporaneous series of studies of natural categories by Rosch and her associates (Rosch, 1973, 1978; Rosch & Mervis, 1975). Employing a combination of experimental studies and anthropological observations, Rosch has adduced substantial evidence that much of the category learning that occurs in ordinary life, with respect both to strictly perceptual categories (for example colors) and more functional categories (tools, foods), can be characterized in much the same terms as the learning observed in studies of prototype formation in the laboratory. With regard to the problem of characterizing the mental representations that underlie categorization, Rosch's work went beyond that of the laboratory studies cited previously by using as evidence not only performance on categorization tasks but also information obtained by asking subjects to list features they believe to characterize categories and by asking for ratings of the degree to which various exemplars typify categories. The converging evidence from these sources has provided substantial support for the idea that representations of natural categories are organized around memories for especially typical or "focal" exemplars. In studies of natural categories, Rosch and her associates have found that exemplars of categories that are rated most typical by subjects are also best recalled or reproduced following learning experiences and classified most quickly and accurately.

The complementarity of these observations to the seemingly more artificial laboratory experiments is brought out especially clearly in a study by Rosch, Simpson, and Miller (1976). These investigators produced collections of three types of materials, dot patterns, stick figures, and consonant/digit strings, by means of variations on arbitrarily defined prototypes. Their subjects were then given learning trials on categorization followed by tests in which the subjects rated the typicality of exemplars of the categories, recalled or reproduced as many exemplars as possible, and performed categorization tasks. Performance in all three of these tasks proved to be strongly related to similarity of the exemplars to the prototypes. The exemplars most similar to the ptototypes were reproduced or recalled most frequently, rated most typical, and categorized most efficiently.

Alternative Models.   Models for the interpretation of studies of fuzzy categories may conveniently be considered in three principal classes. Most novel, in comparison with the more familiar theories of classical discrimination learning and hypothesis selection, are the *prototype* models (Reed, 1973). In a prototype model it is assumed that a learner forms a mental representation of the prototype of a category by, in effect, computing mean or modal values of experienced exemplars or relevant dimensions. Then on test trials the individual determines whether a test stimulus is to be assigned to one or another category by computing its distance on these dimensions from the mental representations of the corresponding prototypes, the stimulus being assigned to the category for which its distance from the prototype is smallest.

This type of model obviously accounts for the main findings about prototype formation summarized previously but does not, in extant forms, account for the sensitivity of learners to the frequencies with which specific exemplars or features have been experienced. The latter findings are accommodated by *feature–frequency* models (Franks & Bransford, 1971). In these, it is assumed that learners store in memory information concerning the frequency with which features or attributes of exemplars occur in members of different categories and then on test trials combine in an additive fashion the remembered frequencies with which attributes of the probe stimulus have occurred in different categories in order to arrive at a categorical judgment. More elaborate variants of the simple feature–frequency models take account not only of the experienced frequency of single features of category exemplars but also of the frequencies of combinations of features, thus providing for relational as well as absolute frequency information (Hayes-Roth & Hayes-Roth, 1977).

The third theoretical approach is that characterizing *exemplar* models (Medin & Schaffer, 1978), in which the basic assumption is that the learner stores in memory not abstracted featural or prototypical information but rather representations of the specific exemplars experienced during learning. On test trials the learner is assumed to assess the similarity of a test stimulus to the memory representations of exemplars in each of the relevant categories and to assign the stimulus to the category to which the computed similarity is greatest.

As presently developed, all three types of models are capable of yielding predictions about relative speeds of learning of different types of exemplars and performance on retention or transfer tests for both old and new exemplars and prototypes. And, roughly speaking, in these applications, the three types of models seem about equally capable of accounting for the principal observed phenomena. It does not appear that specific experimental tests could be decisive at this stage because none of the models discussed have been fully formalized and a number are undergoing continuing augmentation and elaboration.

As a basis for continuing work, the exemplar model seems to offer special promise. One consideration is that the exemplar model of Medin and Schaffer (1978) grew out of an earlier model developed by Medin (1975) in an effort to add an account of the role of context to classical discrimination models and thus offers an advantage of continuity between models for classical discrimination and categorization. A perhaps more important consideration is that the basic ideas of the exemplar model are closer in spirit than those of the other models to the conceptualization of natural categories growing out of the work of Rosch and her associates, Rosch's interpretation of the formation of mental representations of natural categories might, in fact, be taken to be a qualitative counterpart of Medin and Schaffer's exemplar model. Further, feature–frequency models are limited to situations in which categories can be defined in terms of limited sets of features, something not clearly true of many natural categories, whereas the exemplar model has no similar limitation. In the same vein, prototype models can only yield predictions about the course of conceptual learning for situations in which the collections of exemplars are actually generated by variations on known prototypes. The exemplar model also has its limitations, as brought out in the following discussion, but they do not seem to entail restrictions on its potential range of applicability.

SOME CURRENT TRENDS IN RESEARCH AND THEORY

Developmental Stages and Levels of Function

Till about 1970, progress in interpreting the development of discrimination and simple conceptual learning constituted the identification of two distinct levels of function and evidence for a shift with age relative to the predominance of these levels within groups of subjects. The nature of the age shift was seen somewhat differently in two major research programs. In the work of Zeaman and House (1963) the component processes (associative learning of observing responses to stimulus dimensions and of choice responses based on these) were assumed to be the same at all levels of age and intelligence, but with an increasing tendency to observe dimensions in more intelligent and older children. The mechanism responsible for these trends in the use of selective attentional responses to dimensions was unspecified. In the work of Kendler and Kendler (1962), a developmental shift with age was assumed to proceed from a dependence on simple stimulus–response association to more complex chained discriminations with intervening links constituting mediational responses, for example, verbal labels for relevant stimulus attributes. The developmental trend was presumably a consequence of the accumulation of products of past learning with regard to the use of mediating responses.

A decade later we see in Kendler (this volume) a massive influx of data on relevant development trends and an attempt at a comprehensive integration of the old and new findings. In the new framework proposed by Kendler, the simple conception of successive stages (from single stimulus–response to mediated behavior) is replaced by a conception of multiple levels of functioning within the individual. The processes implicated at the different levels are assumed to come into play during cognitive development according to different but overlapping time courses and even in the adult to coexist and compete for dominance.

In Kendler's formulation, cognitive activity involved in accomplishing a categorization task is divided conceptually into a stage or phase of information processing followed by a phase of behavioral regulation, the latter depending on the output of the former. Stimulus processing can occur at a lower, unselective, level essentially as characterized in earlier discrimination theories of Hull (1920) and Spence (1936, 1937), or at a higher, more abstract level in which stimulus information has been encoded into features or other higher-order units. The output of unselective stimulus processing can enter into simple incremental discrimination learning, much as conceived in Spence's theory; more highly encoded stimulus information may also enter into incremental learning but usually leads to hypothesis testing. It is assumed that the two kinds of learning can go on simultaneously in the same individual and that if in a particular case they lead to incompatible choice tendencies, the "stronger" (strength not yet being otherwise defined) takes control of performance. The development of capabilities as a function of age at both the lower and higher levels is assumed to occur by maturation-like processes largely controlled by genetic programming, with the lower level normally completing development first in ordinary environments.

In order to obtain evidence on this conceptualization, Kendler (this volume) combines two methods, optional shifts and assessment of win–stay strategies, that have hitherto been used separately in different types of studies. In the optional shift procedure, subjects first learn to categorize stimuli characterized by values on two or more dimensions (typically color and form) and then are given a relearning series on a shift that is interpretable as a reversal on a relevant dimension. Finally, tests are administered on stimulus pairs chosen so that the subject's choice can indicate whether the learning of the shift problem was accomplished by reversing response assignments on the relevant dimension or by learning new associations between individual stimuli and responses. Evidence of reversal is taken to indicate that the stimulus processing was being accomplished at the higher, selective, level. Evidence of hypothesis testing, as distinguished from simple incremental learning, is obtained by examining individual protocols and determining whether or not the subject consistently repeats successful choices relative to a relevant dimension and shifts only on errors (Levine, 1975; Spiker & Cantor, this volume). In an earlier study, Kendler (1979) obtained results that she interpreted as indicating an increasing tendency with age for children to achieve categorization by learning at the hypothesis-selection level. One of these results was the observation that learning curves showing a gradual decrease in errors prior to the last error on a problem, consistent with incremental learning but not with hypothesis selection, were observed only for young children; another was that the proportion of subjects meeting the criterion of win–stay hypothesis selection increased monotonically with age.

Results obtained on the optional shift task and win–stay performance provided means of separating the encoding and the stimulus processing and behavioral regulation components of Kendler's (this volume) new conceptualization. The measures indexing the two components proved highly correlated at the lowest and highest ages, but for children of intermediate ages a sufficiently large proportion yielded evidence of selective encoding together with incremental learning to indicate that these components are separable. Further, in the large-scale study of verbal labeling and overtraining reported by Kendler, further evidence was obtained that attention to dimensions (selective encoding) as evidenced by reversal shift behavior is not a sufficient condition for hypothesis testing as indexed by win–stay performance. Further, the effects of training on verbal labeling and of overtraining on the categorization task itself appeared to combine essentially additively at all ages. The pattern would seem to fit the interpretation that verbal labeling or some functionally equivalent symbolic activity is implicated in higher-level, selective, stimulus processing and is necessary for learning at the hypothesis-testing level and, further, that an important function of overtraining is the providing of additional opportunities for labeling or symbolization.

Kendler's (this volume) results add substantially to our picture of the age course of appearance of selective encoding and hypothesis-testing behavior and, in addition, provide some indication of the degree to which these are correlated at various ages. Still, some important questions remain open. One of these is whether the age trends observed represent progressive, maturation-like changes in the individual or shifting mixtures of individuals characterized by distinctly different modes of processing. Kendler hypothesizes the former and takes her results to support the hypothesis, but there seems as yet no sharp way of ruling out alternative interpretations. Further, to the degree that the age functions do represent gradual and progressive developmental processes in the individual, do they reflect, on the one hand, maturation or learning of processes or skills intrinsic to the categorization tasks being studied, or, on the other hand, learning that occurs in quite different situations and yields transfer to the experimental tasks?

It may be noted that all the experimental tasks that have yielded evidence bearing on the conceptualizations of Kendler (this volume) and Zeaman and House (1963) present the subject with problems in which correct categorization is definable by simple verbalizable rules. This characterization seems clearly to apply also to much learning that goes on in schools but not, if we accept the arguments of Rosch (1975, 1978) and her associates, to much of children's learning that goes on prior to school age or outside school situations. Thus a hypothesis needing evaluation is that the age trends observed in the categorization studies may depend to some major extent on the fact that with increasing age children are on the average increasingly exposed to school learning involving the same kinds of rule-defined concepts that face them in the experimental tasks. It would be of interest to know whether the age trends in the experimental tasks might in some degree represent by-products of school learning just as, for example, an increase with age in the ability of immigrant children to perform on arithmetical reasoning tasks in school might in part reflect an associated increase in competence with English.

New Evidence on Hypothesis Testing

It seems that a general consensus has emerged that there are at least two distinguishable levels of complexity in the relation between memory and classificatory performance. Also there is relatively broad agreement that the lower level is characterized by the direct connection between stimulus representations and responses that has been assumed in associative learning theories. There is less agreement, however, concerning the nature of the higher level. It is clear enough that, in sufficiently sophisticated adults, categorization in many situations is accomplished via explicit selection and use of verbalizable hypotheses and rules. At the same time it is well known that many aspects of rule-governed behavior can be seen in lower animals, for example, monkeys (Levine, 1959) or even rats (Krechevsky, 1932), which can scarcely be thought to make use of verbal rules. Further, examination of the multiprocess learning models (e.g., Zeaman & House, 1963) that have grown out of research on animals and young children shows that many of the properties of hypothesis testing can be achieved without any use of verbal rules on the part of the learner. Thus it is a difficult problem to determine where in cognitive development literal hypothesis testing appears and under what circumstances it is actually used in categorization.

Spiker and Cantor (this volume) provide a thorough review of the relevant evidence. A major problem running through all the research is the difficulty of ascertaining that techniques designed to detect a learner's mode of processing can be used without, in the process, disturbing the course of learning. Perhaps the only method free of such hazards is that of simply classifying performance patterns to determine whether a learner's series of choices in the categorization tasks conforms to a familiar type, for example, win–stay, lose–shift, which is taken to index hypothesis-governed behavior. However, Spiker and Cantor shows that exclusive reliance on this type of index would be hazardous because under some circumstances (e.g., categorization tasks constructed with the use of pseudodimensions) children may be observed to yield perfect win–stay, lose–shift performance even when it seems clear that they do not have any valid, verbalizable hypothesis.

Other methods of detecting or assessing hypothesis testing all involve some intervention in the learning process. In the blank-trials method of Levine (1975) the normal course of learning with feedback is interrupted by the insertion of a block of trials on which no feedback is given in order to determine whether the learner continues to make a sequence of choices that would conform to a relevant hypothesis. A drawback of the method is that comparisons of learning with and without inserted blank trials show that the procedure itself modifies the course of learning and hence it cannot be taken simply to reveal what the learner was doing without the intervention. Cantor and Spiker (1979) propose that this difficulty is largely overcome with what they term the ''introtact'' method, in which the child engaged in learning a concept is asked at some point on each trial to tell the experimenter what aspects of the stimulus he or she is using as a basis for choice. Cantor and Spiker conclude that this method has less effect on the course of learning than the blank-trials method, especially if the probe is given at the end of each trial (the posttrial probe). Combining the introtact probe with the use of pseudo-dimensions, Spiker and Cantor conclude that even kindergarten-age children under some circumstances yield evidence of genuine hypothesis testing and suggest that the prevalence of such behavior in young children may have been underestimated because it can often be masked by dimensional preferences.

At the same time there is room for considerable reservation concerning the extent to which concept learning in the ordinary life of a young child depends on explicit hypothesis testing and selection. Positive evidence has so far been obtained only in situations where simple and effective hypotheses are not only readily available but suggested in some way by the experimenter. Further, one must recall the evidence of Kendler (this volume) that when young children are instigated to use such devices as verbal labeling, they often fail to continue doing so, even when labeling would be an aid to correct performance. It may be that hypothesis selection should be regarded, not as a pervasive form of learning but rather as a description of an end state of a prolonged learning process that is far from completely understood.

Fuzzy Categories and Exemplar Models

Current work on natural or other "fuzzy" categories centers on the class of exemplar models. It is becoming increasingly clear that remembering and recognizing specific exemplars of categories is an important aspect of concept learning and one not effectively handled in the classical approaches based on rule-defined categories. The role of memory for exemplars may be especially important in children's learning of natural categories and in the early stages of adult learning in novel situations. In one recent study, Mervis and Pani (1980) found that 5-year-old children learned artifical categories faster when their initial experiences were with good exemplars, that is, exemplars possessing many features that have high frequency in the category. Generally learning occurred earlier for good than for poor exemplars. Mervis and Pani also cite evidence that an analysis of some aspects of early language acquisition in terms of memory for exemplars can provide an account of phenomena of overgeneralization that have seemed aberrant from the standpoint of other approaches.

Despite the widespread interest in the learning and use of categories organized around family resemblance of exemplars, formal development of models for learning relative to exemplars is so far largely limited to the work of Medin and his associates. I proceed to sketch the essentials of Medin's model as background for discussion of some recent results and some problems calling for new efforts.

As the model was put forward by Medin and Schaffer (1978), an individual in a discrimination or concept learning situation is assumed to form encoded memory representations of experienced exemplars of categories. These representations are not necessarily complete and they may be influenced by such factors as stimulus salience or perceptual biases. They are, in effect, grouped in memory in accordance with their category assignments in the experimental procedure. When the learner in a test situation encounters either a novel or a previously experienced exemplar, he categorizes the new instance by comparing it to the set of stored representations and forming an impression of the summed similarity of the test exemplar to the exemplar representations of each of the categories in memory. The learner than assigns the test exemplar to the category to which its summed similarity is greatest.

The manner of generating predictions from the model and some of its specific implications can be conveniently brought out in terms of an experiment reported by Medin and Schwanenflugel (1981). The stimuli to be categorized were pictures of faces of women taken from college yearbooks, the pictures varying in hair color, shirt color, smile type, and hair length (as well as other attributes that were not considered in the experimental design and may be presumed to have varied randomly between categories). In the design of the experiment, the attributes of the faces were encoded as binary values on the relevant dimensions (e.g., light hair versus dark hair, short hair versus long hair) although gradations could occur from picture to picture (e.g., degrees of lightness of hair in the pictures encoded as "light" or "dark" by the experimenter). The experimenter defined two categories, A and B, to which the pictures should be assigned and for two groups of subjects assigned three exemplars (pictures) to category A and three to category B. The dimensional representations of the exemplars for groups given training on what are termed *separable* versus *nonseparable* categories are shown in the left-hand portion of Table 12.1 (corresponding to Fig. 7.3 of Medin, this volume). It will be seen that exemplar A_1 for the separable category condition has value 0 for hair color (dimension 1) and value 1 for hair length, smile type, and shirt color, and so on for the other exemplars.

The right-hand portion of Table 12.1 gives the values of a quantity representing the similarity of the row exemplar to itself and to each of the other exemplars in the given condition. These were obtained by raising a similarity coefficient, d (having a value between 0 and 1), to a power given by the number of dimensions on which the row and column exemplar differ. The probability that any row exemplar, presented as a test stimulus, would be assigned to a given category is given in the model by the sum of its similarities to members of that category divided by the sum of its similarities to both categories.

To illustrate, for exemplar A_1 in the first row of the table, the value in column A_1 is unity, because that is the similarity of stimulus A_1 to itself; the value under A_2 is d^2 because exemplar A_1 differs from A_2 on exactly two of the dimensions;

TABLE 12.1
Representation of Picture Classification Experiment in Terms of the
Exemplar Model

Exemplar	Dimension					Identification Response					
	1	2	3	4		A_1	A_2	A_3	B_1	B_2	B_3
Separable Categories											
A_1	0	1	1	1		1	d^2	d^3	d^4	d^2	d
A_2	1	1	1	0		d^2	1	d^3	d^2	d^4	d
A_3	1	0	0	1		d^3	d^3	1	d	d	d^4
B_1	1	0	0	0		d^4	d^2	d	1	d^2	d^3
B_2	0	0	0	1		d^2	d^4	d	d^2	1	d^3
B_3	0	1	1	0		d	d	d^4	d^3	d^2	1
Nonseparable Categories											
A_1	1	1	0	0		1	d^4	d^2	d^2	d^2	d^2
A_2	0	0	1	1		d^4	1	d^2	d^2	d^2	d^2
A_3	1	1	1	1		d^2	d^2	1	d^4	d^2	d^2
B_1	0	0	0	0		d^2	d^2	d^4	1	d^2	d^2
B_2	0	1	0	1		d^2	d^2	d^2	d^2	1	d^4
B_3	1	0	1	0		d^2	d^2	d^2	d^2	d^4	1

the value under A_3 is d^3, because A_1 differs from A_3 on three dimensions; the value under B_1 is d^4, because A_1 differs from B_1 on all four dimensions; and so on. The probability that exemplar A_1 would be correctly assigned to class A by a subject is then predicted to be the sum of the probabilities that it is identified as one of the A_1 exemplars; that is, $1 + d^2 + d^3$, divided by the sum of the values in the row; that is, $1 + d + 2d^2 + d^3 + d^4$.

Some predictions about categorization performance require knowing the value of d, but many may be obtained simply by study of the table. For example, it may be noted immediately that, for both conditions, exemplars A_1 and A_2 should be equally difficult; in the separable category condition the same should be true for B_1 and B_2; for the nonseparable condition, however, B_2 and B_3 should be equally difficult. A little algebra will verify the further prediction that for both conditions the predicted average probability of correctly categorizing instances of category A should be predicted to be equal to the average probability of correctly categorizing instances of category B, regardless of the value of d.

The significance of the property differentiating the two conditions is as follows. In the literature on categorization, considerable attention has been given to the question of whether the sets of exemplars assigned to two categories are linearly separable (Reed, 1973). Two categories, A and B, are said to be separable if a weighted sum of values on all the stimulus dimensions can be found with the property that all exemplars whose sum falls above some cutoff belong to category A and those whose sum falls below the cutoff all belong to category B.

By reference to Table 12.1, it may be seen that for the separable category group, an index formed by taking the value of a stimulus on dimension 1 plus one-half its value on the three other dimensions would yield this complete separability, all exemplars in category A having values of 1.5 or higher and all exemplars in category B having values lower than 1.5. In contrast, for the nonseparable condition no such index is available. Linear separability is a condition for perfect discrimination in all additive cue models and presumably should be an advantageous condition for learning in those models even where perfect discrimination is not possible. Thus Medin (this volume) argues that, according to the independent cue models, categorization learning should be easier for the separable than for the nonseparable condition in this experiment.

Obtaining a corresponding prediction about relative difficulty of the two conditions for the exemplar model requires a bit of calculation, because one cannot know in advance whether or not it turns on the actual value of the parameter d. To investigate the question, I inserted values of d ranging from .1 to .9 by steps of .1 into a computer program that yielded average probabilities of correct categorization of A_i and B_i exemplars for the two conditions shown in Table 12.1. These calculations yielded the prediction that performance should be better on the nonseparable than on the separable condition for all the values of d considered, the difference in probability of correct classification being smallest, and in fact essentially vanishing for $d = .9$, increasing as d decreases to .3, and then decreasing to about .10 at $d = .1$. Reference to the learning functions for this experiment given in Fig. 4 of Medin and Schwanenflugel (1981) will show that during the latter part of learning, the average accuracy of categorization was in the neighborhood of .85 with about a .10 advantage for the nonseparable condition, in excellent agreement with the prediction from our calculations.

The reason, in intuitive terms, why the exemplar model implies that the nonseparable condition should be easier than the separable condition in this experiment is that instances of high similarity exert disproportionate weight on performance because they make it highly likely that the test exemplar will evoke the mental representation of a very similar one, whether that be in the same or the different category. In the separable category condition of Table 12.1, each of the A exemplars is very similar to at least one of the B exemplars (differing on only one dimension), whereas the same property is not to be found in the nonseparable condition.

This summary of the exemplar model is only a simplified account, omitting, for example, consideration of the effects of different saliences of dimensions that may result from differential attention; more extended treatments are given by Medin and Schaffer (1978) and Smith and Medin (1981). To summarize the present status of the model, it may be said that it accounts for the major phenomena of classical discrimination learning at much the same level of detail as the models of Spence (1937) or Zeaman and House (1963) but with the advantage of handling context in a simpler and more systematic manner and accounting for simple conceptual learning relative to fuzzy categories as readily as the learning of simple rule-defined concepts. Also, the model can accommodate some of the major findings regarding prototype formation as, for example, the fact that a prototype never seen by subjects prior to a test trial may be correctly categorized with higher probability than previously experienced exemplars of the category. Further, the exemplar model has consistently proved superior to additive cue models in a series of experimental tests contrived by Medin and his associates to provide differential tests of the two types of models (Medin, this volume; Medin & Schaffer, 1978; Medin & Schwanenflugel, 1981).

Although the performance of the exemplar model in the special test experiments has been impressive, one must note some reservations. One is that all of these tests have been conducted with an experimental paradigm involving repeated presentation of members of small sets of exemplars, the exemplars having been assigned to categories by the experimenter in a manner that would make it difficult or impossible for the learner to form a concept expressable in terms of a set of features necessary and sufficient for an exemplar to belong to a category. Less is known about the relative performance of the two types of models in experiments of the type that additive cue and hypothesis-testing models were originally developed to deal with and nothing regarding situations in which learning is relative to categories comprising large sets of exemplars that do not recur during the course of the experiment.

Some present limitations of the exemplar model suggest that in continuing development it may need to be augmented by inclusion of some processes identical or similar to those that have appeared as components of other models. For example, the exemplar model does not adequately handle an old problem for discrimination theory—the ability of animals as well as human learners to form perfect discriminations even between stimuli that have common components or features. This problem has been noted by Medin on a number of occasions and he has suggested a solution in terms of the development of selective attention to cues or dimensions of high predictive significance, the effect being to reduce the effective similarities between to-be-discriminated stimuli (Medin, 1975; Medin & Schaffer, 1978). With this idea included, the basic exemplar model might be taken to correspond to the lower, incremental learning, level of the schema presented by Kendler (this volume) and the attentional process to correspond to the higher, selective learning process. With such an augmentation, the already demonstrated advantageous features of the exemplar model would be included within a structure of much the same form as that of several other current dual-process models.

A rather elementary problem for the present exemplar model arises from the assumption that decisions as to the identification or categorization of stimuli always represent the outcome of a process in which the test stimulus is compared to sets of representations in memory. The problem is that the model cannot account for the well-known fact that frequently experienced stimuli are recognized with virtual certainty. In the model, such a stimulus would be most similar to and would be most likely to activate its own representation in memory, but also it would tend to activate representations of similar stimuli, with a consequent attenuation of the probability of correct identification or categorization. A possible line of modification of the model that might deal with this problem is suggested by the current work of Medin (this volume) on correlated cues, which evidently tend to acquire greater salience for learners than independent cues and thus to carry more weight in response determination. It may be that combinations of cues that become salient owing either to their correlated occurrence over sets of exemplars or to their co-occurrence in familiar exemplars tend to take on the character of higher-order features or units. Just such a process has been included in discrimination models under the rubric of patterning (Atkinson & Estes, 1963; Estes, 1959) and in treatments of the "unitization" of letters from constituent visual features and of letter groups from constituent letters in reading (Estes, 1975; Smith & Spoehr, 1974).

Though probably all the contributors to the present volume are interested in the way capabilities for categorization emerge in the course of a child's perceptual and cognitive development in ordinary environments, of necessity nearly all the research actually discussed comes from laboratory situations in which categories are prescribed by experimenters. Thus nearly all the empirical material actually available as a basis for theorizing has to do with learning and performance in relation to externally specified lines of categorization. Nonetheless it is of interest to consider whether the models that are emerging and the concepts that enter into them provide any insight into the way categories form in natural environments. The stimulating discussion of some relevant issues by Medin (this volume) suggests that, though few conclusions can yet be drawn, this area presents some major theoretical problems that just may instigate efforts to broaden the scope of the experimental paradigms used in continuing research.

Naturally the first principles one would consider as having potential relevance for natural categorization would be those most central to extant models, among which cue validity and similarity within and between categories are perhaps the most conspicuous. Medin (this volume) considers both of these and draws rather negative conclusions as to their likely role in natural categorization. However, there is room for some reservation about the pessimistic conclusions. Medin takes the validity of a cue or feature for categorization to be determined by the probability that an entity belongs to a particular category given that it includes the feature and, on the basis of this definition, shows that cue validity could not provide a reasonable basis for characterizing the usefulness of categories for a learner in a natural environment. However, I think the definition is suspect, for a reasonable conception of validity needs to include an element of contingency, that is, the validity of a cue should be taken to be something like the difference between the probability that an entity belongs to a given category if it includes the feature and the probability that it belongs to the category if it does not include the feature. With this modified definition, I think cue validity will come out better in an analysis of the kind Medin offers.

A second idea Medin (this volume) considers is that a useful category, or a basic category in the formulation of Rosch (1978), is one in which assignments of exemplars are such as to maximize similarity within the given category while at the same time minimizing the similarity between exemplars of that category and exemplars of other categories. Medin finds that this criterion has some implausible implications, but I think his demonstration turns on a simplification of the problem that may omit an essential element. Namely, Medin considers the situation of a learner in an environment that offers various possibilities of categorizing stimuli with no constraint on the number of categories. Given this characterization, Medin's arguments have some force, but I think the omission of any constraint on the number of categories is implausible and that if the notion of a constraint were included, one would not arrive at the same implications.

One source of relevant evidence regarding an assumption of some constraint on the number of categories in any situation is the large literature concerning capacity limitations on absolute judgments on various stimulus dimensions that accrued in the context of research within the framework of information theory (see e.g., Garner, 1962). There seems little reason to think that the strong constraints known to govern individuals' capability for dealing with categories on simple stimulus dimensions would disappear in the presence of tasks requiring multidimensional categorization. Further, problems of maximization and minimization are in general soluble only under specified constraints. I think current research on natural categories (Rosch, 1975, 1978) and their laboratory analogs (Murphy & Smith, 1982) provides considerable reasons to think that individuals do in general form categories that tend to optimize with regard to cue validity and similarity relationships. A major and relatively untouched problem for continuing research is that of extending laboratory-based models to account for these salient characteristics of natural categorization.

ACKNOWLEDGMENTS

Preparation of this article was supported in part by grants MH 33917 from the United States Public Health Service and BNS 80-26656 from the National Science Foundation.

REFERENCES

Atkinson, R. C., & Estes, W. K. Stimulus sampling theory. In R. D. Luce, R. R. Bush, & E. Galanter (Eds.), *Handbook of mathematical psychology* (Vol. II). New York: Wiley, 1963.
Attneave, F. Transfer of experience with a class-schema to identification-learning of patterns and shapes. *Journal of Experimental Psychology,* 1957, *54,* 81–88.

Binder, A. Effects of altered frequencies upon recognition responses. *Journal of Experimental Psychology*, 1963, *66*, 553–559.

Binder, A., & Estes, W. K. Transfer of responses in visual recognition situations as a function of frequency variables. *Psychological Monographs*, 1966, *80*, No. 23 (Whole No. 631).

Bower, G. H. Choice-point behavior. In R. R. Bush & W. K. Estes (Eds.), *Studies in mathematical learning theory*. Stanford, Calif.: Stanford University Press, 1959.

Bruner, J. S., Goodnow, J. J., & Austin, G. A. *A study of thinking*. New York: Wiley, 1956.

Burke, C. J., & Estes, W. K. A component model for stimulus variables in discrimination learning. *Psychometrika*, 1957, *22*, 133–145.

Bush, R. R., & Mosteller, F. A mathematical model for simple learning. *Psychological Review*, 1951, *58*, 313–323.

Cantor, J. H., & Spiker, C. C. The effects of introtacts on hypothesis testing in kindergarten and first-grade children. *Child Development*, 1979, *50*, 1110–1120.

Estes, W. K. Toward a statistical theory of learning. *Psychological Review*, 1950, *57*, 94–107.

Estes, W. K. Component and pattern models with Markovian interpretations. In R. R. Bush & W. K. Estes (Eds.), *Studies in mathematical learning theory*. Stanford, Calif.: Stanford University Press, 1959.

Estes, W. K. A random-walk model for choice behavior. In K. J. Arrow, S. Karlin, & P. Suppes (Eds.), *Mathematical methods in the social sciences, 1959*. Stanford, Calif.: Stanford University Press, 1960.

Estes, W. K. *Learning theory and mental development*. New York: Academic Press, 1970.

Estes, W. K. Elements and patterns in diagnostic discrimination learning. *Transactions of the New York Academy of Science*, 1972, *34*, 84–95.

Estes, W. K. Memory, perception, and decision in letter identification. In R. L. Solso (Ed.), *Information processing and cognition: The Loyola symposium*. Hillsdale, N.J.: Lawrence Erlbaum Associates, 1975.

Estes, W. K., & Hopkins, B. L. Acquisition and transfer in pattern-vs.-component discrimination learning. *Journal of Experimental Psychology*, 1961, *61*, 322–328.

Foss, D. J., & Harwood, D. Memory for sentences: Implications for human associative memory. *Journal of Verbal Learning and Verbal Behavior*, 1975, *14*, 1–16.

Franks, J. J., & Bransford, J. D. Abstraction of visual patterns. *Journal of Experimental Psychology*, 1971, *90*, 65–74.

Galton, F. Composite portraits, made by combining those of many different persons into a single, resultant figure. *Journal of the Anthropological Institute*, 1879, *8*, 132–144.

Garner, W. R. *Uncertainty and structure as psychological concepts*. New York: Wiley, 1962.

Harlow, H. F. The formation of learning sets. *Psychological Review*, 1949, *56*, 51–65.

Hayes-Roth, B., & Hayes-Roth, F. Concept learning and the recognition and classification of exemplars. *Journal of Verbal Learning and Verbal Behavior*, 1977, *16*, 321–338.

Homa, D., & Chambliss, D. The relative contribution of common and distinctive information on the abstraction from ill-defined categories. *Journal of Experimental Psychology: Human Learning and Memory*, 1975, *1*, 351–359.

Homa, D., & Vosburgh, R. Category breadth and the abstraction of prototypical information. *Journal of Experimental Psychology: Human Learning and Memory*, 1976, *2*, 322–330.

House, B. J., & Zeaman, D. Reversal and nonreversal shifts in discrimination learning in retardates. *Journal of Experimental Psychology*, 1962, *63*, 444–451.

Hull, C. L. Quantitative aspects of the evolution of concepts. *Psychological Monographs*, 1920, *28*, (Whole No. 123).

Kendler, H. H., & Kendler, T. S. Vertical and horizontal processes in problem solving. *Psychological Review*, 1962, *69*, 1–16.

Kendler, T. S. Verbalization and optional reversal shifts among kindergarten children. *Journal of Verbal Learning and Verbal Behavior*, 1964, *3*, 428–436.

Kendler, T. S. The development of discrimination learning: A levels-of-functioning explanation. In H. S. Reese, & L. P. Lipsitt (Eds.), *Advances in child development and behavior*, (Vol. 13). New York: Academic Press, 1979.

Kendler, T. S., & Kendler, H. H. An ontogeny of optional shift behavior. *Child Development*, 1970, *41*, 1–27.

Krechevsky, I. The genesis of "hypotheses" in rats. *University of California Publications in Psychology*, 1932, *6*, 45–64.

La Berge, D. L. A model with neutral elements. In R. R. Bush & W. K. Estes (Eds.), *Studies in mathematical learning theory*. Stanford, Calif.: Stanford University Press, 1959.

La Berge, D. L. A recruitment theory of simple behavior. *Psychometrika*, 1962, *27*, 375–396.

Lashley, K. S. An examination of the "continuity" theory as applied to discriminative learning. *Journal of General Psychology*, 1942, *26*, 241–265.

Levine, M. A model of hypothesis behavior in discrimination learning set. *Psychological Review*, 1959, *66*, 353–366.

Levine, M. Hypothesis behavior in humans during discrimination learning. *Journal of Experimental Psychology*, 1966, *71*, 331–338.

Levine, M. *A cognitive theory of learning: Research on hypothesis testing*. Hillsdale, N.J.: Lawrence Erlbaum Associates, 1975.

Lovejoy, E. *Attention in discrimination learning: A point of view and a theory*. San Francisco, Calif.: Holden-Day, 1968.

Mackintosh, N. J. Overtraining and transfer within and between dimensions in the rat. *Quarterly Journal of Experimental Psychology*, 1964, *16*, 250–256.

Medin, D. L. A theory of context in discrimination learning. In G. H. Bower (Ed.), *The psychology of learning and motivation* (Vol. 9). New York: Academic Press, 1975.

Medin, D. L., & Schaffer, M. M. Context theory of classification learning. *Psychological Review*, 1978, *85*, 207–238.

Medin, D. L., & Schwanenflugel, P. L. Linear separability in classification learning. *Journal of Experimental Psychology: Human Learning and Memory*, 1981, *7*, 355–368.

Mervis, C. B., & Pani, J. R. Acquisition of basic object categories. *Cognitive Psychology*, 1980, *12*, 496–522.

Millward, R. B., & Wickens, T. D. Concept-identification models. In D. H. Krantz, R. D. Luce, R. C. Atkinson, & P. Suppes (Eds.), *Contemporary developments in mathematical psychology: Learning, memory, and thinking* (Vol. I). San Francisco, Calif.: Freeman, 1974.

Murphy, G. L., & Smith, E. E. Basic-level superiority in picture categorization. *Journal of Verbal Learning and Verbal Behavior*, 1982, *21*, 1–20.

Neimark, E. D., & Estes, W. K. (Eds.). *Stimulus sampling theory*. San Francisco, Calif.: Holden-Day, 1967.

Neisser, U. *Cognitive psychology*. New York: Appleton-Century-Crofts, 1967.

Pavlov, I. *Conditioned reflexes*. London: Oxford University Press, 1927.

Posner, M. I., & Keele, S. W. On the genesis of abstract ideas. *Journal of Experimental Psychology*, 1968, *77*, 353–363.

Posner, M. I., & Keele, S. W. Retention of abstract ideas. *Journal of Experimental Psychology*, 1970, *83*, 304–308.

Reed, S. K. *Psychological processes in pattern recognition*. New York & London: Academic Press, 1973.

Restle, F. A theory of discrimination learning. *Psychological Review*, 1955, *62*, 11–19.

Restle, F. The selection of strategies in cue learning. *Psychological Review*, 1962, *69*, 329–343.

Robbins, D. Some models for successive discrimination learning and transfer. *British Journal of Mathematical & Statistical Psychology*, 1972, *25*, 151–167.

Rosch, E. On the internal structure of perceptual and semantic categories. In T. E. Moore (Ed.), *Cognitive development and the acquisition of language*. New York: Academic Press, 1973.

Rosch, E. Universals and cultural specifics in human categorization. In R. Breslin, S. Bochner, & W. Lonner (Eds.), *Cross-cultural perspectives on learning*. New York: Halsted Press, 1975.

Rosch, E. Principles of categorization. In E. Rosch & B. B. Lloyd (Eds.), *Cognition and categorization*. Hillsdale, N.J.: Lawrence Erlbaum Associates, 1978.

Rosch, E., & Mervis, C. B. Family resemblances: Studies in the internal structure of categories. *Cognitive Psychology*, 1975, *7*, 573–605.

Rosch, E., Simpson, C., & Miller, R. S. Structural bases of typicality effects. *Journal of Experimental Psychology: Perception and Performance*, 1976, *2*, 491–502.

Ross, B. H., & Bower, G. H. Comparisons of models of associative recall. *Memory & Cognition*, 1981, *9*, 1–16.

Shepp, B. E., & Turrisi, F. D. Learning and transfer of mediating responses in discrimination learning. In N. R. Ellis (Ed.), *International review of research in mental retardation*, 1966, *2*, 85–121.

Smith, E. E., & Medin, D. L. *Categories and Concepts*. Cambridge, Mass.: Harvard University Press, 1981.

Smith, E. E., & Spoehr, K. T. The perception of printed English: A theoretical perspective. In B. H. Kantowitz (Ed.), *Human information processing: Tutorials in performance and cognition*. Hillsdale, N.J.: Lawrence Erlbaum Associates, 1974.

Spence, K. W. The nature of discrimination learing in animals. *Psychological Review*, 1936, *43*, 427–449.

Spence, K. W. The differential response in animals to stimuli varying within a single dimension. *Psychological Review*, 1937, *44*, 430–444.

Sutherland, N. S. Stimulus analyzing mechanisms. In *The mechanization of thought processes*. Vol. 2. London: Her Majesty's Stationery Office, 1959. Pp. 575–609.

Tighe, L. S. The effect of perceptual pretraining on reversal and nonreversal shifts. *Journal of Experimental Psychology*, 1965, *70*, 379–385.

Tighe, T. J. Subproblem analysis of discrimination learning. In G. H. Bower (Ed.), *The psychology of learning and motivation* (Vol. 7). New York: Academic Press, 1973.

Tighe, T. J., Glick, J., & Cole, M. Subproblem analysis of discrimination shift learning. *Psychonomic Science*, 1971, *24*, 159–160.

Trabasso, T., & Bower, G. H. *Attention in learning: Theory and research*. New York: Wiley, 1968.

Zeaman, D., & House, B. J. The role of attention in retardate discrimination learning. In N. R. Ellis (Eds.), *Handbook of mental deficiency*. New York: McGraw-Hill, 1963.

Author Index

Subject Index